Getting
LOOSE

Getting LOOSE

Lifestyle Consumption in the 1970s

SAM BINKLEY

Duke University Press   Durham and London   2007

© 2007 Duke University Press

All rights reserved

Designed by Heather Hensley

Typeset in Minion Pro by Tseng Information Systems, Inc.

Library of Congress Cataloging-in-Publication Data appear on the last printed page of this book.

Portions of this manuscript have appeared as essays under the titles "The New Middle Classes and the Discourse of Caring: Toward a New Understanding of Cultural Intermediaries" (in *Historicizing Lifestyles: Popular Media, Consumption and Taste Cultures*, edited by David Bell and Joanne Hol-lows [Burlington, Vermont: Ashgate, 2006]); "The Seers of Menlo Park: The Discourse of Heroic Consumption in the *Whole Earth Catalog*" (*Journal of Consumer Culture* 3, no. 3 [2003]); "Every-body's Life Is Like a Spiral: Narrating Post-Fordism in the Lifestyle Movement of the 1970's" (*Cul-tural Studies—Critical Methodologies* 4, no. 2 [2004]); "Cosmic Profit: Countercultural Commerce and the Problem of Trust in American Marketing" (*Consumption, Markets, and Culture* 6, no. 4 [2003]); and in a PhD dissertation titled *Consuming Aquarius: Markets and the Moral Boundaries of the New Class* (New School for Social Research, 2002).

For my parents,

for Dörte,

and for Dave,

who never gave up

Contents

List of Illustrations

Acknowledgments

For their support, patience, occasional perplexity, and over all stoicism in the face of many obsessive years spent on my seemingly unending "hippie project," I owe thanks to many people. As a dissertation at the New School for Social Research, this project benefited from the oversight of Marshall Berman and Orville Lee, and the comments of Stuart Ewen, Don Slater, Jo Entwistle, Randal Doane, Betsy Wissinger, Britta Wheeler, Margarita Palacios, Martin Plot, Anette Baldauf, Stacy McGoldrick, Jorge Capetillo, Jack Levinson, Kim Paice, Jeff Bussolini, Ralph Obermauer, Eric Miles, Elliot Weininger, Julie Ford, Rachel Sotos, Steve Lang, and Dan Cook. The Department of Special Collections, Manuscripts Division, Stanford University, was particularly helpful in allowing me access to the *Whole Earth Catalog Records, 1969–1986*. And most of all, Xenia Von Lilien deserves special thanks for her continued help and support during this time.

Many of these people again showed their generosity as this research developed through painful growing stages into a book project, though many more names were added in these stages as well. These include my editors and staff at Duke University Press, Raphael Allen, Reynolds Smith, Justin Faerber, and Sharon Torian, as well as two anonymous readers who offered encouraging comments on the manuscript at pivotal stages. I am grateful for the comments of my friend and coconspirator Jo Littler, and for the wisdom offered by Todd Ayoung, Eva Illouz, Cas Wouters, Ananya Mukerji, Stephen Miller, Che Hi Choi, Damon Smith, Andrew Haas, Helen Lambert, Zsuzsanna Várhelyi, and Fuyuki Kurasawa. I am forever indebted for the many forms of generosity shown to me by my colleagues at Emerson College, and to Cher Knight, Brooke Knight, Emily Kearns, Eric Gordon, David Bogen, Nigel Gibson, Maria Koundoura, Elizabeth Whitney, Erika Williams, and Linda Peek-Schacht. I am glad for the engaged commentary of participants in the Works-in-Progress Circle at Emerson College, for the help of the staff at the Emerson College Library, and for research support that came to me in the form of a Faculty Advancement Fund Grant from Emerson College in 2006.

There are students too numerous to mention to whom I owe a deep debt of gratitude for sharing moments of insight and discovery. In particular, I am glad for the rigor and inquisitiveness of students in my Identity and Modern Life class (and particularly for the always unpredictable comments of Taylor Block) for prodding me along and letting themselves be carried away by all of this. I am grateful for the many student assistants who have helped me in many ways with this project, including Rylan Morrison, Patrizia Cocca, Andrea Kilkenny, Stacy Anderson—and most importantly Sara Eng and Kendra Brown, for making my life bearable. I am indebted to dozens of Lower East Side sidewalk booksellers and street vendors who hunted down rare items, to online bookstores, to my many friends (both bi- and quadrupedal) at dog runs in Tompkins Square Park, Fort Greene Park, and Boston's Peter's Park, and of course to my writing companion Laika, now happily retired to the 'burbs of Long Island.

Most importantly, I am grateful to those for whom this volume is dedicated: for the devotion and unflinching commitment of Dörte Fitschen-Rath, with whom I have shared many archaeological digs through the debris of recent modernities, tight, loose, and otherwise; for my mother, Paula Binkley, who taught me to interrogate human vanity in all its devious forms; for my father, Robert Binkley, who taught me to interrogate my own vanity in all of its far more devious forms, and for my brother, David Binkley, who never gave up on his own life to the very last. It was he who unwittingly introduced me to the legacy of the 1960s through the relics he left concealed in corners of my parents' home, from records and hash pipes to psychedelic inscriptions. More than anything else, it is to his memory that this volume is dedicated. And finally, I would like to thank the many people of that overlabeled generational cohort that immediately precedes mine, who met with me to relate stories about their dreams of a looser life, and who left records of their adventures in dozens of letters, books, journals, magazines, and publications for me to come along and discover.

Mediated Immediacy

Living in the Now

> I started out talking about how to trip, and then I saw that life was a trip.
>
> So now I talk about how to live.
>
> —Stephen Gaskin, *Catalog of Sexual Consciousness*

In 1971, Simon and Schuster published *The Underground Dictionary* by Dr. Eugene E. Landy, a clinical psychologist and lecturer at the University of Southern California. Dedicated "to my people," the book offered itself as a sort of Rosetta Stone of countercultural slang, fashioning a "much-needed communications bridge between the Establishment and the underground culture" through a detailed inventory of the new vernacular that was rapidly colonizing the popular lexicon of American youth. Most of the entries reflected the technical jargon of drug use and sexual behavior Landy had picked up in his work at a community health center for young people: "Come," we are told, refers to "male or female ejaculate," "Main squeeze: wife or girlfriend," and "Coast" is to "feel the effects of a drug."[1] The *Dictionary* imparts a glimpse into the complex meanings and emotional styles inscribed in everyday habits of living and communicating, described through clandestine and restrictive words: "Up tight: in a state of extreme tension or anxiety; worried, disturbed; upset"; "Groovy: great, fantastic, joyful, happy"; "Cop out: Find an excuse, usually a phony one, to get out of something or a situation" (192, 93, 57).

But Landy's guide to underground slang is more than just language: it unfolds a contentious landscape in which its users could move and live, mediating the opposing emotional and personal styles that defined the dispositions of "the establishment" and "my people." Indeed, the argot of the drug culture projects a tension between two ways of experiencing the sensual world, and of relating that experience to new modes of self-understanding. The blinkered, unknowing, constraining ways of the establishment are undermined by a subterranean flow of expression and experience—a vernacular for a new hedonism, to be sure, but one fashioned on an ambitious program of ethical self-renewal and a singular commitment to the affirmation of feeling and impulse in daily life: "Float: to be under the influence of drugs"; "Boy: heroin"; "Grip: masturbate"; "Hump: have sexual intercourse"; "Rap: talk compulsively while high on drugs" (39, 80, 93, 107, 159). By giving voice to a flow of sensation that coursed through everyday interactions and conduct, the words of counterculture speech released the speaker into a realm of feeling that transcended the anemic and constraining limits of mainstream American culture.

More accurately, hip jargon relates a moral universe organized around the opposing values of self-constraint and self-release. At one end stands a relation of artificially imposed self-limitation arrived at through the passive acceptance of an institutionalized norm:

> Establishment: Those who hold positions of power and authority, such as politicians, police etc.; the dictators of conventional attitudes and values, and those attitudes and values themselves. The Establishment's way of life is regarded as undesirable because of the lack of freedom and hypocrisy. (74–75)

> Mister Charlie: White man, boss, White establishment man. He is one who lives in suburbia, usually has a white collar job, two to three children, a station wagon, and a compact car and a white picket fence. He has short hair and puts the American flag outside his house on patriotic holidays. (133)

At the other end lies its opposite: an affirmation of direct personal engagement as an active force in the fashioning of experiences, realized through a release of the self into the flow of natural impulses, desires and the sensuality and experience of everyday life:

Flower: The philosophy of the flower comes from the fact that the flower is among the most natural of all things in nature; it is free, needing nothing more than the earth, air and sunshine to live. It is peaceful and beautiful and lives its beauty freely. (80)

Tell it like it is: Be open, honest, straightforward; hold nothing back because of fear of hurting someone's feelings. (182)

Soul: an awareness and understanding of life, a naturalness of expression, being in contact with the naturalness of life and the environment, understanding yourself and others. (173)

The world that this new vocabulary unfolds is one in which states of conformity and self-regimentation are undermined, with every utterance, by an awareness and insight into the sensuality and meter of the lived moment—a rupture best conjured with these familiar words: "Hip: Aware, knowledgeable, informed, wise, with a comprehension of; in tune with the times"; "Square: person with a conventional and provincial attitude" (176). Between the hip and the square, then, lay a process of personal change, of loosening up, of becoming loose.

The tensions in Landy's book resonated with struggles around identity, lifestyle, and the appropriate means of self-regulation that were, in the late 1960s and on into the 1970s, transforming the American cultural landscape as millions of young (and not so young) people found increasingly creative ways to loosen themselves up. The loosening of the self provided a popular narrative related in numerous ways with subtle variations. The looser self spoke of a new livelihood, excavated from the stony edifice of tradition and the routines of conventional life. The looser life promised to release submerged, primordial energies long held in check—energies that when freed would empower one with a new capacity to act in and on one's own life. Loosening invoked the idea of a more authentic, innocent, and original source of the self and promised a way of living that was more primary and immediate but also more active and creative. Loose, hip people were empowered to make choices over aspects of their lives that squares, unreflective and constrained by habit, took only for granted. Related through metaphors of eruption, epiphany, and release, the loose life dwelled in the textures of daily life and the minutiae of personal experience. It was lived in the immediacy of *the now*—a real life one could really experience. To "be yourself," to "do what was right for you," to "let it all hang out" was to release a primordial vitality, to become an artist of oneself and of one's identity and to assume responsibility and take credit for what one made of oneself through the crafting of a distinctly loose style of life.

Following the counterculture's halcyon days of the late 1960s, versions of this loosening metaphor would prove immensely popular and infinitely adaptable for a variety of social groups and across a range of locales and lifestyles. In millions of American homes, food would become purer, its naturalness less constrained by additives and processed ingredients; clothing would become more sexual and revealing; home decor more authentic and rustic; sex more orgiastic; relationships more earnest and sincere. Young people would increasingly seek authentic experiences in wilderness trips away from the regimented spaces of the city, while a variety of therapeutic programs would help strip away phoniness by putting people in touch with who they really were. Authenticity was increasingly sought in the foods and garments of presumably less uptight, non-Western peoples, while stress was increasingly massaged and exercised from tense joints and tight muscles. Child-rearing practices embraced the "permissiveness" associated with the new child psychology espoused by Benjamin Spock, while loose, formless beanbag chairs flopped onto lush shag carpets and creative natural fabric wall hangings and macramé compositions adorned living room walls. In the bedroom, couples strove to overcome their hang-ups through open marriages and swinger's parties, while at the office ties were loosened or disappeared entirely, top buttons came undone, hair was allowed to hang down to shoulders, mustaches drooped, sideburns crept, chest hairs peeked and first names began to replace formal modes of address. In the wake of the counterculture of the 1960s, throughout the American middle class, anything whose traditional form could be made to yield to a more impulsive vitality would be worked over and reinvented in a looser way.

Landy's book provides a springboard into the questions that define the parameters of this study: how and why did the loosening motif, as a countercultural pattern of interpersonal style and emotional self-management, migrate from the countercultural fringe to the cultural mainstream? How did the loosening metaphor bridge the distance between Landy's drug center and the citadels of middle-class culture and identity, and why were middle-class people so ready to accept this message, so willing to incorporate the new discourse of loosening into the fabrics of their daily lives? By way of an introduction, I will address these questions in turn, starting with the how, and moving on to the more subtle and provocative question of why this migration occurred.

In the chapters that follow, the diffusion of the loosening motif will be sought in volumes of lifestyle literature—what I term the countercultural lifestyle print culture of the 1970s. While originating in hippie networks and enclaves, these books and magazines rose to national celebrity, disseminating hippie lifestyle themes into the homes and habits of the American middle classes.[2] In the early 1970s, as the youth movement turned its focus from mass mobilization and radical politics to more innocuous lifestyle issues, themes of self-loosening acquired a specifically prescriptive tone applied to a range of lifestyle practices, propagated in volumes of magazines, books, and catalogs, all vaguely countercultural in spirit. As the fires of the 1960s cooled, a small publishing genre rose to prominence in the American book market: books on food, gardening, home construction, ecology, health, spirituality, and relationships, often produced by small offbeat presses on the West Coast, without large distribution deals or production budgets, amateurish and rough in their production quality, brandishing advice on such matters as food preparation, the construction of dwellings, home provisioning, sexuality, collective living, athletics and health, recycling, solar and wind power, exercise, massage, ecology, cycling, jogging, crafts, meditation and spirituality, and hair and clothing. What started as a national network of countercultural presses, bookstores, authors, and critics developed, by the early 1970s, into a powerful presence on the American book market.[3] From a hub of West Coast presses concentrated in the Bay Area, several distinctly Californian titles rocketed to the height of national sales. Beginning with the success of the *Whole Earth Catalog* (an ad hoc collection of product reviews, commentaries, and ecological screeds gathered from hundreds of experimental lifestylists and back-to-the-landers) by the mid-1970s the book market was inundated with titles like *What Color Is Your Parachute, Living on the Earth, Rainbook, The Moosewood Cookbook, Our Bodies, Ourselves, The Massage Book, Domebook, Be Here Now, The Tassajara Bread Book*, and many others.[4] Digby Diehl, book editor for the *Los Angeles Times*, attributed the success of the new Western presses to their engagement with tangible problems of daily life: "Indian lore, Esalen-type therapeutics, ecological alarm, the occult explosion, sex experiments, the counterculture, and various forms of the New Life itself are what readers nationwide are buying."[5] The New Life he described was a loose life lived in the immediate, tangible, and real domain of stripped-down everyday needs and authentic experiences, though it was a life that demanded, curiously, the mediation of an instructional and pedagogical discourse the new lifestyle publishers were only too ready to supply.

Indeed, it was through this New Life and the ceaseless demands for self-loosening it imposed that the counterculture of the 1960s left its most profound imprint on the culture of the American middle class. To participate in the new lifestyle, one had to loosen oneself into the world by overcoming the technological drive to instrumental mastery of nature. One had to loosen oneself into the company of others through honest, open communications, and loosen oneself into one's own body through immersion in the sensuality of the self and an embrace of corporeal experience. Through diet or sexual habits, through daily displays of empathy, or through the way one exercised and cultivated one's body, loosening meant becoming an active chooser of a more authentic self. To be loose was to be mobile in a shifting world, to free oneself of the constraining baggage of tradition, and to sail out across the sea of unmediated experience even as one traveled with one's favored companion, the lifestyle adviser whose prescriptions were always available in the latest journal, book, or magazine on the New Life. In short, to be loose was to choose oneself, and the ultimate truth of that choice lay not in what one chose but in the mere fact of being a chooser—a mobile, flexible and self-responsible self, unconstrained by tradition and collective obligation.

A reflection on the impact of countercultural lifestyle print culture begins to answer the *how* question posed earlier: lifestyle books, largely published on the West Coast, provided a powerful medium for the popularization of a new ethic of the self—a loosening discourse on identity and everyday life. Answering the *why* question, concerning the specific needs and purposes of middle-class people to which the loosening lifestyle responded, is a complicated task requiring a more general overview of the theoretical and historical underpinnings of this study.

Loosening Up

This book attempts to capture a broad trajectory of social and historical change in a thin slice of popular cultural history. The style of life described in West Coast lifestyle literature and crystallized in the jargon of Landy's hippies provides evidence of the changing ways people have, in the name of becoming more modern, fashioned and sustained new modes of self-identity. This study considers profound changes that have occurred in recent years as the basis for selfhood has shifted from the collective and customary forms proper to a traditional society to the individualistic and inventive forms we know today. An old axiom of the sociological tradition tells the story: where in traditional societies individuals were embedded in relatively stable social networks in which questions of self-identity were resolved by fixed cultural and institutional authorities, in today's shaky and changing world we find ourselves compelled to answer those questions on our own through daily improvisations and choices in style of life.[6] Where once the moral guidance embodied by religion and the state, or the sense of affiliation derived from class and community membership, was enough to tell each of us who we were, what we should do, and why our lives were meaningful, today such answers are more often gleaned from individual accomplishments in our careers, our relationships, and in the way we choose to live. Indeed, it is the dissemination of choice in everyday practices (an accomplishment often attributed to our developed culture of consumption) that has so profoundly undermined the stability and permanence proffered by a traditional worldview.[7]

This shift is at the center of a pattern of transformation we associate with modern social and cultural change generally. With the onset of mercantilist trade in early modern Europe, for example, traditional social hierarchies, ordered according to what Arthur Lovejoy termed the "great chain of being" (a unity reinforced by theological certainties) crumpled under the circulation of capital and commodities, a modernizing transformation that substituted the tactile materiality of everyday things for the lofty authority of the cosmic order as an index of prestige and social status.[8] The way one lived in a traditional order was strictly regulated by one's place in this metaphysically stabilized cosmology: to choose a way of life inconsistent with one's social station was tantamount to sin, not just a breach of a personal ethics of well-being but a rejection of the divine plan for man and the world. But with the demise of a social universe undergirded by such a religiously sanctioned worldview and stable system of social caste, the profane, secular world of everyday practices and things emerged as a field of symbolic contest and status competition among highly mobile classes. Today, it is argued, individual choice is enshrined in every facet of identity and selfhood, or, to use the current sociological vernacular, identity has become a reflexive project expressing the individual's capacity to act back on itself with a constitutive force through choices made from an array of equally valid lifestyle options.[9]

In a more contemporary frame, the undermining of tradition and the dissemination of lifestyle choice derives from recent changes in the structure of the modern economy and in the social and personal fabric of everyday life more generally. The uprooting of the industrially based capitalism of the post-war period and the adoption of fluid, flexible, and highly mediated regimes of economic life has brought about the displacement of production and work by consumption, leisure, and lifestyle as a basis for an individual sense of self.[10] Consumption and lifestyle have emerged in recent decades as central to the way people imagine themselves to be agents of their own lives and authors of their own reflexive identities—a turn that has insinuated new forms of flexibility, fragmentation, and fluidity into the very fibers of self-identity. Such lives are no longer tests of character or expressions of devotion to long-term goals requiring the control of impulse and postponement of gratification: they are ongoing projects of the person's own doing expressed in myriad tastes, preferences, and consumer choices, mediated by the phantasmagoria of lifestyle imagery.[11] Consumer lifestyles are feats of self-improvisation in which tradition and collective norms appear not as moral signposts (or what David Reisman called a "psychological gyroscope")[12] pointing the way to virtue, but as remnants of an obsolete mode of self-constraint, an obstacle to be overcome in the fashioning of a more expressive identity. Moreover, in the choppy waters of contemporary life where social bonds are thin, work is flexible, and change comes as quickly as the next fashion cycle, each of us must break free of collective traditions and their cumbersome obligations in order to better surf the waves of perpetual chaos, rolling with the punches of a world in flux. Loosening of the self for the middle classes of the 1970s was part of a reorganization of identity for the conditions of a nascent late modernity, or postmodernity: a reflexive project of self-identity undertaken with the support and guidance of a host of mediators and specialists.[13]

In short, this reconfiguration of the priorities of work and leisure in the postwar period can be read as a moment within a broader dynamic of social change that has operated within Western societies for a very long time—a dynamic of modernity (in a phase variously designated with adjectives and prefixes such as *late, liquid, reflexive*, or *post-*) in which the constraints of tradition are severed in the name of the expressive freedoms of the individual. Landy's hippies, as novel as they may have believed themselves to be, shared more than they realized with the moderns of previous times, just as we, citizens of advanced, twenty-first-century, late modern societies, share more than we realize with them.[14]

None of this, however, tells us why the loosening motif was so welcomed into the homes and lives of middle-class people. Such broad-brush economic and structural considerations, while supplying us with overarching explanations of change on a massive scale, tempt us to read historical events as simple deterministic effects of these changing economic currents. The loosening of the self, it will be argued here, must be grasped on a smaller scale, in the thin cultural slices in which people encountered it in their everyday lives. The modernity of every age is, as Marshall Berman reminds us, a deeply subjective response to the transformations in which one finds oneself immersed.[15] In the case of the peculiar modernity that confronted the American middle classes of the 1970s, the loosening of the self reflected an effort to confront the displacements of modern social change by inscribing this experience within a narrative of unfolding identity. Loosening was a story of personal change designed to allay anxieties resulting from the increasing flexibility of identity and social life: it unfolded a small but intact moral universe in which the undercutting of the traditional foundations of identity and selfhood could be tolerated, even enjoyed, given specific meaning, transformed into a narrative of self-growth and realization told against the backdrop of traumatic twists and turns in the social fabric. What Anthony Giddens calls ontological insecurity, the sense of existential meaninglessness that shadows the construction of identity in modern societies, was resolved, however tenuously, in the project of becoming loose as a narrative of changing selfhood—a reflexive storying of the self.[16]

In this regard, the how and the why questions posed earlier come together in an explanation for the popularity of the loose life: lifestyle publications, as essentially storytelling vehicles, provided the ideal medium both for the transmission of a lifestyle ethic from an underground fringe to the middle-class mainstream, and for the shaping of traumatic change into the purposeful narrative of self-loosening. These lifestyle publications related narrative accounts of a transformed self—loosened, made more real, and opened to a new realm of experience, but not blown away entirely in the maelstrom of modern social and cultural flux. The aim of this book is to capture the many ways in which, for readers of these lifestyle tracts as well as for their authors (hippies, freaks, autodidacts, inventors, and other self-styled entrepreneurs of the New Life), style of life became a story of self-loosening in which the constraints of tradition would be pried open in order that a fuller, more real, less mediated life might emerge, and in which new forms of personal and social uprootedness could be experienced as intentional, purposeful, and meaningful change. In this sense, the present study concerns not just metalevel historical processes and micro-level cultural phenomena, but the interaction of the two in books, texts, and lifestyle advice imparted by mediators of self-identity.

In the lifestyle print culture of the 1970s, the allegorical lesson of self-loosening was related in numberless ways and in many varied combinations: to be loose was to be modern, and to be modern was to tell oneself a story of self-loosening, of a mediated and supervised relaxation of self-control and an acquired talent for the immersion of oneself in bodily sensations, impulses, and the inevitable flow of daily events. The loose lifestyle called upon readers to embrace this modernity in dozens of small yet significant ways: to set aside social inhibitions and express oneself without restraint in groups and relationships; to release oneself from the artificial prohibition on communion with nature enforced by technological civilization and to find oneself in oneness with the earth and its natural products; to release one's body from the protocols of self-presentation by letting one's hair grow or one's jeans wear through, or to cut through sexual mores and pursue one's desires. Indeed, the challenge of properly loosening oneself presented a task of tremendous technical skill and calculation: one had to work on oneself, monitor and supervise the growth of one's new sensibilities, tease out hidden blockages and bottlenecks that prevented one from freely choosing and being who one really was. Diehl's New Life was lived in an immediate relation to the experience of the everyday, but this immediacy was at the same time mediated at every step.

The contradiction between intuition and calculation, or immersion in experiences and the choice and commitment one made to immersion as a general way of life, would provide an active and curious dynamic within the counter-cultural lifestyle movement of the early 1970s, particularly as this dynamic was adopted by a wider segment of the middle class and later still absorbed into the mainstream culture of consumption.[17] As we shall see, this contradiction was reproduced even in the very media through which it was disseminated. Caught in an awkward role as mediators of lived immediacy, the strain of this contradiction gave this literature its distinct character: a roguish refusal of the authority of the traditional expert manual with its objective tone of detached scientific knowledge shaped an intimate and informal mode of advice. Amateurish typographic and formal qualities betrayed the grassroots economic and professional networks from which these books emerged, and the ad hoc production methods by which they were produced testified to a desire to evade the text-as-usual distance from the object conveyed in traditional lifestyle and other literary publications.[18] In this sense, they were loose books relating advice on the loose life in the voice of loose expertise—a discourse in transition from uptight conventions of publication and instruction to livelier, more expressive, and experiential advisory texts. Indeed, the reflexive mode of identity to which these publications spoke was more than advised in the words and pictures that filled their pages: it was tangibly practiced in the binding, the printing, and the layouts that characterized the immediacy and tangibility to which they spoke.

Thus, what is proposed here is a study that brings together a broad-brush theory of modern social change with a detailed rendering of a thin slice of cultural life. While broad-brush analyses and totalizing before/after explanations of social change necessarily entail generalizations and reductions that threaten to stifle more than they reveal, it is hoped that a dialectic of empirical and theoretical work will illuminate such processes within the experienced horizons of everyday social and personal life. Indeed, such explanations often prove unwieldy in the analysis of daily experiences, skipping over the varieties of experience that belong to specific groups and specific locales, while falsely elevating the experiences of one group to a more general status as typical of an epoch. With this problem in mind, it should be stated unequivocally that the loosening of the self, as it is considered here, was an experience particular to one group within the larger mix of American society—a white middle class in which heteronormative and patriarchal sexual and gender norms prevailed.[19] The modernity in question is their modernity, and the anxieties and dreams it evoked were the dreams particular to this group, even as they passed themselves off as much more than that. As Barbara Ehrenreich has pointed out, this group has no proper name, owing to its own presumption of universality and value neutrality, and its enduring, if invisible hegemony as purveyors of America's mainstream. To speak of the postwar middle classes, variously known as the professional-managerial class, the new class, the professional middle class or simply the middle class, is to address this condition of a false universality of values: "Nameless and camouflaged by a culture in which it both stars and writes the scripts," Ehrenreich writes, "this class plays an overweening role in defining 'America': its moods, political direction, and moral tone."[20] Owing to the hegemonic position the middle class has enjoyed and continues to enjoy on the American cultural scene, this group has succeeded in establishing its anxieties and concerns, its modernities and its projects of identity as *the* experience of a time, the backdrop to that of all others. Indeed, while this hegemony cannot be denied, the false naturalization of its own claim to universality can be interrogated and read in the context of the historical predicament within which it developed. As will be discussed in chapter 1, the loosening of the self operated not only in the spaces of middle-class life, but in a set of interactions and appropriations that occurred along the boundaries separating the middle classes from its various others: African Americans, women, gays and lesbians, Asians, and the working class.

But there is another thread woven into this inquiry that serves a separate, though related purpose. The story of the loosening of the self is read here as part of a wider inquiry into the conditions of the present: a genealogy of the flexible and fluid identities so often described in recent scholarship on contemporary cultural change.[21] It will be argued that the lifestyle movements of the 1960s and 1970s contributed significantly to a pattern of cultural change that has produced identity as a highly autonomous, individual accomplishment, mediated by consumer markets and the lifestyle offerings they naturalize as the inevitable frameworks for the choice of self. Identity today is understood as a project undertaken by an enterprising self who cultivates personal autonomy as a career and personal asset in a world mediated by markets and exchange relations.[22] Indeed, careful explanation is provided of the specific continuities between countercultural lifestyle discourses and leading developments in the consumer cultures of the present. Modes of personal autonomy, ways of choosing oneself and making oneself loose, were integrated gradually into the warp and woof of an expanding culture of consumption—at the expense, I argue, of the power these choices hold to excite the imagination and deal reliably with a world of change. This cooptation (to use a rather heavy-handed term) has had the ultimate result of destroying the meaning these lifestyles once held for their practitioners: morphing from lifestyle discourses to prepackaged lifestyle commodities, lifestyles lose their storytelling quality as biographical narratives and shared fictions, fragmenting into isolated actions of purchase and private consumption, most notoriously in the lifestyle brands that came to prominence in the 1980s. The ultimate aim of this study lies, then, with this project of a historical genealogy (albeit one of a rather truncated scope): by better understanding the genesis of the modes of self-understanding we take today to be natural, by tracing them to the specific groups and media through which they were developed and by reconstructing the specific historical horizons against which they were shaped, we position ourselves to better grasp what is missing in our heavily mediated identities and possibly to intervene in and transform them today, to grasp their plasticity in the present, to maximize their potentials and turn them to new and better purposes. In that sense, the aims of this book are quite optimistic: by better understanding the modernities of the past and by seeing with clarity the lineage we share with them, we read our own predicament for the instability and flux, the opportunity and openness it affords.

However, if the intention of a genealogical study is to upset the present by revealing its roots in the past, the imprint of the loose lifestyle on contemporary culture is not always so easy to spot. At first blush, all evidence of the adventure of the loosening lifestyle has either been intentionally disavowed or is preserved only in its most trivial aspects—gestures of rebellion and defiance that, recent studies have revealed, are now innocuous features of everyday capitalism.[23] In the 1980s, as Americans struggled to return the genie loosed by the counterculture back into the bottle of self-discipline and "traditional values," the loosening metaphor would wane in its power to inspire lifestyle adventures, or to draw around itself a discourse of advice and exhortation, while rebellion would become an increasingly common staple of everyday consumption and even corporate leadership.[24] As calls for discipline resonated across public debates from educational policy to government spending, a new tautness was imposed upon the loose life, particularly among the middle-class segment so seduced by the counterculture—the young urban professionals whose lifestyle habits were to leave such an indelible imprint on American consumer culture. Yet in more subtle ways, salient features of the countercultural experiment would be incorporated into the fabric of a new culture of the self. Beyond the most obvious postures of rebellion and defiance (Thomas Frank has written extensively on an unholy alliance between beats, hippies, and rebels and the high-flying corporate magnates of the new economy, inspiring others to question the entire legacy of the 1960s on the remarkably narrow grounds of a critique of adolescent iconoclasm as a political position) the lifestyle experiments of the counterculture fused itself into the fabric of contemporary everyday life. In the yuppie lifestyles of the 1980s, new modes of self-regimentation and control would replace the spirited impulsiveness associated with its historical forbearer, the yippie, but the relation of self to self would remain, acquiring new form and greater purchase on the practice of identity in daily life. Time spent hanging loose or being oneself would be tethered to the tight scheduling of the weekly planner;

therapeutic exercise, once a vehicle of self-exploration, would be praised for its power to enhance productivity, and trips to the gym would tighten up muscles for ever more Herculean feats of decompression from the strains of work.[25] As bell-bottoms and scruffy hair gave way to tapered pants and the mullet (with its controlled reconciliation of a presentable front and unruly back), forms of lifestyle premised on the drawing in of slack were incorporated into a new configuration of the work regime and woven into new patterns of self-identity associated with an economy of rapid growth and change and a consumer culture of increasingly nuanced meaning and ephemeral form.

Even as yuppies shed the outward markings of looseness, they preserved the essentially reflexive character that defined the loose lifestyle of the 1970s, refining it and disseminating it as a general feature of identity and everyday life throughout the American middle class, retooling it for the demands of an increasingly flexible economic and social order.[26] The demand that one live reflexively, that one take responsibility for one's life as the product of one's own artistry, and that one work on oneself to enhance one's authenticity through daily lifestyle choices survived and even prospered during the cultural reforms of the Reagan period, and its purported aim to "roll back" the progressive gains of the 1960s. A countercultural emphasis on expressive self-realization and personal autonomy found an unlikely resonance with neoliberal visions of self-responsibility and enterprise, understood as an ethic of personal accountability and flexibility—values that were enshrined in a thousand yuppie habits from the athletic club to the stock market, and in a conservative contempt for all forms of collectivity from the welfare state to organized labor, as limiting to the full attainment of self-authenticity through achieved self-reliance.[27] Indeed, while the outward forms of looseness have been stripped away, the essential structure of a self-choosing self has remained, transferred from loosely affiliated countercultural lifestyle sages to the halls of department stores, the pages of lifestyle magazines and punchy taglines like "Just Do It."

Identity as a reflexive choice of style of life has been mediated, perhaps since the early 1980s, by a transformed mass market possessing powers of nuance and empathy specifically appropriated from the counterculture of the 1970s. Today, in a culture of consumption whose penetration of daily life is enhanced by new technologies of media, consumer research, and marketing, these mediating discourses are looser for their appropriation of countercultural discourse on lifestyle—capable of speaking in more authentic, intimate tones to more precise market niches and more defined personal needs, and of soothing more effectively the personal anxieties resulting from a world fraught with risk and uncertainty.[28] Incorporated into the lexicon of a more sensitive and humanistic culture of consumption, appeals to self-renewal through lifestyle were drained of any semblance of cultural opposition they possessed as a loosening metaphor, their ideology watered down for less radical audiences and their overall form retooled for a more flexible economy of shallow commitments and deep, but routinely tolerated, ontological insecurity. But more importantly, discourses of self-loosening were flattened out and made trivial as they were transposed from the collective project of a shared community of discourse to the solitary endeavor of the lone shopper. Where loosening, I will argue, was essentially a story or set of stories one told to others and to oneself about one's own development and transformation through daily lifestyle choices, yuppie lifestyles and those that followed lacked such a quality of reciprocity and interlocution, referring instead to private projects of identity providing only an uneasy reconciliation of the problems of the contemporary self. Where loosening up was, as the following chapters will argue, a collective practice involving advice and a shared (if partially imagined) community—what I will call, drawing on the later writings of Michel Foucault, a practice of caring—the reflexive lifestyles of the 1980s and beyond related only bloodless, solipsistic versions of this lifestyle discourse, highly individualistic and narrowly schematic feats crafted into a self-interested, calculating economic individualism that flushed nicely with the neoliberal ideologies of free markets, a radically diminished civil society and only sparse investment in the promise of self-transformation in a shared future.

Today, even as the ethical injunction to loosen up has lost its capacity to invigorate moral discourse, shades of its former meaning surface in unlikely places. The loose critique of the square, for example (of his obsessive workplace rigidity and his timidity in the marketplace), continues to inform a work ethic premised on flexibility and impermanence, and all manners of leisure continue to invoke the value of breaking convention to go with one's feelings, particularly in the activity of impulse buying. Yet looseness, associated with the counter-culture of the 1960s, draws popular rebuke, particularly in the discourse of the political right where "permissiveness" remains a standard rhetorical bludgeon. Four months after the terrorist attacks of September 11, 2001 sent the nation into a spasm of recrimination and giddy patriotism, George W. Bush painted the national mood as one of vigorous moral renewal premised on a lasting and final renunciation of the legacy of the 1960s: "For too long our culture has said, 'If it feels good, do it.' Now America is embracing a new ethic and a new creed: 'Let's roll.'" However one chooses to judge the impact of the lifestyle experiments of the 1970s, it is clear that its central premise was rapidly and lastingly absorbed into the fabric of American society and continues to inform our sense of selfhood and integrity, even from the highest of public offices. In a 2004 Oval Office interview, President Bush, with unwitting yet unmistakable hippie elocution, stressed his wish that the American people "understand where I'm coming from . . . I'm a war president."[29]

The 1960s

The account related here is one that places the counterculture of the 1960s in an unfamiliar perspective. Beyond celebratory accounts of reverie, expressiveness, radical politics and the euphoric momentum of social change, the emphasis here is on the inner capacities for control and decontrol developed in this movement. Against the hedonistic legacy of the 1960s, the focus here is on the simultaneity of internalized control and release, or a controlled story of practiced release, implied by the countercultural lifestyle ethic. Such a focus distinguishes this analysis from more typical histories of the counterculture, even those with ambitious sociological and theoretical goals, which have tended to consider only the immersive, expressive, and sensual aspects, sometimes lumped together under the heading of the Dionysian more generally. More important than the capacity to break down barriers and release new feelings are the specific talents developed for the maintenance of such states of release—talents of self-regulation and self-examination, techniques for the crafting of experiences into biographical identities centered on the loosening of the self.

Inquiries into the moral world of hippies and counterculturals are not new: hippies first showed up on the sociologist's radar as objects of a sociology of deviance approach, or a comparative sociology of religious beliefs. Throughout the 1970s, communes and ashrams were subjected to ethnographic interpretations for the "deviant lifestyles" they practiced, or for the moral standpoints they appeared to endorse, as represented in Steve Tipton's *Getting Saved from the Sixties*, or Robert Bellah's studies of contemporary religious belief. Others have taken a social movements perspective on the political history of the counterculture and the New Left, tracing the political trajectory of the counterculture from its inception at Port Huron to its crest in the riots of 1968 and on to its dissolution in the Nixon years, as evidenced by Todd Gitlin's *The Sixties: Years of Hope, Days of Rage*. More recent studies have sought to link the counterculture with contemporary trends in consumer culture, most notably Thomas Frank's *Conquest of Cool*. Though these works have provided valuable contributions from which the present investigation draws, they largely tend to make the mistake of glossing over the distinct and conflicting agendas within the counterculture itself—differences that came to the fore in a break (often related conveniently to the interval between the two decades) between the fiery militancy of the 1960s and the mellower lifestyle concerns of the 1970s. From 1968 to 1970, between the demonstrations at the Democratic National Convention in Chicago and the first Earth Day, the popular notion of the hippie broadened to include a new set of associations: to the roles of civic firebrand, vagabond, swinger, and LSD mystic were added pastoralist, domestic technician, farmer, technologist, and specialist in the new arts of authentic living.

To loosen oneself in the counterculture of the 1970s was not only to rupture the discipline imposed by the square world but also to evolve beyond the politics and activism of the New Left itself (widely perceived after Nixon's electoral victories and other setbacks as just another form of uptightness). It was to evolve into a form of revolution that was more personal, practical, and immediate, a revolution played out in the practice of everyday life. The concealed continuity between the tight and the loose that is the object of this book developed in that moment where the counterculture of the 1970s assumed a new program and a new priority: the revolution was not something to be fought for, but something to be relaxed into, lived and experienced in the moment. Moreover, as distinct from the explosive lifestyles of hippies in Haight-Ashbury or the high-flying drug cultures of the 1960s, living the revolution did not signal a dissolution of the boundaries of the self in music or psychedelic experiences but provided a coordinated set of living techniques centered on a thematically unified philosophy of life, related in a new advisory discourse on the practicing of a looser and more authentic way of living. Indeed, educated, mediated release would become a technique of self-control, and as such would provide the basis for a new reflexive project of the self.

But there is another sense in which the approach of this book differs from other commonly accepted views on the legacy of the counterculture. In addition to the very different meanings we get from the counterculture of the 1960s and 1970s, there is the question of the specific media through which exhortations of the Dionysian were related. The 1960s counterculture typically evokes the immersive cultures of visuality and sound, and the decentering effects of a carnivalesque culture: psychedelic light shows, colorful fashions, shocking films, Day-Glo face painting, and loud, loud music. The "new sensibility" of the 1960s, as Susan Sontag famously described it, was a reverie of the senses whose proper element was the plastic arts (sculpture, painting, performance) over and against the intellectualism of the old discursive traditions of literature and interpretation.[30] The counterculture itself was a liminal experience, described by Bernice Martin for its ecstatic and transcendent properties that eluded and subverted the traditional categories of institutional life, work, and leisure.[31] Yet if we turn from the light shows and rock concerts to the prescriptive lifestyle texts that became increasingly prominent in the 1970s, a new perspective opens on a culture typically defined by hedonism and irrationalism, by immersive visuals, booming music, and sartorial excess. In hippie books, magazines, and lifestyle publications, the Dionysian explosion of pleasure, sensuality, and enriched consciousness was brought into relation with a host of techniques and procedures whose focus was control and self-regulation, and it was in the form of such a lifestyle discourse, I will argue, that the influence of the counterculture penetrated the lifestyles of the middle classes. Combining a concern with the shifts that occurred between the 1960s and the 1970s from an explosive movement for social change and personal liberation to the more sedate experiments with lifestyle and personal authenticity, with a consideration of the specific modes of ethical discourse related in a lifestyle print culture, we discover that 1960s Dionysianism developed an unexpected alliance with its own Apollonian counterpart: a technique of self-control and self-regulation in which liberation was sketched out as a calculated lifestyle project.

We find that, by the 1970s, for millions of middle-class Americans who had, in their own ways, internalized and routinized the reverie of the 1960s and applied it to a radical renovation of their everyday ways of life, the new sensibility operated within a dynamic of release and constraint: the explosive qualities first celebrated in Haight-Ashbury and in the culture of LSD were soon linked to doctrines of personal growth and techniques of living and experiencing in which eruptions of immediacy and lived experience were transformed into a regular and regulated mode of life. Jimi Hendrix's query "Are you experienced?," once an invitation to step outside oneself into a vertiginous realm of sensation and feeling laced with fear of fragmentation, came to refer to experiences of a much tamer sort—the experience of safety in getting to know oneself through weekends in the woods and jogs on the beach. Loosening, as an ethic and a technique of daily life, provided the overarching metaphor through which the liminality of the new sensibility was tethered to more fundamental needs for regularity, predictability, and ontological security. This tension between the sensual and the discursive, between lived experiences and the efforts of lifestyle specialists to both extend and expand that sensuality through rational techniques, animates the ethic of loosening and the literatures that defined it. As the new sensibility was crafted and shaped into durable ways of living for the new middle classes of the 1970s, the sensuality of the present was transmuted from an immersive experience to a technique of controlled self-release, and ultimately a structuring principle in the organization of time, routines, and a sustained sense of biographical and social identity.

Indeed, a spate of recent books has sought to puncture the myth of the hedonistic 1960s and to trace the links between the supposed carnival of the counterculture and the bacchanal of contemporary consumption patterns. Thomas Frank's study was important in this respect for revealing the buried links between advertising and the counterculture, and the ultimate consequence of the counterculture in broadening the repertoire of consumer identities to include more rebellious postures—gestures of defiance that in no way pose any serious challenge to the economies of consumption themselves. Indeed, the approach of this book agrees with Frank's premise that the 1960s counterculture can be read as the progenitor of contemporary forms of consumption. But the links between contemporary lifestyle consumption and the innovations of the counterculture are far more difficult to trace than Frank acknowledges. To equate the counterculture with rebelliousness per se, and to conclude that contemporary forms of individualistic lifestyle are derivatives of this oppositional stance is to ignore complexity on both sides and to gloss over the process of incorporation by which countercultural lifestyles were retailored for a new economic and cultural configuration. The posture of rebellion and the sensuality of the new sensibility represent only some—and not the most important or lasting—features of the counterculture's legacies for the American popular cultural scene. More important, I will argue, is the fundamental relation to the self as an object of manipulation and choice in the practice of daily life. Such a self-choosing self was developed in the counterculture, exported widely to other groups, and ultimately codified in standardized repertoires of consumption. By emphasizing the introspective 1970s over and against the riotous 1960s, and by taking on the printed word and the written exhortation as against the seductive image and cacophonous sound, the present study describes the fact of reflexivity itself, and the manner in which attention to self is ingrained into the attitudes and identities of people in their everyday lives, as an enduring inheritance of the counterculture.

Plan of This Book

In the pages that follow, the countercultural lifestyle print culture of the 1970s will be read in a holistic manner that takes in all facets of this culture, both material and symbolic. Against the backdrop of a broad historical sketch of the 1970s, and framed by a discussion of the status of expert discourse on matters of lifestyle and identity, dozens of countercultural publications will be considered (though a few will be selected for careful review) in a manner that takes into account all their qualities both as narrative texts and also as material things whose unique formats and design features often tell stories as valuable as the written messages they convey. On a broader institutional level, the social and economic networks through which these publications were produced and distributed to readers within restricted countercultural circles and to wider national audiences will enter in as part of the overall account. All the elements that compose this lifestyle discourse as a print culture, in the widest sense, will figure into the present study: employing Robert Darnton's and Daniel Roche's concept of the "communications circuit," all facets of production, distribution, and reception of printed matters will contribute to this analysis.[32] If countercultural lifestyle discourse espoused a loosening of the control mechanisms imposed on the self, then the microeconomic infrastructure through which this discourse was produced and disseminated, and the very publications as material objects themselves, also functioned as symbols of this lifestyle ethic. The lifestyle print culture's way of producing goods and doing business was analogous with, and served as a metaphor for, the content of its lifestyle message, a fact that is emblazoned on the surface of each of its products in the form of rough layout and amateurish (if more "real") production qualities.

In this regard, this is a study of lifestyle discourse and lifestyle mediation, as over and against one of lifestyle practice. A selected emphasis will fall, therefore, on the texts themselves, as narratives of self-transformation and prescriptive texts on the development of the self through specific choices made in everyday life. A rounded approach more faithful to traditions of ethnography and cultural studies might include a greater emphasis on the ground-level reception of these texts and the extent to which they informed real practices. While such ends are worthy in themselves, for the sake of the economy of my argument I have chosen to stress the prescriptive dimensions of lifestyle as an object of advice, and the narrative content in which a discourse of lifestyle as a set of ethical and normative concerns is spelled out. As much as this is a book about lifestyles, it is also a book about books about lifestyles—about the texts and discourses that inscribed styles of life with specific ethical purposes.

In what follows, heroic accounts of achieved unconstraint will be interpreted in stories of personal loosening and the print artifacts through which they were related—a loosening of self-control that pointed toward a new style of life and a new way of construing identity. The plan of this book will pursue the study of these loosening discourses according to an agenda that first establishes a theoretical and historical framework then moves on to a series of interpretive, descriptive cases. In part 1, "Middle Class in the Maelstrom," three chapters provide a general understanding of the scope of the historical predicament in which a discourse of lifestyle emerged, of the freedoms and anxieties to which it was addressed, and of the specific modes of expertise and the distinct media through which it operated. In chapter 1, "Of Swingers and Organization Men," the fundamental problem of lifestyle is discussed as a personal mediation of the transformations of late modernity as experienced through the erosion of middle-class cultural authority. Calling principally on David Harvey's thesis on the post-Fordist turn, Pierre Bourdieu's theories of cultural capital, and Anthony Giddens's treatments of lifestyle as a feature of late modernity, the case is made for a study of loosening as a specific response to a crisis in middle-class self-understandings in the 1970s and the increasing conditions of individualization in American culture. A consideration of some classic formulations of the changing patterns of self-constraint and self-release provided by American sociologists maps out the shifting conditions that produced a broader openness to experience and an embrace of lifestyle in the early 1970s, leading up to an appropriation and codification of lifestyle as a mainstream mode of consumption in the 1980s. Significantly, as pointed out earlier, this occurred through a pattern of appropriation, emulation, and cooptation of the expressive styles practiced by other groups and other identity movements, principally African Americans and Black Power groups but also women, Asian, Native American, and other ethnic groups.

In chapter 2, "Experts Unbound," the problem of loosening is applied to the more specific conditions of expert discourse and to the changing status of lifestyle expertise through its incorporation of experiential knowledge, particularly for counterculturals. Recalling the expansion of the service sector and particularly the growing fields of health and human services in the 1970s, the case is made here that the changing status of expert discourse enabled a unique mode of exhortation and advice on the topic of lifestyle, one that was capable of instilling daily life choices with ethical and personal significance. In short, newly sensitized loose experts advised on the proper form of the loose lifestyle. Moreover, as popular attitudes toward mass consumption became increasingly skeptical, such empathic modes of address were appropriated into new marketing discourses, espousing a new sensitivity to the values and lifestyles of consumers. In chapter 3, "Book as Tool," the evolving status of the lifestyle expert is traced to the emergence of a countercultural print culture. This emerging publishing category is examined in relation to the changing American book market of the 1970s, and the growing popular interest in small, grassroots publishers, principally based on the West Coast. Clashes between advocates of this emerging market and the loose lifestyle message it embodied and the guardians of the more traditional (uptight) American book trade based in the larger eastern houses are read as expressions of a tension between expressive and repressive, or loose and tight, cultural styles. Throughout, the ethic of looseness is examined as a broadly applied metaphor in this literature, governing everything from the business practices in the loose network of California publishers to the rough, informal techniques of printers and typesetters.

Part 2, "Caring Texts," undertakes a concerted interpretive study of countercultural lifestyle print discourse and of the loosening metaphor divided into three broadly distinct areas: ecology and nature; home, business, and interpersonal life; and self and the body. In each of these chapters, a set of lifestyle concerns provides a framework in which loosening is related through a distinct metaphor of attained unconstraint, or mediated immediacy. Loosening is described through a binary construction contrasting vitality, immediacy, and expressiveness with convention, remoteness, and self-constraint. Chapter 4, "Being One," examines how becoming loose involves freeing oneself of the technological constraints that separate the civilized self from nature. In ecologically inspired lifestyle publications, one releases oneself into the wholeness of the earth through a way of living that is authentic and in touch with the cyclical flows of large ecological systems and the inclusive natural processes that integrate the planet. Several ecological journals are discussed, including *Rainbook* and the *Whole Earth Catalog*, which variously describe a style of life premised on a freer, more intimate relationship with nature, contrasted with the exploitive mentality of industrial society. In chapter 5, "Loving Each Other," the task of loosening is discovered in the injunction to release oneself into the other in the pursuit of trust. Here lifestyle involves learning to let go of egoistic pretenses and immersing oneself in spontaneous and unconstrained social communion and group membership. Trust, as a learned attitude toward social life, is here mediated through a discourse on collectivity and sharing, often defined in opposition to the competitive and instrumental relations of the straight world. Beginning with an investigation of the new sexual ethics of the 1970s (typified by the *Catalog of Sexual Consciousness*), books on communal life (*Celery Wine, Communities*), and geodesic dome construction (*Domebook, Shelter*) describe the loosening of the individual as an intrinsically social problem, involving the affirmation of the self in collective everyday life. The chapter closes with a reflection on the incorporation of loosening into business practices through a study of one countercultural business network (*Briarpatch Book*). Chapter 6, "Letting It All Hang Out," shows how loosening comes to refer to a rejection of the instrumentalized body of mainstream media, and the release of the self into a deepened, more natural sense of embodiment. In the literature on "body work," myriad techniques of relaxation and alternative fitness offered training in the immersion of the mind into the meter and sensuality of a rhetorically deepened body—a goal set in contrast to the regimes of competitive sport and military discipline, which seek only to subordinate the body to the demands of the rational will. Loose forms of embodiment are described in a classic compendium of feminist body work techniques called *Getting Clear*, in several collections on massage and Rolfing, and in a new discourse on jogging and athletics, in which competition itself is redefined as an inward practice of personal identity. This configuration of the athlete, originally the product of countercultural discourse on fitness, ultimately becomes seminal to new forms of lifestyle consumption in the 1980s.

Finally, some clarification of the historical perspective underlying this study is in order. If the line of argumentation presented here smacks of a very old and worn-out story, one that holds up the radical cultural products of the 1960s in order to measure their cooptation by the mass market, I assure the reader that, in what follows, the loosening discourses of the 1970s lifestyle movement will not be celebrated in any romantic sense. While I approach my topic with all the respect a researcher owes to his subjects and subject matter, I make it no secret that, by and large, I am neither a defender nor a critic of this project, at least not on the terms it claimed for itself. The solutions counterculturals delivered lacked historical durability for good reasons: their optimism depended on an ill-considered humanism that was sophomoric at best, sentimental and baseless at worst. The cultural pluralism they espoused banked on a false universalism that did not adequately interrogate its own hegemonic role as a white, largely male, largely heterosexual middle-class value system. This is no nostalgic treatise on lost good old days, much less a call to pick up and carry on where others have left off. But neither is this an occasion for derisive laughter, or a politically moti-vated critique. The empathy that guides this project stems from the imperatives of interpretive research itself, from the willingness to let texts tell their own stories, from the requirement that all stories have to be read against the back-drop of the histories and processes they mediate, and from the responsibilities that come with being a dutiful listener. The loosening of the self expressed an adventure with the modernity of its (and our) time, and what follows is an effort to read these lifestyle adventures as expressions of the deeper logic of a moder-nity we share across the gulf of several decades—a modernity that holds out exciting possibilities for the reshaping of selfhood, even as it grapples to adapt new forms of identity to the strains of cultural and social change. From a gene-alogical standpoint, understanding the intensity and conviction (and perhaps hubris) of countercultural lifestyles as part of a shared modernity allows us to view with fresh eyes the dynamics of our own time, and to perceive the present as a moment within a common arc of historical change—as part of an ongoing modernity, and as therefore available to creative reworking in the present. For that reason I have strained to tie together these lifestyle adventures with the discourses and lifestyles we know today. A history of the lifestyle movements of the 1970s is an important part of the history of ourselves, and of the dilemmas and opportunities we face as citizens of late modernity. This investigation is directed toward the goal of realizing, through historical excavation, the moder-nity within our own present.

Part I

Middle Class in the Maelstrom

1

Of Swingers and Organization Men
Loose Modernities

The moral culture of the American middle class was profoundly shaken by the social conflicts of the 1960s and by the years of economic slowdown that followed.[1] The 1970s is a decade recalled for its dubious legacy of soured hopes and sagging ideals—a mood of "malaise" resulting from the unraveling of cultural and economic structures whose disintegration had long been churning at the heart of American society, now showing itself on the surface of everyday life in forms that ranged from the mundane to the extraordinary. With the decline of manufacture and the emergence of a new service sector, the production of symbolic and informational goods continued a slow eclipse of the old industrial base as the lynchpin of capitalist development, displacing the managerial and manufacturing jobs that composed the core of middle- and working-class economic life. Belief in the ability of the state to act as the custodian of the collective interest was eroded under the scandals of Watergate and the festering of the welfare state, and the idyllic picture of the nuclear family as a respite from social turbulence was shaken by a revolution in values and outlooks, expressed in soaring divorce rates and a devastating generation gap. The crises of the 1970s witnessed a striking erosion in the power of public institutions to command popular faiths and a waning belief in collective solutions to public ills—a sentiment conjured by the *New York Daily News*'s famous headline announcing the federal government's forfeit on the goal of urban renewal: "Ford to City: Drop Dead."[2]

But if these crises signaled the impoverishment of shared public goals, they also hailed a vast and radical expansion of private ones. Recalled as the "Me decade," the 1970s inspired a culture of narcissism, as Christopher Lasch so famously christened it, in which a new emphasis on personal inwardness offered a compensatory safe haven, offsetting the stress of overpowering social and cultural insecurity.[3] The new introspectiveness announced the demise of an established set of traditional faiths centered on work and the postponement of gratification, and the emergence of a consumption-oriented lifestyle ethic centered on lived experience and the immediacy of daily lifestyle choices. Where work discipline, national duty, group affiliation, and professional merit served the "organization man" of the 1950s as the measure of attainment and self-worth, the 1970s produced a morality of self-realization through consumption, leisure, experiential learning, and therapeutic release—a looser morality whose exemplar was undoubtedly the dashing, fun-loving, and flirtatious "swinger."[4] But the slide from organization man to swinger was for many one of atavistic decline: "In the hedonistic life," sociologist Daniel Bell complained, "there is a loss of will and fortitude," and a slackening of conviction and self-control—a sentiment that has occasioned decades of cultural crusades (captured famously in Robert Bork's *Slouching toward Gomorrah*) aimed at expurgating once and for all what neoconservatives consider the self-indulgent residue of the 1960s counterculture.[5]

An inquiry into the emergence of the looser self requires that we evaluate more carefully this slouching trope. It asks that we consider the anxieties and imaginary investments that beset the cultural authority of the middle class and examine the dynamic that set loose swingers and tight organization men in their respective camps. Indeed, this crisis was not unique to the 1970s at all but was expressive of a dynamic of fear and hope, of disintegration and renewal, that characterizes the experience of modern social and cultural change in general. In the pages that follow, the explosive predicament of the crisis decade will be read for the unique modernity it expressed—the modernity of the 1970s— wherein a crisis in public authorities and a passionate loosening of the self related a dynamic of innovation, rupture, and imaginary flight, woven together with a panic at the prospect of a world without moral foundations.

Whitey on the Moon: The Modernity of the 1970s

Modernities are never experienced in a total sense, as the zeitgeist of an age, an epoch, or a civilization, but neither are they merely localized phenomena, scattered across a social surface in disconnected groups. The experience of modernity is felt at the intersection of changing social configurations and in the specific trajectories followed by individuals and groups across preexisting social and cultural boundaries. Such experiences are of the rumbling that accompanies seismic shifts in the ordering of a society, the movement of tectonic plates in the underlying social structure. Modernities must be considered as they develop in their conjunctural specificity, at the interstices opened up by emerging and receding patterns of life, by the concomitant fragmentation and demise of old social groups and the constitution of new ones.[6] Modernities are never the property of one group, much less the unconditioned spirit of an age, but the articulation of moments and temporal trajectories at the reconfigured boundaries between groups. Modernities are, in this sense, "without guarantees" in the meaning given the phrase by Stuart Hall: they express the efforts of individuals to bring their experiences into alignment with structural changes, to articulate everydayness together with changing regimes of power, changing distributions of capital and economy, and changing boundaries between competing clusters of people.[7] Indeed, the reconfiguration of social proximities and spaces is inextricably linked to the way people experience novelty and anticipate its consequences: the experience of the new is often one of disaffiliation and rupture within previously consolidated groups, but also a regrouping, an investment, emulation (or even fetishization) of identity across the boundaries dividing previously competing groups.

What I am calling the modernity of the 1970s was a modernity experienced by a portion of the American middle class that was predominantly white and Anglo-Saxon. This group was traditional in its thinking on sexuality and gender roles, and its regard for other social groups was restrained and suspicious, as evidenced by the xenophobia of American postwar suburban development and the deep-rooted racism and sexism that underscored much middle-class life at that time.[8] The loosening trope that emerged as middle-class youth of the 1960s questioned and ultimately abandoned the narrowness of their parents' worldviews gave narrative form to their own trajectory across social space, from the citadels of middle-class life to the riskier, grittier, and more sensual worlds of hippie hangouts, crash pads, rock concerts, mod neighborhoods, and the like. To drop out was to cross a border, but also to establish a new border where none had previously been: it was to betray one's class and take up with dangerous strangers, to hang out in the neighborhoods one's parents had worked hard to move out of, with the people one's parents had tried hard to protect one from.[9] Among the hip middle class (a group far larger than the hippies themselves), to loosen was to disavow the repressive strictures of the old middle class and to immerse oneself in the expressiveness and sensuality presumed to belong to groups on the margins, from Sufis and jazz musicians to street peddlers and Vietnamese children. Loosening up, as a way of becoming modern, was to participate in a hegemonic modernity practiced by a group that saw itself in very universalistic terms as a vanguard, steering social change from the helm of society's most powerful institutions and from the seat of its economic, social, and cultural engines. Such an insider's viewpoint gave the loosening story an urgency it could not otherwise have possessed: at stake was not just the emancipation of a group, but the fate of an entire world, of all humanity. And the innovations it developed were not discoveries unique to its members, they were breakthroughs on the most fundamental frontiers of human destiny, self-knowledge, and self-authenticity.

For outsiders, however, all of this carried a very different resonance. To the excluded, the modernities of the middle class have seemed quixotic and naive, if not threatening and despotic, particularly where they are premised on a wish to impose reform on others, whether by truncheon or welfare check. During the 1960s, skepticism of the official modernities of the middle class spread to its offspring, disaffected youth who shaped their own insurrectionary visions of social change as students imagined alternative programs for world peace and new, less technologically oriented visions of domestic life. Eagerly comparing themselves to "niggers," middle-class youth drew new lines between their forward-looking social imaginaries and those of their parents, choosing to throw their lot in with a range of oppressed groups as common victims of their parents' twisted and ultimately destructive view of progress.[10] The modernity of the 1970s was in this respect a disordered cluster of narratives and visions of progressive social change, some emerging and insurrectionary, others coping with the loss of their exclusive hold on the future.

Black poet and militant firebrand Gil Scott-Heron captured the hubris and self-involvement of one such middle-class modernity, crystallized in the popular zeal surrounding the early Apollo missions and lunar landings: "The man just upped my rent last night cuz Whitey's on the moon. No hot water, no toilets, no lights but Whitey's on the moon." His verse chides popular enthusiasm for the missions for their blissful failure to focus on the conditions of inner city life: "Y'know I jus' 'bout had my fill of Whitey on the moon, I think I'll sen' these doctor bills, Airmail special, to Whitey on the moon."[11] Whitey's modernity was one of optimism and faith. It prophesized rising standards of living and economic growth, increasing technological wizardry and the expansion of American global power beyond the limits of the globe itself, to new dimensions of colonization and resource exploitation. But for Scott-Heron, Whitey's modernity was clearly not his own, though it was one he understood for having lived all of his life and experiences in its shadow. And it was one against which his own more militant modernity would be composed, albeit his would be tinged with apocalyptic visions of violent transformation coupled with romantic yearning for a recovered precolonial innocence. Indeed, black militants were not the only ones to fashion modern narratives against the backdrop of this official optimism: as the heady days of the Apollo landings receded and the decade of malaise kicked in, Whitey's modernity would itself be eroded by doubts and recriminations as sanctioned versions of the march of progress dissolved into a polyglot of improvised narratives on the authority and direction of change. The modernity of the 1970s summarizes this condition of erosion and doubt, coupled with entrepreneurship and inventiveness in the discourse of modernity.

As such, the modernity of the 1970s was not of the type typically evoked by the term. The 1970s was modern, not in the sense of a unified consensus around a forward looking, optimistic willingness to transgress old taboos in search of new experiences, new forms of life, and new relations to the self and others, or to buck the foundations of tradition with eyes trained expectantly on an emerging horizon. These robust modernities properly belong to other, more heroic decades of America's past, perhaps the 1920s or the 1960s. The modernity of the 1970s expressed the flip side of this gallant modernity: recoiling at the destructive force it had itself unleashed, it was a time of retrenchment and consolidation not through reactionary calls for order and authority (though there were enough of those), but through strained efforts to erect new guidelines and shape new objects of moral devotion to fill the vacuum left by the disintegration of the old. The malaise of the 1970s expressed the hangover phase of the modern adventure: where the rush to change that characterized the 1960s valorized the willingness to overturn cultural and moral authorities handed down from tradition, burning flags and kicking at the edifices of public virtue in a frenzied pursuit of freedom and self-emancipation, the 1970s expressed a desire to retreat from the precipice and withdraw from a freedom that suddenly seemed to overwhelm.[12] The modernity of the 1970s expressed a search for something solid to hold on to in the ether of vaporized foundations.[13]

Particularly for the middle-class youth who had struck out in the 1960s with their own fantastic view of the future, the 1970s brought a new sensibility and a new feeling. In the years between the demonstrations at the Democratic National Convention in Chicago in 1968 and the election of Ronald Reagan, exhilaration turned to vertigo, and new moral strictures and objects of commitment were hastily fabricated to suppress the uncertainty of a life too immersed in all consuming freedoms. "We believed in 'free' in those days," recalls Raymond Mungo, writer, publisher, and unbridled countercultural scribe.

It was our most common and beautiful word, everything had to be free, but most of all life had to be free.

But, for most of us, anyway, the ideology soured as we grew older and learned that *nothing* is free, we can't even lead our own lives unless we can find the money to support it. You're free only if you're willing to live without personal possessions, without a house of your own or a car or anything but clothing and a few personal effects.[14]

Mungo's experience was not at all unique: as the countercultural adventure reached its zenith, as acid trips went bad, as Woodstocks turned to Altamonts and freedom turned out to be, as Janis Joplin sang, just another word for nothin' left to lose, counterculturals desired a more coherent framework within which to shape their lives. It was the sense of such soured freedom, and of the sometimes desperate need to tether freedom to a firmer base, that defined the modernity of the 1970s.

Marshall Berman has related these two moments of the modern experience to what he terms the "Faustian doublebind" at the heart of modernity: an experience of creative change that releases a destructive gale, carrying us at breakneck speed, always threatening to veer out of control, transfixing us with its novelty while inspiring a panicked effort to hold on for dear life: "To be modern is to find ourselves in an environment that promises us adventure, power, joy, growth, transformation of ourselves and the world—and, at the same time, that threatens to destroy everything we have, everything we know, everything we are. . . . it is a paradoxical unity, a unity of disunity: it pours us all into a maelstrom of perpetual disintegration and renewal, of struggle and contradiction, of ambiguity and anguish."[15]

Berman finds his metaphor for this unity of disunity in Marx's and Engels's phrase from the *Communist Manifesto*, "All that is solid melts into air." To be modern is to live in a perpetual state of melting, of transition from fixed and well-defined forms to states of being that lack such form—a liquid or a gas.[16] Another view is offered by Zygmunt Bauman, who describes the transformative experience of what he argues is the most current manifestation of modern life as a "liquid modernity" characterized by flexibility, fluidity, and impermanence in all realms. "Fluids travel easily," writes Bauman. "They 'flow,' 'spill,' 'run out,' 'splash,' 'pour over,' 'leak,' 'flood,' 'spray,' 'drip,' 'seep,' 'ooze'; unlike solids they are not easily stopped—they pass around some obstacles, dissolve some others and bore or soak their way through others still."[17] Yet, Bauman suggests, under contemporary conditions, the maintenance of such fluidity becomes the responsibility of an individual who must impose pattern and form onto realms of life that seem to resist ordering. Lifestyle, and the narrative orders we impose on rapid change, expresses this requirement that we simultaneously become liquid while maintaining liquidity as a form: "Keeping fluids in shape requires a lot of attention, constant vigilance and perpetual effort—and even then the success of the effort is anything but a foregone conclusion."[18]

Mungo's freedom expressed a modernity that could be understood in the terms of such melting metaphors: released from the constraints of an imposed form, he recalls the counterculture as a state of liquidity and mobility, free and without limits. But his eventual disavowal of that freedom expressed the other moment of the modern adventure at which, in Berman's terms, excitement turns to anxiety, or in Bauman's sense, liquidity must be worked into durable states. If Mungo's pure freedom held the promise of renewal and ambiguity, his longing for the creature comforts of house and car sought to give shape to this liquidity, to offset the disintegration, struggle, and anguish that followed shortly after—an anguish that sours even the most robust freedoms.

If the social movements of the 1960s represented, for a significant portion of the American middle class, an emerging modernity of optimism, power, and joy, then the 1970s were characterized by an effort to find stability in the maelstrom, to forge such a unity out of disunity, to be simultaneously liquid and form, to drop new anchors and erect new foundations capable of providing safety and well-being in a world of tumult and disarray. Where such foundations were once furnished by deeply rooted middle-class beliefs in the meaning of family life, career achievement, the authority of institutional and scientific experts, educational credentials, community membership, patriotism, and the promise of rising standards of living (all the trappings of Whitey's modernity), by the 1970s these traditions were overturned in the maelstrom of personal freedom, leaving the boldest of modern people listless and unsure. Particularly for the ones who commanded from the helm of this historical juggernaut, relishing the breakneck momentum of modernity's headlong plunge into oblivion (those identified with the counterculture and the radicalism of the 1960s), the need to inoculate oneself against the uncertainties of a life bereft of moral guidelines was experienced all the more urgently.

As exhilaration turned to vertigo, a craving for safety and security was satisfied (however tenuously) in more coherent doctrines of self-liberation and release. While psychedelic anthems of the 1960s trumpeted the explosion of the self at the limits of madness in a dizzying rupture with everything known and taken for granted, the therapeutic culture of the 1970s presented a more palatable version. The vertiginous psychedelic plunge celebrated by Timothy Leary and his followers was given form and purpose, transformed into a discovery of oneself as a stable object through carefully studied techniques of therapeutic development. Where to "blow one's mind" or "freak out" signified a melting of comfortable ideological blinders, forcing a painful, rapturous, and sometimes joyous glimpse into the ontological paradoxes that lingered just below the surface of routine mental fortifications, a softer mode of self-discovery asked us to "get in touch with ourselves," to "be who we really are," to "let ourselves go," suggesting a warm encounter with a reassuringly stable personal core. In 1974, Berman discussed the paradoxical mellowness of many postradical counterculturals, whose revolutionary dreams of world transformation had been replaced with fantasies of self-transformation in the realm of lifestyle. "The great thing now," Berman writes, "is to be 'mellow,' which means, as you know if you have ever sat through a few minutes of this mellowness, to be empty. The 1960s brought these kids up so high, so fast; now, in the 1970s, they want only to go down slow."[19]

A postradical countercultural thirst for the mellow lifestyle took many forms, among them a faith that the revolutionary teleology projected in the fiery confrontations of 1968 would be transposed onto a mellower narrative of changing lifestyle patterns and personal growth: as America stopped freaking out and got in touch with itself, the age of Aquarius would no longer be fought out on the streets; it would be consumed in holistic foods, healthy leisure activities, spirituality, an ethic of openness and honesty in private and public life. Contra Gil Scott-Heron, the revolution, it turned out, would be televised after all—in fact, its cooptation as a lifestyle doctrine would signal its induction into the canons of middle-class taste. As an approach to living, the spreading changes would occur slowly, through the gradual adoption of new lifestyles and new modes of self-awareness and identity, rather than violently in the flames of conflict and struggle.[20] This narrative was not restricted to the counterculture and its veteran radicals: similar stories of social transformation through individual growth echoed in business, public policy, and a variety of other professional literatures, which variously predicted (accurately) a humanistic turn in organizations from government, education, and the military to the family and consumer culture.[21] A deepening concern with the personal experiences of the individual in social life generally became, in the 1970s, the hallmark of a process of social and personal loosening, of moral progress and modernization, and also as a buffer against the existential uncertainty of modernity's relentless forward thrust.

In short, in the modernity of the 1970s, to be modern was to be loose: to pick oneself over for vestigial constraints of the old regime and to reinvent oneself by simply permitting oneself to *be* in the present. The blasts of consciousness that in the 1960s threatened to fragment the self like a kaleidoscopic light show were transformed into sustained projects aimed at inscribing form onto a self whose freedom had, as Mungo put it, turned unsettlingly sour. The granting of such permission involved the studied relaxation of the old faculties of reason, self-censorship and public protocol, the opening of dikes and levees that dammed up one's truer feelings and impulses—a self-loosening that would release, it was believed, a river of unfettered empathy for one's neighbors (either next door or across the planet), a rich appreciation of nature, a deeper experience of one's body and oneself, and an enhanced sense of the everyday textures that compose routine experience. *Sous les pavés, la plage!* ("Under the cobblestones, the beach!"), recalls a slogan of the Paris uprisings of May 1968: the belief that a better self lay below the artificial constraints of civilization is a dream with a long history in modern social and cultural thought, but in the 1970s this dream took on a very concrete set of programs and practices. The loosening of the self would be lived in the new style of life.

Among a series of postwar decades most frequently referred to by scholars of American poplar culture, the 1970s stands out as a particularly unstable historical construction, a time remembered less for what it created than for how it dealt with what it inherited.[22] The 1970s witnessed the bold social, political, and cultural initiatives of the 1960s whittled down to a shadow of their former promise. During this period the ambitious and ambiguous reformism of the 1960s counterculture was sold to the mainstream in ever more bland derivatives, from pop versions of psychedelic rock to designer blue jeans to insipid exhortations to "have a nice day." The sense of national purpose that had commanded a broad public consensus since the end of the Second World War was badly shaken by the Kennedy shootings, the race riots, the Watergate scandal, the loss in Vietnam, rising inflation, the energy crisis, and surging social and cultural reforms spearheaded by the youth movement. Popular faith in traditional institutions was badly battered, and belief in the national program of combined economic growth, technological development, expanded civil rights, and rising standards of living fell increasingly under a cloud of skepticism and embitterment. Amid soaring inflation and stubborn recession, belief in the capacity of the state to moderate and contain the inevitable swings of an expanding capitalist economy—the cornerstone of postwar Keynesian economic faiths—were regarded with increasing suspicion.[23] Such seemingly disparate scenes as the passage of Proposition 13 in California and the ensuing nationwide mania for tax reform, the bitter struggle over court-ordered busing in South Boston, and the ritual destruction of piles of disco records at a "disco sucks" rally in Chicago dramatized the collapse of a collective vision of the public commons.[24]

Social statistics provide evidence of a profound weakening of popular belief in the power of the institutions and authorities that undergirded middle-class culture in America: a survey of changing attitudes reveals across-the-board declines of roughly 10 percent between 1973 and 1980 in the popular favorable regard for medical, scientific, and financial institutions, education, and organized religion.[25] While these critiques tended to focus on corporate institutions (favorable views of big business declined from 60.2 percent in 1964 to 48.4 percent in 1976, a drop that was felt most severely among twenty-five- to thirty-four-year-olds, who reported a decline from 59.4 percent to 41.7 percent), big business was not the only one to suffer in its popularity: favorable regard for the military declined from 74.4 percent to 67.5 percent, most severely among the group aged eighteen to twenty-four, where it slid from 71.1 percent to 58.7 percent.[26] A study of American social attitudes in 1976 revealed a general sense of uncertainty among Americans concerning their futures: while in 1958, 46.3 percent of Americans questioned gave positive responses when asked if they "usually felt pretty sure your life would work out the way you want it to," by 1976 only 36.7 percent would give the same answer. Similarly, when asked, "When you make plans ahead, do you usually get to carry out things the way you expected?," the 1958 figure of 54.0 percent had, by 1976, dropped to 46.3 percent.[27] The seemingly unending economic crisis was registered in the everyday lives of Americans by the spiraling rate of inflation that, more than any other economic factor, eroded the foundations of middle-class stability.

The causes of inflation were unclear. Traditionally, the American economy had one of the lowest rates of inflation of any industrialized society. From the end of the Civil War to the beginning of the Vietnam War, the rate of inflation hovered somewhere around 2 percent, but by 1979 it soared to 13 percent. The Johnson administration's accumulated war debts, declining productivity, food shortages, and soaring energy costs resulting from the decision of the OPEC nations to enforce an embargo on sales to the United States contributed to a pattern of price increase that, by the end of the 1970s, had doubled prices in many key areas such as food, housing, health care, and other daily necessities.[28] The weakened dollar, energy shortages, and rising interest rates all combined to produce a crisis in public trust the dimensions and impact of which presented an object of public study and speculation. Indeed, the inflationary crisis presented itself as something of a towering public metaphor, a monstrous national Rorschach blot onto which a variety of public and private maladies could be projected and, retrospectively, interpreted.[29]

A study of the emotional toll inflicted on men by the inflationary spiral uncovered a brooding sense of discontent, as reported in the *New York Times*:

> "I feel anxious," complains one middle-aged, middle-class suburbanite. "I'm constantly on edge; I don't laugh much anymore." Asked why, the man responds. "That's the real problem. I don't know."
>
> Increasingly, the answer lies with inflation, resulting in the difficulty of making ends meet. What kinds of feelings are produced in men when

their ability to maintain financial stability becomes threatened[?] ... What can be expected when the social structure denies men the opportunity of achieving their maleness by removing the most accepted, institutionally defined access route?[30]

In the midst of this crisis, a vigorous new discourse on identity and expanded selfhood promised to fill the void left by a declining sense of national community. As a range of groups (women, African Americans, Jews, the elderly) abandoned the happy integrationist model defined by Johnsonian liberals for separatist or multicultural programs, and a new emphasis on the recognition of cultural diversity and the particularity of a variety of American experiences gradually supplanted an ossified discourse on national spirit and unity, focus turned to the recovery of forgotten roots and the extraction of recognition from a blinkered and chauvinistic mainstream. Where the melting pot had beckoned immigrants to shed their traditions and participate in a national culture of consumption and prosperity, the centrifugal culture of the 1970s trumpeted the bankruptcy of the mainstream in its insistence on the irreducible uniqueness of everyone, from liberated women, gays and lesbians, and youth to a range of hyphenated American ethnicities. What Todd Gitlin called the twilight of common dreams combined a growing sense of the irrelevance of a shared national future and a deepening desire to uncover the truth of one's social identity against the grain of the increasingly vanquished American mainstream.

In many regards, this mainstream was represented by the conformity and mediocrity of serially produced goods for mass consumption, while the identities that beckoned to be unearthed presented themselves as vital, authentic, unencumbered alternatives to those ways of living. Having fallen under intense criticism in the 1960s by environmentalists and health and consumer advocates, a generalized suspicion of mass consumption combined disdain for advertising, processed food, and unsafe products into a widely shared contempt for the common fare—a despondency that would dovetail with yearnings for a more authentic experience of self. "I'm afraid my nephews and nieces will grow up to be like Wonder Bread," an Italian American man told a *New York Times* reporter in 1977, "no crust, no identity."[31] While the figure of the affluent worker (bought off with the likes of Wonder Bread) had succeeded in anesthetizing labor unions and lulling the increasingly strident working-class movement of the New Deal period into the "consensus society" of the 1940s and 1950s, this same affluence seemed to drain the meaning of life and selfhood, providing an impetus and counterpoint for a range of new social movements and setting the conditions for a search for a more real way of living.

Despondency with the collective cause and an enflamed desire for "crust" in a style of life removed from the mass culture of Wonder Bread increasingly defined middle-class thinking, sanctioned even by statements from the office of the president. Jimmy Carter's 1979 "malaise" speech chastised Americans for their dependence on "self-indulgence and consumption": "We've discovered that owning things and consuming things does not satisfy our longing for meaning," scolded Carter. "We've learned that piling up material goods cannot fill the emptiness of lives which have no confidence or purpose."[32] While Carter's tact ostensibly reflected popular feelings about consumption and the cultural crisis of the period, his acknowledgment of such "longing for meaning" disturbed many. Carter's call for energy conservation by average consumers seemed to confirm this creeping sense of doubt in the promise of an ever increasing standard of living for the middle class, while pointing to individual solutions as the inevitable way out. By appearing to link arms with the introspective and sentimental yearnings for identity, Carter seemed to sanction the malaise and to endorse the gloomy conditions of the time, effectively preparing his fateful loss to Ronald Reagan in 1980.

In 1979, *U.S. News and World Report* ran a series titled "Is the Malaise Real?" Combing the country for reflections on the current "Crisis in the American Character," the magazine's staff sampled the mood in five communities, uncovering "a marked sense of an economic, social and moral decline." Cited as evidence: "Roaring inflation, tightening energy supplies, threatening recession, deteriorating public services, increasing crime." Feelings of dismay, insecurity, and uncertainty about the future were channeled into a generalized contempt for government: "Carter is telling us to keep our thermostats at 65 degrees," says Camden, New Jersey, grocer Frank Gariano, "but I bet he's not going to go around freezing his tail off in the White House this winter."[33] It seemed the term *malaise* would remain a signpost of the period, a testament both to the real mood of the time and to the mistaken willingness of a president to publicly acknowledge it. These sentiments, which had so badly mired the optimism of a decade ago, seemed to cement the obsolescence of middle-class cultural authority now slouching toward malaise. But if Whitey's modernity had stagnated, that of its traitorous offspring, the maturing counterculturals of the 1960s, now turned lifestyle gurus in the 1970s, seized upon these misfortunes as grist for ever more fantastical projections of their own—modernities configured around the relaxation of self-constraint through the adoption of novel styles of life.

ANOTHER AMERICA

As student activism on campuses across America became the increasing focus of media and popular culture—not to mention the object of fantastic invest-ment by many segments of the traditional left—critic and theologian Ivan Illich composed a stinging criticism of the American educational system. Illich sided with militant students in his 1971 call for a "deschooling society," denouncing the bureaucratic protocols of modern education and marshalling a range of argu-ments for the disentanglement of learning from the provinces of corporate and state administrators, and ultimately its replacement with spontaneous networks of informal learning groups and self-styled pedagogues.[34] Illich envisaged a "learning web" in which educational materials, mentors, learning partners, and advice would be transmitted through local channels of information: "We must conceive of new relational structures which are deliberately set up to facilitate access to [educational] resources for the use of anybody who is motivated to seek them for his education. Administrative, technological, and especially legal arrangements are required to set up such web-like structures."[35]

At the time of his writing, such structures were already partially in place, and expectations for their growth and increasing influence were high. As droves of students dropped out of colleges and high schools, a diaspora of counter-cultural centers for learning, research, advice, and information in many forms sprang up across the country, fostering a colorful culture of print and grass-roots publishing. Some such groups, like the New Alchemy Institute in Woods Hole, Maine, or the National Association of Student Cooperative Organization (NASCO), maintained relatively formal identities as nonprofit organizations, publishing journals and national newsletters with broad popular readerships among countercultural circles and beyond: NASCO's *New Harbinger* and later *Co-op Magazine*, provided important communication nodes in the expand-ing network of communes and "intentional communities," while the New Al-chemists' *Journal of New Alchemy* (later published by Dutton as *The Book of New Alchemy*) became an influential voice on ecological technology and envi-ronmental policy.[36] Overlapping with these were other, less organized circles centered on communes and drop-in centers, which also served as relays in an active network for the dissemination of lifestyle wisdom.

This network coincided with a geographic dispersal of the counterculture in the early years of the 1970s from urban centers and campuses to farms, small towns, and communes. As a once unified countercultural left splintered along diverse ideological, political, economic, and institutional rifts, the turn from mass mobilization to local community building and lifestyle experimentation spurred a migration from inner-city enclaves to disparate rural outposts and regional locations. With the waning of the popular front politics that welded students in a vital social movement in opposition to the Vietnam War and sparked fantasies of a general revolutionary alliance with inner-city blacks, labor, and other oppressed fractions, together with the overrunning of many hippie scenes by homeless and criminal elements, the country seemed the place where experiments in social change could be practiced differently, on a smaller, more intimate scale, directly upon oneself and on one's style of life. Pastoral life, for many counterculturals, promised radical self-fulfillment in an arena sheltered from the turbulent upheavals of modern social life, though lifestyle innovation was also, it was believed, a way of reforming society from within, by *living* the revolution. In the spirit of a contemporary messianism, many counterculturals saw themselves as vanguards of a modern upheaval in human consciousness and sociality that the rest were bound to follow in time.

But life on the land proved to be more demanding than many young visionaries had anticipated: the challenges of food preparation, the disposal of waste, the repair and maintenance of domestic items, and so forth created the need for a new technology of everyday provisioning. The need for information shaped a network for the passing on of survival tips and knowledge, and more generally for enacting a sense of membership and shared purpose among a dispersed lifestyle vanguard. Indeed, the very image of this vanguard group sustained as an object of inspiration and imaginary investment for readers and writers of lifestyle discourse. This membership is described in a popular handbook of countercultural resources, *Networking: The First Report and Directory*, for its nearly empyrean qualities: answering the question "What is Another America?," the authors write:

> Another America is not a place but a state of mind. Touching every area of our lives there is Another America, not often seen on television or read about in newspapers. It is an Emerald City of ideas and visions and practical enterprises that people move in and out of depending on their moods and needs, a domain that is very new, and at the same time very old.

In this special universe, health is perceived as the natural state of the body, cooperation is regarded as an effective way to meet basic needs, nature's ecological orchestra is revered as one unified instrument, inner development is valued as a correlate to social involvement, and the planet is understood to be an interconnected whole.

Another America answers the questions "Whatever happened to the 1960's?" and "Where did people go in the 1970s?" There is Another America and it is pulsating and expanding and unfolding through networking, an organic communications process that threads across interests, through problems and around solutions. Networks are the meeting grounds for the inhabitants of this invisible domain. These flexible, vibrant organizations often exist without boundaries, bylaws or offices. Networks are the lines of communication, the alternative express highways that people use to get things done. In crisis and opportunity, the word spreads quickly through these people-power lines.[37]

In short, tapping into such power lines demanded something unique of its members: an apprehension of ties and bonds so ethereal as to avail themselves only to the well-tuned imagination, a form of cognition best suited to the imaginary sensibilities stirred through the act of reading and circulated through the medium of print. Feeling oneself part of Another America was an experience of modernity in its grandest form, a reprieve from the slouching malaise into which the movements of the 1960s had devolved. In Another America, one looked forward with apprehension and excitement to a transformed future that brought with it a new way of life. But it also meant grasping an experienced simultaneity and shared historical purpose with other readers one did not meet face-to-face. As readers of magazines, books, and journals, this act of imaginary apprehension supplied the stuff of a lifestyle ethic: a fantastic modernity was related in a prescriptive discourse on cooking, windmill construction, gardening, sewing, and bicycle repair. Writing and reading about such mundane problems was, in this sense, anything but mundane: it provided a medium of fantasy and expectation. Some illustrative cases demonstrate the dynamics of imaginary investment excited by such a print culture, and how such investments served these readers as a powerful medium both of historical narrative and for the imaginary projection of a distinct modernity.

In the early 1970s, NASCO's publications, the *New Harbinger* and *Co-op Magazine*, offered a forum for debates on issues of land reform and collective

1. Wigwam Indian Industries, *Community Market Catalog*, 16

living, as well as more practical problems facing cooperative communities and ventures, from economic viability to the management of interpersonal conflicts. In 1971 the organization undertook the publication of a catalogue called *Community Market*, an index of merchandise, services, and goods produced and sold by cooperative groups across the country.[38] The vision of economic life it related was one of dispersion, austerity, and relative isolation—a largely rural network of communes and regional centers for which the circulation of information and tips about the daily challenges of communal life assumed a broad moral purpose. Such advice was both a practical matter of everyday choices, and a medium for collective fantasy about the course of social change.

For example, a listing from the New Life Research Cooperative, an open school located in Kalamazoo, Michigan, attributes to knowledge and information a nearly mystical quality. It advertises its services as a research center for other groups, possessing what it describes as a resource library ("a large number of periodicals, books, catalogs, papers, and manuscripts dealing with areas of social change") a research service ("the information is gathered from the Library and from new resources we are constantly locating") and an access catalogue ("articles and research results concerned with the 'how-to-do-it' problems of rebuilding our world"). Indeed, information as described here is not merely a resource to be shared; it is the medium of a social bond with powerful ethical significance: "The New Life Co-operative concept is not so much something to be talked about as it is a way of talking. It's a way of communicating with our brothers and sisters in a more creative way so that we all might better be able to do what ever we're doing."[39]

A more explicit expression of lifestyle advice as a medium of imaginary solidarity is evident in a newsletter published by a circle of ecologically inspired technologists and scientists: members of the New Alchemy Institute, an East Coast group noted for their research on aquaculture and ecological home design. Founded on Cape Cod in 1969 by biologists John Todd, professor of biology at the University of California, San Diego, and his wife Nancy Jack Todd, the New Alchemists achieved international recognition for their experiments with integrated designs for wind- and solar-powered homes, which included domed ecological systems that preserved solar energy while growing fish and other food sources for the kitchen.[40] In addition to developing several "Arks," or self-sufficient, ecological dwellings, on Cape Cod Prince Edward Island, and in Costa Rica, the New Alchemists also published the *Journal of New Alchemists*, a regular report on their work, their community, and their lifestyles, which circulated widely throughout countercultural reading networks, later compiled in the *Book of the New Alchemists*.

In the journal's fourth issue, published in 1977, an essay by John Todd titled "Tomorrow Is Our Permanent Address" reports on the successful opening of the New Alchemists' Ark on Prince Edward Island, a high-profile event covered in the international press and attended by Canadian Prime Minister Pierre Trudeau. Todd begins his article by affirming an ambitious vision of a global, civilizational change encompassing both personal and social dimensions: "I believe humanity is on the verge of a scientific revolution that will alter our sense of ourselves and our relationship to nature and to the planet. Such a change will transform our understanding of how human communities should be sustained. Sub-elements of knowledge and science which are now fragmented will become linked. Through this process, we shall achieve a more profound understanding of the human experience, our biological past and our place within the natural order."[41] This statement burns with the modernity of the 1970s in its most millenarian mode: the crisis of the present puts us on the cusp of a monu-

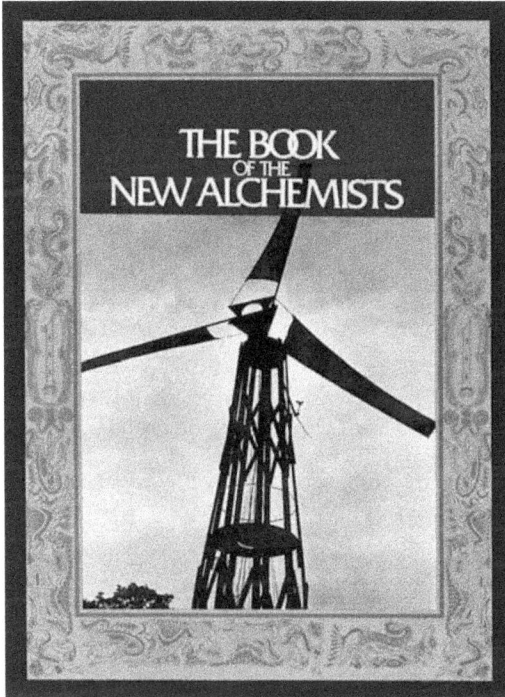

2. Front cover, *Book of the New Alchemists*, edited by Nancy Jack Todd

mental transformation that will bring the integration of disparate, fragmented attitudes and perspectives and will transform the way we live our daily lives.

Yet the apparent futurism of this narrative belies another intriguing variant on modernist themes: an anachronistic longing for the past, expressing a nostalgic, romantic appeal to a preindustrial bond with nature—a yearning that is thematized in the specific medium of the journal itself related in what looks to be Celtic design and typographic motifs. Indeed, the *Journal of New Alchemy* displays a powerful investment in all things organic, described in reports on various projects from composting to the irrigation of home gardens; diagrams and illustrations of new devices and dozens of photographs of participants in New Alchemy experiments (largely young, long-haired, with cut-off jeans and small children), such as the Arks. These futuristic features are woven together with rustic ink drawings, poetry from the New Alchemist group members and, in one case, a quote from Gandalf, the wizard character from J. R. R. Tolkein's *Lord of the Rings.*

NASCO and the New Alchemists were nodes in a network of lifestyle laboratories, and their print culture—their journals, magazines, newsletters, and

3. Back cover, *Book of the New Alchemists*, edited by Nancy Jack Todd

publications—provided the medium through which a specific experience of modernity was contrived and conveyed to others viewing themselves as poised on the cusp of a radically new world. The second part of this book is devoted to uncovering precisely how this modernity and lifestyle were articulated in this print culture, and more precisely how an ethic of self-loosening, as a collective expression of this modernity, was spelled out in its pages. But to properly unfold the meanings they contain, we must first locate this modernity in its historical juncture, in the context of the crises and social changes to which it responded, and the specific reorganization, or melting, of middle-class cultural identity to which the modernity of the 1970s gave narrative form.

Bred in at Least Modest Comfort

The Port Huron Statement, the founding document of the Students for a Democratic Society often cited as the rhetorical opening salvo of the New Left, begins by identifying the class location of its authors: "We are people of this generation, bred in at least modest comfort, housed now in universities, looking uncomfortably to the world we inherit."[42] While it is true that the boundaries of what might be called counterculture are far from fixed, that many countercultural youth fought to sever their bonds with this middle class and that many more crossed class, racial, and ethnic lines to join in the politics, art, and music of the counterculture, it remained true throughout the 1960s and 1970s that the counterculture's core outlooks and identities betrayed origins in the "at least modest comfort" of American middle-class life. It follows from this that the adventures of the counterculture must be understood from the standpoint of this location, and that the modernity of which the counterculture dreamed was crafted at the intersection of overlapping patterns of change in the standing of the middle class. To get at these changes, three areas of middle-class life must be considered: economic life as a domain of work and consumption; cultural life as a set of tastes and canons of distinction, and social life as a set of unspoken though keenly felt social and cultural boundaries established between the middle classes and other outsider or subaltern groups. It was at the historical conjuncture established by intersecting transformations in these three realms that the loosening of the self assumed its unique vision, that it evolved and proliferated its unique modernity, and that it ultimately colonized the mainstream of middle-class life.

POST-FORDISM

Perhaps the most popular symbol of the mood of crisis and despondency that characterized the modernity of the 1970s was the national economy, whose decline was read in highly metaphorical terms that resonated with anxieties and stories of personal and national backslide, replete with metaphors for slackening discipline and diminished virility. The combined blows of "stagflation" (the unlikely coupling of high inflation and high unemployment), a devastating oil embargo, and rising costs of living had put an end to three decades of postwar expansion that had guaranteed increased material rewards and upward mobility for each succeeding generation in exchange for the acceptance of a regime of labor discipline demanded of an expanding economy.[43]

But while the crises of the 1970s are often linked to the economic problems of the time, the truth is that most Americans did fairly well during this decade. Real disposable income rose 28.5 percent during the 1970s, compared to 30 percent for the previous decade. In spite of its problems, the American economy remained the strongest in the world: it produced $15 trillion in goods and services, while Americans consumed $1.5 trillion worth of products. Its GNP remained 50 percent higher than that of the Soviet Union, and double that of Japan, its nearest competitor.[44] Yet instability in the economy fueled a crisis of confidence that reverberated throughout the society, impacting most powerfully the identity and position of the middle class. To fully grasp the emotional toll of this crisis and the new prominence it gave to personal style of life, the problems of the 1970s must be read against a larger pattern of postwar economic growth—a pattern of change many commentators have mapped along a trajectory leading from Fordist, or work-centered, to post-Fordist, or flexible and dispersed economic structures in which consumption and leisure play leading roles.[45]

A trajectory of social and economic change leading from the postwar industrial and manufacturing economies to what has been termed cultural or consumer capitalism is often described as a shift from the highly centralized methods of Fordist mass production, mass marketing, and mass consumption to the dispersed, flexible, and culturally nuanced forms of a post-Fordist economic order.[46] The Fordist order rested on a coordination between economic, cultural, and social spheres traceable to the compact imposed in 1914 by Henry Ford on workers at his Dearborn, Michigan, plant—a five-dollar, eight-hour workday in exchange for compliance to the thoroughly administered work regimes demanded by his assembly-line method of manufacture. Under management regimes developed by F. W. Taylor, which imposed a rigid separation of planning from execution in all areas of the work process (effectively reducing the worker to a functional appendage of a planned system of production), Ford understood that such volumes of mass production and such conditions of workplace alienation could succeed only if consumption were concomitantly increased to keep up with supply, both to guarantee sufficient levels of consumer demand and to quell worker unrest. This required, in short, an extension of the rationalizing imperatives of production from the workplace to the private lives of workers and consumers, incorporating both work and leisure into a totally administered way of living, shaped to meet the needs of a vast and highly rationalized economic and social system.

"Postwar Fordism," David Harvey writes, "has to be seen, therefore, less as a mere system of mass production and more as a total way of life," shaped largely around the tooling of one's labor power for a highly rationalized industrial or administrative work force, and the tooling of one's leisure time for an equally rationalized culture of mass consumption.[47] For the Fordist "affluent workers" and the experts who supervised them, this compact was not without economic and material rewards: U.S. gross domestic product rose 4.4 percent a year during the 1960s, and median family income grew from $14,000 in 1949 to $28,000 in 1969.[48] But more significant was the psychological and personal respite this life afforded from turbulence and uncertainty, albeit at the expense of creativity, individuality, and expressive self-fulfillment.

Indeed, the moral universe of the Fordist society supplied the basic tenets of the worldview I have already identified with the square: faith in expert knowledge, acceptance of the authority of remote administration, and a willingness to subordinate one's desires to abstractly conceived functions and remote goals. The tautness of character imposed by this system was the focus of much sociological and psychological speculation, most notably recorded in *The Organization Man* by William H. Whyte, in his account of the "man in the grey flannel suit," whose social ethic was premised on the functional imperatives of the large organization, and whose relationship to himself was shaped around the demands of adjustment and conformity to these collective goals. Whyte describes this ethic: "A belief in the group as the source of creativity; a belief in 'belongingness' as the ultimate need of the individual; and a belief in the application of science to achieve this belongingness."[49] Whether in the realms of work or leisure, this social ethic provided both a moral worldview and a mode of daily ethics: constrain oneself to the protocols and functions of the large organization, adjust to social norms, and the world will remain safe, solid, and purposeful. In one of dozens of countercultural accolades to the square, Ray Davies of the Kinks famously captured this routinization of experience in "The Well-Respected Man":

> 'Cause he gets up in the morning,
> And he goes to work at nine,
> And he comes back home at five-thirty,
> Gets the same train every time.
> 'Cause his world is built 'round punctuality,
> It never fails.

As Davies understood, by the late 1960s, the square ways of the organization man appeared as a house of cards, vulnerable to challenges from the expressive, swinging self.

Theorists of the post-Fordist turn have pointed to the economic breakdown of the early 1970s as the culmination of a long-brewing process of disintegration and decentralization of the economic, social, and cultural organization of Fordism. Two general areas of crisis prompted a shift of priorities from Fordist to post-Fordist economies and a breakup of the total way of life demanded of the Fordist system: in the sphere of production and in that of consumption. A broad shift of manufacturing from the old industrial centers in the Northeast to the emerging economies of the "sunbelt" states accompanied a wider deindustrialization of urban centers and contributed to a variety of bruising political and cultural problems developing in the inner cities, devastating what were once stable working-class neighborhoods and exacerbating already painful racial and ethnic antagonisms. In the area of production, increased foreign competition, shifting market demand, and unreliable supplies of raw materials (principally oil) demanded a slimming down and decentralization of the old hierarchical structures that had defined the work worlds of the old Fordist system, and their replacement with less centralized, and more mobile and adaptable horizontally structured organizations.[50] As the American economy became increasingly internationalized with a steady influx of foreign-made goods from Japan and West Germany, from the early 1970s on flexibility was developed with respect to the manufacturing processes (with a turn to just-in-time and small-batch production) and a shift to smaller, less centralized firms staffed by non-unionized and temporary employees. With the decline of the manufacturing base, the breakup of traditional working-class communities and the erosion of job security for an increasingly mobile and flexible work force, the world of work waned in its power to lend meaning to the lives and identities of working- and middle-class people.[51]

In the area of consumption, similar processes were at work, though with contrasting results. A saturation and fragmentation of the old mass markets and an acceleration of product cycles together with an inundation of electronic, primarily visual media led to an intensification of the semiotic and ephemeral quality of consumer goods and services. Another form of flexibility was apparent in the expanding consumption process and growing domestic markets, with the intensification of design innovation, market segmentation, personalized and nuanced advertising campaigns and, as will be discussed in the following chapter, the emergence of an occupational group of professional mediators in the realm of consumption and human services (e.g., specialists, consultants, and innovators who together fashioned a supplementary discourse on consumption somewhere between state and market). Most importantly, with the demise of mass markets, consumption became, in the post-Fordist phase, more individualized, more personalized, and more centered on the subtle and nuanced meanings underpinning lifestyle choices than on the narrower material needs of the rationalized, mass-market consumer.[52] The conspicuous consumption of positional goods, once tied to the prestige aspirations of the new, postwar middle classes, was allowed to float from these rigid systems of status classification and address itself to the changing, flexible needs of a personal identity. Less disciplined by the semiotics of one-upmanship or positioning on a ladder of status rankings, consumption patterns came to refer to the choosing selves themselves, as reflections of personal choice, evidence of the individual identities of personal choosers of a particular way of life. The rise of the yuppie signaled the new, individualized consumer of the post-Fordist era: distinguished from the masses not by the fixed highbrow criteria of the old cultural elite, but by a more mobile awareness of personal and individual lifestyle needs and a drive for authenticity and the reality of immediate experiences in one's choice of lifestyles.[53]

In short, the unified world of work and leisure, organized around the axis of functional rationality and the supervision of remote administrative experts gave way, in the post-Fordist world, to a flexible and ephemeral world in which work was temporary and shifting and the symbols of leisure were increasingly released from the structures of class hierarchy, addressed ever more to the freedoms of the self-choosing self. In *The Cultural Contradictions of Capitalism*, Daniel Bell commented on the wider effects of this shift from production to consumption on the moral composition of the American character. The ideology of immediate gratification, closely linked with the injunction of self-expression and personal self-realization through the granting of licensed pleasure, has produced a culture of "kicks, highs," sexual experimentation, undeferred pleasure and self-fulfillment as the ideology and culture of the new capitalist society—a theory Bell turns to a critique of the progressive cultural gains of the 1960s. For Bell, the surge of hedonism embodied by the counterculture, cloaked in avant-garde sensibility, reached its apogee with the hippies of the 1960s and rooted itself in the common culture during the 1970s through the influence of a cohort of cosmopolitan lifestyle elites, pretenders to the mantle of cultural modernity. Bemoaning the modern condition that has turned us over to a "spiritual crisis [in which] the new anchorages have proved illusory and the old ones have become submerged,"[54] Bell attacks the culture of hedonism for having lured Americans away from the tried and true wellsprings of moral character—those qualities of self-denial and hard work cultivated in an earlier phase of industrial capitalism. The new culture of consumption has, according to Bell, "sought to 'express' itself by denying restraint and seeking release. What has occurred today is that restraint has gone slack, and the impulse to release finds no tension—or creativity. More to the point, the search for release has become legitimated in a liberal culture and exploited (as in the music industry) by commercial entrepreneurs who affect a 'mod' life-style of their own" (145).

Slack, for Bell, is the result of a progressive commercialization of civil society and the expansion of market values into the most intimate realms of subjectivity, leaving little redeeming in its wake. The gratification of consumer impulse has been elevated over the principled deferment of pleasure and the staid commitment to work and civic responsibility that once laid the foundation of American civilization. Inundated with appeals to hedonistic release, the new self emerged as an insatiable surface for sensory stimuli, hungry for sensations without moral lessons. Under such conditions, Bell writes, "One is to be 'straight' by day and a 'swinger' by night" (72). Notably, Bell was not referring to the core membership of the American middle class, but to a particularly influential fraction within it: the young, educated group whose zest for experience was traceable to the rhapsodic days of the 1960s counterculture. For this group, being modern meant not being like one's parents: square, efficient, dependent on institutional supervision and divorced from the sensual world. This refusal is most apparent in those places where generational battles were slugged out most noisily: in the realm of culture, where canons of middlebrow connoisseurship were made to yield to more sensual, expressive, and immersive forms.

CULTURE

Culture, in the sociological sense, defines a set of schemes and frameworks for the classification of symbols and objects, and concomitantly for the classification of the one doing the classification—the consumer of culture who displays a certain status by exhibiting taste.[55] In fact, taste, as a system for classifying objects of consumption, serves the less apparent function of marking a social space defined by proximities to other social groups expressed through gestures of acceptance and refusal, keeping boundaries clear and easy to read. "Taste classifies the classifier," as Pierre Bourdieu has famously written, and the classificatory schemes contained in culture often coincide with the needs of distinct classes to emulate their superiors and distinguish themselves from their inferiors, thus maintaining a sense of self within the space marked out by these social differences.[56] The skills one requires to make such cultural classifications are expressed in Bourdieu's phrase "cultural capital": the foreknowledge that makes it possible for one to properly classify objects of taste and pleasure (i.e., classify them by consuming them properly), in such a way as to distinguish oneself from those lacking these competencies. In addition to the realms of work and leisure discussed earlier, middle-class identities are consolidated by canons of taste and modes of cultural classification codified in forms of cultural capital. Not quite elite, but strenuously distinguished from the vulgarity of mass culture, the American middle classes were long thought to possess middlebrow tastes, displaying a penchant for products of high culture though allegedly lacking the cultural capital to properly derive their content. Middlebrow striving for a more sophisticated practice of cultural consumption defines what can be termed middle-class cultural capital, and a version of it prevailed in the American middle classes throughout most of the twentieth century.[57]

It follows, then, that middle-class cultural capital has been, from its inception, an unstable and volatile mix, frequently the object of ridicule from both above and below. Janice Radway has revealed the manner in which literary consumption among the American middle class has depicted the emergence of middlebrow sensibilities through the specifically emulationist regard they displayed toward classic literary works.[58] The prominence earned by the Book-of-the-Month Club, whose popularity reflected rising literacy rates and the increasing status demands of an expanding middle class, sparked criticism from an older cast of elites by distributing classic works to wide audiences at relatively low cost. Such readers were vociferously ridiculed by cultural critics like Dwight MacDonald, who condemned the travesty of middlebrow aspiration as a "cancerous growth on high culture."[59] "There is slowly emerging a tepid, flaccid Middlebrow Culture that threatens to engulf everything in its spreading ooze," wrote MacDonald. "All this is not a raising of the level of Mass Culture as might appear at first, but rather a corruption of High Culture. There is nothing more vulgar than sophisticated *kitsch*."[60] Indeed, modes of middlebrow cultural capital would prove increasingly volatile as the decades of the postwar period wore on, particularly as the economic, political, and social crises of the 1960s and 1970s exacted an increasingly painful toll.

Cultural capital, like economic capital, does not circulate freely and evenly throughout society: like money, culture depends for its universality and general acceptability on filtering mechanisms capable of sifting out the authentic from the counterfeit, the wheat from the chaff, thereby conferring legitimacy on certain patterns of choice while denying it to others. Cultural capital derives its validation from an array of authorities and centers of culture that select, screen, and keep the gates of their respective domains: editors, curators, critics, reviewers, commentators, and other culture specialists whose job it is to classify and reclassify what is "interesting," contemporary, and worthy of attention to "serious" audiences.[61] If the filtering process by which museums, universities, and art houses sort out the legitimate from the illegitimate is held in high regard, if there is consensus on the canons of taste and the institutions and experts who maintain them, cultural capital remains stable and uncontested, as do the identities of the groups who use such cultural capital to position themselves in society. But where rapid social change, the emergence of competing groups or the proliferation of alternative tastes undermines the consensus on these institutions and the classifying talents they administer, the question of who has good taste and who is uncouth becomes unclear.[62] For MacDonald, the boundary between high culture and the "ooze" of sophisticated kitsch was easy to draw, but by the mid-1960s, with the popularity of pop art and rock and roll, under the pressing demands of African Americans and other groups, and amid the escalating clamor of media saturation and myriad style explosions, the boundaries cordoning off high from low became increasingly an object of dispute. Coextensive with the overproduction of symbolic consumer goods linked to the post-Fordist turn, a crisis in the legitimacy of its own cultural canons submerged middle-class tastes in a blizzard of ever more meaningful, if unstable, cultural products.

Mike Featherstone, Scott Lash, and others have described this unraveling of the cultural authority of the middle classes in terms of the collapse of an elite canon of taste premised on an aesthetic of distanciation.[63] Drawing on Bourdieu's analysis, such canons are ordered by an implicit hierarchical schema in which distance, reserve, and a contemplative withdrawal from the immediacy and impact of cultural materials affirmed the aesthetic distance displayed by a cultivated taste, which held itself at one remove from the direct, practical, and unmediated appreciation of more vulgar cultural products. Bourdieu's formulation is well known: while working-class sensibilities express a taste of necessity, preferring straightforwardness and directness in styles of art and culture, elite tastes and their middlebrow emulators express an aesthetic of distanciation, characterized by a reserved, contemplative, and thoughtful response to cultural products.[64] However, under the blows of cultural saturation, amid the declining consensus on the respectability of the gatekeepers of legitimate culture, the sheer clutter resulting from the overproduction of symbolic goods, and the resounding clashes of competing social groups both inside and outside the boundaries of the middle classes, canons of taste buckle and succumb to demands for revision and democratization. The classification of cultural goods, rather than staying restricted to the codes dictated by a universal standard, becomes an open field rife with experimentation, entrepreneurship, and dilettantism. Particularly for the emerging younger fragments within the middle class—a group variously referred to by Bourdieu as the new petit bourgeoisie, new intellectuals, or the new cultural intermediaries—a process of social dedifferentiation (the collapsing of class boundaries) results in a taste scheme premised on a cultural dedistanciation (the collapse of a reserved distance on the directness of cultural products and their effects): a new classificatory scheme that repudiates classification in general through the recuperation of a presumably unclassifiable immediacy and lived experience as legitimate taste, foregrounded in authentic experiences of individuality and selfhood.[65] The new intellectuals "see themselves as unclassifiable, 'excluded,' 'dropped out,' 'marginal' anything rather than categorized, assigned to a class, a determinate place in social space. . . . Guided by their anti-institutional temperament and the concern to escape everything redolent of competitions, hierarchies and classifications . . . these new intellectuals are inventing an art of living which provides them with the gratifications and prestige of the intellectual at the least cost."[66]

To live the loose life, then, was to open oneself up to a wide range of goods and activities whose power to designate oneself within the categories of traditional middle-class social classification was weakened by a reconfiguration of the standards by which cultural capital could be measured. These changes can be summarized: while the old bourgeois disposition valued contemplation over sensation and thoughtful reserve over emphatic investment in cultural goods, a new, emerging fraction within the middle class (a younger, more cosmopolitan group) embraced the immediacy of real moments, understood here as learning processes and exploratory adventures in presumably unmediated experience, personal being, the exoticism of cultural "otherness," and the sensuality of the body. Hippies, young people, and other progressive groups became, in this regard, champions of dedistanciated cultural capital in everyday experience. They encouraged others to let themselves go, to live in the now, to choose themselves (as opposed to earning themselves), eroding distinctions between social classes in their openness to novelty and exoticism, and in their attention to the undervalued realm of the everyday. They found artistry in the most mundane places (the body, food, nature) and they collapsed the alleged "distance" demanded of middle-class connoisseurship in their embrace of immediacy, sensation, adventure, and experience—reclassified as "self-development," "self-realization" or "fun."

However, dedistanciation, like the quest for immediacy in everyday experience, was not as impulsive as it first appeared: it presumed its own skills at classification, consumption, and taste, supplied in its own subterranean channels of cultural capital. Drawing on the words of Cas Wouters, Mike Featherstone describes the calculated hedonism of this dedistanciated taste formation: "The increasing capacity of the new middle class to display a calculating hedonism, to engage in more varied (and often dangerous) aesthetic and emotional explorations which themselves do not amount to a rejection of controls, but a more carefully circumscribed and interpersonally responsible 'controlled de-control' of the emotions . . . necessarily entails some calculation and mutually expected respect for other persons."[67] The row over the emerging taste for dedistanciation, its relevant status as either emergent genius or spreading "cultural ooze," is reflected in many of the cultural skirmishes that troubled the middle classes in the 1960s, though none so clearly as the storms that greeted the Beatles, the civilizing vanguard of rock, in the late 1960s, particularly with the release in 1967 of the album *Sergeant Pepper's Lonely Hearts Club Band*.

"Rock n' Roll has become a meaningful form of personal expression for many young people," announced an article in *Downbeat Magazine*, cited in a 1967 *New York Times* piece on the increasing seriousness of rock music as a cultural form. The central demand expressed in the article's title, "It's Time to Start Listening," drew support from other critics' assertions that rock and roll was becoming legitimate culture—"the medium in which some of our best young poets have chosen to express themselves," as one critic put it. Indeed, no less than Leonard Bernstein's words are cited in the article to support this claim: "Don't try to escape Rock n' Roll, try to understand it," Bernstein was quoted. "It has something to tell adults."[68] These comments indicate the spirit with which rock music of the late 1960s, with its growing poetic ambitions, penchant for social commentary, and its slowly inflating sense of its own importance as a medium of artistic expression, was welcomed into the canons of middle-class taste. With trepidation the new guest was invited to the table of legitimate culture, though this invitation was barbed at every turn with qualifications and reservations.

Sergeant Pepper is renowned for having brought this tension to a head. As a rock album, *Sergeant Pepper* is indisputably adventurous in pushing the boundaries of the genre, in part due to its departure from conventional rock arrangements centered around the guitar and its use of electronics (the Moog synthesizer), orchestration, and other studio-specific engineering devices, but also owing to its thematic ambitions as the first of rock's many concept albums. Its allusions to drug use notwithstanding, the popularity of this record penetrated the very citadels of high cultural commentary: in "Learning from the Beatles," Richard Poirier's thorough analysis of the albums' lyrics in the *Partisan Review*, Poirier concluded that "sometimes [the Beatles] are like Monteverdi and sometimes their songs are even better than Schumann's."[69] But other critics were not so warm, often intent on rebuffing the Beatles' incursions into legitimate culture, gingerly escorting the interlopers to the door: "The Beatles have a tendency to build phrases around unresolved leading tones," wrote one *New York Times* critic, "this precipitates the ear into a false modal frame that temporarily turns the fifth of the scale into the tonic, momentarily suggesting the Mixolydian mode."[70]

The dilemma posed by *Sergeant Pepper* and other albums was immediately traceable to the generational disputes that were fast consuming the American middle class, pitting musical styles—classical music on the one hand, popular rock on the other—against each other in a heated competition for legitimacy. This dispute employed competing, or at least contrasting modes of aesthetic valuation: where classical music was serious, contemplative, and sophisticated, rock was popular, occasionally insightful and displaying potential for talent, but limited in its capacity to manifest true artistry owing to its impulsiveness and spontaneity. Another *Times* critic contrasted classical music's rule-governed methods to rock's sensuality and expressiveness, made possible by the former's dependence on keyboard and the latter's use of guitar in composition and performance:

> In Rock music there is a lack of commitment to voice leading, inner lines, modulations and variations, the very staples of western, keyboard-oriented concert music. . . . [It is] a vehicle for the fingers, bringing into

play touch and a general kinetic response to beat. Above all, it utilizes the ear with a sense of abandonment. "Serious" musicians, on the other hand, stress control, and, rather than depending on the ear alone, place a special emphasis on the mind and the eye. Even the aleatoric or improvisatory music I have played has been so riddled with rules that a sense of abandonment was almost impossible. Rock, like jazz before it, is player's music, composed collectively and put together by ear.[71]

Along a border dividing the ear and the finger from the mind and the eye was a traffic in cultural legitimacy, a reclassification of cultural capital, that was at times conciliatory, but more often contentious and acrimonious. With increasing thrusts, the dedistanciated, insurrectionary sensuality of the finger threatened to erode the authority of the distanced eye, and with it the canons of taste and sophistication that had heretofore assured the middle class of their place in the larger mix of American social classes. In other words, with rock and roll, a looser music challenged the hegemony of the mindful arts, and the transition from one to the other defined a sense of heightened anticipation and hope in the future of an expanding art form, but also a nervous anticipation of unknown consequences. The emergence of the loose life and the modernity it envisioned occurred along the boundaries of a receding ethic of work and an emerging culture of leisure and consumption, and at the border of two canons of taste, one distanced and thoughtful, the other sensual and immediate, each pinned to declining and ascendant fragments of the middle class. Like the moral declines described in Bork's slouching narrative, the collapse of middle class cultural authority has remained the bane of conservative critics, most notably Allan Bloom, whose *Closing of the American Mind* lamented the atavism of taste in what passed as the loosening of cultural codes. Yet there was another important axis of border play along which this particular modernity was fashioned, one not configured vertically in a competitive play for the mantle of true art, but outwardly in a gesture of desire, emulation, and fetishistic attraction to the mysterious properties of the exotic.

THE OTHER

The clash between the internalized self-discipline of the organization man and the expressive self-realization of the swinger reverberated throughout middle-class culture as waves of a younger, more mobile (or more "liquid," to extend Bauman's metaphor) people fled the citadels of the middle class for more authentic, immediate lives. The loosening of the self appeared as a crisis of middle-class authority as divisions appeared within groups that had previously shared a consensus on the value of culture. An older postwar middle class whose primary orientation was to work, community, and the sacrifices demanded of each faced off against a younger group more oriented to style of life as a source of social identity. But the loosening of the self occurred along other boundaries external to the middle class itself as this younger group embraced a pattern of orientalism—a romantic investment in the relaxation of social boundaries excluding a range of subaltern groups that included African Americans, Native Americans, Asians, workers, homeless people, revolutionary third world groups, drifters, mystics, homosexuals, women, and children.[72] Loosening was not just a gesture of patricide, it was a treasonous act of affiliation with various others populating the margins of middle-class existence—a logic of emulation summarized in the phrase *We Are the People Our Parents Warned Us Against*, the title of Nicholas Von Hoffman's study of the Haight-Ashbury scene, where to become loose was to be like the Negro in one's passion and expressive argot, like the laborer in one's vulgarity, like the Indian in one's communion with nature, like the Asian in one's sense of the spiritual, or like the beggar in one's willingness to sleep and panhandle in the park. Von Hoffman recalls the comments of a hippie he interviewed for his book: "It was always the dream of the white man to live in a natural state, and that's what we got to do. The Polynesians, the black man, every race has done it but the white man . . . it's a free frame of experience, that's what it is."[73] Such an embrace of the social others one was raised to avoid would define much of what it meant to live in the immediacy of the present: loose men would betray the discipline instilled in them by their fathers, releasing themselves from the armature of masculinity to discover the emotionalism typically attributed to women, or a flamboyance assigned to homosexuals.[74] White middle-class people would abandon their inhibitions (if only for an evening of marijuana smoking) and find their true selves as hipsters and what Norman Mailer described as "White Negroes."[75] Lifestyles, in this sense, were conceived against the grain of deeply embedded patterns of middle-class status and exclusion: to practice a lifestyle was to open oneself to the way others live, in an anthropological sense.

As youth came to increasingly emulate the mysticism of the East, to copy the cuisine of ethnic groups, to assume the effeminacy of queens and cross-dressers and to don the blue jeans and wide-brimmed hats once associated with Dust Bowl farmers, a process of middle-class disloyalty promised to release young middle-class people from the constraints of privilege and intrinsic dispositions of calculative self-regulation it bequeathed, opening a new realm of immediate experience. As the refinement and temperament once associated with the distanciated taste and the educated character was increasingly displaced by the self-knowledge gleaned from adventures in America's gritty social underbelly, spontaneous outbursts, tosses with the pigs, introspective LSD sessions, and other "real" experiences (as opposed to tastes gleaned from proper aesthetic educations), as all the techniques of self control and cultivation that were once the mark of middle-class pride and distinction were gradually recast as repressed, colorless, and "square," the relaxation of self-constraint and the embrace of the everyday was described in terms of a transgression into the prohibited zones of America's marginalia. Cas Wouters has uncovered links between what he terms a process of "informalization," as a "conscious effort to relearn more primal and concealed impulses and emotions," and a changing class dynamic, a "proletarization of the bourgeoisie." Citing Orwell, Wouters writes: "The attraction of the greater directness, vitality and spontaneity, exerted across the barriers of established class differences, has been given an extra dimension in Orwell's description of the 'proles' in his *1984*: 'the proles have stayed human. They had not become hardened inside. They had held on to the primitive emotions which he himself had to re-learn by conscious effort.'"[76]

Loosening was, for many, a narrative of class treason and disaffection—a disavowal of the aesthetic hierarchy and the forms of intentional communication and self-constraint that undergirded class stratification in American society, but it was also a romantic affirmation of the other as the source of a more fundamental, expressive, and primitive humanity, whose qualities, according to Orwell, one could "re-learn by conscious effort." In many cases, however, this relearning did not seriously challenge or revalue the inferior status to which the subaltern was relegated, but inscribed instead a heroic inferiority on these groups. Von Hoffman relates his observations of another Haight-Ashbury figure, Tom, an acid head whose episodes of infantile regression and whose lax hygiene suggest an odd inversion of the middle-class values with which he was raised. "One of the reasons Tom is so filthy," Van Hoffman writes, "is that he has reversed the running of the reels of his life: now he can play with the Freudian bowel movement his Mom would not let him touch. In the hip world, there is a great crying out against not only the plastic but the hygienic. Asepsis is condemned as artificiality."[77] Loosening provided a relation to oneself as always in a state of communion with a prohibited or devalued (and consequently revalued and reclassified) realm of materiality and sensual experience (sometimes, as in this case, the excremental), which is always the property of a social other who remains in this subordinate role. The story of self-loosening is one of becoming more like this other. As in the realm of economic life where one loosens oneself from the regimes of the working day into a life of leisure and consumption, or in the realm of taste where one permits oneself to stray from a distanciated connoisseurship into the here-and-now of sensual, emotive art, so in social life one grants oneself permission to cross over into the forbidden realm of exotic others. To be loose is never to be sedentary in one's middle-class state, always loosening, but never quite loose—or never loose enough.

Identity: The Jogging Path of Life

The loosening of the self expressed a moment of heroic modernity, gallantly rupturing the confining total way of life imposed by the Fordist society in an impassioned drive for sensation, freedom, and self-realization. But it also expressed a desire to recoil from that departure, to pull back from the precipice into a more secure narrative of selfhood and authentic identity. To live the loose lifestyle was thus to incorporate the conflicting imperatives of disintegration and renewal constitutive of the modern experience into a single moment or story, to relate the distressing momentum of modern flux and all of its incumbent freedoms to a reassuring narrative of meaningful growth and personal discovery. Indeed, the domestication of such ambiguities is expressed in techniques we apply to ourselves in our style of life, and in the personal narratives of change and development we use to describe these lifestyles as practices of a reflexive project of identity.[78] Such projects are feats of narrative, not unlike the work we perform on a story or text as we weave together discordant elements of our biographies to form a coherent account. "Self-identity, as a coherent phenomenon," writes Anthony Giddens, "presumes a narrative: Keeping a journal, and working through an autobiography, are central recommendations for sustaining an integrated sense of self. . . . Yet autobiography—particularly in the broad sense of an interpretative self-history produced by the individual concerned, whether written down or not—is actually at the core of self-identity in modern social life. Like any other formalised narrative, it is something that has to be worked at, and calls for creative input as a matter of course."[79]

The production of such narratives defines the self as a reflexive project:

something we work on every day in our most insignificant lifestyle choices, from clothing and food to vacations, careers, furniture, and romantic partners, each of which carries embedded within it a tiny story of the chooser herself and her development over time. The narrative of the loosening self provided one such project: to be loose was to *become* loose, to be always in the moment of becoming more real and more authentic, more in touch with the real meter and moment of one's daily experience. This narrative was told and retold in dozens of tiny decisions, exhortations, and techniques: the choice to grow sideburns, to experiment with natural foods, to loosen one's top button all told small stories of who one was becoming and how one was developing a new unmediated rela- tionship to the self, achieved through the learned relaxation of self-constraint.

Indeed, the mood of the 1970s is most popularly summarized with the re- flexive pronoun, *me*—the Me Decade, as Tom Wolfe famously christened it, was a period of reflexivity, introspection, and investment in the trajectory of a changing self as the single touchstone of moral meaning, at least among the more cosmopolitan segment of the American middle class.[80] The moral dis- putes of this period were deeply linked to the larger processes that conflated moral meaning with the experiential realization of the individual, understood as an open-ended process of disclosure, exploration, and learning. The growth process of the individual became itself an object of moral obligation and daily work—a narrative of learning and developmental self-knowledge that posed an alternative to the fixed edifices of traditional morality. Wolfe summarized the striving for self-transformation that characterized middle-class longing during the Me Decade: "The old alchemical dream was changing base metals into gold." Wolfe writes: "The new alchemical dream is: changing one's personality—re- making, remodeling, elevating, and polishing one's very self . . . and observing, studying, and doting on it. (Me!)"[81]

The new sense of individualism was reflected in many areas of social life: climbing divorce rates, the enhancement of career objectives for women, the re- laxation of sexual mores and widespread rethinking of traditional family struc- tures and roles, together with an extension of the traditional boundaries of "youth" (defined as a period of expressive authenticity) well beyond their previ- ous limits, all stressed the fulfillment of the individual through the removal of outmoded conventions as the center of personal livelihood and as the keystone, or the narrative thread, running through larger biographical trajectories. Be- tween 1970 and 1979, the number of people living alone increased by 60 percent, comprising 23 percent of households by 1980, and between 1950 and 1978, the

rate of divorce increased from 3.1 percent to 7.1 percent.[82] The on-air collapse of
the Loud family during their nationally televised weekly documentary *American Family* (an ordinary household that surprised audiences with the mother's
emphatic on-camera demand for a divorce and the coming-out of their teenage
son), together with such shows as *All in the Family*, seemed to confirm the obsolescence of the nuclear family itself — a sign of increased personal liberty to
some, but a frightening indicator of larger processes of social uprootedness and
moral confusion to others. This inward shift in the source of authority was not
evenly distributed throughout American society, nor was it confined to a specific social group or class. Such outlooks were clustered in an educated middle
class in largely urban northeastern and West Coast parts of the country, though
its origins were indisputably to be found in the lifestyle networks of the counterculture.[83]

In a culture of weakened economic, religious, and sexual norms, Americans
turned to both novel and traditional values to regulate those parts of their lives
that had come so badly unhinged. In 1976, a Gallup Poll survey of Americans
involved with "spiritual experimentation" found 12 percent of Americans practicing either Transcendental Meditation, yoga, "the Charismatic Movement,"
mysticism, or an Eastern religion.[84] By the end of the 1970s this trend had become widespread, and such highly individualistic narratives of personal change
were increasingly common: studies from Daniel Yankelovich indicated that 72
percent of Americans spent a great deal of time thinking about themselves and
their inner lives; 70 percent of Americans said that while they have many ac-
quaintances, they have few real friends, and that 41 percent said that they now
had fewer close friends than they had in the past.[85] Of course, the inwardness
of the 1970s was itself a vastly developed version of older forms of reflexivity
developed earlier in an odd intersection shared by Negro jazz musicians, teenage delinquents, and Greenwich Village bohemians seduced by Eastern mysticism. These groups shared a common embrace of real experience and sensuality, and a dismissal of protocol, abstraction, and formal knowledge as a basis for
self-discipline and the deferral of gratification—a sensibility with diverse roots
in American culture, but whose chief exponent in the early 1970s was undoubtedly the counterculture, and its lifestyle variants.

HIP

"Hey, Johnny, what are you rebelling against?" asks Marlon Brando's dancing
partner in *The Wild One*. "What do ya got?" comes Brando's curt rejoinder—a

reply that speaks volumes on what it means to be hip, to share in the vibrancy and sensuality that permeated, in different forms, the beat culture of the 1950s and later the counterculture of the 1960s and 1970s. Refuting dogma and ideology, hip resides in the immediacy of the lived moment and the concrete expressions of language and style. As Norman Mailer famously mused in his account of the "White Negro," hip abjured instituted morality, seeking only to "do what one feels whenever and wherever it is possible ... to open the limits of the possible for oneself, for oneself alone."[86] For the beat generation, smitten with jazz, Sartre, and Freud, hip preserved or renewed a primitive vitality that had all but disappeared under the work regimes and repressive niceties of mainstream American culture, channeled into subterranean streams of nuance and expression where it lived as a buried pulse on the fringes of society. Hip people were the ones who "never yawn or say a commonplace thing, but burn, burn, burn, like fabulous yellow roman candles," as Jack Kerouac famously wrote, people who released, rather than suppressed the vital energies that others kept pent up and controlled. In the decades that followed, the valorization of an unmediated present championed by the beats would provide both a rhetorical template and an ethical framework for dozens of related experiments: while psychedelic rock and rollers lived reality and immediacy through the ritual destruction of instruments and spontaneous musical compositions, burgeoning students of Eastern mysticism pursued a search for truth through efforts to "live in the now," and minions of backpackers, hitchhikers, and hippie gurus celebrated the lived present over the deferred future.

But the hip self also presented a timely response to changing social conditions that demanded new ways of being in a social and moral world in which work (and deferred gratification) was declining in its ability to structure biographical narrative and confer group identity, and leisure and consumption (the experience of the moment) provided increasingly powerful vehicles for mental and imaginary transport. The hip self was an impulsive self, to be sure, but it was also a chosen self, one that explored the adaptability of reflexive narratives of the self for more durable states of being. And at the center of the hip life was the demand that one become an active chooser of one's own way of living, and by extension of one's own sense of personal and social self. In the liberatory rhetoric that characterized the counterculture of the 1960s and its discourse on lifestyle, the fact of choice itself assumed the form of a support for a new kind of self. Charles Reich, in his countercultural classic *The Greening of*

America, illustrates the significance of personal choice in a comparison of Consciousness II (the uptight mindset of America's mainstream) and the emerging Consciousness III (the looser outlook of the young generation):

> Consciousness II believes more in the automobile than in walking, more in the decision of an institution than in the feelings of an individual, more in a distant but rational goal than in the immediacy of the present....One of the central beliefs of Consciousness II concerns work. The belief is that the individual should do his best to fit himself to a function that is needed by society, subordinating himself to the requirements of the occupation or institution that he has chosen. He feels this as a duty, and is willing to make "sacrifices" for it. He may have an almost puritanical willingness to deny his own feelings....
>
> [Consciousness III] is a liberation that is both personal and communal, an escape from the limits fixed by custom and society, in pursuit of something better and higher. It is epitomized in the concept of "choosing a life-style"; the idea that an individual need not accept the pattern that society has formed for him, but may make his own choice. It is seen visually in the growth of the student-gypsy world, a new geography of hitch hikers, knapsacks, sleeping bags and the open road: not a summer vacation or a journey from one fixed point to another, but a new sense of existence in the immediate present, without fixed points. It can be heard in the song from the rock opera "Tommy" by the Who, "I'm Free."[87]

Choice is here aligned with a story of becoming a chooser through the loosening of internalized mechanisms of self-control, and a willing immersion of the self into the meter of daily life. At the heart of this repudiation of "distant but rational goals" through an immersion in the "immediate present," was a process of loosening, letting oneself go, "turning on, tuning in" and most importantly, "dropping out"—releasing oneself into what Timothy Leary described as the rhythmic nature of the nervous system. Potentially devouring freedoms were transformed into intentional acts of freedom, choices of immediate living through reflexive choices that were, more than anything else, choices of the freedom to choose itself. The hip choice was of a less constrained, more real and immediate way of living ("dropping out" meant letting oneself fall into the present), whose function it was to carve ontological insecurities into reassuring and meaningful narratives of identity.

As the 1970s wore on, the choice of hip was developed into a broader technique of self-choice centered on the uncovering of personal authenticity, reflected by Jerry Rubin in his book *Growing Up at Thirty-Seven*, a rich, confessional document of his trek from the heights of countercultural celebrity through the crowded marketplace of therapeutic and spiritual regimes, treatments, and techniques. Rubin plumbs the depths of his own self-transformation, spinning a narrative of growth from the constraints of public responsibility (in this case, the responsibilities of an antiwar activist) to the inner authenticity of a true self: "There were many things I refused to see in the sixties because I hid behind the radical leader image; my personal life was at the service of a public existence. As long as I had an investment in being Jerry Rubin the image I could not grow. I had to free myself from my self-image, my public image; I had to kill Jerry Rubin to become me."[88] If Rubin's confessional testimony remains, as Christopher Lasch wrote, "mired in liberationist clichés," producing "few indications of self-understanding, personal or collective,"[89] its narrative of radical self-transformation nonetheless expresses a story of developmental change, from public phoniness to personal authenticity. And, importantly, the new truth of the self was in part a product of new ways of living: Rubin goes on to describe his adventures through a range of therapies and health regimes, from Rolfing, bio-energetics, and health food to jogging and a variety of personal therapies. Lasch, who singled out Rubin's book in his study *The Culture of Narcissism*, reads Rubin's journey as a decline into self-indulgence, though for others it signaled a rigorous way of life in which the challenge of self-authenticity was confronted as a daily task: one had to learn to relax through the mastering of a set of techniques one shared and practiced with others, related in a developmental narrative of evolutionary progress from artifice and constraint to personal self-realization.

Another story from the pages of the *Briarpatch Review*, a small newsletter for countercultural entrepreneurs that circulated throughout the Bay Area in the mid- to late 1970s, tells a similar story of personal and social growth.

> Like a lot of other folks, I had my consciousness raised (directed is perhaps a more accurate word) during the political struggles of 1968–1971. I became impatient for change, worried that we had little time left to "save" ourselves, our communities, and our planet. I wanted "revolution now!" I thought in terms of large-scale projects; government, private, or university funding; even nationwide organizations and impacts.

Five years later I find myself persuaded that most "revolutionaries" will only succeed in replacing one centralized, intolerant, authoritarian regime with another. So I am seeking a change theory which recognizes the necessity of evolutionary change based on human values.[90]

For this author, there is a rupture between the late 1960s and early 1970s that separates a dogmatic revolutionary agenda (one that "directs" rather than "raises" consciousness) from an alternate program of change that incorporates personal, "human values" into an inevitable evolutionary trajectory. Later the author reflects on this sense of moral equilibrium that has replaced the strident, inner conflicts brought by revolutionary strife: "Gurdjieff says that fundamental personal change comes only through lifelong work. Barry Stevens reminds us, 'Don't push the river; it flows by itself.' The Beatles sing 'there will be an answer, let it be.' And the steady tortoise crosses the line ahead of the dashing hare."[91]

Letting the river flow by itself is achieved by releasing oneself and the controlled pace of daily existence from the constraints of instrumental thinking into the meter and pulse of one's style of life. It assumed a stabilized pattern of duration and change that engulfs the will of the individual, soothing the anxieties of a worldview lacking any clear sense of what is worth striving for yet heavy with intense personal and political aspirations. Learning how not to push rivers required one to expunge oneself of the egoism and intentionality of the square world of work and the snobbery of middle class taste by emulating non-western peoples, even where such squares and snobs masqueraded as revolutionaries and radicals. In a similar spirit, one back-to-the-lander found these words to relate the political trajectory of the lifestyle movement to its roots in the social movements of the 1960s, in terms of a learned ethic of inner release: social change "is not something we can make happen, though it is something we can **let** happen. . . . You can't change [society] by reform, you can't topple it (without instituting another just as bad). These were the lessons learned in the streets of Chicago in 1968. You can only withdraw."[92]

This theme of an intentional letting is reflected in the comments of another author, Marilyn Ferguson (a New Age–inspired brain science researcher and author of *The Aquarian Conspiracy*, a guide to the New Age cultural and social network in America), who locates the transformed outlooks apparent in the new lifestyles in such a capacity for cultivated release. For Ferguson, "deliberate letting . . . as when we deliberately relax our grip on something," defines a new view on life as a learning experience. "The grip is the contraction of our consciousness, our psychic spasm, which must be loosened before anything can change. These psychotechnologies are designed to free that tight hold so that we might become buoyant, the way a lifeguard detaches the panicky grip of a drowning person so that he might be rescued."[93] Such "deliberate letting" involves a process of learning to let things happen (as opposed to making them happen) and relates a narrative of moral growth from the radicalism of New Left militancy to an acquired talent for self-surrender to the present and the cultivation of a sense of self in one's daily style of life. In all these cases, emancipation is here written as a technique of relaxation, to be sure, though one that defied the authority of traditional scientific experts and opened itself to a rich variety of lifestyle mentors and moral entrepreneurs in an effort both to distinguish themselves from the rigidity of their square parents and to produce for themselves a place of solace and sense of moral purpose amid the turbulent modernity of the 1970s. These lifestyles developed around a broad theme of relaxation and release—a form of self-storying expressed in the broader loosening of self-constraint.

YUPPIES

While an overt rhetoric of loosening as a vanguard lifestyle practice had largely vanished from the cultural horizons of American popular culture by the closing years of the 1970s, the imprint left by this episode on lifestyles and consumer markets has proven permanent and lasting. Within these lifestyle networks, there had developed modes of identity centered on the sovereignty of individual choice and the problem of lifestyle that exhorted the individual to forego convention and shared cultural norms in the pursuit of private meanings and rewards. From the early 1980s, even as overt invocations of the looser lifestyle receded, a sense of the plasticity of identity, of the self as an object of ongoing manipulation and control, had already been grafted onto the ways millions of Americans thought about their lives and their overall life trajectories, and themed into the ways Americans spent money on dozens of lifestyle accoutrements. What occurred was a gradual absorption of these invocations to relaxation and to the creative tending to the self—the structures of a reflexive project of self-identity—into the language and discourses of marketing, advertising, and consumer culture, and into the very fabrics of everyday lives for citizens of advanced capitalist societies. Where in the loosening discourse generally, and in the reflexive project of the self in particular, identity was interpreted as an active process, an intentional giving shape to the narrative that constituted one's identity or to the formlessness that made up the sense of self, by the late 1970s and early 1980s such self-cultivating activity had been metonymically substituted with another: the making of purchases and the consumption of services. The choice of oneself, shared and mediated in a culture of print, was subsumed under the broader activity of choice between mass-marketed commodities.

The incorporation of the counterculture began early—in fact, as has been pointed out, the counterculture and the mass market were never entirely distinct. Since the early 1960s, as Thomas Frank has shown, gestures of insurrection were already well integrated into advertising discourse, and throughout the 1970s new, looser codes of dress and styles of personal appearance were formulated to incorporate potentially disruptive styles into stable forms of professional protocol.[94] One notable area was that of hairstyle: in 1974, the *New York Times* announced "The Doubts Linger, but the Longhairs Are Being Trimmed," describing a growing trend among men, who were cutting their hair and seeking a more tidy appearance: "I wore my hair long since 1970 . . . I got tired of it. In the places I hang out, the longhairs are beginning to look creepy." The article featured several before-after pictures of men, transformed from rough and ragged hippies into what seems the more recognizable "1970s haircut"—medium length, neatly brushed and blow-dried.[95] The domestication of loose styles took many forms, none more memorable than the open, unbuttoned shirt as acceptable professional attire, which contrasted with the excessively constrained buttoned up shirt with necktie: "Is Groovy Groovy or Ghastly over Forty?" asked one journalist: "More and more middle aged men are dressing in the so called groovy style initially favored by men in their early 20's." Groovy, we are told, involved certain discernable features: "A body shirt opened anywhere from the second button down to the navel, with necklaces, pendants and/or beads displayed on a background of chest hair." The men interviewed for the article complained that everything, from leisure to professional life, was increasingly youth-oriented, and they were forced to adopt groovy styles in conformity with these new institutional norms: "If you don't look young, you're not anything," one man explained. Indeed, for most of the men interviewed, the key feature of their presentation was revealed chest hair, adorned with necklaces. One man is described: "He too wears necklaces and pendants—usually an imposing rough hewn chunk of metal bouncing decisively along the colorful terrain of his chest and/or belly. His large round face wears a curious expression—an improbably but somehow appealing mix of Maharaj Ji and Dennis the Menace."[96] If such exposed and burly chests, opposed as they were to the "uptight" buttoned-up style of the straight suit-and-tie look, allowed these men to assimilate into a professional environment dominated by youth, it was precisely through such a reconciliation of a dialectic of novelty and familiarity, or expressive release and an imposed constraint. Looseness had become institutionalized as an everyday mode of lifestyle.

But for the incorporation of the loose lifestyle to be complete, the essentially reflexive character of the identity it instituted would have to be stripped of any outward opposition to new consumer markets and changing regimes of work. Looseness, in short, would be tightened up—a process that began in earnest after the election of Ronald Reagan, and with the emergence of a professional class with unmistakable roots in the counterculture, yet decidedly opposed both to the radical social objectives of the New Left and to the expressive life-style programs of the 1970s.

It was a defining moment for the incorporation of the loose life when *News-week* announced in a memorable cover story that 1984 had been "The Year of the Yuppie."[97] That year marked the arrival of a new class of aspiring, urban young people who had abandoned social conscience for the pursuit of social prestige and career success, yet had brought with them all the personal and cultural as-sets of the countercultural lifestyle experiment, centered on individual choice and personal authenticity. The year of the yuppie unfolded a narrative of shriv-eling moral conviction and exploding self-interest as yippies famously aban-doned programs of both social reform and personal transformation, embrac-ing instead the far narrower pursuit of wealth and social power, albeit through the use of interpersonal skills, techniques of self-maintenance, and expressive leisure styles once thought to hold a far greater moral promise. As an instru-ment of social advancement, reflexivity would shed the loosening telos and re-invent itself as a tool of upward mobility: work on the self would be harnessed to skills for a competitive labor market, to the expansion of networks of social capital whereby contacts could pass on investment tips and job opportunities, and to the practice of conspicuously inconspicuous consumption with a spe-cifically cosmopolitan flare—a developed taste for authenticity, customization, and cultural pluralism in a consumer market that was quick to shed its outward appearance of mass production for consumers hungry to see their unique indi-viduality reflected in their purchases. The entrepreneurial self—the highly mobile, self-reliant, self-choosing player in the world of neoliberal economics and accelerated consumption—was composed from the cultural and ethical legacy of the counterculture.

The moniker *yuppie* was first used in print in 1983 by *Chicago Tribune* columnist Bob Greene to describe Jerry Rubin's "networking" parties (informal social gatherings roughly modeled on countercultural consciousness raising groups, but created solely for business hobnobbing), though demographers and sociologists would struggle to clarify the precise boundaries of this new social group. Typically born between the years 1946 and 1964, earning $30,000 per year if living alone or $40,000 if married, employed in a professional or managerial occupation and located in or near a city of 100,000 inhabitants or more, yuppies constituted only a small portion of their generation—5 percent by the mid-1980s. They were thought to be liberal on social issues, tolerant and accepting of social differences, adventurous culturally, and antiauthoritarian in their outlooks but conservative on economic issues such as taxation and the role of the federal government in reducing poverty and managing the economy. Yuppies, it is argued, displayed these double commitments in the Democratic primary of 1984 by lending a hefty boost to the candidacy of Gary Hart, but they later abandoned the party to vote for the candidate of prosperity, Ronald Reagan.

At the center of the yuppie myth was a shift that some would read as a betrayal, others as a process of maturation, and still others as an extension of an original project through a new strategy: yuppies would develop a distinct nonchalance about the sacrifice of personal morality for the pursuit of wealth. The *Newsweek* story quotes Amy Caplan, a thirty-year-old sales manager for CBS who abruptly quit her job as a social worker when she saw her first paycheck: "I realized that I would have to make a commitment to being poor to be a social worker," Caplan explains. "Eventually, I was able to shed the notion that to prove to everybody I was a good person I had to parade around as a good person by being a social worker." Caplan's formulation is classic: shared morality is an obstacle to the development of personal authenticity—a goal better pursued in the open market, where the integrity of the profit motive demands no ruse. Indeed, if moral introspection threatened the clear and decisive control of the self, no risks would be taken at all: in a clear reversal of a psychedelic agenda which demanded that one drop out of deeply habituated patterns of thought through an LSD-induced freak-out, yuppies, Jerry Rubin explained, abjured drugs as counterproductive: "They don't want their minds altered by introducing a substance that might lead them to question what they're doing." Indeed, the pursuit of career and the ostentatious display of wealth would so clearly replace the goals that had inspired the "conscience constituency" that many would be led to conclude from this seeming contradiction the bankruptcy of all that the counterculture stood for. With the yuppie, the adventure that had characterized the struggles of the 1960s, later domesticated in the modernity of the 1970s, would be written off as a flight of fancy, a youthful pipe dream dispelled with the first cold winds of economic crisis or touch of gray hair.

As the imperatives of earning and spending eclipsed those of self-discovery and social reform, the ultimate ends of this process of self-cultivation would shift markedly: loosening of the self into the immediacy of daily life would succumb to a program aimed at the elimination of all forms of social dependence, an endless optimization of the individual and his survival skills, both in the realm of work in a highly flexible economy and in leisure and culture, where reliable codes of taste and status had worn thin. In the yuppie lifestyle, bonds with others would be shed, personal energies would be maximized, pleasures intensified, functions rationalized, and self-reliance enhanced. As the increasingly competitive demands of new labor markets, the ever more tenuous nature of emotional commitment, and the more nuanced symbolic universe of a changing consumer culture came increasingly to define the lives of yuppies, self-cultivation became less a project of relinquished self-monitoring toward greater self-integration, and more one of enhanced control for challenges one would confront alone in an unstable world. Navigating the increasingly choppy waters of professional and social life required a steady hand and keen eye, and what better goal to commit oneself to than the cultivation of these techniques of self-mastery. "For all their sometimes frenzied consumption," Newsweek explains, "yuppies can display a certain emotional austerity that keeps them from slipping on the jogging path of life. [One interviewee] sees a therapist, although less for any specific problems than because he is driven 'to be better, to excel,' in accordance with the Yuppie Golden Rule: 'If it ain't broke, improve it.' "[98]

For yuppies, life itself emerged as an object of ever more strident scrutiny, control, and regulation through innovative regimes of self-tightening that spanned the domains of work and leisure. Yuppies, it was believed, regulated time more efficiently than other groups through the use of new devices and products, from Filofaxes to Rolodexes and later Palm Pilots and cell phones. Anticipating the yuppie trend, a 1979 Newsweek story described the rising phenomenon of the "workaholic," as evidenced by twenty-four-year-old Marilyn Machlowitz, a recent Yale business school graduate who was described lounging on the beach at Martinique's Club Med hunched over a computer printout with a calculator in hand, adding up statistics for her new book—a study on workaholics. "To date, alienated workers have received most of the scholarly attention," explains Machlowitz, later to become a staff psychologist for New York Life Insurance. "I thought we could learn about work from people who like it, too."[99] Like Machlowitz, yuppies were always too busy for the loose moments of daily life but their diligence was a project entirely of their own doing.

While the lifestyle discourse of the 1970s had celebrated the liberation of the body from regimes of competition in new expressive sports, yuppies recuperated the body in a regime of competitive fitness training. While the consciousness movement of the 1970s had sought transcendence, the yuppies of the 1980s explored the possibilities of New Age therapy for the expressed purpose of increasing productivity at work and the expansion of social networks yielding greater access to a variety of rewards.[100] Even as the discourse of a loose lifestyle had been left behind, the founding principle upon which such a discourse was based nonetheless persisted: that life *was* a style, that one could participate in the styling of life, that one chose oneself by choosing how one lived.

The crucial difference, however, lay in the degree of collectivity involved. While the loosening of the self was something one shared through a culture of print, the tightening of the yuppie self was something one engaged on one's own, with only a mass market in consumer goods to consult for advice. While yuppie consumption was widely viewed as emulative in the classic Veblenian sense (imitative of the postures of the old aristocracy), the truth is more than this: it expressed the valorization of self-control and reflexive choice in the shaping of a personal style of life—themes that were celebrated in a range of newer, more individualistic consumer goods in the 1980s, such as Apple's Macintosh computer, which, in 1984, flattered its users with the freedom to glide over a real "desktop," selecting icons with a "mouse."

In 1977, a year remembered for low consumer confidence, the highest level of sales were recorded in products identified with new fitness fads and other lifestyle trends: Cuisinarts and other kitchenware, jogging suits, raw wood furniture for painting at home, and biorhythm kits.[101] Indeed, in the late 1970s, the kitchen emerged as a vital new field of exquisitely cultivated techniques and gadgets, all testifying to the agency of the user, radically distinguished from the passive mass-market consumer who simply warmed up whatever was passed along. A growing consumer interest in specialized kitchenware, spearheaded by the popularity of the French Cuisinart, induced several restaurant-supply firms to open retail stores for the public, one reported in *Businessweek* to have drawn four hundred customers on its first day of business.[102] When the Cuisinart was introduced in 1973, its sales remained lackluster until it was endorsed by *Gourmet Magazine* in 1975, after which it quickly took over the food-processor niche, providing dozens of choices between various blades and settings, professionalizing the simple act of cooking for a creative lifestylist. Manufactured by Robot-Coupe, the Cuisinart was the first French-built product to capture a major share of the American home appliance market, selling more than 500,000 items in 1977 alone, for as much as $225 per unit. Citing what he called a growing trend toward home-prepared foods and "cooking consciousness," a Cuisinart sales representative predicted increased sales in coming years, in spite of gathering competition from American firms.

In short, as the success of Cuisinart and Macintosh suggest, the power of personal choice, of the loose lifestylist to freely choose herself, so vigorously lauded by Charles Reich as central to the expanded consciousness of the new generation, had been absorbed into the choices offered by kitchen appliances, computers, and other consumer goods. Yuppies succeeded in stripping the rhetorical forms of much countercultural discourse, reversing, in many cases, the objectives and problematics of its holistic, collective, and hedonistic appeals, while at the same time preserving the core features of this discourse: the framing of a view of the self as malleable and reflexive, and the self's way of life, in its details and habits, as a venue for the improvisation of a personal identity. If yuppies eliminated the overt form of loosening, what they preserved was the injunction of total self-responsibility, the choice of self through the choice of a way of life, even as they trained this responsibility on the demands of changing labor markets and the requirements for upward mobility. As such, stripped of its character as a shared rhetorical and discursive practice, reflexivity ceased to operate as a narrative form. In the relatively detached world of mainstream consumption, however niched, remote from the quality of collective deliberation and conscious intentionality, stripped of the forms of mutual telling that define reflexive identities as narratives of loosening, yuppie lifestyles no longer supported the reflexive crafting of biographical narrative described by Giddens.

In the chapters ahead, these new lifestyles will be considered through the various areas of life they addressed: as marriage and relationship literature, they promised self-renewal through the relaxation of self-censorship in social relations; as ecological and recreational literature, they espoused the removal of rationalist prohibitions on an instinctive communion with nature and wilderness, providing techniques for friendly uses of renewable energy and the consumption of more natural foods. As therapeutic instruction, the new lifestyles offered a hedonistic release of the self into the sensuality of the body or the body of others. As career counseling, the looser life encouraged intuitive choice and impulsiveness in the choice of career paths. The loosening of the self provided an easily transferable motif between all these discourses, wherein new lifestyles of self-renewal were marshaled against the restrictive codes of self-monitoring, snobbish distance, and instrumental self-control associated with an earlier generation of experts, workers, teachers, police, and other more detached lifestyle specialists.

The narrative of loosening defined a powerful and attractive motif, or a transposable metaphor around which, for millions of middle-class Americans, personal identities were constituted. In the words and advisory literatures of nontraditional lifestyle experts and in the lifestyle doctrines they produced from Rolfing to acupuncture, meditation, swinging, whole foods, and macramé, a narrative of self-renewal and discovery related the demise of older forms of self-constraint to the release of new energies and potentials. While conservatives would later record this process through metaphors of "slouching" and "closing," for lifestylists of the 1970s, it signaled a narrative of personal growth and modern progress—an experience of the modernity of the 1970s. One never simply *was* oneself, nor did one make oneself: one *allowed oneself to become* oneself by letting go of old hang-ups, old forms of repression, and self-monitoring, by rejecting the controlling influence of the mass market, and by learning how let oneself be who one really was. This loosening embodied a technique of the self, a way of caring for the self that drew one into a web of relations with others. And, it will be argued, each of these problematics of loosening was incorporated ultimately into a marketing category or an advertising strategy that significantly reconfigured key themes, serving up the choosing self not as a shared discourse on a way of life, but as a product ready for private purchase. While resisting romantic arguments against incorporation or the cooptation of culture, I will argue that, in this form, the potential of lifestyle as a reflexive narrating of the biographical identity was debased and compromised.

In the next chapter, the specific identities of these lifestyle experts and the unique mode of address through which they imparted their loosening advice will be discussed. If, as I've suggested, hedonism was not a condition one simply slouched into, but a technique one mastered, then the question remains: who were the new lifestyle experts that administered the new discourse on hedonism, the new intellectuals and cultural intermediaries charged with the task of improvising the new discourses on deliberate letting and learned relaxation? How did they qualify their expertise? Through what media did they work? What business networks supported and marketed their products? Who were their audiences, and how did they interpret and internalize such loosening ordinances into their personal identities and ways of life? If, as I contend, the loosening of lifestyle was a collective venture in which grassroots media played an important part, who were the producers of this media, and how did it circulate?

❷

Experts Unbound

Intimate Professionals and the Value of Lifestyle

The experience of modernity has been described as one of liquefaction. Along the fault-lines of shifting economic, cultural and social life, identities are torn apart and made fluid, but also recovered and refashioned into more durable forms. A modern life, it has been argued, is one which manages this contradiction, giving form to one's own liquid state by grafting accounts of transformation into stories of purposeful, personal becoming. The loosening of one's life offers one such story, replete with techniques and methods one can incorporate into personal existence on a daily basis. But this story-making is not a task one faces alone: in the lifestyle literature of the 1970s, personal becoming was mediated and assisted by a host of lifestyle experts who understood the dilemmas of modern life in an intimate way.[1] To grasp the mediating function of these lifestyle texts, we must inquire into the manner of discourse through which these authors spoke, the kind of authority they claimed for themselves and the positive form they gave to their advice on matters of identity and everyday life. To understand self-loosening as a mediated accomplishment, we must understand the specific relationship such mediators established with their readers and practitioners. This relation, and the trust upon which it was fashioned, I will argue, was one derived not from the authoritative, institutionally qualified discourse of traditional expertise, but from a new kind of expert and a new way of talking and writing about selfhood and everyday life. In the lifestyle discourse of the 1970s, the new mediators practiced an ethic of caring, in the sense used in the work of Michel Foucault.[2]

In one of his most provocative works, *The Care of the Self*, Foucault offered a detailed and descriptive exploration of the many ways in which subjectivity in the Ancient world was shaped and produced through subtle techniques and methods pertaining to such domains of everyday practice as family and kinship, political activity, eating, sexuality, sleep, the interpretation of dreams and the care of the body, all of which were addressed in volumes of ethical advice and written correspondence. Foucault examined prescriptive texts which outlined for practitioners the ways in which the self might be taken as an object of cultivation and ethical development — a care of the self convened as a collective endeavor through discourses shared and circulated among practitioners and advisors.

> Around the care of the self, there developed an entire activity of speaking and writing in which the work of oneself on oneself and communication with others were linked together. Here we touch on one of the most important aspects of this activity devoted to oneself: it constituted, not an exercise in solitude, but a true social practice. And it did so in several ways. It often took form within more or less institutionalized structures ... the interplay of the care of the self and the help of the other blends into preexisting relations, giving them a new coloration and a greater warmth. The care of the self — or the attention one devotes to the care that others should take of themselves — appears as an intensification of social relations.[3]

While Foucault had no interest in hippies or their lifestyles per se (indeed, in his years lecturing at Berkeley he held nothing but distain for what he termed the "California cult of the self"[4]), and neither did he intend his analysis for the problems confronting modern people, his insights into the dynamics of caring as an ethical relation between individuals mediated by writing help to illustrate the caring relation established in lifestyle print culture. Lifestyle literature of the 1970s achieved a similar "intensification of social relations." It drew people into caring relations with each other, in which the project of self-identity became a shared daily undertaking, mediated by caring texts. Particularly as this discourse is registered against the liquifying effects of a collapsing middle class culture, the care of the self captures the ways in which techniques of self cultivation derive from creative experiments shared between writers and readers across a bond of trust and reciprocity. Caring embodies a "new coloration" in Foucault's words, in which the reflexive project of the self is practiced as a collective improvisation — a coloration that is eroded and compromised as such discourses pass over from vanguard networks and bohemian circles to mainstream patterns of consumption.

Toward this end, the two chapters that remain of Part I will sketch, in broad brushstrokes, the development of such a caring discourse, the changing basis of its authority as a mode of expertise, and the rise of a print culture capable of addressing the wider project of self-loosening through the medium of the caring text. While chapter 3 will concern itself with the properties of the text in an emerging lifestyle publishing network largely based in California, chapter 2 will explore the more general institutional and social basis for such a caring discourse with the expansion of the service sector in the 1970s. Amid a tide of caring professionals, advice, pedagogy and exhortation on the proper style of life assumed a new, loose form.

Loose Expertise and the Caring Professions

In *The Fall of Public Man*, Richard Sennett lamented the rising popular enthusiasm for personal authenticity that characterized so much public culture in the 1970s. He described the decline of conventionalized public identities and the new hegemony of the intimate: "Convention is itself," Sennett writes, "... the single most expressive tool of public life. But in an age wherein intimate relations determine what shall be believable, conventions, artifices, and rules appear only to get in the way of revealing oneself to another; they are obstructions to intimate expression."[5] Though Sennett's comments were directed at the conduct of public officials in the post-Watergate era, their relevance to the lifestyle expert is apparent: at a time of fading institutional faiths, the expert had to overcome the stumbling blocks of his own conventionality to attain a measure of legitimacy for his reader. He had to be humanized and individualized, and the basis for his knowledge had to be dislodged from the distanced, remote, and abstract pedagogy of the old Fordist managerial supervisor and fashioned again as real intimate knowledge—the kind that can be gained only from direct experience, learning, and personal growth in one's own life.

Zygmunt Bauman attributes these qualities to a figure he terms the counselor:

addressing herself to the "unfinishedness, incompleteness and underdetermination" of individual identity immersed in a world of collapsible meanings and scattered and incommensurate life choices, the counselor offers a framework in which coherent self-identity might be accomplished through specific ways of living. But the intimate standpoint adopted by the counselor, having renounced any extrapersonal criteria, can only refer to her unique and highly personal experience, to her own accomplishments in her own programs of self-making and to her highly personal mode of disclosure as the basis for such expertise.[6] Bauman (citing the work of Hilary Radner) mentions Jane Fonda, whose popular workout video and book played significantly in defining a new discourse of lifestyle expertise in the popular culture of the early 1980s, as one who embodies the personalistic authority of this figure: "I like to think a lot of my body as my own doing and my own blood and guts," Fonda tells her readers: "It's my responsibility."[7] Her instructional voice is not one that separates planning from execution, in the classic Taylorist sense, nor is it one that parades about in conventionalized form. It is one that collapses knowing, doing, and personal being in an intimate mode of address—a caring discourse on lifestyle that chooses itself and in so doing instates responsibility in its readers. It is a discourse that derives its legitimacy from the only recognized authority remaining in a post-traditional world: an individual's choice of style of life.

In short, a loose ethic of lifestyle would have to adopt a loose mode of discourse, one emerging from the authentic experiences of a practitioner, shared in a spirit of compassion and genuine heartfelt concern, and whose ultimate application would be to the real meter and pace of a reader's everyday life. In loose lifestyle discourse, convention is read as a constraint on vital intimacies bursting to be shared, and the looser, more intimate expert is the one capable of breaching those constraints and "telling it like it is." As such, lifestyle discourses often suffered from the pathologies Bauman and Sennett point out: an expertise riddled with triteness and superficiality bordering on narcissism. Yet if one delves into concrete cases, one discovers other elements at work. Gestures of leveling and reciprocity also invoked an element of care. In fact, instances of such caring discourses infused the lifestyle literature of the 1970s, though their insinuation into the broader national culture derived from deep structural changes in the American economy and workforce, which saw the emergence of nonhierarchical interpersonal communication skills and lifestyle concerns as an occupational priority, rivaling and replacing an earlier professional ethos centered on the more traditionally defined orders of employment. Over the course of the 1960s and 1970s, a new basis for these caring professionals developed with the expansion of public sector jobs in health, education, and human services, and with the emergence of a range of civic and countercultural networks. While this expansion would be rolled back in the 1980s, the topography of lifestyle and the posture of earnest caring it mapped out would be quickly taken up in an ever more compassionate culture of consumption.

THE SERVICE SOCIETY

Daniel Bell has linked the rise of the new institutional specialist of the 1970s to a wider account of the changing composition of the American labor force. In *The Coming of the Post Industrial Society*, Bell described the demise of manufacture, the eclipse of the goods-producing sector of the economy, and the emergence of a professional, technocratic class whose principal product was not things but knowledge and ideas. He counted these new workers as part of the emerging service sector, a category stretched to include such varied activities as personal services (retail stores, laundries, beauty shops), business services (banking and finance, real estate), transportation and communication, and a cluster of what he defines as health, education, research, and government. "And this is the category," Bell writes, "that represents the expansion of a new intelligentsia—in the universities, research organizations, professions, and government."[8] Indeed, it was in the government sector (specifically in local government), more than in the realm of marketing or advertising, that Bell identified the largest growth in services: a 150-percent rate of growth in government services from 1947 to 1968 was expected to continue at a rate of 52 percent by the year 1980, with 17 percent, or 17 million people, working in some form of government-administered service. While the rate of growth at the federal level had actually declined from 3.5 percent in 1947 to 3 percent in 1968, services on the local and state level had risen from 7.5 percent to 13.9 percent in the same years (132).

Bell's postindustrial knowledge worker rose to prominence in the years since the Second World War with the emergence of a new class of professionals and white collar workers (clerical workers, managers), whose numbers had increased by 38 percent between the years 1964 and 1975, while traditional blue-collar workers (craftsmen, foremen, laborers) had grown by only 17 percent (18). The leading sector within this group was the scientific and engineering professions, whose ranks had nearly doubled between 1960 and 1975. "Theoretical knowledge," Bell writes, "increasingly becomes the strategic resource, the axial principle of a society" (26). Bell's postindustrial thesis remains a benchmark in theories of late-twentieth-century social change, though it has not been without its detractors, then or now. Critics at the time pointed to his overemphasis on the white-collar, administrative, and bureaucratic sectors in various branches of state employment at the expense of other forms of expertise, manifested in webs of human services, health services, and educational professionals, whose numbers within local governments had seen much growth in the 1960s and 1970s. For the teachers in Illich's learning networks or the citizens of Another America, as well as for workers in the expanding sectors of marketing and life-style mediation, the principal service skill was not abstract theoretical knowledge but a hands-on grasp of the meaning of human experience in the course of everyday life. These were mediators of personal needs and interpreters of personal meanings, and the reign of theoretical knowledge in Bell's account failed to take in the developing new personalist sensibility that was coursing through the culture, undermining the foundations of traditional institutional specialization.

Expansion in education, health, and human services was the subject of a lesser-known study published in 1974 by Alan Gartner and Frank Riessman. *The Service Society and the Consumer Vanguard* assessed the growth of service providers and professionals in a range of fields, including "women's counseling, hotlines, halfway houses, rape counseling, sex therapy, family planning, encounter groups, retirement counseling, special services for the dying, vocational rehabilitation, day care, marriage encounters, abortion counseling, alternative education centers, community schools, peer counseling, and self help groups such as Alcoholics Anonymous, Synanon, Recovery Incorporated, Weight Watchers, human potential groups and so on"—jobs that, they argued, were growing on the level of local and state governments and were particularly appealing to young, educated, and idealistic workers whose moral sensibilities were formed in the movements of the 1960s.[9] But the significance of such a humanistic service sector went beyond the professionals themselves to include the consumers, recipients of nonmarket services whose relevance was directed to the immediacy of personal well-being in daily life. Such consumers (youth, minorities, women, and others pushed to the margins of the modern economy) did not depend on market exchanges but on the right to services of various kinds (such as health care and welfare), which included the right to participate in decisions affecting these services. Thus, service providers and their consumers formed a radical axis outside traditional market relations: they tended to eschew the hierarchical discipline of the traditional work environment and lived according to real, not perceived daily needs. Their habits of consumption were framed not by market persuasions but by an authentic engagement with the necessities of daily life, mediated not by advertising images but by their own experiences, filtered by discourses administered by these service professionals. Indeed, these authors tell us, it was in the expanded sector of local government service professions, the health, education and welfare sector, which included helping services of various kinds, that the humanistic spirit of 1960s activism continued to develop.

As distinct from the cohorts of specialists and knowledge professionals studied by Bell, these human service professionals displayed an irreducibly humanistic approach to matters relating to individual quality of life: their aim, in opposition to market-driven services (whose function it was to diminish personal satisfaction with life and to induce, through desire and fantasy, cravings for always newer products), was to enhance or increase the quality of personal well-being by deepening self-understanding and self-knowledge. Theirs was a discourse on caring, to be sure, expressed in what the authors term a "service consciousness" or a "service society ethos," which distinguished these professionals from their counterparts in the market: a greater openness to the needs of recipients of such services, a greater sensitivity to issues relating to personal existence and style of life. "Counseling, tutoring, and health education are examples of what we mean," they wrote; "each of them involves a one-to-one interpersonal relationship, they do not necessarily produce a tangible product or necessarily involve any physical object between server and served, and they are directly beneficial in purpose" (18). Indeed, while Bell's postindustrial society centered around the ascent of formal, abstract knowledge held by scientists and engineers, the service society would be one in which a new humanistic psychology held sway as the overarching principle of the rapidly expanding frontier of human services. Outside the traditional occupational structures of blue-collar and white-collar employment, the new service providers possessed a greater sense of the human stakes of their work, leisure, and daily life, cultivating an egalitarian, nonhierarchical regard for clients and consumers of service work. This ethic, the authors argued, reflected a general cultural transformation in American society: "It is no wonder, then, that the basic values of our time—

which are increasingly invading the older industrial segments of the society, the older middle class and the traditional working class—are service values having to do with the humanization of work, for example, the improved quality of life and the environment, the expansion of consciousness, the reduction of hierarchy, bureaucracy, authority, and centralization and the development of self" (34).

Not only would this consciousness serve as a replacement ethic for a moribund middle-class and industrial worldview, it would serve the needs of those excluded from such market economies generally—the poor, minorities, women, and others for whom the consumption of such services opened up ways of living that were distinct in kind from the regimes of work and consumption imposed by the dominant order. Such "unnecessary people," "characterized by much more unbounded time in which the individual as agent feels freer to make choices, to do one's own thing, to live one's lifestyle," stood in a position to shape styles of life that were more authentic and enriched and potentially exportable to wider social groups. "He/she can be less concerned with organization, hierarchy, tradition. The consumer [of public services] role permits more interest in growth, self-development, expression, liberation, personal rights, the environment, nature" (106).

The networks Gartner and Riessman describe, which encompass public-sector professionals and other community groups often with countercultural affiliations, are important for our understanding of the changing discourse on lifestyle and the evolving status of the caring expert: these networks provided a prolific base for the development of new ways of relating advice and exhorting individuals to new, more authentic and meaningful ways of living—ways of speaking and caring premised on a vital intimacy ceaselessly referring to personal, not institutional, grounds for its legitimacy. Amid such loosened institutional strictures, the origins of a reflexive discourse on lifestyle were shaped for broad popular consumption. Some examples of this empathic discourse illustrate the reflexive quality of the new intimate specialist.

INTIMACY

In 1961 Richard Alpert was the classic figure of a Fordist institutional specialist, the type of professional whose swelling numbers Bell equated with the arrival of a new social class, a psychologist holding multiple appointments at Harvard University. Alpert and his colleagues were what he recalled later as "9 to 5 psychologists: we came to work every day and we did our psychology, just like you would do insurance or auto mechanics, and then at 5 we went home and were just as neurotic as we were before we went to work."[10] Like many other workers under this regime of production, Alpert felt alienated and empty in his work. But following experiments with LSD in a series of regulated sessions conducted with Timothy Leary and others, he began a transformation from Harvard psychologist to spokesman for the psychedelic experience and finally to countercultural celebrity and apostle of a uniquely countercultural version of Eastern mysticism—the latter under the moniker Baba Ram Dass. "There are three stages in this journey that I have been on!" wrote Alpert, "the first, the social science stage; the second, the psychedelic stage; and the third, the yogi stage. They are summating—that is, each is contributing to the next. It's like the unfolding of a lotus flower."

The story of Alpert's transformation is one of the seminal narratives of the counterculture's historical trajectory, charting a path from the constraints of institutional convention to a more profound engagement with the unmediated experience of reality and personal identity. It is one of awakening, of dropping out and becoming loose, but also one of transformation from one kind of knowledge specialist to another: as Alpert developed from "'hip' therapist to the hip community at Stanford" to enthusiastic lecturer and proponent of the clinical and therapeutic use of LSD to a bearded, beaded devotee of the Indian guru Bhagwan Dass, the expertise of this Harvard psychologist evolved a spiritual and practical insight into the deeper meaning of life, together with a heartfelt ability to communicate this meaning to others. Baba Ram Dass's spiritual journey was recorded in a testimonial tract published in 1971 by a small New Age press in San Cristobal, New Mexico, the Lama Foundation, and titled *Be Here Now*, what later became a classic text in countercultural mysticism. *Be Here Now* is a compendium of philosophical musings and slogans interspersed with psychedelic scribbles and diagrams, printed in block capital letters on colored brown paper stock and introduced by Dass's own recollections of his transformation. While these scattered statements do not compose a consistent doctrine of faith of any sort, they converge on a theme central to Hindu mysticism that dovetailed conveniently with the objectives of the counterculture more generally: the celebration of immediacy and the lived moment, and a conviction that such immediacy could be shared only through media that were powerfully personal. Dass wrote,

Nobody is going anywhere
nobody is coming from anywhere
we're all here
we're all here
in eternal time & space
we're always going to be here
we're just doing lila rasa
the divine dance we're dancing.

Yet, as Dass argues, such an immediacy did not avail itself to everyone, and it required the mediation of an expert spiritual guide capable of putting his cards on the table and sharing lessons learned on his own voyage. Dass describes his reasons for writing this book:

Now, though I am a beginner on the path, I have returned to the West for a time to work out karma or unfulfilled commitment. Part of this commitment is to share what I have learned with those of you who are still on a similar journey. One can share a message through telling "our-story" as I have just done, or through teaching methods of yoga, or singing, or making love. Each of us finds his unique vehicle for sharing with others his bit of wisdom. For me, this story is but a vehicle for sharing with you the true message . . . the living faith in what is possible.

Another such voice aimed more squarely at the practice of lifestyle is found in an influential anthology of writings on "bodywork," a therapeutic manual incorporating massage, yoga, and other methods for achieving relaxation and a heightened sense of one's own body in daily life. Anne Kent Rush's *Getting Clear: Body Work for Women*, developed from her activities with other body therapists in the Bay Area counterculture of the early 1970s, was published by a small Berkeley-based press called Bookworks in 1973, and was later picked up for national distribution by Random House. Rush begins her anthology with a section: "Starting with Myself," in which she clarifies her own feminist standpoint as a basis for a personal mode of expertise:

I am writing for women because I am a woman and can tell you what tools have been useful to me. . . . The philosophy behind all these therapies is different from the premise of most traditional kinds of therapy in which the attitude is that the "patient" is "sick," the therapist is the all-knowing "authority," and he "cures" the patient by imposing an outside world system on him or her. In contrast to this, the basic premise of Gestalt and most body therapies is that each individual has her own truth, and her "cure" is within herself, that the path to clarity and personal effectiveness is through self-awareness and integration of one's inner feeling with one's outer actions. . . . By learning tools for self awareness, you can integrate the "therapeutic" process into your life so that you continue to develop and grow consciously.[11]

The author's qualification of her specific mode of expertise, distinguished from "traditional kinds of therapy" by its intimacy and relinquishing of an instrumental distance, enables a unique relationship between author and reader, or expert and practitioner of an ethically enhanced way of life. They are both, in a sense, practitioners of an ethical life. The voice is a caring voice, and it induces the reader to care for herself. The measure of internalization she invites could develop only from a much deeper dimension of trust and intimacy between a traditional specialist and a reader-practitioner, mediated by a uniquely informal discourse.

A third example illuminates this intimate discourse as an active mode of expert address: in 1970, Shambhala Publications of Boulder, Colorado, published a cookbook written by a young monk at the Zen Mountain Monastery in Tassajara Springs, California, with a cover illustration by Anne Kent Rush. The *Tassajara Bread Book* combined bread recipes with philosophical ruminations on cooking and simple, contour sketches of monastic life. The book soon soared in popularity, drawing many imitators from a variety of small presses. In the book's introduction, the author muses:

Bread makes itself, by your kindness, with your help, with imagination running through you, with dough under hand, you are breadmaking itself, which is why breadmaking is so fulfilling and rewarding.

A recipe doesn't belong to anyone. Given to me, I give it to you. Only a guide, only a skeletal framework. You must fill in the flesh according to your nature and desire. Your life, your love will bring these words into full creation. This cannot be taught. You already know. So please cook, love, feel, create.[12]

In the Zen approach, the breadmaker is told to surrender one's instrumental rationality, to release oneself into the process of cooking itself—into an experience that is not instrumental in the traditional sense but that immerses and dissolves the agent into the moment of doing. And such a nonrational immersion requires a very different kind of instruction from that of a traditionally task-oriented exercise: the practitioner must be coaxed through empathy and care to surrender oneself intuitively, rather than directed to apply oneself instrumentally to the purposes at hand. Similarly in other lifestyle discourses: the constraints of accomplished doing are replaced by a release of oneself into the moment of experiencing—a possibility one uncovers only in a space well outside the restricting canons of middle-class recreation, home hobby, and craft practices. The roots of this new discourse on lifestyle originated in countercultural networks and soon fed into the expanding service professions, though it was not long until inflections of intimacy and a deeper, more humanistic concern with personal well-being and style of life would begin to color more mainstream marketing and advertising messages. A more far-reaching assessment of the changing role of expert discourse in American advertising reveals the incorporation of a discourse on caring into a more general discourse on lifestyle mediated by a mass market.

Bridging the Credibility Gap

A staple of national advertising has long been the testimonial endorsement of experts drawn from a variety of professional fields. The commanding, paternalistic tone of the white-lab-coated, clipboard carrying, pipe smoking, spectacled "expert," stroking his beard while instructing the consumer on the latest research on a range of topics, has for a long time influenced popular perception of brands and lifestyles. But by the 1970s, the stature of this authority on issues of daily life was increasingly undermined by a broader crisis in the credibility of institutional expertise, and by the emergence of a more intimate and humanistic voice that seemed to speak more directly to the practice of lifestyle as a meaningful endeavor. Even as advertising discourses turned from words to images over the course of the twentieth century, the voice of the credentialed specialist on style of life was increasingly supplanted in the 1970s by ways of speaking that depended less on a professional distance between theorist and practitioner, and more on a spirit of equality between copractitioners of shared ways of life. While advertising and marketing professionals in the 1960s and 1970s struggled with a crisis in the legitimacy of such expert discourses, they managed to repair their credibility by reaching out to other realms—to the informal, humanistically inclined service professionals who had learned to discuss lifestyles in ways that purported to address the real needs and experiences of consumers themselves.[13] Media historians Leiss, Kline, and Jhally discuss the enhanced intimacy implied by lifestyle advertising of the 1970s with reference to a Nice n' Easy hair color magazine ad, featuring a photograph of a wide-eyed woman with a sincere expression next to a handwritten note: "My name is Lisa. I've just used Nice n' Easy for the first time. My hair looks and feels silky—and the color's so natural I look like myself—only better! I like it a lot. It lets me be me!"[14] The contrast with expert discourse is telling: direct experience with the use of products in one's life and an openness in the relating of advice convey the values of personal authenticity—letting me be me. It was through these channels, through an advertising and marketing industry and through a culture of consumption more generally, that the loosening of the self became hegemonic within middle-class leisure and consumption patterns, and that personal identity became increasingly redefined as a reflexive practice of voluntary choice.

TOUGH CONSUMERS

In 1967, citing a study that found the American public discounting 40 to 50 percent of what it heard from advertisers and politicians, Senator Philip Hart of Michigan called upon advertisers to address the conditions of what he termed "psychological disbelief," or a wide skepticism held by consumers for the vast bulk of advertising messages.[15] Market strategists strove to understand the "credibility gap" that had opened up between producers and consumers, and to address with greater sincerity the challenges confronting advertisers: "The consumer market is becoming increasingly complex," one analyst wrote. "Increased discretionary incomes and the vast proliferation of consumer products have multiplied the number, value and variety of transactions; consequently, opportunities for consumer deception are far more abundant than ever before."[16] Resolving this crisis in trust with a skeptical buying public would prove a daunting task for the advertising industry throughout the 1970s, as it would for a variety of state agencies and others with vested interests in the regulation of style of life.

In the realm of consumption, this crisis had several sources: newer goods made from a wider range of unknown and sometimes untested materials posed enormous challenges for advertisers and package designers, especially under the conditions of increasing demand for information and advice. By the mid-

1960s, nearly half the products on the market were less than twenty years old, making consumer education a paramount challenge in the new markets.[17] Ten years later these conditions were exacerbated by several crisis factors: the successful mobilization of consumer interests under the consumer movement and the "Naderites" galvanized public scrutiny and distrust of the manufacturing and marketing process. A wave of litigation, investigative journalism, and legislative reform revealed a rising level of consumer distrust of the entire market system.[18] Under the added strains of the inflationary period, which saw consumers scrutinizing prices and product labels like never before, advertisers and product and package designers realized the demand for frank, informative statements, transforming daily acts of consumption into highly reflective, highly discursive affairs.

Several groups stepped in to answer the demand for information, among them the Consumer Union (the most vocal organ of the new consumer movements and publishers of *Consumer Report*), and its most recognized national figure, Ralph Nader, whose grassroots drives for fairness in pricing, advertising, and product safety transformed the face of modern marketing. Under Nader's leadership, a network of state and local consumer organizations, largely staffed by volunteers and part-timers, were successful in pressing their concerns to the forefront of the national debate. As his final term came to a close, a war-weary Lyndon Johnson was only too happy to use popular concerns with consumption to deflect attention from price increases caused by the mounting costs of the Vietnam War, and in 1966 he sent a "Consumer Interests Message" to Congress calling for legislative action—a trend continued in Nixon's proposal for a "Buyer's Bill of Rights" and the establishment of an office of consumer affairs, which led ultimately to the creation of the Consumer Protection Agency.[19] On a grassroots level, the consumer movement displayed considerable muscle: when meat prices spiraled in the early 1970s, the combined efforts of consumer food cooperatives were successful in returning prices to affordable levels.[20] However, while its highly publicized legislative victories were significant, the core achievements of the consumer movement lay in the changing of popular attitudes toward goods and in heightening the demand for education and information about products.

Under the added strains of the inflationary period, which saw consumers scrutinizing prices and product information like never before, advertisers and product and package designers answered to the demand for frank, informative copy and factual data. Goods were increasingly sold with testing data and endorsements from the scientific establishment, and consumer guidebooks emerged as a means of approaching the "tough customer," offering a way for retailers to "sell with facts instead of baloney," as one commentator put it.[21] Yet mainstream advertisers and marketing professionals remained puzzled during this period by the strong cultural sentiment underpinning a broad rejection of the mass marketing approach by consumers contemptuous of the shallowness of consumer culture itself: citing Thorstein Veblen, one *Advertising Age* writer fretted in "70s Consumer May Spurn Status of Consumption":

> Many [of these new consumers] are the young who will be taking their places in the American productive machinery during the next ten years [and] who think this kind of motivation is nonsense. They really do not care that they drive Fords while others buy Cadillacs. After all both are good cars with power and room and pleasing design. Why sweat for the extra dollars when the Ford will do just as well? No one really cares whether a man's suit comes from a mass production factory or Bond Street tailor. Both are serviceable and, besides, only a few people could tell the difference anyway.[22]

Marketing experts widely accepted the authority of these judgments, often attributing them to a superior moral sensibility that was gaining momentum within American society. Skepticism was attributed to the influence of the "socially conscious consumer" or "self-actualizer": using Abraham Maslow's theory of personality and moral hierarchy, researchers identified a consumer that had already solved the basic needs of survival and sought deeper satisfaction in meaningful moral self-fulfillment—a purpose that necessarily demanded a critical view of marketing.[23] Possessing deep self-knowledge (and consequently nearly market-proof), Maslow's self-actualizers were described as "autonomous, resisting enculturation, and maintaining an inner detachment from the culture in which they are immersed, coming to their own decisions."[24] Self-actualizers cared about things like carbon monoxide emission levels in new cars and high phosphate content in detergent products, nonreturnable bottles, and nondegradable ingredients in products, and they demanded more in-depth information about products on labels, in advertising, and in consumer education initiatives. By 1972, studies revealed that high-phosphate detergents could lose as much as 12 percent of their market share in simulated experiments,[25] a loss significant enough to frighten producers into greater disclosure of product contents and to excite strategists with the prospect of a new market segment.[26] Calls for across-the-board reforms in consumer education and "responsible consumption"[27] were tempered by appeals for the segmentation of ecological concerns in limited products and markets, since, researchers argued, the ecological consumer defined only one set of demands that should not be generalized throughout the entire consuming public.[28] Objections to the wastefulness and duplicity of marketing were, in some cases, easily absorbed into the vernacular of advertising rhetoric itself, driving one *Advertising Age* writer to complain of a rash of "ecopornography" in recent advertising, evident in such products as "eyecology" false lashes, "Sunarspecs Ecological Systems for the 70s," a line of office furniture, and "Ecology cough syrup."[29] But in other ways these criticisms were not so easily brushed off, stimulating passionate debates within the marketing business itself.[30]

Criticisms of marketing within the business establishment came in many forms, ranging from narrow economic concerns with the utility of advertising as a profit-generating scheme[31] to assessments of the wider social role of marketing as an agent of socialization, a warden of race relations and ecological well-being, and the bearer of honest and fair opportunities for consumers.[32] Indeed, the marketing establishment underwent what one author termed an "identity crisis," or a crisis of moral purpose, which it sought to resolve by reaching out to a range of fields from the social sciences and psychology, as well as from social movements for racial justice, ecology, and environmentalism, marketing sought to broaden the scope of its responsibilities and applications, embracing a variety of human needs not reducible to the narrow category of consumer demand.[33] Criticisms of "marketing myopia" led to appeals for a "broaden[ed] concept of marketing" among advocates of a "social marketing" approach—a call to extend the purview of marketing to include many of the objectives defined by the public-sector service professions: educational, nonprofit, and broader issues of personal well-being. One commentator tried to minimize the differences distinguishing the marketing profession from other providers of human services in the nonprofit sector: "What in marketing is selling in the school is teaching, in the church 'proselytizing,' in politics 'propagandizing,'" suggesting that the marketing establishment incorporate lessons from all of these areas, perhaps recovering public trust as it addressed itself to purposes of greater human significance.[34]

Such internal moral interrogation conjoined with more pragmatic debates about the effectiveness of current marketing schemes in the face of changing social and cultural conditions, and new possibilities presented by new consumer attitudes. A 1969 article titled "Marketing Science in the Age of Aquarius" reflected on the challenges posed by demands for a more authentic approach to consumption from the counterculture and other groups:

> "Will these children of affluence grow up to be consumers on quite the same economy-moving scale of their parents?" Professor Lazer has suggested that such a trend may open up new "markets based on social concern, markets of the mind, and markets concerned with the development of people to the fullest extent of their capabilities." The point is that the line marketing manager who may see his primary responsibility as moving television sets, toothpaste, or midiskirts [sic] is nevertheless compelled to come to terms with the fundamental pattern of value change in America, and probably the world as well.[35]

The belief that "television sets, toothpaste, or midiskirts" would prove inadequate to the emerging "markets of the mind" anticipated a wider acceptance of the need for consumers to relate lifestyles to a deeper sense of moral purpose, or to a more profound level of lifestyle wherein consumers could express themselves "to the fullest extent of their capabilities." As lifestyles loosened, the marketing profession had to learn to speak the language not of conspicuous consumption but of a more profound realm of human meaning. Such a discourse was already developing in the expanding networks of human service professionals discussed earlier, but also spread across a wide network of countercultural groups, businesses, community centers, and publishers. By way of illustration, it is possible to trace one path along which an intimate discourse on lifestyle was absorbed into a mainstream marketing practice: this path leads from an informal network of countercultural lifestylists concerned with the promotion of what they termed "voluntary simplicity," to a popular marketing philosophy known as Values and Lifestyles.

VOLUNTARY SIMPLICITY

Throughout the 1960s and into the 1970s, the Stanford Research Institutes International (a breakaway think tank from Stanford University, based in Menlo Park, California, and known by the acronym SRI), brought together an eclectic group of policy researchers and thinkers whose ideas shared on odd resonance with countercultural thought. Their aim was to develop a specific policy platform by which humanistically inspired long-range planning concepts could be introduced to state, federal, and business planning. Their first significant project began in 1972 when the Kettering Foundation awarded SRI a broad research assignment on the long-term future of education. Willis Harman, an SRI researcher who had conducted studies in extrasensory perception and LSD-based mysticism, was selected to head the team, joined by two others, Duane Elgin and Oliver Markley. The study marshaled the efforts of an interdisciplinary team of researchers from the humanities and social sciences, as well as from engineering and physics, who spent eight months compiling a study that was released in 1974 only in mimeographed form, and published in print only in 1983. *Changing Images of Man* set out to study how certain "images of the nature of man in relationship to the universe" had changed over time, and how these images had put modern industrial civilization on a destructive path, requiring a wholesale reorientation of human consciousness from an egoistic industrial image to one fashioned on a holistic relationship with nature patterned on Eastern mysticism. In spite of its obscurity, the message of *Changing Images of Man* resonated across a range of policy groups and think tanks, surfacing in policy debates in the public and private sectors.[36]

In the volume's third chapter, largely written by Duane Elgin, the study discussed the specifically economic images of man that predominate in contemporary society and suggested positive alternatives for business and marketing, with strong implications for modified views of consumption and lifestyle. In essence, the industrial image of mankind, which linked mass production with mass consumption, was deemed inadequate to the social and environmental realities faced by contemporary man and required a new "image." Calling for a wide transformation of consumption habits in a postindustrial civilization, the report offered an image of man more conscious of the interrelatedness of mind and body, cause and effect, work and play, and of the individual's relationship to his or her terrestrial environment expressed in everyday lifestyle choices. Such an image was not the accidental outcome of changing fads; rather, it was necessary to the development of the species from lower to higher forms. More precisely, business, the study argued, would play a leading role in easing the transition to such a higher level. This widely read mimeographed manuscript established the conceptual groundwork for two important studies of the changing form of marketing and consumer culture: Elgin's *Voluntary Simplicity*, and later Arnold Mitchell's ambitious and influential *Nine American Lifestyles*,[37] which inspired a widespread shift in marketing practice, dubbed the Values and Lifestyles methodology.

At the same time as *Changing Images of Man* was drafted, Duane Elgin had been refining his own observations on changing popular attitudes toward lifestyle for SRI's Business Intelligence Program, drawing on materials from a wide body of research collected from dozens of small, countercultural lifestyle groups and studies (among them Arthur Gish's *Beyond the Rat Race*, the GAMMA Group's *Selective Conserver Society*, and *Taking Charge* by the San Francisco Simple Living Collective). The resulting study was completed in collaboration with Mitchell and titled "Voluntary Simplicity" (a portion of which was published in *CoEvolution Quarterly*, a spin-off of the back-to-the-Earth bible the *Whole Earth Catalog*). The phrase acquired immediate popularity as an expression of the optimistic narrative of the counterculture, packaged as a moderate way of middle-class life.

Elgin came across the term *voluntary simplicity* in a 1974 reprint of an article first published in 1936, written by a Harvard student named Richard Gregg who left America to study with Ghandi in India. The piece first appeared in the *Visva-Bharati Quarterly* but was resurrected twice in the 1970s, first in the journal *Manas* and later in *CoEvolution Quarterly*. Elgin was struck by the article's relevance to the contemporary problems facing American consumer society: "The way of living Gregg described intended the integration of both inner and outer aspects of life, it affirmed the role of simplicity, and it was written by a man whose learning drew deeply from both Eastern and Western cultures."[38] The product was a popular study of recent consumer trends, which, it was argued, the business community desperately needed to understand. In fact, the success of "Voluntary Simplicity" prompted Elgin and Mitchell to begin a lecturing tour in April 1977, which, following on the equally successful appearances of the environmentalist E. F. Schumacher, author of *Small Is Beautiful*, drew attention from both the business community and federal and state officials. But it was not until 1981 that Elgin published the volume as *Voluntary Simplicity*—a title that was to establish the "simple living" movement that grew in the 1980s and 1990s and to initiate a broad discourse and sustained market niche of lifestyle practices aimed at reduced consumption levels. Such a movement would gather momentum moving into the new millennium with magazines such as

Real Simple, Simple Living, and, one could argue, in the formidable success of such firms as Martha Stewart Living and the Body Shop. As with *Changing Images of Man,* Elgin located his account of the emerging lifestyle movement squarely within a countercultural evolutionary narrative of spiritual enlightenment and changing values, centered around the importance of personal choice:

> By the early 1970s, it was clear that sweeping social changes were not going to materialize. . . . a whole generation's trust in leadership had virtually collapsed, and the sense of national integrity and purpose had been shaken to the core. Not surprisingly, the national mood turned inward. People wanted to restore some semblance of "normalcy" to their lives after a decade of wrenching change.
>
> . . . For the more persistent among this pioneering culture, the agenda shifted from transforming society to finding new ways of living at the grass roots level of society. Instead of continuing the seemingly fruitless struggle to change dominant institutions, many among this forerunner group began to concentrate on their immediate lives—the domain where they had genuine control and could make a visible, if seemingly small, difference. At the local level, countless small experiments in living began to flourish.[39]

Elgin's thesis located changing forms of consciousness in consuming patterns that included conservation, recycling, self-maintenance, and the popularity of an assortment of home provisioning crafts and techniques. But more importantly, his ecological premise identified his own personal experience with transformed habits of consumption as universally shared with readers and practitioners—they were all united, both author and reader, around the concerns they shared as cohabitants of planet Earth, and with the shared desire to care for this shared object through acts of stewardship exercised over oneself. "We have entered a time of transition as a human family," Elgin writes; "we are being pushed by hard necessity and pulled by enormous opportunity to fundamentally reconsider the way in which we choose to live our daily lives" (7). Indeed, throughout the countercultural discourse on lifestyle, personal choice was central to the new ways of living, for it was through personal choice that the individual shared in profound, world-historical processes of global transformation, which were themselves tied in with experiences of the realization of self: "This book is premised on a [belief that] the manner in which we live our ordinary lives *does* make a difference . . . my overriding concern has been with how we can make small and practical change in our everyday lives and thereby contribute both to the quality of our personal existence and to the well-being of the entire human family" (7–8). But while Elgin's exhortation of such "small practical changes" may have intended a broader moral program of personal and social change, it nonetheless proved a practical discovery for a marketing industry hungrily searching for more and better ways to insinuate goods into the personal lives of consumers, and to address such consumers in a sincere and intimate manner. In the values and lifestyles methodology, the making of small practical changes was elided with the making of small but meaningful purchases.

VALUES AND LIFESTYLES

While the SRI reports made inroads into both countercultural discourses on business and lifestyle and mainstream marketing efforts to grapple with the "credibility gap," it was with Mitchell's *Nine American Lifestyles* that the focus on personal values identified by Stanford researchers was to find its form as a marketing manifesto. What came to be known as the Values and Lifestyles (VALS) approach, in which consumers were broken down into types based on deeply held personal inclinations (experiencers, achievers, strivers . . .) was developed from Mitchell's earlier lifestyle studies published in 1973 as *Life Ways and Lifestyles*—a work that provided the impetus for the foundation of SRI's prestigious and influential VALS program in 1978.

Mitchell's VALS typologies incorporated a countercultural vision of a broad societal shift defined by an emerging attitude toward consumption and consumer choice as an expression not of class, race, gender, or ethnic backgrounds (the types applied by earlier marketing studies), but of unique and deeply personal moral sensibilities.[40] The influence of the counterculture is apparent in Mitchell's weighting of the VALS typology in favor of certain attributes of character: VALS maps a tension between two value systems, one endorsing the individualism, competition, and acquisitiveness of mainstream American society and another stressing the expressiveness, ease with oneself, and earnestness associated with youth and the counterculture. Borrowing from David Reisman's studies of changing American character, Mitchell describes the outer-directed groups' concern with "signals," and their status associations, more committed either to bland conformity or to the pursuit of celebrity through heroic acts of accomplishment. Meanwhile, the inner-directed groups, mostly members of the postwar generation, holders of good educations and professional jobs, tended to be "self-expressive, individualistic, concerned with people, impassioned, diverse, complex."[41] Importantly, Mitchell's inner-directed types possessed a greater capacity for the individual choice of their own lifestyles, and a deeper sensitivity to others, deriving from their enhanced awareness of their own feelings—a sensitivity that left open channels for new and more sincere (or intimate) marketing messages. It was possible, Mitchell argued, to address the deeper meanings invested in lifestyle choices by this vanguard group, whose habits would inevitably become the universal norm.

Indeed, by the mid-1980s, the VALS methodology was the buzz of the marketing world, influencing research and market planning for major firms such as Avon, Timex, Sanka, and American Airlines, shaping retail strategy and affecting the content of advertising and promotions.[42] Exercising greater understanding of the deeper values that defined its various markets, and capable of investing products with a deeper sense of personal relevance to the goals of self-selected lifestyles, VALS explored pathways from the impersonal and remote methods of the mass market (supervised by the distanced, credentialed specialists) to a more personalized way of eliciting the trust of consumers represented by intimate lifestyle practitioners. "When the marketer deals at arm's length with millions of people, VALS is a better way to humanize those people than many of the conceptualizations currently available," one analyst wrote.[43] In a 1983 article in *American Demographics*, an influential marketing director was quoted praising the uniquely personal approach of VALS: "'VALS makes it possible to personalize marketing and to understand the target we're trying to reach better than any other piece of research.' We've moved away from the world of individual contact with the customer, but VALS restores some of that personalization."[44]

The group to which Mitchell attributed the greatest promise in his optimistic prediction of changing American social values were the experiencers— an influential 5 percent of the American population who "seek the authentic, the active, the daring—whether it is mountain climbing or artistic expression. They prefer natural products to synthetic, shop in organic food stores, grow their own flowers and vegetables."[45] The vanguard of things to come, the experiencers eschewed material goods for intense transforming moments capable of cultivating a deeper sense of personal livelihood. Just as hippies extolled the dawning of the age of Aquarius, so marketers in the 1970s foretold of the rise of the experiencer consumer—looking forward to the 1980s, Mitchell hailed the coming "decade of the real thing."

But as the discoveries of the VALS researchers became more integrated into the consumer culture of the 1980s, as the momentum of the counterculture lost steam and the young lifestylists were replaced by far more politically and morally innocuous yuppies, the injunction to authenticity and sincerity implied in this humanistic renovation of marketing was soon shorn of its overtly moral pretenses. For James Ogilvy, a longtime collaborator with Mitchell and director of the SRI program, the emergent experiencer segment was read less in terms of the moral openings it provided, and more as a vanguard of an emerging consumer style that was shaping a new sector of retail—an experience industry—which, he predicted in 1986, would permanently redefine the consuming habits of Americans by stressing the consumption of experiences, in place of more concrete goods or services. Trumpeting the relevance of Mitchell's VALS typology for the new marketing challenges brought by an increasing demand for sensory experiences, Ogilvy writes: "The experience industry cultivates through education, broadens through travel, allows escape through entertainment, heals through psychotherapy, numbs through drugs and alcohol, edifies through religion, informs through reading and enraptures through art."[46]

Experience could be as mundane as a trip to the 7-Eleven (Ogilvy cites the testimony of a convenience store executive: "We are not in the grocery business, we are in the convenience business"), or as dramatic as a whale-spotting tour off the coast of British Columbia. In either case, Ogilvy writes, "The quality of the experience has as much to do with the person as with the product" (29). Once marketers are enriched with a deep understanding of the individual needs of the consumer, Ogilvy explains, lifestyle experiences can be extended into all areas of manufacture, sales, and promotions. In a comment that recalls the lifestyle sentiments projected onto the Cuisinart, Ogilvy wrote: "Kitchen appliances can enhance the cooking experience. Food and beverage companies are really in the dining-experience business. Camera companies don't just sell cameras or film—they sell memories of experiences. And automobile manufacturers are doing more than providing the means for getting from one place to another. They sell the driving experience" (53).

Toyota's "Oh, What a Feeling" campaign stands out for Ogilvy as an example of experiential marketing at work: for consumers looking for experiences of speed and intensity (character-building experiences combining hedonism with expressive learning), the Toyota ad "stresses the experience of ownership rather than the features of the automobile . . . consumers can feel the lightness of the car when accelerating, braking or turning" (29). Employing the interpretive skills of uniquely sensitized marketing directors, the logic of the market was extended into the most intimate realms of personal experience, where the agency of the reflexive lifestylist was made synonymous with that of the consumer. As the voices of the intimate experts were incorporated into the cultures of mainstream consumption, assertions of empathy with the deeply felt needs, values, and experiences of lay consumers became increasingly central to the selling of goods and services. If the aim of the counterculture had been to equate being with choosing, the aim of experiential consumption and other marketing and advertising rhetorics of the 1980s was to extend the analogy by equating choosing with buying. The "new coloration" of lifestyle as a collaborative practice of self-cultivation was replaced with a solitary practice of consuming, even as the essentially reflexive character of this lifestyle was preserved.

❸

Book as Tool
Lifestyle Print Culture and the West Coast Publishing Boom

The loose discourse on lifestyle derived from a repositioning of the lifestyle expert as a loose professional—a change that occurred in social networks stretching from publicly employed providers of human services to countercultural hubs where lifestyles were elaborated and advised upon, interrogated and re-invented. In chapter 2, we visited some of the professional sites where this discourse was disseminated and considered how a humanistic discourse on daily life was incorporated into the fabric of mainstream consumer culture. In the chapter that follows, we will consider the specific medium—the countercultural lifestyle print culture—through which loose lifestyles were propagated. Beginning as a localized and marginal publishing phenomenon, a countercultural discourse on everyday livelihood soon attained national stature as an alternative to the stale living patterns of the postwar mass consumer.

This loosening of self was a process often written about, woven into stories of constraints removed and hang-ups freed, unleashing spontaneous vitalities and modes of feeling—a biographical narrative of becoming loose that offset the scattering effects of an accelerated culture of modernity and the uprooting of middle class cultural heritage. Through advisory narratives on diet, relationships, exercise, home furnishing, travel, sex, home economics, cycling, recycling, gardening, massage, home birth, and Volkswagen repair, readers were exhorted to relax into their immediate experiences and live themselves in the daily flow of events, always under the ordinances of a novel form of expert advice. But this exhortation was not just related through words on a page: it was literalized in the material products of grassroots publications and through the informal networks whereby books, magazines, catalogues, and journals were produced and circulated to their readers. The loosening motif was performed in all the elements that composed a print culture in the wider sociological sense. The concern of this chapter, and of the three chapters that comprise part 2 of this study, is with the broader phenomenon of this print culture: with the small-scale economic networks and the webs of writers, readers, editors, distributors, printers, and illustrators that composed this culture of print, and with books and publications wherein looseness was represented and dramatized as a caring discourse on everyday life.

An inquiry into the emergence of this particular print culture reveals in greater detail the passage of a lifestyle discourse from a peripheral fringe to a mainstream center. We uncover a process of incorporation that took place along a tense and unstable boundary separating competing camps in the competitive market for books, each bringing its own distinct products to market, and each implicitly advancing its own valuation of culture. On the one hand is a countercultural, grassroots publishing network centered largely in the Bay Area, and on the other a traditional publishing and literary establishment with deep roots in the East Coast intellectual centers of Boston and New York.[1]

Within the West Coast culture of print, the loosening metaphor was dramatized by the informal links that tied writers, printers, distributors, and readers in an imaginary bond with remote audiences and authors—Another America to be sure, this time with a consolidating business interest and national ambitions. The reality of these bonds was concretized in the rough-hewn covers, amateurish typographic styles, crude saddle binding, and scattered layouts, all testaments to the immediacy of personal experience they proselytized. Their narratives of loosening assumed a wider importance, encompassing not just a personal but a social and global story of universal transition. Loosening was not just something one did to oneself, it was something one shared with imaginary, contemporaneous readers, writers, and others—a great, encompassing process of world change one participated in with a host of unseen colleagues, all readers of the same materials. Indeed, the purpose and narrative form ascribed to lifestyle by such an advisory discourse depended on the assumption of a collective project, a purposeful movement toward a goal of social change. Yet frequent invocations of the invisible multitudes, accessible to the imaginations of readers, perhaps of a national, perhaps of a global scale, gave the new lifestyles a resonance that could be derived only through purely mental figurations—the imaginary bonds one forms through the act of shared, contemporaneous reading. The first part of this chapter will offer a window into such networks and shed light on the way an imaginary membership bound by a shared discourse of care was rendered in the minds of readers, while the second part will investigate the emergence of one particularly prolific hub of lifestyle publishing on the West Coast, for whom the loosening metaphor signaled a mark of distinction that had to be negotiated, or struggled over, against the dominant publishing and bookselling authorities in the east.

Remaking Real Life through the Culture of Print

In the midst of what was euphemistically termed the "urban crisis" of the 1970s, Urban Alternatives (or UrbAlt) formed as a nonprofit group based in Worthington, a suburb of Columbus, Ohio. A network of vanguard, urban experimentalists with the aim of putting into practice the social visions developed in the counterculture of the 1960s, the group addressed the bleakness of modern urban life through the exploration of new forms of collective living and personal lifestyle. UrbAlt had existed for several years as a clearinghouse for research and resources from various nonprofit community groups across the country, sponsoring workshops, conferences, and seminars on a range of living and organizing approaches covering legal and economic aspects of urban issues, and more broadly sharing views on the quality of life in America's cities. Meetings were sometimes held at university campuses and community centers across the region, but more frequently the group met in a downtown Columbus location called "A Place to Be, a unique downtown educational center developed by the Reverend James Bills" as part of a local church in downtown Columbus.[2]

Issues of their newsletter, *Doing It!*, started to come out in 1976. A regular, letter-sized publication usually containing eighty pages, *Doing It!* was printed on inexpensive newsprint with two wide columns of large type, interrupted with shadowy black-and-white photographs and sketchy, amateurish but expressive cartoons, diagrams, and illustrations. The bimonthly magazine cost $2 per issue, $10 annually. Advertising ran $100 for a full-page ad and 5 cents a word for a classified. Over the magazine's ten issues during two years of publication, advertising picked up, moving from a few quarter-page ads packed at the back of the publication to as many as a dozen, some a half page in size. Indeed, ads featured announcements and notices from a variety of national alternative lifestyle groups, extending to a network of readers from across the country. Advertisers include: *Communities*, a regarded organ of the commune movement based in Virginia; *Win Magazine*, a political broadside from Brooklyn, New York; *Alternative Source of Energy Magazine* from Minnesota; *Green Revolution*, a directory of communes and co-ops based in Pennsylvania; and *Mothering*, a journal on natural mothering, home births, and midwifery published in Colorado. Similarly, classified ads suggested that the markets and the readerships *Doing It!* had accessed were not restricted to the Ohio region, but extended through networks of mail-order correspondence to retailers and producers across the country:

NATURAL CLEANSING DIET, help your body heal itself, eliminates excess mucous and toxins. $1; SELFHEAL-5A, 1817 Hayden Lane, Tempe AZ 85282

GAMES WITH A DIFFERENCE! Non-competitive card and board games for children and adults. Play together not against each other. Free catalogue. Family Pastimes, DI Perth, Ontario, Canada K7H 3C6

SOLAR ENERGY PRODUCT DESCRIPTIONS, with prices. Differential thermostats, storage tanks with integral heat exchangers, and many more necessary solar system components. Send 13 cent stamp for HELIOTROPE GENERAL product data. 3733 Kenora Drive, Spring Valley, CA 92077.[3]

Doing It! was not unique in any respect. It was one of hundreds of such publications, often short-lived ventures with small, widely dispersed, but deeply committed reading audiences. This one continued to publish from May 1976 until September 1977, when it changed its name to *Humanizing City Life*, a title it kept for two issues before folding in April 1978 with its tenth issue. In a statement on the inside jacket of this issue, the editors discuss the problems the journal faced running at a loss of $2,000 per issue; the failure of a promotional mailing sent to 24,000 readers taken from assorted borrowed mailing lists, which failed to draw more than half a percent of responses; and the prospects of turning the magazine into a newsletter for UrbAlt members. Yet the purpose it set for itself and the image of its own audience it related was quite revealing. The first issue of *Doing It!* defines these objectives with this editorial statement, printed on the inside of the front cover:

> The structural arrangements of society—government, business, human services, educational and other institutions—seem to be afflicted with gi-antism and are out of scale with people's lives. We turn away, alone and alienated from a society that has reduced us to numbers. Loneliness in a crowd is the most telling metaphor for modern urban life.
>
> Yet all over the country there is a trickle of movement going the other way. People who are staying in the cities, unwilling or unable to escape to the country, are trying to gain control over their lives and their environ-ment. Some do no more than join food co-ops in order to get closer to the process of obtaining food, in the company of like-minded compan-ions. Some go so far as to join in living and working collectives, taking a radical step away from prevailing customs. In between all sorts of other things are going on—urban food production, informal education, parent support groups, citizen action groups, networks of independent crafts-people, and so on and on. They are as diverse as the human imagination can conceive and involve people in the most formidable creative act: the remaking of real life.[4]

This statement is a classic affirmation of the significance of the personal in the face of the depersonalizing currents of modern social life, typical of many lifestyle magazines from this time. Personal significance had to be rescued from the anonymity imposed by scale, and the route to this new intimacy was a col-lectively renewed style of life. Yet in spite of its emphasis on the particularity of the local in opposition to the gargantuan structures of mainstream society, *Doing It!* celebrated the reader's membership within a larger network of readers and lifestylists that was uniquely inaccessible to the immediate senses—a senti-ment expressed in an article on a countercultural community index called the *People's Yellow Pages*. Quoting one of the organizers of a *People's Yellow Pages* from Ithaca, New York, the article states:

> A People's Yellow Pages profiles an emergent new world as it appears in a particular geographic chunk. It is an articulation and celebration of the tangible aspects of our dreams of a free world. It's something we can hold in our hands, that proves that others also have struggled, are struggling, and are experiencing victories. It begins to sketch, with faint, halting lines,

a totality—a community where we share, overcome, and build. And it helps us to know who is with us, and what they are doing.[5]

The materiality of the publication and the ephemerality of the network are linked: this statement's appeal to "tangible aspects," "something we can hold in our hands," which "proves the existence of others," reiterates the tension and longing for an imagined community implicit in this print culture through a veneration of the materiality of the print product itself. The imagined readership and the real magazine are both less and more than real things: the irreality of the readers are evidenced in the palpability of a thing read and shared by numbers too many and too disparate to be known face to face. Such imagining is central to the coherence of a print culture and indispensable to the storying of the loose self as a narrative of personal identity. Moreover, the capacity of print cultures to affirm communities and establish relationships is seminal to its functioning as a medium of intimate expertise, and to its properties as a caring text. To grasp this, we must take into account the unique ways in which print cultures circulate meanings, and specifically the unique status of print as registered against other electronic and primarily visual media.

PRINT CULTURE

Media scholar Joshua Meyrowitz has contrasted the relative exclusivity of print culture to the vast publicity of television. Exclusive and marginal forms of print media, in contrast to mass market electronic media, impose automatic filtering functions on the selection of their audiences merely by the prerequisites they require for their consumption. Where television reaches a wide and undifferentiated mass of viewers by posing only one degree of interpretive complexity (the reproduction of sights and sounds that can be easily selected from a range of channels), print cultures define their audience with a far greater degree of precision and distinction with materials that are already highly coded, differentiated into "introductory and advanced" levels.[6] Meyrowitz writes, "The stages of learning required to master complex information in print support many distinct groups, many stages of socialization into each group, and many levels of status and authority."[7] Countercultural print media, with their roughshod quality and slang, are coded in a manner that presumes certain reading competencies and certain ethical agreements on what a mass media product (a book or magazine, for example) should look like and thus suggests an audience bound by these shared understandings. Themes central to the identity of this group and its way of life are manifested in the format of the medium itself: the qualities are roughhewn and thus more intimate, posing a powerful contrast with the mainstream model typified by television, a medium constrained by a unidirectional flow of content from a bureaucratized, hierarchical production machinery doling out content to a passive, anomic mass-market consumer.

In the pages of this literature, a triumph of the personal was literalized in the leveling of the status of the lifestyle expert, but also in the leveling of the production hierarchy that drew readers, producers, distributors, and retailers into a diffuse network unified by a grassroots local economy. Indeed, evidence of this leveling was everywhere apparent: readers frequently contributed personal letters, articles, and ads; the production techniques betrayed the layman skills of producers who were no better skilled than readers; and the networks of distribution were personalized to suggest that all were involved in the same lifestyle described by the text. The caring ethic was more than just proselytized in the content of lifestyle texts, it was enacted in typography, layout, and physical features, and it was dramatized in the loose business arrangements and retail networks through which texts were passed along to their audiences. Thus, these reading networks, like the "imagined communities" described by Benedict Anderson,[8] share a contemporaneous reading experience with the same people who fabricated the various magazines, periodicals, and newspapers, but also the distributors, retailers, and contributors.

One important vehicle for this theme was the use of chirographic (handwritten) as opposed to typographic (printed) use of space. Walter Ong has described the differences between manuscript and print texts in their ability to summon antitechnological sentiments:

> Print situates works in space more relentlessly than writing ever did. Writing moves words from the sound world to a world of visual space, but print locks works into position in this space. . . . Printed texts look machine-made, as they are. Chirographic control of space tends to be ornamental, ornate as in calligraphy. Typographic control typically impresses more by its tidiness and inevitability: the lines perfectly regular, all justified on the right side, everything coming out even visually, and without the aid of the guidelines or ruled borders that often occur in manuscripts. This is an insistent world of cold, non-human, facts. "That's the way it is"—Walter Cronkite's television signature comes from the world of print that underlies the secondary orality of television.[9]

The print culture of the countercultural reading network, ever undermining the typographic control of space with the intimacy of chirographic ornament, sought to represent, metaphorically perhaps, a certain social informality, intimacy, and group membership against the anonymity and authority of the "cold, non-human facts" propagated by traditional experts. In sloppy and uneven paste-ups, scrawled illustrations, and ornate handwritten letters, the tensions between formal and experiential expertise, and between uptight and loose ways of living, were, quite literally, spelled out on the page. The spirit of this contemporaneousness loosening was not confined to a few scattered groups like Urban Alternatives but animated a lively and influential development in the American book publishing industry.

West Coast Publishing:
Classifying the Advisable Life

As the years of radical confrontation became increasingly remote, and as new challenges posed by energy shortages, inflation, and an increasingly diverse market in "health"-oriented products came to dominate the national agenda, many student radicals drifted into a dispersed rural network whose bonds were maintained through an expanding print culture, devoted to practical instruction in matters of personal well-being, daily provisioning, home construction, and so on. From their battles on university campuses, where many student radicals had written and edited campus broadsides, counterculturals brought journalistic, editorial, and production skills that could be adapted to the more innocuous purposes of advising on gardening, small business, handicrafts, and food preparation.[10] The importance of the underground press in the student movement is well documented: in San Francisco such newspapers as the *Oracle*, the *Tribe*, and the *Berkeley Barb* coalesced readers in the Haight-Ashbury scene, while on the East Coast, the *East Village Other* and *Rat* set out to organize hippies into a coherent readership. The *Kaleidoscope* in Milwaukee, *Distant Drummer* in Philadelphia, the *Seed* in Chicago, and the *Avatar* in Boston made antiwar activism and the use of psychedelic drugs into topics of weekly reading. But with the demise of many of these scenes, the skills gleaned in the production of such newspapers would be applied to publications with a much wider circulation and a less political emphasis on style of life.

Developments on the side of business and technology aided in this shift: the availability of an easily rented computer typesetter (by the mid-1970s an IBM

Selectric typesetting machine with interchangeable typefaces could be rented for $150 a month) enabled shoestring publishers to freely manipulate and paste down cold-type compositions, allowing hand-lettered headlines, drawings, and any kind of graphic experiments that might emerge during the typesetting process. Such technology spawned dozens of home press projects, leading authors and editors to undertake their own production, editing, and design. Moreover, the proliferation of multiple publishing centers eager to fill "open" print time between major jobs with smaller runs on less expensive accounts gave small presses access to inexpensive printing services. The result was a small renaissance in amateur publishing. A *Rockford Sunday Magazine* correspondent described the phenomenon: "They are mostly trade paperbacks, communicative in content, reflecting new trends in ideas that originate on the West Coast, lavishly illustrated, colorful and appealling to a young audience."[11] While many of these books and magazines would have trouble penetrating mainstream book markets, marked as they were with "gremlins," typographic gaffes, crude layout, and amateurish design, a few would attract lucrative contracts from the big East Coast houses, some rising to the level of national best sellers.[12] Indeed, as the 1970s unfolded, this category would expand in profitability and prestige. When in 1977 Harper & Row relocated its religious books division to San Francisco, the move was hailed by the publishing industry as a symbol of the emergence of these peripheral publishing networks to a new position of national prominence.[13] The first to blaze this trail from West Coast enclave to national market was the countercultural, ecologically conscious "access catalogue" *The Whole Earth Catalog*, a countercultural index and commentary listing resources, though dozens of imitators would seek to network readers in similar ways, providing forums, advice, and counsel on new approaches to everyday life.[14] Their names are as diverse as their contents: *CoEvolution Quarterly, Journal of Community Communications, East-West Journal, Guide to Cooperative Alternatives, New Games Resource Catalog, Rain: A Journal of Appropriate Technology, Self-Reliance, Seriatim: The Journal of Ecotopia, Whole Earth Papers, The Whole Person Calendar, Briarpatch Review, Journal of the New Alchemists, Doing It! Source Catalog, Humanizing Urban Life, Womanspirit, New Age Journal, Place, Alternatives, Appropriate Technology, People's Yellow Pages, New Harbinger, Mother Earth News, Green Revolution, Communities, Cascades,* and dozens more.[15]

The story of their debut on the national scene is largely one of the emergence of the west as a viable publishing and bookselling market, in an affront to the traditional bastions of American publishing based in New York and other eastern cities—a clash that expressed competing criteria for the value of a literary product and of the nature of intellectual legitimacy more generally. While West Coast publishing was driven by the desire to break down the conventions of commercial publishing, to swing wide the doors of access, and to share "information" within local networks of self-selected authors and readers, the traditions of the east sought to make profit through the mass production and sale of products from specialized authors to a wide and anonymous market. In a clash of cultures that reproduced those same ruptures within middle class cultural authority that we have already visited (clashes between traditional distanciated taste on the one hand and the new valorization of immediate sensation on the other), publishers in the west sought to elevate everyday knowledge and experience, while their counterparts in the east sought to promote only those products bearing literary worth and the value of true talent.

THE WEST COAST

The West Coast publishing boom was itself part of a wider demographic shift from eastern and midwestern cities to the West and the South—a pattern of business migration that eroded the traditional monopoly of New York publishers and created marketing opportunities for small presses nationally. While in 1977 almost 40 percent of publishing firms (businesses with an employee identification number, at least one employee, and whose primary business was selling books) were located in the New England and mid-Atlantic states, by 1987 that portion had declined to less than a third, while the South and the West grew from 10 to 13 percent and 20 to 27 percent respectively. Los Angeles was, at the start of the 1970s, the nation's second largest book-buying center, with San Francisco the fourth. If existing trends continued, critics maintained, the West Coast would supplant the East as the nation's foremost book market by the year 1980.[16]

Indeed throughout the decade, the West Coast market was presented in the publishing trade press as an opening frontier defined by an entirely new kind of book consumer bearing an entirely new sort of literary value, one that was attended to by local publishers practicing a new business ethic: a study commissioned by the *San Francisco Chronicle* in 1972 revealed that Northern Californians were educated, literate, and young: 41 percent of Northern Californian adults had attended college; 74 percent had attended high school, and

65 percent were between eighteen and forty-nine—the age group most agreeable to spending money on books. By the early 1970s, large retail booksellers based in the east were beginning to respond to this opening market: B. Dalton Booksellers, Doubleday, and Brentano's all moved to expand their presence in mall and shopping districts across California, challenging the independent booksellers who had been steadily expanding their clientele over the last few years. Throughout the decade, major houses from the East opened offices in West Coast cities to better reach those markets, most notably the move in 1976 of Harper & Row's religious department.[17] The move made sense, a company spokesman argued, because 60 percent of the authors on its religious books list lived west of the Mississippi, with 30 percent living on the West Coast.[18] "Besides," the commentator continued, "it's not part of publishing that depends on the New York literary scene." Sales from Harper & Row's religious book list, a diverse category that had included authors from Dr. Martin Luther King to Martin Heidegger, had totaled three and a half million dollars that year.[19]

However, as appealing as the West Coast may have been to many eastern firms, it was nonetheless often perceived as an immature market, fraught with risks and logistical problems that hampered its full development. Distribution and promotion stood out as two specific areas of concern: difficulties in reaching across such wide expanses to often far-flung outlets put strains on sales representatives, many of whom had to cover wide markets with limited personnel. While New York distributors enjoyed a relatively concentrated market of the greater New York area, Connecticut, and New Jersey, distributors covering the "Western region," composed of the "eleven Western states," had to negotiate greater expanses of space, slowing the responsiveness of suppliers to hard-to-reach retailers (stores often had to wait four to six weeks for titles that might be in daily demand), compounded by the problem of returns, poorly selling titles sent back to the publishers.[20] With the larger share of warehousing and printing of trade books still done in the East, and with cities west of the Mississippi increasingly "bookish" in their demands, wholesalers and distributors complained of an excessive burden, and East Coast firms puzzled over the problems posed by this new opening of the West: the West was often derided in the East as a "supermarket culture," whose potential book-buying market was more connected to media outlets defined by mass entertainment (Hollywood films) and consumption (shopping malls and mass retail outlets), than to the intellectual and cultural centers through which book sales were generated.[21] Perceiving the

West as lacking in a consistent reading and book-buying population, many East Coast houses relied exclusively on the most traditional media for the introduction and promotion of new titles: large advertisements in the *New York Review of Books*, for example, or author appearances on network television talk shows hosted by Merv Griffin, Dinah Shore, or Johnny Carson. With the difficulty of planned author tours in the inaccessible markets of the West, East Coast firms tended to rely solely on these mass-market mechanisms, often with the result of slower sales, which themselves seemed to confirm the perception of the West Coast as simply not literate enough to be worth the effort.[22]

But defenders of this "supermarket culture" offered a very different analysis of its potentials, largely hinging on a definition of the book consumer that eluded the traditional mass-market model imposed by eastern houses. While the West lacked the traditional intellectual centers where titles received praise and recognition, it possessed powerful local networks and informal centers where books were discussed and promoted. The mass-market promotional strategies that East Coast firms brought to the West ignored what one marketing specialist insisted was unique to the West Coast book market: the local networks, centered around independent bookstores in smaller urban enclaves, and the vast college system. Indeed, a range of new developments contributed to a strong book-buying public that escaped the traditional marketing radars of East Coast houses: the emergence of an influential underground publishing network, new literary supplements in college newspapers as well as other suburban dailies and regional publications; the increasing publicity given locally produced titles directed to specific timely and regional issues on local news and other media outside the usual book promotion spots; and the more active and cooperative role of independent bookstores in arranging author tours and speaking events, and in cooperating in larger promotional plans.[23]

Moreover, the view of the West as lacking in the intellectual stature of the East was a claim that carried with it more than a dash of eastern chauvinism: lacking the intellectual capitals and hence the cultural nuance and cultivation that would enable a properly mature market for books, the West Coast could support sales in trendy titles related to lifestyle and spirituality, but not the serious literature that supported a real publishing business. One visiting publisher described the market as strong in "best sellers, how-to, pop-psych, self-help, occult—and most of them in trade and paperbacks. But not much hardcover, not much fiction, very few literary works of 'heavy' nonfiction. It's an unsophisticated audience, and yes, it buys a lot of books, but it's not as varied or diverse or consistently responsive as general statistics might indicate."[24] While charges of faddishness were received with indignation, western commentators responded with an alternative axis of cultural valuation, celebrating the spontaneous and informal network of the readers, writers, and booksellers, and the everydayness of its literary content. In other words, while the East labored between the traditional distinction of elite and mass culture, casting the trendiness of the West as a mass-market driven phenomenon, the West acknowledged its penchant for novelty, associating this interest not with the mass market, but with an intrinsic creativity and openmindedness, one that was unschooled, perhaps, but all the more authentic for it.

Indignation and a rejection of the chauvinism of the East Coast establishment was part and parcel of the identity of the West Coast publishing culture—a sentiment described by Digby Diehl in a special issue of *Publishers Weekly* on the emerging West Coast scene. Diehl, photographed for the article on the beach, bearded, surfboard in one hand, arm full of books and typewriter in the other, clearly removes himself from the cultural hierarchies he identifies with eastern publishing, asserting that "In New York, I am often treated to the joke that I was chosen Book Editor of the *Los Angeles Times* because I was the only person in California who could read without moving his lips." He goes on to compare the discussion of the relative appeals of the New York and Los Angeles literary worlds to a party game familiar to many men ("that old Male Chauvinist Pig game, 'If You Could Have Any Woman In the World . . .'"). Who would be the ideal woman? Diehl immediately stakes his claim: Elizabeth Taylor—a move which surprises many East Coast literati friends, who, as he tells it, prefer the more subtle intrigue and intellect of, say Eleanor Roosevelt. But Diehl is unapologetic: "There is something about her overripe sensuality," he claims, even while he anticipates the objections of his New York friends: "But what would you talk to her about[?] . . . she's so—*vuhl*-gar." Diehl is untroubled by this charge:

> Ah, yes, the secret word is out: vulgarity. It's what the West has that everyone else seems to want in startlingly increasing proportions. No doubt it will be the secret of how the East was won. And in its best form—such as Elizabeth Taylor—it is something to be joyously embraced . . . There is an energetic ferment in the Western book world that is revitalizing the national mainstream. This ferment has, in many ways, brought publishing out of its quaint New England cloisters to . . . the edge of history.

Indeed, western vulgarity, Diehl argues, provides a much-needed tonic to the insular, eastern-dominated world of publishing. The old establishment, cloistered in its sophistication, stands to benefit from this infusion of electric, if vulgar, energy. He calls upon readers to recognize the West as a "celebration of vulgarity" and to salute the "stud service of the West which has brought fresh blood to an industry suffering from the mutations of several hundred years of inbreeding. Despite my flippancy, I hope that my praise of Western vulgarity is understood with the seriousness intended, for this vulgarity is not only vitality, but a sense of commonality often missing in our elite, high educated and snobbish book circles (from 'Vulgus, L., common people')."[25]

These sentiments are characteristic of West Coast publishers' attitude toward the power and authority vested in the New York–based publishing establishment. A *Publishers Weekly* survey, mailed out to professionals in the book industry in twelve western states, innocently inquired whether book-buying audiences in the West were "unsophisticated." Answers ran roughly five to one as "no," with often heated commentary. One respondent defiantly asserts the value of such lack of sophistication: "But I say hooray for all that; let's keep our 'less sophisticated' audience, and all the new money and market the hell out of them. If I can use the fads and cults as a cushion, I'm more able to go with the risks that are worth taking—and that includes, by the way, small press stuff, first fiction, unknown authors, essayists, good philosophy. What I want to know is, what's their cushion in the East?"[26]

Indeed, the classification of the West Coast reader as lacking sophistication and thus closer to the mass market consumer, defined by her willingness to follow fads and latch on to the next going thing, is here linked with the asset of greater flexibility and independence of the publisher. Just as the Beatles had flustered music critics at the *New York Times* by toying with notions of musical genius, so the "supermarket culture" of the West subverted the taste canons that had defined the exclusivity of middle-class taste.

Questions about the reclassification of the West Coast book market extended beyond questions of the sophistication of its readers: the West Coast was also appealing to eastern publishers as a source for the titles that were developed locally by small presses—titles that had proven their appeal to western audiences and, some in the East speculated, possessed powerful marketing potential on a national scale. West Coast publishers and the local authors they developed were, by the early 1970s, becoming the object of much eastern curiosity: smaller-scale operations, formed of informal networks of writers, editors, and distributors, these firms seemed to suggest an alternative way of doing business—a view of the West that was illustrated in a *Publishers Weekly* article featuring a photograph of a group of smiling book people sitting around a table on an outdoor deck overlooking the Pacific, accompanied by a caption reading: "An editorial conference California style."[27] In short, the West Coast was desirable to the East not only for its readers, but for a nascent grassroots publishing and bookselling industry of its own, one that seemed to conform to very different rules, covering everything from the development of content to production and distribution. Nowhere is the uniqueness of this industry better illustrated than in the case of the Bay Area publishing and bookselling business.

THE BAY AREA

Just before Christmas in 1972, San Francisco's Golden Gate Park was host to a gathering that in many respects resembled dozens of others over the preceding years. Organic food stands set up next to bookstalls, rock bands and poets performed from an open-air stage, and pot smoke wafted through the grounds while bottles of wine were surreptitiously passed between groups of vendors and their customers. But this was not a be-in or gathering of the tribes in the tradition of the Haight-Ashbury scene: it was the First International San Francisco Book Fair, described in its brochure as "a revival of craftsmanship, a reverence for beauty, above all, a personal commitment to the spirit embodied in a book rather than merely a commitment to the publishing business." The Book Fair was meant to showcase some of the hundreds of small presses that had emerged over the preceding years, publishing often short runs of innovative fiction, practical, how-to paperbacks, and other lifestyle tracts. "If any East Coast publisher had showed up," Frederic Mitchell of Scrimshaw Press recalled to a *Publishers Weekly* correspondent, "he would have flipped out. The atmosphere was unpetty and cooperative. It was something new in publishing and we all knew it. There was a sense that we had the double whammy on New York. We're not only managing to make a little money off our books, but we're having fun too."[28] The book fair provides a window into the publishing and bookselling industry emerging in the Bay Area in the early 1970s, characterized by Diehl as a "frontierland of transplants [that] has generated a contemporary mythology of its own, and with it, the re-examination of all our national values."[29]

Book publishing in the Bay Area had long been of a very regional character, home to several small presses specializing in historical nonfiction, as well as activity guides and tour books aimed at West Coast residents. Among the earliest distinguished features of this market was the region's fine book publishers, most notably a rather exclusive network of printers clustered in the Bay Area, including Grabhorn-Hoyem Press and others, whose devotion to traditional presswork techniques and binding methods carried national reputations. A publishing and bookselling tradition can be linked to a network of Bay Area entrepreneurs, intellectuals, writers, publishers, distributors, and luminaries, traceable to the legendary beatnik poets and writers of the 1950s and the small businesses that fostered their rise, most notably City Lights Bookstore and Cody's. Throughout the 1960s, this nascent circle of poets and writers expanded as the spectacle of a psychedelic tribal community beckoned to youth across America, drawing droves of hippies and others to San Francisco's notorious Haight-Ashbury and other scenes. Out of this network, distributors and publishers like Bookpeople, Shambhala, North Point Press, Chronicle, Ten Speed, Nolo, and Sierra Club came to define the literary and commercial world of the countercultural publishing while making slow but steady advances into the mainstream of American book sales. This world constituted a mixed bag: a broad gamut of poetry, fiction and nonfiction, trade and mass-market books. More paperback than hardcover, the books were considered marginal and fringy by mainstream tastes. "These West Coast publishers are attracting a lot of attention now because they are not tradition-bound," said one commentator from a publishing firm based in the East, "instinctively they're willing to try new things."[30]

Yet despite their marginality, publishers on the West Coast soon became attractive to readers nationally, drawing East Coast houses to a trove of innovative works, ripe for the plucking from small publishers and distributors unable to manage large national markets. Indeed, as countercultural lifestyle themes became more popular among the American middle classes, the national potential of seemingly offbeat countercultural books sent the eastern houses scouring the West for popular books that could be repackaged and distributed on a far larger scale. A few titles stand out: *Fifty Simple Things You Can Do to Save the Earth*, *What Color Is Your Parachute*, *Creative Visualization*, and, in particular, *The Whole Earth Catalog*.[31] A *Publishers Weekly* article recalls the specifically organic professional and ideological core of West Coast publishing in the 1970s, the genesis of which is attributed directly to the influence of the *Whole Earth Catalog*.

In New York, people have traditionally gone into publishing as a "career choice." On the West Coast, publishing developed as a side effect of a particular interest. Individuals interested in hiking, Buddhism, juggling, meditation, starting a business, getting a divorce, nature, ecology, computers, gay and lesbian issues, or simply how to cook a salmon would look around for a book, fine none, then go on to publish in that category. From this stemmed the Bay Area concept of the book as a tool. Here again is the legacy of *The Whole Earth Catalog*: books are objects to use, places to find practical information about things that publisher's neighbors care passionately about.[32]

Indeed, the *Catalog* was edified in the 1970s as the pioneering work that opened the category of countercultural, ecologically conscious "access catalogs" (countercultural index publications listing resources for those pursuing new, holistically responsible lifestyles) and opened the West to the national market.[33] The *Catalog*, which developed from a small circle of ecologically inspired back-to-naturists working in a garage in Menlo Park, south of San Francisco, offered detailed commentary on dozens of items useful to the former commune dweller, or maybe the suburban hobbyist with like aspirations. Its cluttered pages, crudely pasted down with blocks of type and found images, buzzed like an Eastern bazaar with myriad new ways of doing ordinary, taken-for-granted things, from shoe repair to stargazing, accompanied by informal product reviews of hardware, clothing, and books loosely clustered around the practical problems of living in the modern world. The startling success of the *Whole Earth Catalog*, purchased from local Bay Area distributor Bookpeople by Random House and sold nationally, defined the model for West Coast books: offbeat, grassroots, and suggestive of new ways of life.

An overview of the Bay Area publishing scene of the early 1970s shows how style of life, in the hands of these nontraditional experts and entrepreneurs, would be contrasted with other institutionalized, hierarchical classifications of expertise and cultural competence. There are several figures and presses whose contributions stand out in this respect, though few as deserving as Don Gerrard, who in 1968 founded Bookpeople, a small book distributor based in San Francisco. He and a partner started with short list combining local authors and titles with national paperbacks, relying on their own mail-order catalogue "with a funky, anti–New York stance." Within a year and a half Bookpeople mushroomed into a $2 million business with twenty-five employees, carrying a list of

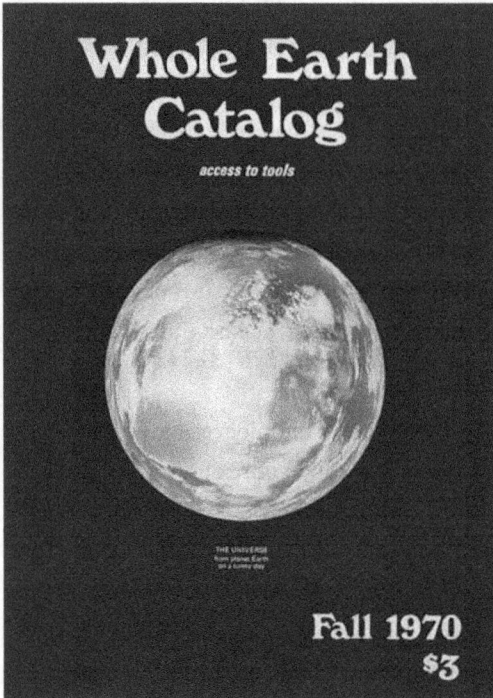

Fall 1970

$3

4. Cover, *Whole Earth Catalog*, edited by Stuart Brand

mostly how-to titles, catalogues and manuals and drawing eager interest from the larger East Coast firms. John Muir's *How to Keep Your Volkswagen Alive: A Step by Step Manual for the Complete Idiot* sold 125,000 copies, Jeanie Darlington's *Grow Your Own: An Encounter with Organic Gardening* sold 56,000 copies, and Alicia Bay Laurel's *Living on the Earth* sold 10,000 copies in its first four months, and, like the *Whole Earth Catalog*, was quickly picked up by Random House, where it became a national best seller. Bookpeople was ultimately to split into a distribution arm, Bookpeople, owned and operated by its staff, and Bookworks, Gerrard's own operation, which, in tandem with Random House, published titles such as *The Massage Book*, *Vagabonding in Europe and North Africa*, and *No More Public School*, an instructional manual on home schooling. Bookpeople, meanwhile, persisted as a collectively owned, cooperatively run enterprise, acting as an umbrella for dozens of small presses in the Bay Area and beyond.[34]

Living on the Earth was the product of a twenty-one-year-old woman living at Wheeler Ranch, a commune in California. Alicia Bay Laurel (her real name is Kaufman, though she preferred to be named for her favorite tree) penned, quite literally, the manuscript in her own handwritten script while living communally on the ranch in 1969. Without so much as a table of contents, the book contains page after page of instruction on the myriad problems that confront the natural lifestylist in the course of daily life: how to make a lantern for a candle from a tin can; how to build an ice chest; how to make your own baby food from organically grown fruits and vegetables; how to tie-dye; how to deal with troublesome neighbors (moths, rats, ticks); how to cure a cold. The serendipitous ordering of all this advice is accented with Bay Laurel's own drawings: flowing childish, Matisse-like line drawings, depicting every variety of subject matter to illustrate her instructions. Smiling moons look down on a sleeping-bagged couple snuggled in tall grass; naked gardeners till soil; a bearded figure strums a guitar. In her introduction, Bay Laurel explains the ordering of the book:

> This book is for people who would rather chop wood than work behind a desk so they can pay P.G.&E. It has no chapters, it just grew as I learned; you may find the index your only guide to this unmapped land. However, if you have a feeling for the flow of things, you will discover a path: from traveling the wilds to the first fence, simple housing, furnishing, houses, crafts, agriculture, food preparation, medicine—not unlike the development of our ancient ancestors. When we depend less on industrially produced consumer goods, we can live in quiet places. Our bodies become vigorous; we discover the serenity of living with the rhythms of the earth. We cease oppressing one another.[35]

The book was produced with no typesetting, no galleys, and no revisions: on the recommendation of Stewart Brand, editor of the *Whole Earth Catalog*, Bay Laurel took her collection of folios to Don Gerrard, who had been looking for something that would follow the success of the *Whole Earth Catalogs*, but most of what he had seen, he told *Publishers Weekly*, was too commercial. "She came in with her book in a little blue suitcase," Gerrard recalls. "We took it home and read it and flipped out." Calling it a "turn on book," Gerrard said that "if you could impersonate the Little Prince as a chick, you'd have Alicia." Originally published by Bookworks, the title was eventually picked up by Random House as a Vintage paperback, with a first printing of 100,000 copies. A two-page spread on *Living on the Earth* in *Publishers Weekly* mimicked the book's chirographic style: in meandering script, a reviewer lavished praise on the book's

5. Cover, *Living on the Earth*, by Alicia Bay Laurel. Copyright 1971, Alicia Bay Laurel. Reprinted by permission of Random House, Inc.

authenticity and simplicity: "We decided that we couldn't tell you about it in stodgy type, because then you might not realize the rather startling statement this book makes about the making of books: It is still reasonable to simply write a book, print it, bind it and sell it. As someone once said, the only thing Gutenberg had over the scribes, after all, was the novelty of a justified line."[36]

Shambhala Publications earned its reputation as a press dedicated to New Age spirituality, the uniquely countercultural version of Eastern mysticism associated with many West Coast houses. Started in 1968 by two Berkeley graduate students in the basement of a bookstore they owned and operated, Shambhala's mission was to be "a house dedicated to exploring and mapping man's inner world and expressing creatively the potential of Man's evolution." After only three years of operation, Shambhala had over thirty titles in print, including *Mandala*, *The Tassajara Bread Book*, and *Meditation in Action*, an instructional manual on meditation and Eastern mysticism written by Chogyam Trungpa, a Tibetan monk. *Meditation in Action* was assembled in the basement of the bookstore in 1969, and by 1972 it had proven an indisputable hit for Shambhala, selling over 26,000 copies. But a more sensational experiment for Shambhala

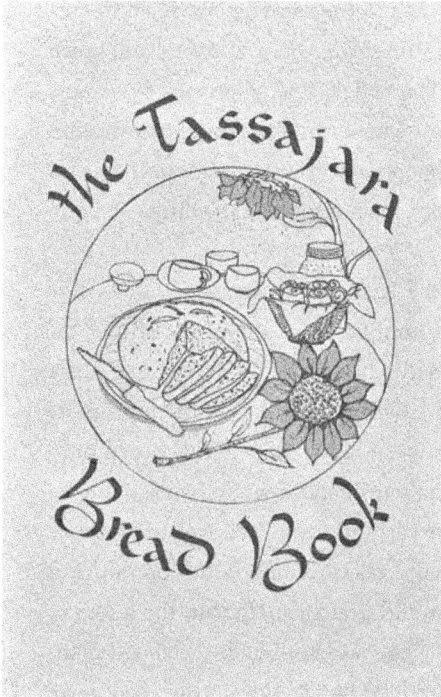

6. Cover, *The Tassajara Bread Book* by Edward Espe Brown

was *The Tassajara Bread Book*, whose gentle pedagogical tone we explored in chapter 2: a collection of recipes, sketches, and philosophical ruminations on bread preparation written by Edward Espe Brown, a monk at a California Zen retreat called Tassajara.[37]

Written on a $100 advance and printed in an initial edition of 3,000 copies, by the mid-1970s sales of *The Tassajara Bread Book* would reach 300,000, ultimately passing 750,000 and securing it an enduring legacy as a classic in cooking and bread baking instruction. The book's rustic, earth-tone cover of brown cardstock gave it a rootsiness that was complimented by titles and chapter headings written in swirling calligraphic form, seemingly drawn with quill pen, accompanied by illustrations of monastery scenes and diagrams of bread baking techniques drawn with casual but steady contour lines. Woven throughout these instructions was a consistent reflection on mundane tasks as intrinsically meaningful, even in their minutiae: "Bread makes itself," an opening statement explains, "by your kindness, with your help, with imagination running through you, with dough under hand, you are breadmaking itself, which is why breadmaking is so fulfilling and rewarding."[38] Brown, who moved on to prominence as a chef at Greens, a restaurant owned by the San Francisco Zen Center, was to follow this success with two other titles: *Tassajara Cooking* and, much later, *The Tassajara Recipe Book*, all with Shambhala, and all greeted by readers eager to spice up their drab middle-class kitchens with exotic non-western foods. By 1976, Shambhala had left Bookpeople and gone to Random House for distribution, and with eighteen titles in 1977, the house was exceeding $800,000 in trade sales.

Closer to the political objectives of the New Left of the 1960s was Glide Publications, later New Glide. Glide was, until 1977, the publishing arm of the Glide Memorial Church, a progressive Methodist ministry devoted to a range of causes from gay and lesbian issues to environmentalism and feminism. As the church became the focal point for activism in the 1960s, Glide began publishing titles dealing with what were then considered touchy issues: *Battered Wives* and *Living Women/Loving Men* are early efforts at political and lifestyle perspectives on gay partnering and abusive relationships. "Our commitment was to produce responsible books that would deal squarely with the issues of social change, no matter how unpopular those issues might be," claimed managing editor Ruth Gottstein.[39] But in 1977, Glide Publications, which had never published commercially, broke with the church to become New Glide. Titles such as *Word Is Out: Stories of Some of Our Lives*, *Incest: The Last Taboo*, and *Chutzpah: A Jewish Liberation Anthology* maintained the press's commitment to "issue" topics, though with a focus on personal life and individual identity. But New Glide also expanded into new areas: a series of books on emerging artists, and a manual on beekeeping titled *Curative Properties of Honey and Bee Venom* would point the way to broader issues of culture and lifestyle for the press as it began its appeal to a larger market. In 1978, New Glide published *The Briarpatch Book: Experiences of Right Livelihood and Simple Living*, a collection of articles from the *Briarpatch Review*, a newsletter circulated among a network of countercultural businesses in the Bay Area and beyond. Like *The Tassajara Bread Book*, *The Briarpatch Book* wore its authenticity on its sleeve: the volume's deep brown cover and rough pages resonate with a bucolic innocence that is confirmed with the rich brown ink used to print text. Naive drawings are interspersed with articles documenting the struggles of counterculturally-oriented small businesses, from restaurants to clothing stores to auto shops.

More typical of the West Coast's go-it-alone spirit, however, was San Francisco–based Scrimshaw Press, an outfit composed of a former publisher of *Ramparts*, a radical left magazine, and a recreational climber and photographer.

7. Cover, *Briarpatch Review*

Scrimshaw earned a reputation as a publisher of high-quality photo books, often regional in character, which tapped in to the prevailing ecological and pastoral yearnings of the time and earned them several awards in design from the American Institute of Graphic Design. This category, first opened up by Sierra Books, long a publisher of awkwardly-sized environmental picture books (featuring the works of Ansel Adams and others) was at first received with some reserve by distributors and booksellers in the East (the format won't fit the shelf sizes of most stores, one retailer complained), but soon the glossy, large format of the picture book became more accepted. Several titles tell the story: *Delta West: The Land and People of the Sacramento–San Quentin Delta*, a lush photographic study of regional California culture, *Gift of Place, Antigua Black, Image Tibet*, and most successfully, *Handmade Houses: A Guide to the Woodbutcher's Art*, a collection of whimsical photographs of personal, idiosyncratic structures created from wood. The success of *Handmade Houses*, editor Fred Mitchell recalled, was due to its diverse appeal to a variety of people involved in creating their own homes: "It rattles around in a lot of pickup trucks and lumber yards, because it's directly useful for people who want to loosen their minds."[40]

Another important leader in the Bay Area publishing field was Straight

Arrow Books, the publishing arm of *Rolling Stone Magazine*. Straight Arrow's corporate motif, an image of a uniformed Boy Scout, eyes optimistically and obediently fixed on the distance, seemed at odds with the informal professional culture fostered by Straight Arrow's staff, and by Alan Rinzler, the thirty-three-year-old Harvard graduate hired to run Straight Arrow in 1971. Housed in a loft south of Mission Street near San Francisco's waterfront, Straight Arrow's offices, Alan Hislop reported in *Publishers Weekly*, were "eclectic with hand-built furniture, antiques and pieces from junk shops. The staff of about 60 off-beat young people, most of whom work for both the book division and the magazine, seems incongruous surrounded by the latest technology of computers and instant typesetting machines." Against this backdrop, Rinzler himself provided a further touch of countercultural bravado, "splendid looking in embroidered levis which are decorated with bits of patchwork." The tension between straight and loose was imprinted firmly in the content of Straight Arrow books. Titles such as *Body Count: A Confessional Memoir*, and *Mindfuckers: Source Book on the Rise of Acid Fascism* identified the press with far-out, difficult, and fringy material. But from its inception, Straight Arrow had its eye on a more substantive list: "We've begun to send out heavier vibes," Rinzler said in 1973. "It's harder to publish literature than message books, but that's what we're trying to do. We're interested in publishing culture and serious books of investigative journalism, books of information and enlightenment, useful functional books for being alive in America." These objectives were realized with titles such as *Lennon Remembers*, a collection of interviews from *Rolling Stone, The Connoisseur's Book of Marijuana*, and a book of graphics titled *Cosmic Bicycle*.[41]

While the lists of each of these publishers are varied, and any generalizations as to their content are necessarily partial, it is nonetheless possible to identify a general concern with style of life as a concerted practice—a project to be pursued under the care of an intimate discourse on personal authenticity. One particularly powerful motif runs through these injunctions to lifestyle: the metaphor of the tool, or the "book as tool."

BOOK AS TOOL

The concept of the tool, made apparent in the *Whole Earth Catalog*'s byline, "access to tools," which appeared on the cover of each issue, stressed a belief in lifestyle not as the passive accumulation of objects, but as the active, creative, and highly individual choice of a meaningful life. The motif proved infectious:

an article in *Country Woman*, a feminist access catalogue inspired by the *Whole Earth*, relates the "tool" concept to the underlying meaning of goods as elements of a larger way of life:

> Walking to the bathhouse today, holding my new twenty-ounce hammer, I suddenly understood the Whole Earth Catalogue meaning of "tool." I always thought tools were objects, things: screw drivers, wrenches, axes, hoes. Now I realize that tools are a process: using the right-sized and shaped object in the most effective way to get a job done. It's having a well-balanced hammer and knowing how to hold and swing it that makes it a tool; changes the whole work process from a struggle to a pleasure.[42]

Resonant with a countercultural emphasis on process over product, this author relates tool to a view of task, and lifestyle, as performative rather than instrumental in essence. Most importantly, the *Catalog* conveyed an insight into the practical use of goods, not as static possessions but as tools in a larger process: against the acquisitiveness of traditional modes of middle-class consumption, the *Catalog* stressed a deeper understanding of goods as parts or moments in a larger temporal and lifestyle continuum.

Initially handled by Bookpeople, the *Catalog* took the publishing industry by surprise when its surging popularity brought in sales of over 100,000 copies, leading Random House to purchase the *Catalog*'s final issue, *The Last Whole Earth Catalog*, and turn it into a million-copy best seller. Its popularity nearly caused pandemonium in 1972 when it was handed the National Book Award for current affairs, beating out several more traditional titles and drawing the resignation of one of the judges, author Gary Willis, who was angered that an edited collection would be awarded the prize while other "important books" by "serious writers" were left out.[43] Unswayed, Brand accepted the award: "As you know, the 'Whole Earth Catalog' is less a book than it is a public event. A considerable population of unlikely people made the catalogue. I think they are honored by your award. All I can do is agree wholeheartedly with your estimate of them. And if the award encourages still more self-initiated, amateur, youth-based, non–New York publishing, good deal."[44]

The *Catalog*'s success forever transformed the West Coast publishing industry, drawing endless scouts from East Coast houses in search of "the next *Whole Earth Catalog*," and, it can be argued, carrying a discourse of lifestyle far beyond Bay Area countercultural circles. By the early 1990s, several market categories traceable to the West Coast publishing explosion that began two decades earlier had been opened up for informational, instructional publications: cookbooks (Chronicle's *Little Cookbook* series sold more than 2 million copies), computer manuals (Peachpit's *Mac Bible* claimed to break the New York mold by "showing people how to use tools"), travel (Lonely Planet, Moon, Ulysses, and Foghorn books incorporated environmentalism into vacationing), and New Age (Shakti Gawain's *Creative Visualization* sold more than 2 million copies by 1992).

Though books and magazines were certainly not the only media through which discourses of looseness were propagated (many would object that music, film, and other more powerful vehicles of popular culture were far more influential), printed discourse provides a window into the ethical meaning of loosening that other media do not. As a mode of discourse, the injunction to unconstrain oneself is presented in a more rigorous mode of articulation: it is ironed out, rationalized, and made sense of in a way that the sensual experience of rock music or the charisma of the film star are not. The loose lifestyle, as a means of tempering the dissipating effects of modern change, of mediating, in a single way of life, the exhilaration and anxiety that accompanies dramatic transformation in the economic, cultural, and social positioning of the middle-class, provides a counterweight for personal identities threatened with the scattering effects of contemporary life. Loosening, or reading about loosening, and the repositioning of lifestyle expertise as intimate and immediate discourse of caring, was achieved in a print culture that trumpeted these qualities on every page, and in the social and economic networks through which such media are circulated. Such a lifestyle discourse related a caring effect replete with ethical and practical lessons and a powerful sense of the unfolding of the self as a narrative form. With the broader historical backdrop of this caring discourse in place, and the more general arc of a cultural and social turn generally provided, we can turn now to the thin cultural slice with which we began: with the publications themselves wherein the problematic of the loosening self was literally spelled out. What constraints had to be removed, what precisely was to be loosened, and what sort of transformations of the self could be expected?

Part II
Caring Texts

4

Being One

From Knowledge to Consciousness in the Spaceship Society

In the preceding chapters we have viewed lifestyles as daily activities in which people fashion stories of personal growth and
change through seemingly mundane choices and preferences.
Amid economic, cultural, and social realignments, middle-class
lifestylists of the 1970s found that becoming loose offered a structuring narrative that suppressed the anxiety and foreboding of en-
gulfing social change by lending significance to everyday patterns
of choice, inscribing them as expressive vehicles of a developing
subjectivity. In the lifestyle movement of the 1970s, where thrilling
possibilities for the choice of style of life were shadowed by doubts
and uncertainties as to the ultimate purposes to which such lives
were directed, loosening offered a highly mobile and transposable
metaphor for the consolidation of a durable sense of self. Though
the specific areas of lifestyle in which loosening was invoked were
wide-ranging and diverse, they shared a common theme and related problematic: life had to be released from civilizational constraint and loosened *into* something else—a precivilization, authentic, rawer, and more immediate domain of experience. The demand
that one remove constraints imposed upon oneself was a requirement that presumed a field of sensuality and livelihood into which
one could dissolve oneself, though the identity of this field varied
radically as the problematic of loosening was posed differently as a
dilemma of leisure, domestic life, travel, cuisine, social life, hygiene,
and fitness. In the chapters that follow, I have chosen to group these

objects into three general clusters: by rethinking and reliving one's relationship to nature, to others, and to one's own body, one could discover ways to be become looser, freer, less constrained, and more oneself. By dissolving the inhibitions that prohibited communion with these neglected or undervalued domains, identities could become enriched and recentered, shaped against the prevailing forces of an all-consuming modernity. Moreover, each of these realms, it will be shown, was the object of an advisory discourse and a print culture that addressed its readers in a uniquely personal and informal tone. A discourse of caring, related in these caring texts provided ethical advice on the proper techniques of self-cultivation and care, issued in honest, modest, and loose narratives to their believing readers.

The caring text, as I intend the term, develops a relationship between readers and absent others who collectively attend to the problem of what Bauman termed the "unfinished" business of identity under the conditions of modern life. Amid the torrent of commodities and sensations, changing economies, redrawn social boundaries and new ways of life that beset the American middle classes in the 1960s and 1970s, basic habits of personal identity were crowded out of the mental space demanded for the thinking of a stable sense of self. Such a modernity was one of explosive impact and seduction through the dissipation and distraction of the cognitive focus necessary for self-monitoring and self-restraint, resulting in the collapse of moral distance—the space for thinking—one takes on oneself when one sees one's life as a biographical narrative. While such distractions are a threat to traditional regimes of work, they are endemic to expanding cultures of consumption and leisure. Seduction, writes Bauman, "is best achieved if the consumers cannot hold their attention nor focus their desire on any object for long; they are impatient, impetuous and restive, and above all easily excitable and equally susceptible to losing interest."[1] Under such conditions, "the life itinerary of most individuals is likely to be strewn with discarded and lost identities,"[2] and the production of new ways for cultivating self-attention is left up to the inventive methods of individuals themselves, occasionally banding together on collaborative works of improvised lifestyle practice.

In short, care expresses such shared efforts at the cultivation of self-attention aimed at instilling a reflective distance on the self in everyday conduct—a purpose realized through discussion and correspondence with others engaged in like practices. Caring texts are those specific media through which collaborative efforts are undertaken remotely: they attend to the problem of distraction by lifting us out of everyday life in the reading and writing experience, making us think about our choices in the mediation of everyday lifestyles. As mentioned earlier, the loose lifestyle, as an object of caring, poses an interesting paradox: one gains reflective distance in order to better immerse oneself in experience (the mediation of immediacy), yet the purpose of caring remains the same: caring texts institute a thoughtfulness about everyday choices that allows for a reflexive narrating of events and shaping of biographical stories of self-becoming. In Foucauldian terms, this dynamic of reflexivity and everyday conduct can be described as a mode of "self-problematization," a holding up of some aspect of one's daily conduct as the object of serious ethical scrutiny and concern, at the center of which is a discourse with others on the appropriate shape of such behavior for the purposes of an ethical goal of one sort or another.[3] As Foucault's studies have revealed, the discourses that comprise ethical problematizations often employ forms of writing and reading uniquely suited to this purpose—techniques of ethical caring embedded in practices of reading that, I argue, are relevant to our understanding of contemporary reading practices of the caring text.

Indeed, the experience of writing and reading provides a medium for this retrospective integration of the self through a narrative, available to others, which veers close to the function of pedagogy—a quality Foucault uncovers in the ancient use of personal notebooks, or *hupomnemata*, kept and circulated among a cultivated ethical elite. Citing Seneca, Foucault discusses the specifically ethical character of writing in this manner, which works both to counter the fragmenting effects of a life tormented by passions aroused by the distractions of the present, by relating one's attention to lessons learned in the pasts of everyday life: "The hupomnemata resists this scattering by fixing acquired elements, and by constituting a share of the past, as it were, toward which it is always possible to turn back, to withdraw . . . the practice of the self involves reading, for one could not draw everything from one's own stock or arm oneself by oneself with the principles of reason that are indispensable for self-conduct: guide or example, the help of others is necessary."[4]

The recounting of such daily practices to another allowed one to focus more clearly on oneself, to store experiences for later retrieval, and to lend continuity and coherence by relating a practice to a narrative form. This dynamic, I argue, defines the practice of the caring text as an ethical problematization of distractions foisted by the speed, fragmentation, and tempo of modern life. In the chapters that follow, such efforts will be considered in three general areas of lifestyle where specific loosening projects were undertaken, each defined by a specific object, a primordial field of experience and immediacy into which the uptight self could be released. First, the loosening of the self is framed as a development in consciousness on a global, ecological scale in which the instrumental constraints of civilization are loosened and an enriching communion with natural, organic, ecological systems is allowed. Loosening into the earth required a shift in perception and awareness: with the demise of a traditional industrial worldview centered on an instrumental relation to the natural environment, a new ecological worldview emerged in which man and nature were seen in a holistic, integrated cosmic totality—a shift of consciousness lived out in a set of ecologically informed styles of life. Next, in chapter 5, the domain of interpersonal relations (sexual life, domestic cohabitation, and ultimately business and commerce) is the site of a loosening practice in which unmediated access to the experiences and emotions of others provides an object of self-loosening. As the conventions of interpersonal protocol and the social contract gave way to spontaneous expressions of authentic feeling and love, being truthfully and freely in the company of others presented a technique of loosening richly described in volumes of lifestyle literature. In chapter 6 the maintenance of the body provides a third arena of self-loosening as the mental constraints imposed on muscle tissue and the sensuality of bodily movement were relaxed in a therapy of personal wellness. Rolling back the censuring functions of an intellect that had hitherto harnessed the body for work or competition, advisory narratives on yoga, massage, and alternative sports presented the body itself as a thing into which one could, with skill, loosen up. The loosening motif is related in each of these domains in a prescriptive print discourse and a caring text, whose aim was to instill awareness of daily life through the accumulation of experience for later telling in a community of contemporaneous readers.

In this chapter, the object of loosening appears with the individual's daily relationship with the natural world through habits of consumption and routine provisioning. In the ecological discourse of the early 1970s, age-old constraints imposed by the conventions of the industrial worldview were overcome through the transcendence of a Western rationalism that portrayed man in an oppositional and instrumental relation with nature. Whether in the form of a frontier narrative of human settlement and conquest or in a technological-scientific discourse on space exploration, a classically modern narrative depicting man's struggle with his environment was superseded by a new "holistic" consciousness offering a deeper understanding of the human predicament: man stood not against and apart from nature, but deeply integrated with the earth's profoundly interwoven patterns of resource use, disposal and renewal, understood as a broad, barely perceptible "whole system." A powerful desire to affirm a tangible sense of this wholeness with nature shaped a wide variety of ecological habits and lifestyles, from recycling to home gardening, where, it was thought, one could release oneself into the loving spirit of a replenishing earth and all of its interdependent systems, if one could sufficiently open one's mind and reform one's habits.

Indeed, in the lifestyle discourses of the 1970s, this longing for union with the earth assumed a unique narrative form, unfolding its own distinct modernity. Particularly in the literature of ecological futurism and in the writings of its various countercultural adherents, the holistic expansion of consciousness was contrasted with the linear progress of knowledge, in the traditional enlightenment sense: for a mind to see beyond the blinkered specializations of Western science, one had to apprehend the totality of man's various knowledges and his living unity with a broad planetary and cosmic entity—a seismic shift in the character of knowledge itself that demanded a new institutional and practical basis for expertise, research, and advice on style of life. Ecological consciousness was reflected in a new set of practices of daily life, from the use of renewable energy sources, recycling, and home fabrication of clothing and other goods, to a new naturalistic cuisine. Advice on such techniques was related through dozens of ecologically inspired texts and publications, the most influential of which were the access catalogues mentioned in chapter 3, countercultural listings of resources and instruction on the practical use of ecological consciousness. The first and most influential of these listings was without a doubt the *Whole Earth Catalog*, though many others would follow its lead.

Fashioning the Grand View

Jean-Francois Lyotard has described the importance of "metanarratives" of progress for the culture of modern societies. In such societies, stories of tremendous span and significance tell of colossal patterns of growth toward desirable goals: grand narratives of developing rationality, humanity, egalitarianism, and scientific advance lend a sense of momentum and legitimacy to modernity's unruly and uprooting tendencies, imposing meaning and purpose on the lives most radically reshaped by modernity's destructive thrust.[5] For Lyotard, the postmodern condition is characterized by an unraveling of such metanarratives, which confront increasing skepticism from broad segments of humanity and give way ultimately to far more limited, heterogeneous, localized accounts of historical time. Such a crisis of metanarrative has become a touchstone of postmodern theoretical discourse, although surprisingly little is written about the cultural moment of this crisis itself, which, if one considers Lyotard's historical periodization, falls in the later quarter of the twentieth century. And of the many insurrections and breakdowns that defined this crisis, certainly one of the more colorful came with the counterculture's assault on the authority of the scientific expert—the institutional helmsman whose rationality and base of specialized knowledge served as a navigation tool in the unfolding of modern progress—and the claiming of that mantle for the uniquely sensitized individual, guided only by her highly personal, experiential sense of direction. Progress, in the counterculture of the 1960s and 1970s, was personalized and sensualized, no longer limited to a process of civilizational development toward more rational forms, but extending to her own personal growth (albeit on a global scale) of the individual's feeling for herself and her changing involvement with her world. This challenge is captured in the wide use during the 1960s and 1970s of the term *consciousness* to describe an evolving awareness of the individual's relationship to society, and the deeper meanings of human history.

For Charles Reich, *consciousness* fit into a wider vocabulary that tied a personal ethics and political sentiment into a program for reform and social change: "Consciousness, as we are using the term, is not a set of opinions, information, or values, but a total configuration in any given individual, which makes up his whole perception of reality, his whole world view."[6] More than just a state one sought to acquire, consciousness was a story one told oneself about one's personal development from Consciousness I through II and III, and its growth across the population plotted a story of increasing awareness toward more modern states: "[Consciousness III] is now in the process of rapidly spreading to wider and wider segments of youth, and by degrees to older people, as they experience the recovery of self that marks conversion to a different consciousness. The new consciousness is also in the process of revolutionizing the structure of our society. It does not accomplish this by direct political means, but by changing cultures and the quality of individual lives, which in turn change politics and, ultimately, structure."[7]

The basis for this narrative of social change was not, as in traditional modernist tropes, the spread of enlightenment and rationality, but the awakening of an intuitive feeling for things, for others, and for oneself. In their studies of the counterculture and New Age movements of the 1970s, Robert Bellah, Steve Tipton, and others have tied the new consciousness to what they describe as a holistic moral tendency that arose as a rejection of the old utilitarian and individualist tenets deeply rooted in the American moral tradition.[8] Where the traditional view of science was dualistic, positioning man at a distance from nature and other objects of knowledge, the new consciousness was holistic: it saw man and all human efforts as part of larger natural and cosmic processes, bound by deep underlying but barely perceptible systems of cause and effect. The historical origins of this dualistic view are found in a centuries-old dialogue between biblical religiosity and utilitarian instrumentality, which together established the characterological foundation for an industrial middle-class professional ethos, defined around administrative expertise and credentialed, Taylorist managerial supervision. Where the Protestant biblical tradition stressed self-restraint and the control of impulse in deference to the will of God, the utilitarian tradition required these same measures of self-control in accordance with the inner demands of one's rationally calculated interests, acted out in real world markets, frontiers, and industries.[9] With the onset of industrialism and the ascendance of utilitarianism over biblical morality, Tipton explains, "technological reason— the rationalization of means to maximize given ends—replaced conscience as a moral guide."[10] A dualistic opposition separating self and other, self and world, impulse and norm fueled an emergent instrumental rationality among middle-class professionals, crystallized in what we have encountered as the uptightness of the square.

But while the dualism of what became the square world positioned the individual outside of and against the world, the counterculture celebrated a monistic view in which actions and ends, agents and objects, feelings and behaviors were dissolved into an inclusive holism. Drawing freely on themes from Eastern mysticism, psychedelic discourse, romanticism, and ecology, the monism of the counterculture projected an underlying totality binding self with a social and natural world whose linkages eluded the categories of traditional knowledge. The individual was tied to nature by deep bonds that had to be sensed rather than known. Apprehension of the overarching totality of the universe, of the deep linkages binding actions and outcomes that revealed the ultimate futility

8. Diagram, *Utopian Eyes* 7 (1977), 16

of effort and action in the old instrumental sense, eluded the squares—it was a sensibility bestowed upon those capable of thinking beyond the old Cartesian categories of reason and objectivity, and for those capable of letting themselves go into a direct experience with real life. In its more explicit countercultural forms, the freeing of the self from the old categories of science released one into the world, into a flow of events one could not control, but didn't have to. Holistic consciousness allowed one to immerse oneself into the fabric of the universe where one could recover and constitute the full unity of one's own character— to be a fully "whole" self. As unscientific as its premises may have been, media-tors of the new consciousness nonetheless sprang up from an assortment of quasi-scientific centers, variously issuing edicts on new directions for civiliza-tional progress. A graphic rendition of such a narrative is found in *Utopian Eyes*, a New Age lifestyle journal published by a communal group based in the Bay Area.

With diagrammatic clarity, the mode of holistic consciousness is related to a developmental view we acquire of the events that define our lives: from dis-jointed and discontinuous "iceberg-like objects, all separated from one another by water," to a state of consciousness in which "the appearance of separate-ness between various thoughts, feelings, actions etc represented by the iceberg islands is now seen to be unreal," and the underlying totality of events lends continuity to lives and biographical narratives, read as moments within an unfolding, deeply integrated totality.[11] A discussion of holistic consciousness, as the basis for a countercultural discourse on lifestyle derived in part from the field of natural ecology, and was developed in the 1970s into a far-reaching metanarrative on the deeper purposes underlying the advance of modernity.

ECOLOGY

The science of ecology was introduced to America by Aldo Leopold in his 1949 book *A Sand County Almanac*, a collection of rural natural history studies of the American landscape, emphasizing the interdependent organization of environmental regions from coastal areas to deserts. By the 1950s, ecology had emerged as a scientific discipline in the United States with complimentary developments in the social sciences in the area of "human ecology." But it was in 1962 with Rachel Carson's *Silent Spring*, a wide-ranging study that marshaled substantial scientific evidence of the threats posed to the global environmental condition by pollutants and overpopulation from atomic weapons to DDT, that the discourse of ecology moved in the direction of an inclusive critique of industrial economic policy. By the mid-1960s, both Carson's and Leopold's books had found a broad popular readership, galvanizing environmental concerns about the concealed health hazards of industrial pollutants and materials and the overall social, personal, and environmental consequences of industrial growth.

A series of highly publicized environmental catastrophes (a massive oil spill off the coast of Santa Barbara in 1969 pummeled television viewers with images of oil-soaked sea birds and contaminated beaches) focused public concern on environmental issues, bringing ecology to the forefront of a student movement already preoccupied with civil rights and opposition to the war in Vietnam. Ecology, in the hands of student radicals and others, opened a broader political horizon, fusing problems of economic and industrial policy with deeper notions of selfhood and personal well-being. Ecology and environmentalism presented a program so ambitious as to transcend conventional political divisions entirely, yet so modest as to reach deep into the most intimate aspects of everyday life—a blend of personal and political whose debut in public discourse came with the events of Earth Day 1970.

In 1969, inspired by the antiwar teach-ins that had done so much to galvanize the student Left of the late 1960s, Wisconsin senator Gaylord Nelson sought to replicate this model around the increasingly popular theme of environmentalism. Nelson incorporated a nonprofit organization called Environmental Teach-In, pledged $15,000 of his own money to organize a network of student environmental groups, and hired twenty-five-year-old antiwar activist Sam Brown as national coordinator. Out of this network emerged Earth Day, April 22, 1970, an event that mobilized an estimated 20 million Americans in activities as diverse as spontaneous street cleaning, political demonstration, and activism, suffused with a moral discourse on holistic responsibility.[12] Artist and conservationist Alan Gussow, speaking at an Earth Day event, expressed this program in a narrative of human development toward greater holistic forms: against the linear march of progress related in conventional modernizing stories, Gussow envisioned a progress defined by an all-encompassing circularity: "Such a view of the future is circular like the whole Earth. A circular future means that we cannot escape from whatever it is that we do here and now. Life is not linear, it is round. If we pollute the Earth and others do the same, the pollution will come up over the horizon one day and destroy us."[13] Such themes of circularity and return were reiterated by Barry Commoner (dubbed the "Paul Revere of ecology" on the cover of *Time Magazine* in 1970); LaMont Cole; the brothers Eugene and Howard Odum; E. F. Schumacher, author of *Small Is Beautiful*; Buckminster Fuller, who contributed the phrase "Spaceship Earth"; and later James Lovelock, who supplied the richly spiritual concept of "Gaia" to describe the planetary ecosystem as a single, animate force, not unlike an ancient deity.[14] It was Fuller's "Spaceship Earth," however, that would offer one of the most lasting metaphors for the ecology movement, linking holistic sentiments and a new mode of consciousness with an alarmist warning of pending environmental catastrophe.

In Fuller's work, the term *spaceship* related an image of the earth as an enclosed unit, an immensely complex machine populated by terrestrial "astronauts," all caught up in the task of successfully operating and navigating this craft through the universe without destroying it in the process. Significantly, the spaceship's resources were limited: it did not contain water, air, and raw materials enough to support man's permanent residence on its surface without significant feats of engineering. Fuller's metaphor was extensive: lacking a user's manual with which to operate the spaceship, man had to figure it out himself. He had to discover how to make Spaceship Earth work, how to conserve its resources and limit his own growth using the one piece of special hardware uniquely designed for the purpose: his intellect. Fuller wrote, "The designed omission of the instruction book on how to operate and maintain Spaceship Earth and its complex life-supporting and regenerating systems has forced man to discover retrospectively just what his most important forward capabilities are. His intellect had to discover itself."[15] The discovery of this intellect meant the discovery of the Earth as a limited resource—a spaceship—into which man had to properly integrate himself and his civilization if the catastrophe of depleted resources was to be headed off. Such a task could not be trusted to the old categories of scientific specialization, Fuller warned, which examined natural phenomenon only in parts: it demanded the collapsing of compartmentalized modes of knowledge into a totalizing consciousness of the planet as a whole entity.

Such apocalyptic themes were taken up in 1970 when a group of thirty scientists, economists, and others met in Rome to discuss what they termed the "predicament of man," with the aim of devising a research plan for confronting a pending environmental disaster stemming from the reckless extraction and use of natural resources. The group published three volumes of findings, describing three distinct world-future scenarios, the most widely acclaimed being *Limits to Growth*, published in 1972.[16] The mammoth research project was constructed on an elaborate plan devised by MIT professor Jay Forrester, which used computerized data to plot the various interwoven effects of global resource depletion correlated with rising pollution, population, and other factors of "exponential growth."[17] Published with reams of cryptic charts and graphs depicting everything from rising DDT levels in body fat to global food production to changes in desired family size, the research concluded that, unless present levels of economic growth and consumption were drastically curtailed, environmental resources would be entirely depleted within the next hundred years, probably much sooner, leading to starvation, suffering, and civilizational collapse. Only a small window of time remained for the quick implementation of a new economic pattern.

Importantly, these findings were drawn not only from the conclusions of Forrester's systems dynamics models, but from the insights of a unique frame of mind, a consciousness (as opposed to knowledge in the traditional sense), possessed by those capable of synthesizing broad swaths of data, of assuming a great distance on the narrow imperatives of the present, and grasping, with the aid of the imagination, the larger arc of human history and civilization. While

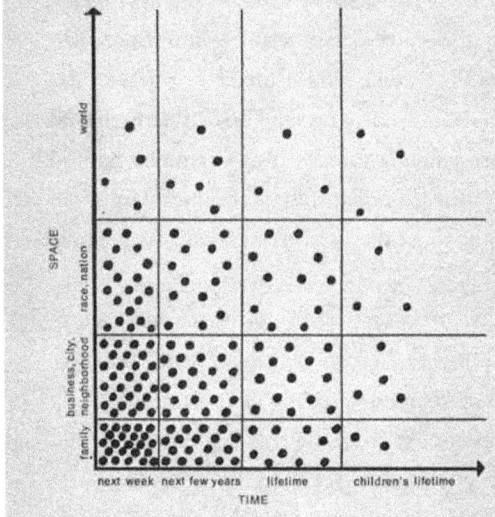

24   THE LIMITS TO GROWTH

Figure 1 HUMAN PERSPECTIVES

9. Human perspectives, from *Limits to Growth*, by D. H. Meadows et al.

such a shift in consciousness remained limited to a small circle of experts, it was urgent that it be taken up in the daily practices of consumers worldwide. A diagram of human perspectives located this attitude on the coordinates of time and space awareness, with the greater, more inclusive perspective occupied by those at the extreme ends of both the space and time axis.

The release of perceptual constraints and the discarding of cognitive blinders imposed by daily struggles for survival opened up new vistas and wider horizons from which great stories could be told. Loosening into the wider perspective, one acquired a consciousness of history as a great, unfolding story, though one which was just now coming to the hazardous moment of a dilemma: "Utopia or Oblivion," as Fuller proposed. Either man would learn to see and live his residency on Spaceship Earth responsibly, or he would surely perish. Importantly, one could participate in this narrative through one's everyday habits as a consumer and stylist of a chosen way of life.

In the late 1960s and early 1970s, the ecological movement inspired economists to theorize a "steady state" economy, in which the extraction of raw materials and the disposal of waste would be adjusted to the processes of replenishment required to maintain a state of system equilibrium with the natural environment. Pollution, waste, and environmental depletion resulting from reckless extraction of resources (common occurrences in expanding capital-ist economies) would be replaced by ordered and responsible ways suited to a closed "whole system," limited in its ability both to supply raw materials and to absorb refuse. This meant a reduction of consumption and production, new "alternate" technologies adapted to specific environments, localized markets and networks, and a changed attitude toward the purchase and use of goods. As more and more people acquired this expanded awareness of their relation-ship with nature, this closed system economics, called the "spaceman economy" by ecological economist Kenneth Boulding, would replace the older "cowboy economy," in which nature was regarded as an open horizon or a plateau for the capture, a replenishing source of goods always ripe for extraction, infinitely able to absorb what ever human debris might be heaped on her. Boulding writes:

> The closed earth of the future requires economic principles which are somewhat different from those of the open earth of the past. For the sake of picturesqueness, I am tempted to call the open economy the "cowboy economy," the cowboy being symbolic of the illimitable pains and also as-sociated with reckless, exploitative, romantic and violent behavior, which is characteristic of open societies. The closed economy of the future might similarly be called the 'spaceman' economy, in which the earth has become a single spaceship, without unlimited reservoirs of anything, either for ex-traction or for pollution, and in which, therefore, man must find his place in a cyclical ecological system. . . . The difference between the two types of economy becomes most apparent in the attitudes towards consumption. In the cowboy economy, consumption is regarded as a good thing and production likewise. . . . By contrast, in the spaceman economy . . . [t]he essential measure of the success of the economy is not production and consumption at all, but the nature, extent, quality and complexity of the total capital stock, including in this the state of the human bodies and minds included in the system. In the spaceman economy, what we are primarily concerned with is stock maintenance.[18]

As Boulding suggests, the transition from cowboy to spaceman economies in-volved more than a change of economic policies. It called for a wholesale shift in the attitudes and perspectives of all economic actors, most importantly consumers, carrying a significant cognitive component: one had to apprehend an object of dizzying proportions, a "whole earth" as a closed system, the dimensions of which exceeded the comprehension of the immediate senses and the traditional methodologies of science. One had to maintain the sense of this immense object in one's attitude toward small lifestyle choices within the narrow space and time of everyday practice—a task for which a host of entrepreneurs and lifestyle mediators stood by ready to lend a hand.

Among the most obvious countercultural lifestyle discourses to advance these goals was one dealing with food and culinary practice, picked up by droves of middle-class consumers through dozens of cookbooks and restaurants and later insinuated into mainstream consumption patterns in the form of an ersatz appeal to nature, natural ingredients, and environmentally friendly products. "Food was a medium for broad social change," writes Warren Belasco, historian and chronicler of the countercultural food movement. "Unlike sporadic antiwar protests, dietary rightness could be lived 365 days a year, three times a day."[19] Belasco's study of countercultural innovations in cuisine describe a broad political and cultural network incorporating communes, health food stores, and hippie restaurants into a creative engine for the production of culinary alternatives, loosely themed around the desire to incorporate an authentic bond with nature into one's daily life. A quote from Frances Moore Lappé's *Diet for a Small Planet* illustrates this goal:

> Previously, when I went to a supermarket, I felt at the mercy of our advertising culture. My tastes were manipulated. And food, instead of being my most direct link with the nurturing earth, had become mere merchandise by which I fulfilled my role as a "good" consumer. But as I gained the understanding that I have tried to communicate to you in this book, I found that I was making choices, choices based on real knowledge about food and about the effect on the earth of different types of food production. It was a gradual process in which there was no question of a sacrifice in giving up meat. Rather as new types of food combinations became more attractive, shopping for food and cooking was no longer unconscious and boring, but a real adventure. The adventure was the discovery of ways, the best, most delicious ways, of making the most of the earth's productivity.[20]

Diet for a Small Planet combined vegetarian recipes emphasizing the importance of protein with commentary and information meant to furnish a broader ecological, historical, and geographical understanding of the world food system, and of the wastefulness resulting from the cultivation of livestock at the expense of wheat and other vegetable products. Among the dozens of counterculturally inspired cookbooks to pick up on these themes were such titles as *The Moosewood Cookbook*, a handwritten edition of recipes and commentary from a natural foods restaurant in Ithaca, New York, and *Laurel's Kitchen*, a thick compendium on vegetarian recipes including information on cooperative purchasing of ingredients and home gardening.[21]

But food was not the only realm wherein holistic consciousness could be imported into lifestyle choice. Perhaps no other fad of the 1970s better illustrates the packaging of holistic motifs for mass consumption than the Earth Shoe, invented in the 1950s by Danish yoga instructor Anne Kalso, who brought her shoe to America in 1970 and named it for the Earth Day phenomenon. Available as clogs, hiking shoes, or sandals, the shoe's negative heel promised to replicate the sensation of walking barefoot on a beach—a more natural and healthy way to experience nature and one's own body. An ad for Earth Shoes linked the experience of walking more firmly on the earth with a powerful, personal feeling of balance and unity with one's body: "Inside every Earth brand shoe is a brilliant invention. The Earth sole. An invention that guides you, inch by inch, through a unique experience which we call 'pure walking.' A path of motion designed to balance, focus and concentrate your own natural forces so that you will walk, perhaps for the first time, with continuous, comfortable easy power."[22] The appeal to the personal benefits of this product, like a therapeutic cure, promised to elevate the simple act of walking to the level of dance or sport by setting the user in a more profound relationship to the earth. Underscoring these claims was the appeal to a special kind of expertise: a nontraditional lifestyle consciousness that owed more to Eastern spirituality and nontraditional therapies than to Western technological know-how.

Whether through food or shoes, such a sense of the earth demanded advice and guidance of a kind that had never before been offered. Learning to relax the boundaries of the constricting categories of science and to view one's consuming habits within a larger continuum of need and resources, to taste Mother Earth in one's lunch or to feel her in one's stride, demanded a mode of specialist discourse that was itself holistic, unbound from the traditional distinctions and methodologies of the Fordist professional. Framed by the narrative of pending crisis, and under the advice of a body of invitive specialists, consumer choice became a high-stakes game. The solutions proffered by the new lifestyle experts found increasing legitimacy in an emerging lifestyle print culture already responsive to the demands of the new ecologically conscious consumer. Such terms as "voluntary simplicity," "appropriate technology," "soft technology," and other lifestyle adaptations meant to guarantee a life of "right livelihood" all testified to the increasing influence of a countercultural vanguard on mainstream consumer markets of the 1970s. An important and influential source of this holistic rhetoric was a budding lifestyle print culture, and specifically a series of grassroots, locally compiled resource catalogues listing supplies, techniques, and short manifestos on the urgency of practicing the holistic consciousness in daily life.

ACCESS CATALOGUES

One effect of the economic turbulence and domestic penny-pinching of the 1970s was a dramatic increase in the volume of in-home shopping, particularly among an educated, middle-class, catalogue-reading public. Market researchers of the time recorded the story: as a market segment, in-home shoppers grew from 9 percent of total general merchandise sales in 1964 to over 11 percent by the mid-1970s. By 1971, in-home shopping topped $10 billion in total retail sales.[23] In-home spending rose again between 1969 and 1973 by another 55 percent (against a general 45-percent gain for general merchandise sales through stores).[24] By 1974, catalogue sales at Sears, Ward, and J. C. Penney ran 20 percent ahead of the previous year, compared to an 8 percent increase in retail sales, with Montgomery Ward alone reporting a 40 percent increase in catalogue sales by August 1974.[25]

Several explanations were offered for the sudden take-off of catalogues, though there was a consensus that this was largely a phenomenon of the novelty-seeking middle-class shopper: the in-home shopper was judged to be "above-average in socio-economic status as measured by household income level, social class, education and occupation of household head."[26] Some researchers suggested that women outpaced men in this category, due in part to their new responsibilities as professionals and decreased time for shopping, while others pointed to the lag in price hikes necessitated by the lengthy catalogue production and distribution process, or the appeal to suburban consumers looking to save gas money by cutting trips to the shopping mall. Another strain of research linked catalogue sales to deepening demands of consumers for more personalized goods, responding to changing values and lifestyles, and an increasing emphasis on the uniqueness of personal lifestyle needs: "Mail-order shopping's strength lies in providing the new, the unique, the personalized products," to a "more cosmopolitan, cultured and value-conscious, convenience-oriented and generally more demanding" consumer.[27] These shoppers were more flexible, visited stores more often, were more subject to impulse purchases and discretionary buying, and responded to the experiential character of shopping as a meaningful personal activity.

Moreover, the catalogue market was itself highly differentiated, appealing to a range of niches and tastes. Noting a wider shift from traditional, general catalogues to smaller, supplemental, specialty catalogues, one prominent researcher supposed that "the current and future strength of the catalog lies in those items that are unusual, new, and fashionable—those that provide the uniqueness or distinctiveness that appeals to the self-confident and venturesome frequent catalog buyer."[28] By presenting well-planned product shots accompanied by expert testimonies and advice, catalogues provided a retail space that was highly discursive and thematized around particular lifestyle and value concerns, whose intimacy was intensified by a written discourse on the consuming experience. Moreover, testimonies and product descriptions had to cultivate a greater measure of trust than did traditional retailers in order to entice in-home consumers into taking risks on products that they had not actually seen through dealings with retailers they had never actually met. Such a degree of trust demanded an intimate expert narrative at odds with the anonymous, boisterous, and aggressive salesmanship of traditional mass-marketing discourse. Catalogue retailing contained an additional appeal for middle-class consumers as the medium of communication for the dispersed countercultural lifestyle communities that, by the early 1970s, had formed a powerful subeconomy and lively print culture espousing the virtues of a "holistic" lifestyle ethic.

It was into this climate that a wide assortment of countercultural lifestyle catalogues emerged, widely touted as "access catalogues" (named for the subtitle to the *Whole Earth Catalog*, "access to tools")—lifestyle guides packed with sources, references, and advice for the aspiring ecological lifestylist. This phenomenon was captured in a 1974 editorial piece in the *New York Times* spoofing the catalog craze and the lifestyle phenomenon it inspired. Composed by Alix Nelson as a lengthy work of tortured prose, the piece summarized popular views on the new lifestyle discourse, with commentary on several of the most influential catalogues. The verse begins:

Without leaving your Eames chair, you can now order:
A kit to purify drinking water,
A guide to the construction of swimming pools,
A complete set of carpenter's tools,
A list of the latest not quite Free Schools,
Theses on harpsichords and geodesic dome rules.

. . . .

Oh there's a plethora of aphorisms, advice and data
On every imaginable passing fada,
And on each new technological appliance
Designed to further "self-reliance."[29]

The verse goes on to describe a list of catalogues of note: *The Whole Earth Catalog*, *The Whole Earth Epilogue*, *The Connection* (whose pages featured listings for "incense and camping tents, humming bird feeders, a hand carved flute"), *The Goodfellow Catalog of Wonderful Things* ("purses, pipes and rings"), *People's Yellow Pages of America* ("a directory of names and resources for crashing, tripping, hitchhiking and hostelling"), *The New Woman's Survival Catalog* ("a woman-made book"), *Survival Scrapbook* ("shelter, helter skelter, build your own anything—there's a welter"), *The Good Earth Almanac* ("it's the ticket for getting lost in forest or thicket"), *Public Works* ("schedules and fares of planes, bus and rail"), *Super Catalog of Car Parts and Accessories* ("for the car freak who has everything"), and *The Gardener's Catalog*. Nelson's prose testifies to the variety of journals, periodicals, catalogues, and popular books that carried commentary and advice for the consumer confronting the ecological "crisis" and seeking a new relationship with nature and the wider planetary ecosystem. A careful look at one publication shows something of the social networks and economic circuitry underpinning the production and distribution of a typical access catalogue.

Rain: A Journal of Appropriate Technology was an Oregon-based magazine featuring various materials on appropriate technology (AT): diagrams and instructions on the construction of wind power and solar power generators, composting, recycling techniques, and so on. Cofounded by Steve Johnson, a researcher at the Environmental Education Center at Portland State University, and Lee Johnson (no relation), a returning Vietnam War veteran with a background in economics and an interest in wind power, *Rain* soon attracted other important members with backgrounds in environmentalism and ecology: Tom Bender, from the University of Minnesota School of Architecture in St. Paul, and his wife Lane De Moll, an environmentalist whose father had been one of the early solar power researchers in the 1950s.[30] Funded by the U.S. Department of Education's Fund for Environmental Education, *Rain* collected various energy tidbits and tips on environmentally friendly technology for circulation to non-profit project organizers and research centers, but after a few years the editors sought to expand the scope of their coverage to include larger political and policy issues and more in-depth coverage of new research, for which it sought to garner a subscription base that would enable them to sustain themselves independently of federal support. By the mid-1970s, this base, while still not much over 5,000, included the names of many of the movers and shakers in the field of appropriate technology and alternative sources of energy, as well as leading figures in the commune movement and other alternative-lifestyle groups. Leaving their offices at Portland State University, the staff of *Rain* moved into a house on the outskirts of Portland, where they took turns editing respective issues.

The house of the *Rain* editors became a national center for dialogue and hobnobbing, attracting visits from luminaries in the alternative energy field, the Peace Corps, editors of other cooperative living magazines such as *Communities*, and even a visit from Jerry Brown, the environmentally concerned governor of California. *Rainbook* was published by Schocken Books in 1977 and became an instant classic not only among the readerships of AT publications, but also for a range of communal and cooperative networks and back-to-earthers, as well as professionals in energy research, community planning, and ecological development.[31] The catalogue's cover reveals the extent to which these narratives of technological change were related to changing habits of consumption: a downtown street is transformed into a holistically responsible community, as parking lots are replaced by food co-ops, power-generating windmills dot the skyline, and nature, in the form of foliage and urban agriculture, takes its vengeance on technology.

Interestingly, *Rainbook* uses a holistic metaphor to describe a deep, barely detectable totality that extended to include not just the ecological balance its technologies sought to address, but the readership itself, the contemporaneous, imagined reading publics to which its catalogue is addressed. Defining the project of appropriate technology, the *Rainbook* editors write: "We are taking a

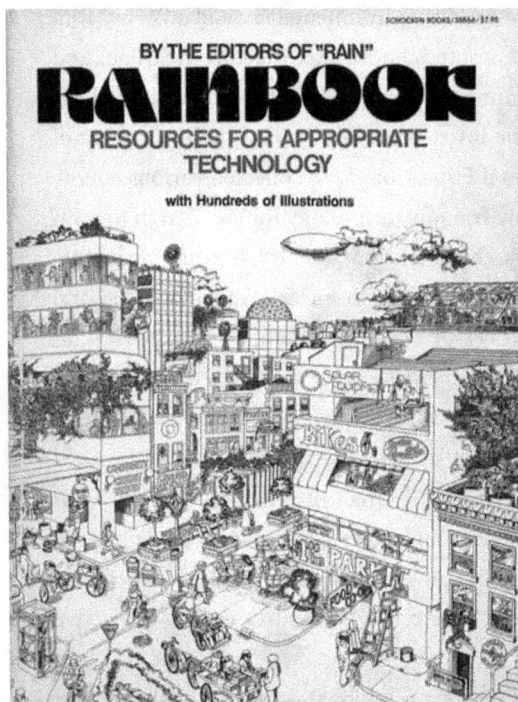

10. Cover, *Rainbook*, edited by Lane De Moll

broad view of technology here, for what 'appropriate technology' adds to technology is the question 'What is Appropriate?' That question requires that we get into the intricately interconnected web that links everything together—a web where a small change in something seemingly far removed can allow big changes in what you're concerned with."[32] The catalogue listed dozens of journals, newsletters, research groups, books, conferences, environmental organizations, directories, information centers, and national resources that composed this web. *Rainbook* became the vogue among intellectuals, critics, and commentators interested in preserving or extending the project of the New Left, such as the noted environmentalist and former SDS leader Kirkpatrick Sale, whose lukewarm review of *Rainbook* for the *New York Times Book Review* was enough to stimulate wide interest, prompting Schocken to invest in promotion and advertising enough to carry *Rainbook* onto the shelves of public libraries, environmental research centers, and other public and private think tanks.[33] A review of *Rainbook* in *CoEvolution Quarterly* described the publication as a "finely sifted collection of what has proven to be good and useful in the baffling tangle of what's available. The sifting is done (as usual with this crew) by persons who are actually working with the subject of the review, giving a quiet honesty that permeates the entire Rainbook."[34] This "baffling tangle" is loosely mapped in a section of the catalogue called "networks," followed by another, "making connections," which reflect the density and complexity of the social networks that constitute the wider reading public of *Rainbook*. In a deeply personalized prose style, an editor explores the individual, experiential aspects of network membership and maintenance, acknowledging the limits of printed communication:

> I guess if I wanted to carry further the art of being a communicator, or connector, in the sense of facilitating communication between myself and the world, and others, and others and the world, and others with others and all of that, it would be more interesting to move into non-verbal areas. Written history leaves out the thing most important about how we perceive things. . . . The moment the catalog (this one) is published it's a historical document as opposed to being a life connector to current information. So much so that I think of it as an art form. It does more in what it communicates about how things are related to other things than actually giving life information. It's a view or a map from a point of view.[35]

The figment of networked participants this text imagines served an important function in rendering, in the minds of readers, an economic and cultural community that doubled as a conduit for advice, shared experience, and what was variously referred to as "information," "resources," or "connectedness." Most importantly, however, it was the *Whole Earth Catalog* that early on established lifestyle as an important realm for the pursuit of holistic, ecological objectives, and, under Stuart Brand's direction, carried this agenda through the late 1970s and 1980s in subsequent publications, *CoEvolution Quarterly*, published from 1974 to 1984, and later the *Whole Earth Magazine*.

THE WHOLE EARTH CATALOG: ACCESS TO TOOLS

The insights that inspired *The Whole Earth Catalog* crystallize the philosophical hubris of the counterculture: in 1966, Stewart Brand, the *Catalog*'s founder and editor, conceived the idea for the *Catalog* as he came away inspired from a lecture delivered by Buckminster Fuller on man's emerging awareness of the earth as a holistic, integrated system. That evening, an LSD epiphany led Brand to the insight that a single image of this planet taken from space, widely reproduced and disseminated, might help inspire an awareness of the entire planet as a single integrated whole system, and of the human priorities such integration implied for people in their everyday life. This insight compelled him to begin a campaign calling upon NASA to deliver a photograph of the entire surface of the Earth. The button he distributed to select senators and members of Congress, NASA officials, and Soviet space experts posed the question "Why Haven't We Seen a Photograph of the Whole Earth Yet?" and achieved wide enough circulation, Brand alleges, that the first photographs of the planet were later released to the mainstream press.[36]

The image of the whole Earth became the motif of countercultural environmentalism, and was adopted by the radical environmental group Environmental Action for the first Earth Day. The phrase "whole Earth," which was never copyrighted by Brand, was taken up by dozens of stores and products in the 1970s and after, from the "Whole Earth Access" store in San Francisco to "Whole Foods" and "Earth shoes." As the political banner of a rising movement, the insignia of a whole earth represented a deepened understanding of the inner meaning of lifestyle as a global responsibility, enfolding the personal needs and the place of goods in an integrated planetary system tied directly to the larger moral obligation of a terrestrial steward. Importantly, the figure of the whole Earth became a lifestyle reference as it adorned the cover of the *Whole Earth Catalog*. Published under the auspices of the Portola Institute, a nonprofit educational research group directed by Dick Raymond and based in Menlo Park, California, the *Catalog* combined information, resource listings, and product reviews of various equipment and tools required for the ecologically conscious lifestylist, from wood-burning stoves and garden hoes to computers and Moog synthesizers. Notably, the *Catalog* juxtaposed and combined the two philosophical and intellectual programs that ran through the center of the counterculture's historical sensibility: a romantic naturalism and a futuristic technophilia. Theodore Roszak writes: "This catalog clearly meant to project a consistent vision. It seemed to be saying that all human ingenuity deserved to be celebrated—from the stone axe to American Indian medicine to modern electronics."[37]

Throughout the period of the *Catalog*'s existence, Brand considered his project a vanguard development, destined ultimately to influence the mainstream.[38] Between 1968 and 1970, the *Catalog* was published twice a year with a circulation of about 15,000 copies. Between issues, two supplements were printed in editions of roughly 35,000 copies each. The initial series ran from

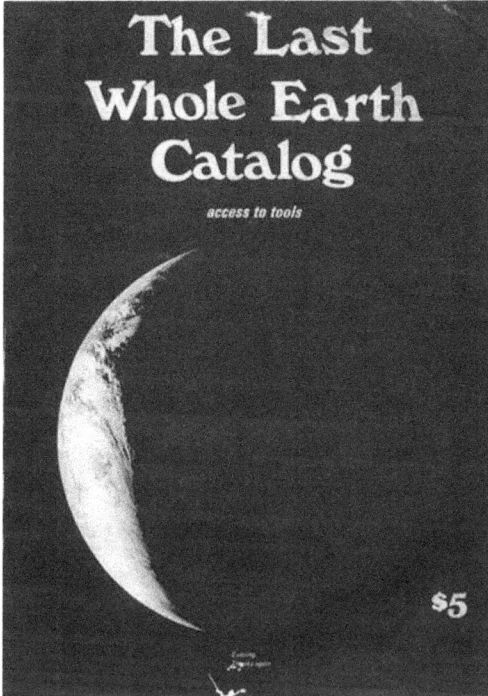

11. Cover, *The Last Whole Earth Catalog,* edited by Stuart Brand

1968 to 1971, growing from 31 to 447 pages by the time of *The Last Whole Earth Catalog* in 1972 (followed by the *Whole Earth Epilogue* in 1974 and the *Next Whole Earth Catalog* in 1980). In 1972 alone, the *Last Whole Earth Catalog* sold 380,396 copies of a 400,000-print edition, and in 1973 the total climbed to 1,178,048—a figure that was to top 1.5 million copies both domestically and overseas by the end of 1974.[39] In 1973, Brand received a National Book Award for his project, earning him countercultural celebrity and acceptance among the East Coast publishing establishment, as well as interest from market researchers and retailers across the country.[40]

READING

While the *Catalog* appealed to a wide readership (who "seem to dig it mainly as literature") the supplements were, according to one observer, for the "Whole Earth faithful, those scattered homesteaders and communers and isolated experimenters in life-style who first called the *Catalog* into being and who remain its essential audience."[41] During the counterculture's heyday, the *Catalog* captivated readers with its stunning diversity of products, advice, commentary, and incongruous features and spreads, crammed together on crowded pages amid hackneyed pasteups and uneven type—a flotsam and jetsam of back-to-the-land hardware unified around an elusive moral insight into the underlying connectedness of personal cause and cosmic effect in the consumption process.

This theme was reiterated in a *Time Magazine* feature on the *Whole Earth Catalog*, which included a photograph of Brand poring over a book next to a page spread of the *Catalog*. Noting its broad market appeal, the article continues: "Although it is specifically aimed at 'technological dropouts' (in the words of its authors), the catalogue's phenomenal success shows it has a far vaster range of appeal. It is a sort of Sears, Roebuck–Consumer Report for the minorities of the cybernetic age."[42] The serendipitous allure of the *Catalog*'s holistic abundance captivated both countercultural and mainstream consumers with the interpretive puzzle it appeared to pose: what could such a diverse collection of things have in common? To what deeper purpose were they directed? What kind of new story of human civilizational advance did such a fusion of antiquarian and futuristic technologies relate, and what kind of new way of life did they suggest? An article in *Harper's*, featuring several pages reprinted from the *Catalog*, relates the reader's fascination with these pages.

> The very quality of the *Whole Earth Catalog* that most delighted and charmed me as a reader [was] the incredible variousness of it, the bewildering profusion of its content, the enigmatic capriciousness of its format ... Because the whole diffuse business, it had always seemed to me, was held together by some mysterious principle of internal dynamics, some inscrutable law of metaphysics which I simply didn't understand, which no one who hadn't actually been close to the very center of the entire Whole Earth operation could even begin to define.[43]

Disorganization and typographic glitches, it was argued, transformed passive readers into active interpreters of cryptic, if sincere, lifestyle discourses. When, in 1974, *Harper's* turned over several pages of its "wraparound" section to Brand for a unique *Whole Earth*–style editorial spotlight, the editors introduced the pages: "Brand is not looking for editorial perfection and is especially loath to correct (or, as he sees it, to compromise) the tone of readers' letters. Besides, he feels discovering mistakes may give the reader a sense of participation."[44] The agency of these new consumers, however, was as much a real-world activity

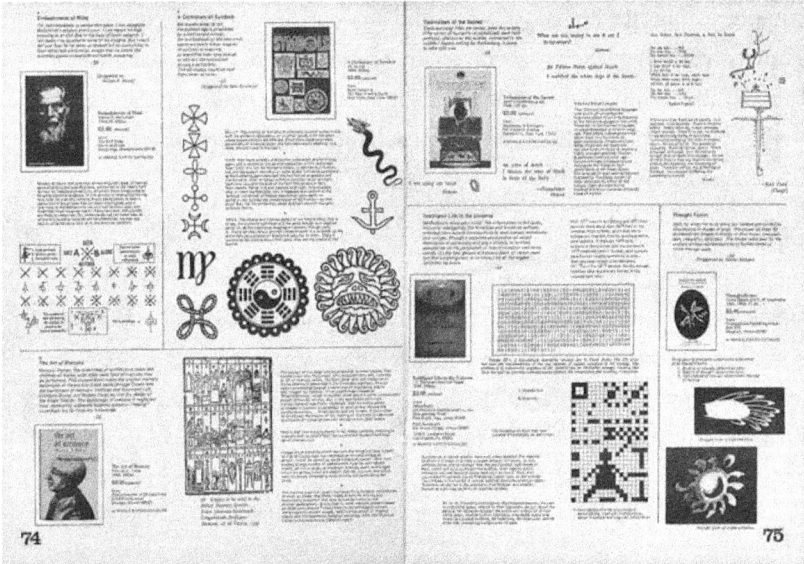

12. Page spread, *Whole Earth Catalog* (1970), 74–75

as an imaginary flight of consumer daydreaming: a note sent to Brand in 1979 requests the "Whole Earth" namesake for the author's own upstart project, to be titled the *Whole Earth Travelog*: "The audience is intended to be those people with escapist tendencies who might wish to shop for a unique vacation or study experience, or, as with the Whole Earth series, to simply thumb through it while sitting on the john before another day of work."[45]

Most importantly, the *Catalog* conveyed an insight into the practical use of goods, not as possessions but as tools: against the shallow acquisitiveness of mainstream modes of consumption, the *Catalog* stressed a deeper understanding of goods as parts or moments in a larger temporal and lifestyle continuum. With the folding of the *Catalog* in 1972, assets from the project were channeled into Brand's nonprofit Point Foundation, set up to distribute grants to the hundreds of *Whole Earth*–inspired endeavors that cropped up throughout the 1970s. In its first two years, as proceeds from the *Whole Earth Catalog* rolled in, the Point Foundation casually doled out over $1.5 million to a wide range of experimental nonprofit groups and launched on its own publishing endeavors which included *Soft-Tech*, a listing of appropriate technology sources, *Space Colonies*, an anthology of writings on the long-term implications of the space program, and, most notably, *CoEvolution Quarterly*, a journal of commentary and resource listings for holistic projects and analysis. Several fan letters testify to the intensity with which readers invested the *Catalog*, not just as a source for novel goods, but as the wellspring of nontraditional advice on lifestyle and consumption. Many of these letters are undated, handwritten, often accompanied by drawings and scribbles:

> Dear Stewart—
>
> I cannot put into words my admiration for what the Next Whole Earth Catalog accomplishes. It defines a new cultural convergence as significant for our time as utilitarianism was. It says: "here are the important parallels of science, action, life, spirit, thought." May God grant you and all who work with you long life, ever renewed freshness, continuing industry, clear ecosystems and good fortune.[46]

> Dear Company,
>
> I admire you all so much for your dedication to your work and the ideas behind it. You make dreams; no, you have dreams and rather than mold them to the practical, you bring the practicality to them. You continue to be an inspiration to me. I wish you all were my friends.[47]

For these readers, the *Catalog* invested everyday lifestyle choices with a unique historical sense: ostensibly relating to the challenges of rural homesteading, the majority of these readers were inspired by the impression of profundity implied by an underlying "whole system," whose balance was effected by our everyday mundane choices. As such, consumption acquired a moral and personal stake: one could help or hinder the life of the planet through one's daily decisions. As the vehicle of a "new cultural convergence as significant for our time as utilitarianism," the *Catalog* infused a new intellectual discourse with an injunction to take up practical projects in daily life: "You make dreams; no, you have dreams and rather than mold them to the practical, you bring the practicality to them." Lifestyle, as a field of philosophical and historical meaning, infused consumption with deep significance for a more authentic mode of lifestyle.

Throughout the 1970s, Brand remained at the center of an influential hub of holistic lifestyle experts, offering infusions of cash in the form of small grants to various individuals and groups providing commentary and criticism on the public crises of the 1970s, on the relevance of holistic concepts to such varied fields as biology, physics, energy technology, horticulture, urban planning, and psychology, and on various lifestyle alternatives demanded by changing social and environmental conditions. The informal intellectual climate of this network is reflected in one of dozens of scribbled notes from Stewart Brand's files, this one sent in late November of 1974 by Ira Einhorn, a veteran SDSer turned New Age consciousness seer (later jailed for allegedly murdering his girlfriend), inviting Brand to an informal conference at the Institute for the Study of Consciousness in Berkeley:

> Our focus will be twofold: 1. To attempt to reach some agreement on the nature of the new paradigm that is emerging from the study of consciousness, physics, & parapsychology—the nature of the paradigm should avoid closure and get some of those who will be there to consider theories other than their own, 2. To develop some strategy for encouraging people in a wide range of disciplines to consider writing on a new paradigm. No papers will be presented, no preparation is required, people have been invited to just come and share space with focus on the two above presented problems.[48]

Einhorn's note typifies the utopian narratives evidenced in dozens of correspondences: a convergence of specialized fields into a single "paradigm" expressed an "emergence" whose pure form would transcend the dogmatism of formal scholarship for the direct, experiential face-to-face interactions of inspired seekers. Brand's unique mode of nontraditional expertise was not confined to debates within this circle of critics: personal correspondence with a range of figures from the academic scientific establishment, politics, industry, and government suggest the breadth of his audience and the respect attributed to his unique blend of postcountercultural, holistic expertise and ironic, anti-institutional candor. Most notable is Brand's acquaintanceship with California governor Jerry Brown, who, after years of correspondence, appointed Brand a special consultant at a salary of $2,000 a month.[49]

Brand's role in the Brown administration was, according to an undated article from the *Sacramento Union*, unclear. Quizzed on his responsibilities, Brand is reported to have replied: "Oh, I've been thinking of doing thus and such . . ." The article includes a photograph of Brand (described as "thus and such man") riding a bicycle out of Brown's office, a demonstration of his proposal for the distribution of bicycles to all state employees for travel between their offices and their homes. The article goes on to quote Gray Davis, then the governor's chief of staff (later elected governor of California):

"The governor doesn't believe ideas should stem from the center of power" Davis says. "Ideas should extend from the periphery to the center. Stewart Brand could accelerate the process. It may be hard to quantify his job. We've asked him to review bills the governor acted on last year and initiatives undertaken in the past two years to see if they stimulate ideas for the future from Brand . . ." When encountered in the Capitol hallway, Gov. Brown says that Brand has done "lots of things around here." Pressed for details, he adds "Oh, don't be so linear. Don't be so linear . . ." [50]

Dozens of notes, letters, and correspondences between Brand's office at *CoEvolution Quarterly* and the governor's office testify to the odd alliance between a countercultural lifestyle guru and a mainstream politician with verbose countercultural pretenses drawn together by their shared opposition to "linear" thinking. Such a holistic, nonlinear discourse on the profundity of minute choices in everyday life (such as the riding of bicycles to and from work) is observed in the pages of the *Catalog*, where experiential expertise is applied to daily patterns of product choice.

PAGES

New issues of the *Catalog* came out roughly on a quarterly basis, with supplements appearing at infrequent intervals. Thickening with every issue, the *Last Whole Earth Catalog* stands out as the fattest and most widely circulated volume. The tabloid-sized cover typically featured an image of the Earth, though some issues portrayed pictures of galaxies, planets, or other astronomical images. Inside, a wide range of goods were crammed onto pages jigsawed by uneven borders into oddly shaped wedges and blocks.

Like other issues of the *Catalog*, the *Last Whole Earth Catalog* was divided into sections, beginning with "Whole Systems," a portion devoted to scientific, ecological and spiritual publications promoting the concept of integrated systems. As in all issues and supplements, the works of Buckminster Fuller are featured prominently: *Nine Chains to the Moon, Operating Manual for Spaceship Earth, Untitled Epic Poem on the History of Industrialization, No More Secondhand God*. A range of ecological texts follow, including *The Subversive Science, Challenge for Survival, Resources and Man, The Population Bomb,* and *Ecotactics,* interspersed with straightforward science texts like *The Character of Physical Law* and *Laws of Form,* historical works like *The Rise of the West* and spiritual publications such as *The Tao of Science* and *Tao Teh King*. Following "Whole

Systems" are other sections that break down the range of goods into specific categories: "Shelter and Land Use" offers kits for the construction of geodesic domes and a wide range of Fulleresque constructions such as the "Futuro," a UFO-shaped fiberglass dwelling sufficient for family residence, deliverable to any location in the United States. Additionally, more straightforward manuals, parts, and hardware for home construction such as the pouring of concrete, electrical wiring, carpentry, and other tasks are featured in this section. Under "Industry and Craft," a variety of items from butter churns, pottery wheels, and macramé kits to mundane mechanical tools like hammers, pliers, and wrenches are interspersed with nostalgic lithograph images showing Depression-era farm laborers, women working at looms, and other oddities.

A "Communications" section includes books on art, a typographic representation of an "interstellar communication" (a dense block of tiny 1s and 0s), tarot cards, posters of Escher drawings, a Moog synthesizer, a guide to filmmaking, and a standard book on electronics repair. The "Community" section features cookbooks (including *The Joy of Cooking*), a manual on home canning, the magazine *Mother Earth News*, the Earth flag, the writings of Malcolm X, and an impressive array of manuals on everything from home birth to "simple burial." "Nomadics" lists goods more generally identified with camping, travel, and outdoor recreation: sleeping bags, Coleman stoves, archery sets, hide-tanning equipment, scuba gear, and pup tents. Finally, a section titled "Learning" presents an array of manuals and how-to books: *American Boy's Handy Book*, *Children's Games in Street and Playground*, a manual from the Edmund Scientific Company, a "Valtox drug identification kit," and a book on Gestalt therapy. In all cases, items in these sections are reviewed by the *Catalog* staff, and often by Brand himself, whose reviews always conclude with the personal notation ubiquitous throughout the *Catalog*: "—SB."

The tone of these reviews is consistent: first-person-singulars pepper the short prose, often drifting into personal anecdotes, humorous asides, cautionary notes, or open statements of the reviewer's lack of knowledge about the product. In cases where the producers of the goods are known personally to the reviewer (as with most cottage-industrially-produced goods), reviews are warmed with affirmations, encouragements, and endearing exhortations. Unrelated pictures appear throughout these pages just as poems, statements from various groups and organizations, and other miscellaneous elements supplement the display of goods. The *Catalog* closes with a series of paid advertisements, all clearly labeled according to their price: $25 ad, $10 ad, $75 ad, and finally, a short section called "Business," comprising a full financial disclosure of the *Catalog*'s production and distribution budget, photographs of the Portola offices, and a form for submitting suggestions for items to be reviewed in future issues. The charm of the *Catalog* derives from this quality of mesmerizing bricolage: the contrast and hybridization of unlikely items confirms its intimacy as a homemade publication, and the lived totality—the totality of an individual lifestyle—within which all these elements might be brought together.

Throughout there is evidence of instruction and expertise: diagrams of quilt patterns, embroidery stitches, cross-sections of underground pumps, small engines and lean-tos, designs for canoes, tepees, and hammocks, sketches of stinging nettles and ginseng, cutaway renderings of the mouth of a cow (for telling its age), a birth control handbook with instructions on the application of spermicidal preparation and the insertion of a contraceptive diaphragm—the *Catalog* leveled the specialized knowledges and taste distinctions that normally compartmentalized interests and activities, merging a rich range of activities into a general injunction to act and to live with one's own nature and with one's own natural world. In 1972, Brand reviewed a popular ecological book, Paul Swatek's *The User's Guide to the Protection of the Environment*. Praising Swatek for finding "daily virtuous behavior toward ecological Good," Brand neatly summarized the *Catalog*'s unique ethical and ecological attitude toward lifestyle and consumption: "The consumer has more power for good or ill than the voter. All of us ecologically-concerned citizens have frets of creeping hypocrisy when we enter the supermarket all unknowing or half-knowing about the effect of our purchases and refusals to purchase. This book is a fret reducer."[51] Swatek's book, which details a wide range of domestic ecological measures from garbage disposal to lawn maintenance, calls upon consumers to take seriously the environmental and ecological consequences of their everyday habits as consumers, an exhortation Swatek premises on the ubiquity of vast systems of ecological and environmental interdependence.

Throughout the *Whole Earth Catalog*, the experience of perceived totalities (which are always in some way related to the purchase of goods) is depicted as an unstable, if euphoric moment, sometimes rapturous, sometimes fleeting—a close kin to the paradigmatic countercultural mode of insight celebrated in psychedelic discourse. In his review of Howard Odum's *Environment, Power and Society*, Brand describes the pleasure of holistic consciousness as condensed in a moment of revelation, yet presenting an ongoing challenge for the untutored: "Beautiful work. Energy language is the simplifier we've lacked to see our systems whole. When the cosmic yum comes by, you get the ONE! alright, but that may not particularly help you work with connectedness. The terms and understanding in this book can" (8). What Brand terms the "cosmic yum" is a holistic insight and an understanding, though its relevance is to the larger reflexive project of self-renewal and personal growth—a project demanding techniques of self-management and control. This tension between a highly individualistic experience of holistic connectedness and the techniques through which connectedness is cultivated and controlled is the topic of much expert advice, and is reflected in the "Purpose" statement that appeared inside the cover of every issue of the *Whole Earth Catalog*. Here Brand described the stakes of one's choice of lifestyle as an instance of profound self-understanding:

> We are as gods and might as well get good at it. So far remotely done power and glory—as via government, big business, formal education, church—has succeeded to the point where gross defects obscure actual gains. In response to this dilemma and to these gains a realm of intimate, personal power is developing—power of the individual to conduct his own education, find his own inspiration, shape his own environment, and share his adventure with whoever is interested. Tools that aid this process are sought and promoted by the WHOLE EARTH CATALOG. (1)

For the reader of the *Whole Earth Catalog*, separating the deficits from the assets of technological civilization was an urgent task requiring the advice of experts and holding out the promise of new thresholds of self-reflection and self-experience. This advice and the character of this holistic expertise was consolidated and elaborated throughout various publishing ventures sponsored by the Menlo Park group, and ultimately informed a rich discourse on environmental responsibility in everyday lifestyle choice. The stakes for the holistic consumer, enveloped in the whole system of social and planetary convergence, were high, and demand the guidance of nontraditional lifestyle experts.

COEVOLUTION QUARTERLY

With the demise of the *Whole Earth Catalog* and the *Catalog's* original publisher, the Portola Institute, a new circle of counterculturals, practitioners and experts in various fields pursued the *Catalog's* holistic social agenda through an entity Brand created out of profits generated by the *Catalog*: the Point Foundation. The Point Foundation maintained the *Catalog*'s focus on lifestyle issues and networking functions, but also initiated a funding program meant to disseminate money throughout the movement the *Catalog* had fostered. The Foundation combined the rhetoric of holistic science, business savvy and technical know-how on new domestic and lifestyle developments, read in the context of a larger trajectory of evolutionary social change. Most influential of the Foundation's projects was *CoEvolution Quarterly*, the first issue of which was intended as a supplement to the second volume of the *Last Whole Earth Catalog*, titled the *Whole Earth Epilogue*, published in the fall of 1974. As Brand remarked in the fourth issue, what distinguished the *Catalogs* from *CoEvolution* was the latter's endorsement of a holistic evolutionary narrative, expressed in a wider conceptual shift, from the Cartesian scientism of such 1960s countercultural gurus as Fuller, Marshall McLuhan, and Herbert Marcuse to the holistic rhetoric espoused by the likes of ecologists and naturalists Howard Odum, Ivan Illich, and E. F. Schumacher.[52]

In contrast to the *Catalog*, *CoEvolution Quarterly* aspired to the prestige of a scientific research journal: extending the *Catalog*'s discourse on environmental activism through lifestyle and consumption, the *Quarterly* added lengthy articles from commentators and specialists in the applied science and research fields, as well as reports from the fields of business, philosophy, and mysticism and a range of local and community activists. Like the *Catalog*, the *Quarterly* filled its pages with reviews of saleable goods from do-it-yourself manuals for the construction of wood-burning stoves or compost units to survivalist hardware items like down vests and axes. But the *Quarterly* also included feature articles from a galaxy of countercultural intellects: Duane Elgin and Arnold Mitchell, the two Stanford researchers who devised the notion of voluntary simplicity, a piece by the British anthropologist Gregory Bateson, James Lovelock on the Gaia hypothesis, Richard Baker-roshi, abbot of the San Francisco Zen Center, a piece called "Surviving in Small Business" by Paul Hawken, position papers from a mind/body conference, an excerpt from Herman Kahn's *Problems of Transition to Postindustrial Society*, an essay on appropriate technology, a piece on the New Games Tournament, which saw hundreds of hippies converging on the Marin Landheads outside San Francisco for a weekend of "earthball" and other New Games, and an article titled "2025, If . . ." by Buckminster Fuller.

The unorthodox scientism of *CoEvolution Quarterly* and its supplements was founded on a historical narrative of inevitable evolutionary development toward an ultimately holistic future. The specific shape of this future was debated and prophesized in articles on utopian experiments and an incredible array of activities and reports from across the country and the world, though the most sustained debate was undoubtedly one that developed around the colonization of space. Orbiting space colonies, it was argued, would provide ecologically designed habitats for humanity in a postapocalyptic age of depleted resources—a proposal that raised questions concerning the ecological and practical aspects of such a venture, and ultimately its feasibility as a policy proposal in the economically pinched context of the economic recession.[53]

Indeed, throughout the 1970s, *CoEvolution Quarterly* entertained a lively discussion on the topic of space colonization, prompting Brand to compile a special supplement, *Space Colonies*, in 1977. The debate over space colonization brought together speculations on the renewal of daily life through holistic technique with a grand modernist narrative on human destiny. The cowboy economy, having run its course, had already drained the earth of resources (or certainly would soon), thus necessitating a rapid migration to space. In dozens of articles and speculative accounts of life on board such orbiting stations, the apparently apocalyptic narrative brought into play a stock of countercultural concerns with personal release and emancipation, realized in a promise of literal "weightlessness." In the new space colonies, people would live in what was described as "free space"—the baggage of outmoded traditions, social hierarchies, and "hang-ups" would be left permanently behind, quite literally at a great distance, allowing the new pioneer to live and drift freely on a new frontier.

In an introductory statement to the supplement, Brand presented the wider question of space colonization as an opportunity to "take Space personally," to invest it with one's own imaginary anxieties and yearnings, and on this basis to elaborate a new arena for concern and advice on the proper way of life. Brand urged his readers to "see Space as a path, or at least a metaphor, for their own liberation": "The subject is FREE SPACE. That's the technical term for everyplace outside the Earth's atmosphere. It's a political term—and increasingly, as exploration and argument proceed into orbit, a political reality."[54] Brand's use of "FREE SPACE," the "technical term," sets the tone for this special issue of *CoEvolution Quarterly*. On the cover of *Space Colonies* is an image that summarizes this liberatory vision: what might pass for a fairly run-of-the-mill romantic pastoral landscape depicts rolling hills and greenery wrapped on the inside

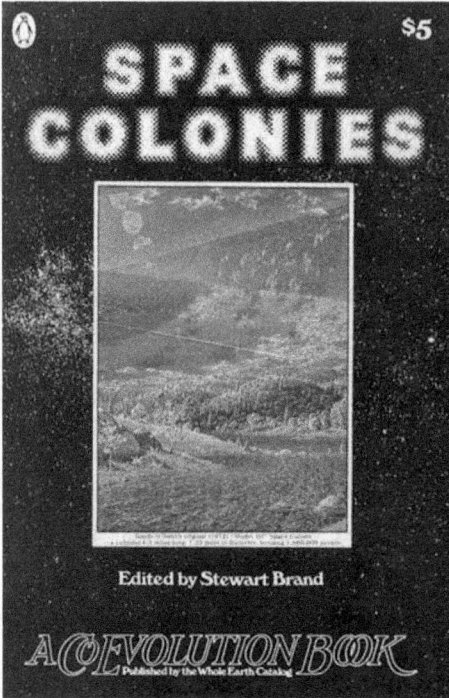

Edited by Stewart Brand

A COEVOLUTION BOOK
Published by the Whole Earth Catalog

13. Cover, *Space Colonies*,
by Stuart Brand

of a gigantic tube, suspended in space. Children play and birds soar over a green forest, restored to gravitational stability by the slow rotation of the immense enclosing hull of the space colony: a technological, naturalistic heaven. Life on the orbiting space station provided the ultimate lifestyle option: departure from the Earth itself to a sustained life on one's own "whole system," where one was permanently loosened from the hang-ups of the old society. The *Whole Earth Catalog* and *CoEvolution Quarterly*, like the many ecologically-oriented access catalogues that followed their example, described the individual's location within such larger holistic entities as an object of inspiration and feeling available to those possessing an expanded holistic consciousness (or with access to the advice of one who did). Being one meant releasing oneself into that larger entity—a task one chose for oneself, even as one carried it out under the guidance and supervision of a lifestyle discourse. Immersed in such caring words, readers saw their own lives from a distance, investing them with the narrative coherence supplied by a story of self-loosening.

These themes, of course, did not vanish with the closing of the 1970s, but became interwoven with our contemporary culture of consumption and style of life. On the one hand, they offer nothing specifically new: promises of a renewed bond with nature have appeared in advertising discourse since the beginning of national campaigns in the nineteenth century. Advertising historian Jackson Lears has described how themes of nurturing abundance defined advertising's most common fables for a largely agrarian society, later displaced by themes of efficiency and productivity with the onset of industrialization.[55] Yet the crisis in Fordist models of consumption reintroduced themes of nature in the guise of a counternarrative to dominant modernities, a nostalgia for a lost innocence and vitality defiled by industrial society's blind drive for progress, which doubled as a personal story of individual and historical development, providing a source of stability beyond the hectic regimes of consumption itself. By the 1970s, advertising discourse was replete with such themes: one thinks of the famous "crying Indian" public service announcement that aired on the first Earth Day, in which an (Italian American) actor portraying a Native American paddles his canoe past belching smokestacks and litter-strewn highways, turning to the camera to shed a single tear at the environmental damage done to his native earth. Nature, as an object of consumer longing, was generally integrated into the vernacular of advertising in the 1970s and made a staple in the decades that followed.

As the 1970s rounded the corner and what came to be called the "decade of greed" set in, invocations of the natural would reshape such industries as cosmetics, where organic ingredients would draw droves of consumers from traditional brands in search of natural materials—a need that was satisfied with the use of such ingredients as jojoba, an extract from a wild desert plant that began appearing in skin moisturizers in the early 1980s. American eating habits were increasingly attracted to the natural, most notably in the mid-1970s with the introduction of the granola bar category, which started as a natural alternative to traditional sugary candy bars for children and teens and grew at annual rates of up to 56 percent throughout much of the 1970s, led by General Mills and its Nature Valley Brand.[56] Throughout, the new eating patterns were related through metaphors for the natural authenticity of ingredients: in 1984 a restaurant critic commented on changing culinary patterns in the United States, attributing an increasing appetite for natural foods to "a process began at least 15 years ago with the ecology movement's conviction that what we eat affects not only who we are but also the earth and its resources," citing as support several trendy Manhattan whole food restaurants, including Naturworks, Whole Wheat 'n Wild Berrys, and Au Natural. As the demands of a distinct mode of holistic consciousness were minimized and the phrase "natural" became an ever more familiar, if never quite clearly defined commodity attribute, the deeper importance of a renewed bond with nature, attained through a specific way of living, was replaced in a matter of years with a range of products and services that served up the natural as a package. No longer was it necessary to engage a community of co-practitioners to consult self-styled experts, to listen, or to read. Becoming natural was no longer part of a discourse on becoming loose: products from granola bars to cosmetics, and, in the years that followed, Jeeps, bottled water, and credit cards could, according to some usage of the term, be described as natural.[57]

⑤

Loving Each Other
From Phony to Real in the New Togetherness

For many counterculturals, nature provided an elusive object of nostalgic longing, recoverable through a technique of self-loosening. The natural world, represented by scenes of undefiled vegetation and crystal-clear waters, was a thing one could dissolve oneself into by learning to live within the natural cycles of the seasons, and by expanding one's comprehension of the universe beyond the constraints of tradition and the utilitarian focus it imposed. But there were other domains of replenishment one could loosen oneself into: there was the human world, a world of feelings and sensibilities into which one could set oneself adrift, if one could master the technique. This chapter will consider these human objects for the manner in which they held out a promise of self-renewal through a cultivated technique of release. To truly be with others, to feel them, trust in them, and share oneself with them, one had to loosen oneself from the strictures of tradition, overcome the fear of social sanction and opprobrium, and recover the immediacy, the sensuality, and the experience of a truly shared moment. One had to plumb the depths of one's authenticity, setting aside egoism and phoniness, avoiding cop-outs and put-ons, and release oneself into the unmediated immediacy of the other—a task for which a host of expert mediators stood poised with advice and counsel. The lifestyle culture of the 1970s expressed the reflexivity of the self in the domain of managed, interpersonal relations where one had to work hard to reveal oneself to others as one really was.

The explanation that follows builds on a tradition of sociological insight into the changing nature of interpersonal relations in traditional and modern contexts. In contrast to traditional relationships, interpersonal bonds in modern societies are freer, more disembedded from the constraints of institutionalized moral authority, and consequently are regarded more as the individual accomplishment of the two consenting parties—a bond that depends for its durability on a technique of relating that each party has to master in order to practice effectively. But modern relationships are also diluted in their durability, subject to patterns of tumult and upset that come with social mobility and the liquidity that defines modern conditions in general. They are weakened in their staying power over time and subject to feelings of anxiety and insecurity. The waning ability of modern relationships to provide a lasting sense of trust and comfort frustrates individuals in their efforts to craft durable identities. Indeed, trust, a scarce resource in societies of flux, becomes central to the maintenance of self-assuredness in posttraditional societies and to the suppression of ontological insecurity: while in traditional societies trust was elicited from individuals on the basis of personal face-to-face interactions, under the conditions of radicalized modernity (and under advanced consumer capitalism), trust is increasingly placed in less stable "'absent others'—people one never sees nor meets but whose actions directly affect features of one's own life."[1]

Indeed, the trust one places in others is seminal to the maintenance of a biographically coherent sense of self: one needs others to talk to, to tell one's stories to, and by doing so to shape one's experiences into sustainable personal narratives. With the erosion of such bonds, the retrospective fashioning of biographical selves wanes in its power to give form to the liquidity of modern life.[2] Modern relationships present themselves as objects of care, and as such demand a whole apparatus and technique for their maintenance and cultivation, even while they remain ultimately diluted in their ability to allow partners to forge narrative through interlocution and shared telling (the term *high-maintenance* applied to a relationship usually refers to an uneven ratio of investment and profitability in this regard).

In this way, modern relationships are reflexive endeavors: friendships and marriages, even family ties, derive their validity not from their faithfulness to duty and collective purpose, but from the artfulness with which they are produced and maintained by participating parties. It is the quality and skill invested through inputs over time, and no other factors, that have made these relationships what they are. Modern relationships earn the trust of those who bear sole responsibility for their creation—a task that is faced daily in the mundane habits of life, a key feature of which is the emergent plasticity of interpersonal bonds as objects of informed technique and skilled craft. Indeed, much of what we call style of life is taken up with this effort to cultivate and sustain the trust we desire from others and to supply that trust in return—a task made all the more challenging by radical upheavals in the norms governing sex and gender roles, shifting class boundaries, and the rewriting of conventionally defined narratives around which biographical trajectories are mapped. While the new creative openness in contemporary relationships is doubtless exhilarating for the possibilities it affords and liberating for the power structures it challenges, the anxiety and insecurity that accompany this tumult and upheaval cannot be denied. It is a fact of everyday life that has generated voluminous literature on marriage, dating, sexuality, obligation, friendship, and the microphysics of etiquette and interpersonal transaction.

Moreover, a central purpose in the cultivation of trust (as we saw in chapter 2) is the disclosure of the self before the other in all of its authenticity and truth. With the scattering of hierarchies and the collapse of traditional authoritative roles, the revealing of one's intimate side, of one's authentic needs (in order that the other may know what she must do to satisfy them), shapes the core of modern relationships, or what Giddens has called the "pure relationship"—one that sustains without traditional supports and stands premised only on the emotional rewards it can supply to each partner.[3] Giddens writes that a pure relationship is "entered into for its own sake, for what can be derived by each person from a sustained association with another; and which is continued only in so far as it is thought by both parties to deliver enough satisfactions for each individual to stay within it."[4] Trust is the glue that holds together this pure relationship, attained through the revelation of individual authenticity to the other, but it is a trust that must stand on its own feet, in the absence of any external support: "Such trust presumes the opening out of the individual to the other, because knowledge that the other is committed, and harbours no basic antagonisms towards oneself, is the only framework for trust when external supports are largely absent."[5] In the modern context generally, and within the modernity of the 1970s in particular, the cultivation of trust through the opening out of the individual formed a central feature of lifestyle and its attendant discourses, demanding a courageous willingness to loosen the bonds of tradition and the artifices of conventional social roles (discarded as egoisms) and release oneself without hesitation into the space of the other.

We saw in chapter 1 how, throughout the Me Decade, the quest for the self became a national preoccupation and the basis for an insurrectionary narrative of modern progress, at least among an influential segment of the middle class. For the most part, realization of personal authenticity meant disentangling oneself and one's relationships with others from the debris of other, hegemonic forms, from the egoistic "cop-outs," or the pride that defined the competitive, honorific self, or from the instrumentality through which interpersonal relations were defined in the workplace. In the counterculture and the lifestyle movement, one could experience oneself and others with a new vitality, freed from the ossifying constraints of convention, tradition, and edifice. Getting over hang-ups meant being real, having the courage to make oneself vulnerable before the other in order that each party might better know and better meet the other's emotional needs. To earn and supply trust, one had to loosen up, to free one's authenticity from the phoniness, cop-out, and conceit imposed by the old order.

The chapter that follows deals with the problematic of interpersonal loosening as it relates to this feature of lifestyle as a reflexive project of the self: the maintenance and stabilization of interpersonal relationships and the refurbishing of trust in those relationships as a task of everyday livelihood and an object of instructed care. Such a revelation of personal authenticity resulted from the studied removal of inhibitions and hang-ups. Learning to unearth one's true feelings from the crumbling edifice of the square world was conceived as the domain of the nontraditional lifestyle adviser within a countercultural lifestyle print culture—a discourse that takes us to the heart of one of the counterculture's most fundamental aims, with the renewal of interpersonal relations generally, and a recovery of the empathy, closeness, and intuitive bonds between individuals that had been sundered under the cold bureaucracies and petty interests of industrial society. In what follows, two threads of lifestyle discourse will be considered for the way they expressed a renewal of interpersonal relations though a prescriptive narrative of caring: first, in a discourse on sexuality and sexual technique the call to overcome prohibitions and hang-ups, to lose oneself into the act of lovemaking and to please one's partner through displays of authentic passion, allowed one to better relate to others by developing a more transparent relationship with oneself and with one's own desires. Later, in a realm of instructional and resource literature devoted to the communal movement and cooperative living that expanded into a much wider discourse on business and professional life, commentary on the sharing of spaces and chores in daily life spoke to a renewal of trust embodied in the dishing out of tasks and in the construction of shared living quarters, and ultimately on an alternative ethic of sales and management. Trust here is related to a deep sense of openness and sharing between coworkers, retailers, merchants, and customers. It is through this last realm of advice, I will argue, that a specifically countercultural discourse on trust and interpersonal relations was infused into a new culture of consumption and streamlined for a new mode of highly autonomous, reflexive individuality. Under the aegis of a humanistic philosophy of business management and retail emphasizing trust, authenticity, and openness, the reflexivity of countercultural lifestyle was insinuated into the institutional life of a kinder, gentler capitalism and appropriated by an entrepreneurial style of selfhood, for which work was understood as a mode of self-expression.

The New Openness: Plastic Sexuality

At the peak of its hubris, the counterculture summarized its objectives with one simple word—*love*. Love was all you needed, a flexible catch-all phrase incorporating views on all levels of human cooperation, from global military conflicts to romantic spats, into a way of living—a personal ethic one could practice in all of the most mundane features of everyday life, from family and friends to encounters with bank tellers and policemen. All you needed was love: this message filled the airwaves across the world on June 25, 1967, as the Beatles gave the summer of love its musical anthem and a seductive rhetorical tool in the first global satellite television broadcast: against the backdrop of the war in Vietnam, rising domestic violence in American cities, and the anomie and isolation fostered by societies of mass consumption and remote organization, the Beatles sang of a spontaneous, impulsive, and deeply personal renewal of unconstrained social solidarity, seemingly there for the taking. Love, it was believed, if released from the iron cages into which it had been consigned, would flow freely across all social divisions once the constraints of a teetering institutional edifice were kicked aside. "The great organizations to which most people give their working day and the apartments and suburbs to which they return at night," wrote Charles Reich, "are equally places of loneliness and alienation. Friendship has been coated over with a layer of impenetrable artificiality as men strive to live roles designed for them. Protocol, competition, hostility, and fear have replaced the warmth of the circle of affection which might sustain man against a hostile universe."[6]

To overcome this condition, all the lonely people had to do, all the Eleanor Rigbys of the world, was release themselves into the world of true feeling. "It's easy . . . all you need is love," the Beatles sang: just let yourself go. Love expressed the counterculture's monistic tenets in a pure and versatile metaphor: one had to overcome the artificial distances and ruptures forced between individuals by the modern technocratic order and conceive of oneself together, bonded with a larger social unity that overflowed the false barriers suppressing our natural, truer humanity. Easy as it was however, love, and the new programs of interpersonal trust it inspired also demanded a technique of personal authenticity: to love was to assume responsibility for being real in all one's behaviors, to wean oneself of habits of pretence and appearance that safeguarded the facade of the social self, obscuring authentic sentiment with conventions of recognition and honorific regard. By the early 1970s, as the ethic of experience and feeling that defined the hippie became codified in a durable middle-class lifestyle discourse, an overt rhetoric of love had largely given way to more adult discussions of sensitivity, understanding, and a "service ethos," as discussed in chapter 2. The area of everyday life most dramatically affected by this call for a recovery of an unfettered, primordial empathy was that of sexual life and the patterns of marriage and kinship that formed around it.

Arguments for the social causes of the new sexual freedom cite factors ranging from an expanding media and entertainment industry that gradually coaxed censors and legislators to relax regulations and reform obscenity laws, to more varied developments in housing and employment opportunities that allowed greater autonomy for women and youth.[7] But central to the new sexual freedom was the ready availability of birth control, and what feminists termed the uncoupling of sexuality from reproduction—a shift that opened the sexual realm as a vast field for self-exploration and recreation, and as a new terrain for the practices of self-disclosure and reciprocity.[8]

Giddens's account of the pure relationship gives special priority to the sexual domain as an autonomous realm of experimentation and reciprocal fulfillment, and as the basis for the cultivation of new forms of trust. Under contemporary conditions of relative sexual equality implicit within modern forms of kinship, what Giddens terms the "confluent love" of the pure relationship defines a bond in which mutual satisfaction is central, providing an operative basis for ongoing commitment.[9] Indeed, with the reciprocal meeting of needs as the foundation for continued obligation, the confluent relationship depends heavily on the expression and interpretation of those needs—a condition that is guaranteed by continuing practices of disclosure and revelation between partners. Giddens writes: "Confluent love is active, contingent love . . . [it] presumes equality in emotional give and take, [and it] only develops to the degree to which each partner is prepared to reveal concerns and needs to the other and to be vulnerable to that other" (61–62). For this reason, the confluent relationship, for which the practical technique of mutual need satisfaction is paramount, calls upon a range of techniques and methods: "Confluent love for the first time introduces the *ars erotica* into the core of the conjugal relationship and makes the achievement of reciprocal sexual pleasure a key element in whether the relationship is sustained or dissolved. The cultivation of sexual skills, the capability of giving and experiencing sexual satisfaction, on the part of both sexes, becomes organized reflexively via a multitude of sources of sexual information, advice and training" (62–63).

Moreover, the choices implied within the pure relationship are deeply entwined with the development of what Giddens terms "plastic sexuality": sexual behavior as an autonomous object of manipulation and creative play, a pleasurable end in itself, but also a technique of self-realization and mutual exploration through its perfection as a craft. Plastic sexuality is that paramount area of daily life through which needs are explored and met, and through which authenticities are revealed. As a feature of the pure relationship, plastic sexuality offers a means of fashioning a stable relationship premised on the mutual satisfaction of deeply personal needs through a reflexive technique of need satisfaction—a project that is, as we shall see, heavily advised in a genre of lifestyle discourse that made a noisy entry on the American cultural scene in the early 1970s. In the midst of the sexual revolution, sexuality was redefined not only as a legitimate feature of a loose lifestyle, but as the primary arena of interpersonal self-loosening, whose advocates and mediators undertook a uniquely loose posture in the larger field of expert discourse on lifestyle.

SEX

"Compared with what came before," David Vandor, the porn czar for the New York City mayor's office remarked in a discussion with a reporter, "'Deep Throat' is an excellent film. It is better than most situation comedies or C rate comedies."[10] Vandor's comments referred to what is by contemporary standards a relatively inoffensive porno flick that transformed obscenity standards in the United States in the early 1970s: *Deep Throat* was among the first to venture beyond the stale recipes of traditional pornography into a humorous portrayal of the travails of a young woman, played by Linda Lovelace, afflicted with an odd physiological curiosity: her clitoris, she discovers, is located in her throat, a predicament that she explores in the film's long sequence of fellatio scenes. For this measure of artistic vision, the film was awarded a unique status in the canons of art, film, and tabloid gossip: the *Times* dubbed it "porno-chic"—the first pornographic film to be deemed worthy of interest for a vanguard audience thought to hold taste and sophistication in the realm of culture. "This quality, coming at a time of permissiveness, is apparently enough to persuade a lot of people that there is no harm or shame in indulging the curiosity—and perhaps even their frankly prurient interest—by going to see 'Deep Throat.'" The article goes on to name some of these people, who include Johnny Carson, Mike Nichols, Jack Nicholson, a group of French United Nations diplomats, some off-duty cops, and a gaggle of reporters from the *New York Times*, from both the news staff and later from the office of the *Review of Books*. The story of *Deep Throat*, the porno flick elevated to the status of high art only to be hounded by Nixon's Justice Department and ultimately disavowed as a record of "rape on film" by Lovelace herself, offers a unique view of the insurrectionary sexual culture of the 1970s. Sexual life, the penultimate realm of sensuality and dedistanciation, assumed for itself a new legitimacy that threatened to upset the taste hierarchy of the old middle-class culture, most notoriously through the visual media (film and photography) through which it declared its presence, but also through a print discourse describing the new techniques of sexual life.[11]

The explosive sale of sex manuals during the 1970s was a reflection of the wider boom in lifestyle discourse and the changing status of experts in this area. Following the groundbreaking success of such titles as Alex Comfort's *Joy of Sex*, *The Sensuous Woman*, and later *The Sensuous Man* and others, the first few years of the 1970s saw the open discourse on sexuality catapulted onto bestseller lists all over the country.[12] The consensus throughout this literature was that sexual lifestyles were to become less constrained by restrictions and inhibitions inherited from the older middle classes, but only as such practices were the object of educated choice. Most importantly, the new discourse on sexuality dropped its institutional credential and became unrelentingly personal: while a century of "marriage manuals" had related the medical advice of detached specialists, the new discourse was confessional, expressive, and playful. Expert discourse on sexuality had traditionally been the domain of health specialists whose message was one of self-control. "An ardent spur-of-the-moment tumble sounds very romantic," explains the author of *The Sex Technique in Marriage*, published in 1933.[13] "However, ineptly arranged intercourse leaves the clothes you had no chance to shed in shambles, your plans for the evening shot and your birth control program incomplete."[14] Such detachment from the experience and spontaneity of the sexual encounter would contrast sharply with the hedonistic doctrines of a few decades later. Indeed, the contrasting injunctions to control or to release oneself into the sexual experience would draw upon very different modes of expert discourse.

In 1973, Mopsy Strange Kennedy, a freelance writer from Boston writing in an op-ed piece for the *New York Times*, attempted to distinguish the styles of expert advice on the topic of sexuality that were saturating American popular culture. The author picked out the "No-Nonsense School" for contrast with what she called the "Please-Give-Me-Back-My-Nonsense School": "The No-Nonsense School of clinically observed activity which tells us what is, and presumably what should be, in the beds of us all. This one has made way for the other school, the Give-Me-Back-My-Nonsense School, which says do your own thing. . . . There is no right or wrong in the dark, light some incense, don't listen to what people tell you to do—except us of course."[15] In this first category belong, not surprisingly, the traditional specialists who advised on matters of sexual life through a posture of scientific detachment: Alfred Kinsey, Masters and Johnson, Van De Velde's *Ideal Marriage*, and other clinically qualified sexological studies; while in the second category are the nontraditional experts, who classified everyday conduct as a valid form of freely chosen expression and self-exploration: "Xavier Hollander and David Reuben, author of *Any Woman Can*, and *Cosmopolitan Magazine's Love Guide*"—publications whose authors have "confessed in the first person to every Byzantine act." The new specialists on sexuality advocated a release of sexual spirit from the constraints of tradition, but also a recovery of sex itself as a refined and cultivated practice. Indeed, the effort to reclassify, and thus valorize, the realm of sexuality is spelled out plainly in the most notorious sex manual of the 1970s: Alex Comfort's *Joy of Sex: A Gourmet Guide to Lovemaking*, published in 1972 by Crown Publishers, set out to lend to the sexual adventurer the legitimacy traditionally afforded the connoisseur of fine foods. Unplanned sexual encounters, which had to an earlier generation of sex counselors threatened to disrupt one's evening plans and the neatness of one's attire, were for Comfort and others the wellspring of spontaneity and the love of the moment. "The quickie is the equivalent of inspiration," Comfort writes, "and you should let it strike lightning fashion, any time and almost anywhere, from bed in the middle of the night to halfway up a spiral stairwell: anywhere that you're suddenly alone and the inspiration is bilateral." [16] *The Joy of Sex* was among the first of a wave of such books, whose flippancy, irony, and personal tone were emulated across this newly opened publishing category.

Throughout Comfort's book sexual acts were judged according to standards of connoisseurship typically reserved for fine foods. The book's contents are arranged under the categories one might find in a cookbook—"Starters" offers a variety of forms of foreplay from the use of "gadgets and gimmicks" to rolling on a condom; "Main Courses" lists mutual masturbation, kissing, and a wide range of coital positions, a section titled "Sauces and Pickles" explores such areas as biting, discipline, dancing, and a variety of non-Western techniques from Japanese and Indian to Chinese Styles. Notably, the first two chapters of the book define the strategy of legitimation to be applied: a chapter called "the Art of Lovemaking" includes a collection of fine art plates, gushy watercolor renderings of a hippie couple making love, interspersed with erotic Japanese prints and other images from non-Western culture. The section "On Advanced Lovemaking" describes the progress in "getting over hang ups" that have occurred in the past few years, with more basic inhibitions and problems being dealt with by the baser clinical literature that came out since the 1950s, such as Masters and Johnson, whose readers are getting over hang-ups "so basic that in past generations the folk tradition would have taken care of them." Moving beyond these fundamental needs, however, what was needed now was a fuller, more sophisticated approach:

> Chef-grade cooking doesn't happen naturally: it starts at the point where people know how to prepare and enjoy food, are curious about it and willing to take trouble preparing it, read recipe hints, and find they are helped by one or two detailed techniques. It's hard to make mayonnaise by trial and error, for instance. Cordon Bleu sex, as we define it, is exactly the same situation—the extra one can get from comparing notes, using

some imagination, trying way-out or new experiences, when one is already making satisfying love and wants to go on from there.[17]

For Alex Comfort, Cordon Bleu sex was distinguished from the crass desires of the sexual hedonist by the discourse of taste and cultivation woven into the judgment of sexual practices themselves—a form of expertise and special counsel that departed radically from the stodgy distance of the traditional medical expert. Indeed, the crossing of this boundary between formal and experiential knowledge as the basis for lifestyle advice defined sexual life as a field for learning and growth in which one explored one's deepest sexual needs and appetites with another. This was no easy task: one had to learn to immerse oneself in the newly discovered continent of sexual experience. Indeed, this learning process defined narratives of personal and moral growth toward more relaxed, more loose, and less hung-up stages of life, and as such was something best supervised by an experienced mentor or a knowing guide.

If Alex Comfort, by analogizing sexual experience to the consumption of fine foods, had brought sexuality into the realm of legitimate taste, the debate over the professional status of sexual therapists reveals important disagreements about the medical and scientific authority that framed the new discourse on sexual lifestyle, and particularly that of the freelance sexual-therapeutic practitioner. Such therapists debuted on the medical field in 1970 when William Masters and Virginia Johnson published *Human Sexual Inadequacy*, an expansive report reflecting years of investigation into the various sexual problems and dysfunctions plaguing American society.[18] Developed from research at the St. Louis clinic the couple founded to investigate such dysfunctions as frigidity, impotence, premature ejaculation, and other travails of the middle-class bedroom, *Human Sexual Inadequacy* built on notoriety earned four years earlier with *Human Sexual Response* and focused a broad popular debate on the ethical and professional quandaries surrounding the clinical treatment of sexual problems—treatment that often involved couples having sex in clinical environments, or, in some cases, single (often male) clients having sex with trained surrogate sexual partners. The book inspired the commercial field of sex therapy, which exploded in the years following its publication. By 1974 there were estimated to be between 3,500 and 5,000 clinics of various kinds offering some variety of sex therapy, some financed by foundations or small hospitals, and others supported by fees charged directly to clients. Fees ranged upward from $40 an hour per couple for a ten- to twenty-hour program, to $2,500 for a two-week program with up to five years of follow-up if needed. In many cases, therapeutic seriousness gave way to quackery, profiteering, and thinly masked prostitution. "The opportunities for charlatanry are abundant," William Masters cautioned. "Once there is a breakthrough in a medical finding, it takes a time for legitimate training to occur. Meanwhile, the promoters leap in."[19]

The blueprint for sexual surrogate therapy is found in a brief chapter of *Human Sexual Inadequacy* titled "Replacement Partners and Surrogate Partners," which proposes a two-week package of talk, history collection, and "individual body-work therapy" in which the administering doctor would develop the therapeutic discourse with the presumably anxious male, whose apprehension and self-consciousness in the sexual act prevented him from performing comfortably with others. Only at select moments would a female surrogate be brought in to advance the bodywork therapy to the stage of sexual contact.[20] The aim of this treatment was, throughout, the relaxation of the client through the distraction of his attention from the sexual performance itself through the development of an easy and comfortable relationship with the surrogate. "The anxious male must first be placed at ease socially," write Masters and Johnson. "He develops this ease from firsthand knowledge of the partner surrogate through observing her personal appearance, preference in food, drink, manner of dress and of social conduct, and the way she verbally communicates with him" (152).

The root of dysfunction, for most men, was "response anxiety" or "performance anxiety," which clients could overcome as they were encouraged to lose themselves into the sexual experience itself. This involved turning their concerns from their own pleasure and focusing primarily on the sexual pleasure of their partner, the surrogate. "An impotent man," the authors write, "should never attempt to give pleasure to his wife with only the concept of receiving pleasurable stimuli from her in return. He must give of himself to his wife primarily for her pleasure, and then must allow himself to be lost in the warmth and depth of her response, and in so doing divest himself of his impersonal spectator's role ... When the male loses himself in the giving, the female's sensate return will be reflected by positive interdigitation of his biophysical and psychosocial influences, and the erection he has tried time and time again to force will develop freely when least expected" (198).

Yet the achievement of such relaxation was not the province of the administering doctor per se. In a classically Taylorist separation of concept and execution, sexual surrogate therapy would maintain a strict distinction between talk therapy and bodily contact, placing supervising doctors on one side and a trained practicing surrogate on the other. But as the recommendations of *Human Sexual Inadequacy* were variously adopted and adapted to a range of cultural and commercial purposes, this distinction was questioned as alternative models of the surrogate therapist allowed a wider range of interpretation and a more colorful and individual application of the treatment methods. By 1972, William Hartman and Marylin Fithian published *Treatment of Sexual Dysfunction*, arguing for greater leniency for self-styled surrogates who would be allowed to conduct the entire therapeutic process themselves, emphasizing physical technique over talk therapy. Hartman's and Fithian's studies, based on work at the Berkeley Sex Therapy Group, attracted a large following of practicing surrogates and inspired the American Association of Sex Educators, Counselors, and Therapists (AASECT) to establish clinical and ethical guidelines and a modest certification process by which surrogates could attain accreditation and establish their own practices. By the mid-1970s, the clinical practice of sexual surrogate therapy had spawned a small cottage industry of widely varying techniques and approaches, freely incorporating themes from Eastern mysticism, New Age healing, post-Freudian analysis, and other sources. Many of these clinics displayed vague countercultural affiliations, and they drew legitimacy and an expanded notion of expertise and therapeutic practice from a broader discourse of advice and commentary disseminated through a culture of print. Sexuality would be a realm of personal self-loosening and an instrument of caring, mediated by a discourse on interpersonal relations and human trust as a fundamental, primordial potential.

CATALOG OF SEXUAL CONSCIOUSNESS

In the counterculture, sexuality was, as Giddens described, reinvented as a plastic object of choice and artistry. One's sex life became a thing of creativity and technique but also an arena of daily life wherein one might cultivate and share a deeper, truer, and more authentic sense of who one really was, and by doing so inject a more profound sense of trust in relationships whose only basis lay in their ability to supply reciprocal emotional satisfaction. This ethical purpose is defined in an influential anthology of materials edited by Saul Braun, together with his wife Peggy and a team of writers, sex educators, photographers, and therapists. The *Catalog of Sexual Consciousness* was a collection of materials and resources compiled for readers "committed to the idea that people have a right to determine for themselves the growth and development of their sexual consciousness."[21]

Published in 1975 by the New York–based Grove Press (the press credited with taking down America's censorship laws following court rulings on the publication of *Lady Chatterly's Lover* and *Tropic of Cancer*, but whose lists included such luminaries of the New Left as Malcolm X and Che Guevara, as well as a daring array of literary erotica, with titles such as *The Softness on the Other Side of the Hole*), the *Catalog* fit the access catalogue mold nicely and quickly sold out its first print run of 10,000 copies. Fashioned precisely on the large size and busy layout developed by the *Whole Earth Catalog*, the *Catalog of Sexual Consciousness* professed its intent to provide "a comprehensive non-judgmental selection of access materials in human sexuality." A devotional tribute to the *Whole Earth* project appears on the inside cover, along with a reproduction of the cover of the *Last Whole Earth Catalog*: "We would like to acknowledge a debt of gratitude to the Whole Earth Catalog. Their purpose is our purpose." Like the *Whole Earth*, the pages are filled with haphazardly arranged citations from recognized books on a range of topics related to human sexuality, together with listings of organizations and resources, found photographs and graphics, magazine pages lifted from various sources, illustrations and erotic art, reproductions of flyers, posters, and book covers, and a running commentary from the editors, presented in a dialogue format: the voices of Saul, Ziva, Stella, and others assure the reader of the intimacy and personal investment of the editors in the object of their advice.

Dozens of references and sources listed in the *Catalog*'s 288 pages confirm its devotion to this purpose—an improbable collection combining insights from the New Age and human potential movements with more seedy contributions from *Screw Magazine* and Manhattan s-m dungeons. Under categories like "Gestalt," "Yoga," and "Body Therapies," listings include organizations such as the Guild for Structural Integration headed by Ida Rolf, developer of the Rolfing technique, and the Integral Yoga Hatha Center in Boston. Elsewhere listings for services of a more clinical nature cite the Kinsey Institute, abortion and sterilization services, and a range of hotlines, from a rape counseling center to sex information lines. In still other areas, more classically countercultural interests are reflected in books on marijuana use and underground comics, featuring the scatological illustrations of R. Crumb; and finally, sources for materials and

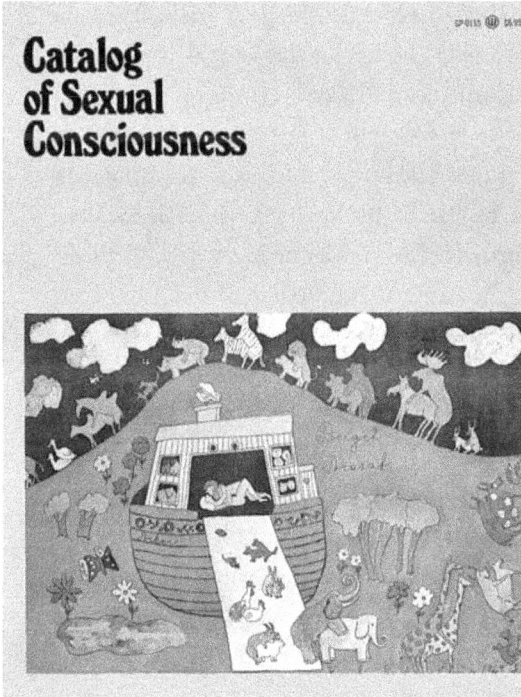

14. Cover, *Catalog of Sexual Consciousness*, by Saul Braun

services related to a seemingly less ideological sex trade describe prostitution services in San Francisco, pulp pornographic novels, bondage gear, and sex toys. For the editors themselves, however, these disparate themes are tied together by a common, deeply humanistic project in which they themselves share a profound personal investment: "A lot of strong, caring energy went into creating this book, and we feel sure you're going to love it," the editors tell us, "We also think it will be helpful no matter what place your head is in."

The *Catalog of Sexual Consciousness* is unmistakable for its adherence to the resource catalogue format and its implicit endorsement of the reader as independent lifestyle practitioner. The independence is reproduced in the autonomy and creativity with which the reader skims the *Catalog*'s pages: "This book is a Resource Tool: It will help you get in touch with as many aspects of sexuality as you want in an open atmosphere free of judgments." A section preceding the table of contents advises us of the different modes we might employ: "Random Access: You can look through the book, pick what you like, and let the rest go by," or alternately, "Systematic Access: If you are interested in getting a total view of sexuality in all its aspects you can start at the beginning and read through to the end. You will be exposed to a complete range of material in some depth." And finally, "Experiential Access: The catalog format makes it possible for you to freely bridge the gap between idea and action. Here are places to visit, workshops to attend, teachers to study with, books to read, products to buy, alternatives to experience" (6). It is this final way of reading, perhaps the most thoroughly engaging, that defines the *Catalog* for what it is: a lifestyle medium, which hails the creativity and reflexivity of the reader on every page—a reader whose choices, unconstrained in the carnival atmosphere of the listings, are entirely and only his or her own.

The materials are divided into three general groupings. Part 1, "Body Is Self: An Introduction to Sexual Consciousness," concerns itself with "the body as the vehicle for sexual experience. The body gives us a wealth of information about ourselves in a variety of ways which help us discover who we are sexually. ... Resources in Part One deal with self awareness, learning how our bodies communicate to us and how to attend with a joyful seriousness and care to the messages we receive" (6). Materials in part 1 cover topics ranging from masturbation and self-pleasuring (with a list of educational films such as *Feeling Good*, *One on One*, and *Early Morning*), erotic art (with reproductions of erotic Japanese prints and other images of non-Western art), a list of workshops (including one called Sexual Being held at Riverside Church in New York: "Sexuality in its most basic expressions—loving, touching and love-making ... emphasis on personal growth of the participants, who are encouraged to bring a 'significant other' with whom to share the experience"), and a long section on sex ed (with advice on setting up sex-education programs through local school boards, the training of sex-education staff, and other items).

Part 2 is titled "The Body Politic: A Catalog of Sexual Consciousness" and offers an "attempt to put together in some kind of order the complexity of relationships on all its levels in the social and political environment. Use this section to develop insight into relationships and their sexual rewards" (6). Part 2 begins with a long section called "The Western Heritage" (containing a discussion of Christianity and witchcraft and concluding with a smiling photograph of Richard Nixon, accompanied with a statement from the president on his National Commission on Obscenity and Pornography), and moves on to a discussion of the law; a lengthy statement on s-m largely composed of illustrations and fliers from a variety of s-m clubs and comics; a section on rape with contact information for several crisis centers, and another long section titled voyeurism, featuring ads lifted from various girlie magazines. These ads include bondage gear, crotchless panties, bar glasses with nude models on the sides, and a *Playboy Magazine* pinup. Following this are several sections on sex surrogates and sexual therapy, and sections on sex for the disabled, the retarded, and the elderly.

The third part of the *Catalog* is titled "Spirit: Expansions of Sexual Consciousness." This section, the editors tell us, "comes full circle to Part One where we started, with the body, but in another perspective. Possibly the ways of relationship discussed in Part Two will have led you to the realization that what we're relating to in sex is not body-as-object but the physical self as a medium of spirit. Use this last section to explore the idea that body and spirit are one, different yet as inseparable as male and female, the two halves of an endlessly mysterious wholeness, forever unfolding and discovering itself" (7). A long section on "grass" (featuring a range of testimonials on drug philosophy and smoking techniques) is followed by one on underground comics, psychedelics, dance, yoga, and meditation.

It is in the continuing dialogues between the authors, however, that the *Catalog of Sexual Consciousness* best expresses its view of sexuality as a technique for cultivation of trust between partners. In an opening statement titled "Talkin' to Ya," the editors offer a series of comments outlining their antirepressive ideology: "To begin with," Stella tells us, "we are taught not to touch ourselves or to play with each other's genitals."

> We are taught to be ashamed of our naked bodies, our desires, our fantasies, and when we are allowed to express ourselves, it is only through traditionally sanctioned modes. The message is this: deny your body and pleasure, nurture your intellect and powers of self-control. In essence, as we succumb to our training, we make the intellect a dictator which imposes rules to live by and roles to function by. We learn to say no to ourselves and yes to the system. We are at war within our bodies. (10)

The undoing of this primal repression, however, is the object to which the *Catalog* devotes itself. Stella returns later to announce the vanguard new culture of sensuality and expressiveness: "What we are describing is nothing short of total revolution, a revolution of pleasure and love that can take place within each person. We are the transitional people, effecting an evolutionary leap of consciousness within our own beings in our lifetimes. We are born into one age only to die in another" (11).

Yet this evolutionary leap is envisioned not as a social movement in the traditional sense, but as a personal development of deeply rooted, fundamental energies and life forces. Ziva tells us: "Our view is that sexual feeling is an energy; it has a life-force, and the capacity to connect us more acutely to ourselves and to one another." But it is an energy premised on a feat of liberatory self-development, as Stella describes: "Growth is a revolution on the personal level. It involves overthrowing our intellect-dictator. In so doing, we are not giving up the intellect, but according it a more democratic function within us, balanced and integrated with emotions and sensations." And notably, this task is one for which the individual practitioner himself takes full responsibility, and to which the advisory discourse of the *Catalog* relates itself only as a facilitator, never a legislator—or, as Saul writes: "The book claims its authority from natural laws, not from any religion, science or other institution. The only authority over your body is you, yourself. The only expert who knows enough to tell you what to do or not to do is you, yourself" (11).

Most importantly, liberated sexuality is described as an arena for enhancing interpersonal connections through the sharing of intimacy and deep, sensual contact, as Stella advises: "The experience of opening up to other people and sharing what's really there is a way of getting support, a way of learning to fulfill oneself with other people. Revealing oneself to others is the best self-revelation. Our friends are our mirrors" (16). Indeed, this sense that the mysterious vitality that constitutes sexual consciousness is at odds with distancing conventions that maintain an artificial sense of sociality is everywhere suggested in the pages of the *Catalog*. Elsewhere, in a quote lifted from a book titled *Hot Tubs: How to Build, Maintain and Enjoy Your Own*, the powers of a completely loosened sense of one's own bodily pleasures allow one to break down artificial distances and form powerful emotional bonds:

> Discord and uptightness gets washed away by hot water. Sink into the tub, and you'll begin to shed the dead skin of your previous person and find a smoother one underneath. It happens when you sit around with naked friends and neighbors for a few hours. Suddenly you realize that you love that person. Next time you meet you put your arms around each other and say, "remember when we were in the womb together?" and he or she says, "yes, yes," and squeezes you and sighs a big sigh. (17)

The "dead skin" referred to here is often implicated in the institution of traditional marriage—a bankrupt holdover from an earlier age. A section on monogamy describes the emptiness of traditional marriage and the possibility of reinvigorating relationships through a greater measure of self-knowledge gained through enhanced sexual consciousness. An exchange between *Catalog* editors Peggy and Saul (who, we learn, are married) reveals the dichotomous relation between states of rigidity and conventionality identified with the traditional monogamous marriage, and the looser state identified with heightened sexual consciousness, wherein intimacy flows freely—a difference defined by heightened states of knowledge of the needs of the other.

> Peggy: One of the possibilities always present in a committed relationship—marital or otherwise—is that of "knowing" another person. Knowing in this sense suggests an alive interaction, an experience of the Other and of yourself with the Other. This kind of knowing implies acceptance and love. Not being static, this knowing keeps on transcending what is known.

> Saul: It is a fluid experience . . . that is a very open relationship which lets you keep digging for your missing parts. (158)

Indeed, such digging, undertaken within the context of a shared relationship, is nonetheless a highly autonomous affair to which established traditions have little to offer:

> Saul: The problem actually is that most people seem to expect the solution to the dilemmas of life and marriage to come from some system or other. Whereas the answer is completely in the exercise of observing yourself in operation. The movement away from the rigidity is going to evolve out of that kind of watchfulness . . . the critical thing is movement, increasing your flexibility. The big benefit of that is increased intimacy. The rigid marriage is not intimate. Intimacy is in the exposure of whatever is spontaneous and of the moment in the relationship—the thing that *happens* between us. (158)

With rigidity on one side and intimacy on the other, the ethical choice was clear: the conventions of marriage were sundered by the embrace of the real, the intimate, and the immediate—the thing that *happens*. While the domain of sexual life defined an area wherein the advice of experts like Saul and Peggy demonstrated its ethical intent most forcefully, we find in other realms similar efforts to excavate trust from the debris of the old culture through the practice of new ways of living and the shaping of new kinds of relationships. In the movement toward cooperative living and later in alternative business practice, where love and trust were to be practiced on a more mundane level, another very different kind of advice developed around the planning and building of collective homes and on the myriad problems confronted in the running of a small business.

Cosmic Profit: Finding Trust in Everyday Life

In the late 1960s and early 1970s, voluntary communities or communes proliferated across the country: one survey estimated 2,000 rural communes and 5,000 collectives by the mid-1970s, while dozens of popular books celebrated the networks of collective groups, most composed of young people living together under shared ideologies of trust and personal authenticity, animated by a spirited desire to reinvent interpersonal life daily through the shaping of a shared sense of trust.[22] "When I wake up in the morning, I'm happy," said one commune dweller, "I never felt that way before. I know people love me. It's really groovy waking up and knowing that 48 people love you. It gives you all sorts of energy. You're standing alone—but you're standing with 48 people."[23] Communal life, represented in various forms, thematized a narrative of self-transformation through the learned capacity to release oneself into the authenticity of real relationships embodied by collective ways of living. The division of household chores, the maintenance of domestic enterprises from craft production to small-scale farming, the preparation of food, and the construction of new facilities provided occasions for creativity in the improvisation of new modes of interpersonal trust. Dozens of publications sprung up to tie this network together and to relay advice on these collective tasks: with names like *Green Revolution*, *Small Town*, *Akwasasne Notes*, and *Workbook*, these magazines and catalogues stressed the practical aspects of collective living, while exhorting readers in the new ways of solidarity. The case of *Communities Magazine* is illustrative.

Late in 1972, seven communal groups who together published four underground journals covering the commune movement—*Alternatives* (formerly the *Modern Utopian*), *Communitarian*, *Communitas*, and the *Journal of Walden Two Commune*—came together to form a magazine that would pool all their energies and reach an entire national network of communal groups. *Communities* sought to forge links between isolated communes scattered across the country, enabling the sharing of experiences and reflection on the outcomes of various experiments in social planning, cooperative living, and ecological, domestic technology. In 1974, the group published a *Commune Directory*, the first of a series of efforts at a detailed inventory of the commune movement that would culminate in 1979 with the efforts of a group of editors from the Community Publications Cooperative, Paul Freundlich, Chris Collins, and Mikki Wenig. With funds from two nonprofit groups, the Center for Studies of Metropolitan Problems and the National Institute of Mental Health, the group focused their energies on what would be their most far-reaching directory of communal and cooperative organizations: the *Guide to Cooperative Living*.[24] An editorial statement preceding the listings describes the historical predicament to which the book is addressed: "If the 60s message was 'Be here now, for flower power, end the war now, enlightenment is right around the corner'—the question for the 70s became, 'How?' How to live lives which support rather than contradict our spiritual and political quest? How in the face of vast complexity and confusion to follow the light of our truth into a new age?" The question is resolved in the concrete ways of living the network espoused: "In little pockets of community around the continent, people have been redefining how we can make our lives together. We call them food coops and child-care coops, block organizing, intentional communities, ashrams, collectives, communes, centers of healing and liberation of women and men: we could as well call them 'classrooms.' In them we use cooperation and consensus, appropriate technology and simpler living—but mostly we learn by doing."[25]

Indeed, the learning-by-doing such classrooms inculcated in their students involved the development of new relationships with others and new forms of trust premised on novel forms of openness, transparency, and empathy—what has been previously identified as a discourse of caring. This lesson was taught in many ways in relation to various daily tasks.

TRUST

One such lesson is related in a chronicle of communal life, *Celery Wine: Story of a Country Commune*, by Elaine Sundancer. Published in 1973 by Community Cooperative Publications, Sundancer's memoirs trace her reasons for joining a commune and describe the kind of life she lived there, though she dismisses any reading of her book as a prescriptive or instructional text in any traditional sense. In the book's opening pages the author presents her chronicle as a work of advice, a response to steady demands for information and counsel from novices in the world of communal organization and living, though "advice," Sundancer cautions her readers, "is a shit-word." "When you say, 'give me some advice,' you are saying, 'tell me what your eyes see,' and often you are saying 'I trust what your eyes see, more than I trust my own,' That's foolishness. Your own eyes are the only eyes that can see for you. What you see, what you experience, is what's true for you, more than anything anyone can tell you."[26] Sundancer's posture here is an odd one: at once imparting advice while at the same time disqualifying the basis of her advice, she summons the experience of the reader as the final court of judgment in all matters, locating trust in the practice, and the reflection of the practice in unmediated testimony of one who has been there. Her role as specialist, as she sees it, garners a higher degree of trust for what it openly betrays about itself: in a discourse in which all knowledge is valid only in the realm of personal experience, the counselor freely admits her limits, even while she puzzles over the apparent paradox of such nonadvice: "I am not responsible for the use you make of my words, you are. Do what you will; if I say 'Do your own trip' that in itself is a form of saying 'do what I say'" (163).

Sundancer's path to communal living is revealing. It begins with the sudden departure of her husband, Ted—a crisis whose traumatic effect was initially devastating, but which soon developed into an opening for a transformative experience of growth and release from conventional identities and lifestyles: "All my life I had been living within certain forms, certain limits; I had been held down by tethered ropes. 'My house, my husband, my son, my books, my cooking pots' . . . my tethered rope had snapped and I was in a new universe . . . When Ted came back a week or so later, ready to talk again about our problems, I didn't want to talk. I had just been let out of a locked room, and I had a new world to explore" (18–19). With Ted's departure, Sundancer joined a circle of Berkeley hippies and others devoted to the idealistic promise of a new collective life: the group formed and began stripping down their lives, sharing housing, dispensing with extraneous possessions, and planning for an eventual move to the country. Collective living was experienced as a relaxation of the constraining boundaries of an urban, possessive individual, but also as a process in which the merging with a collective group enabled the recovery of an authentic sense of self: "Sharing my apartment didn't bother me the way it once had. I had relaxed. I was no longer trying to control the space around me. My boundary line was clear now. My actions were definitively my own. I didn't need territory; I possessed myself" (22).

15. Cover, *Celery Wine: Story of a Country Commune*, by Elaine Sundancer

However, what began as a liberating embrace of shared living developed ultimately into a test of personal resolve. Throughout, Sundancer's memoirs give the sense of a weakened and needy personality whose relationships with others are defined by timidity, an irksome vulnerability to criticism and competition, and a pining for safety from the pressures of group membership and what she perceives as the torrents of modern social life. Communal living, for Sundancer, is less an experience of love with every waking morning, and more a troubled effort to resolve disputes through relentless appeals to honesty and compassion, and a desperate yearning for happiness in nature. Yet it is still a place for self-cultivation and self-work—a classroom of sorts where more profound dimensions of trust are sought to allay anxieties resulting from a condition of mobility and drift. Puzzling over the question of why the commune presented her with such an environment for "going through changes," Sundancer speculates, "For me, the farm is a place where I can work on myself, a place where it's okay to go through changes. Maybe it's because here I'm living with people who'll let me change—and if I need to do something unusual like being silent, or going without my glasses for a while, or curling up under a blanket and being scared, no one minds" (106–10). And most importantly, such conditions were, above all else, loose: all planning and intentionality was subsumed in the flow of events and experiences, in the daily texture of passing time: "We had no clock, no telephone, very rarely a newspaper. I learned to tell time very roughly by the sun. I learned to hang loose, to adjust to what happened as it happened—there was no way to make appointments or tie down the future. . . . The days seemed long and slow and quiet, not divided into little boxes, and I moved from one activity to the next without asking myself whether I was using my time wisely" (42). The technique of such laxity extended from her execution of daily tasks from food preparation, the canning of perishables, gardening, and washing, to private practices of reading, writing, and walking in the woods. And most importantly, laxity was an interpersonal skill, an enterprise of collective endeavor with huge returns of self-knowledge for the one best able to loosen up. Commune members helped each other overcome hang-ups, become less uptight, and release themselves into the fabric of a mutually accepting community. Sundancer writes:

> One time Claudia snapped at me, and I felt hurt and angry. I waited until late at night when the house was quiet, and then I started to tell her how I was feeling. I half expected her to snap at me again, but instead she winced and said "Oh, that's a part of myself I've been working on so long, but it still keeps on happening." Once Mike said "If there's anything I'm doing I want you to let me know about it, the same way that if I had something caught in my beard and I couldn't see it myself I'd want you to tell me about it." (106)

From Sundancer's account, and from other testimonials from a range of communal experiments, the dynamics of collective self-work provided a backdrop for much of what went on daily. This message was conveyed in a number of publishing genres, perhaps most influentially in an emerging discourse on the construction of dwellings. Communes were, among other things, places where people conceived and built new homes, and in so doing reassessed social proximity on a concrete spatial level, thus requiring advice and instruction in the techniques of construction and architectural design—hip planners with imaginary solutions to the newly defined problems of cohabitation and authenticity in daily life.[27] Among the most noted and influential of the publications were a series of instructional catalogues espousing the construction of the geodesic dome as an architectural form: *Domebook I,* and *Domebook II,* with *Domebook*

16. Cover, *Pacific Domes: Domebook II*

III appearing as a supplement to a later publication called *Shelter I,* followed by *Shelter II*—all large-format access catalogues, close in dimensions, typographic layout, and content to the *Whole Earth Catalog.*[28] These publications related advice on the replenishment of interpersonal trust through two broad injunctions: live intimately with others (and find spaces, preferably round and domed, appropriate to this intimacy) and build things yourselves, collectively and cooperatively, in ways that develop the cooperative and expressive potentials of the group.

In pages and pages of instructional material, the *Domebooks* and *Shelter* books argued that the design and construction of houses should originate from the spontaneity of an impulsive human effort, like children playing with building materials. As with other access catalogues, this message was reflected in the amateurish typesetting and pasteup that characterized the publication itself. New homes were to be built by those who lived in them, using materials that were at hand and knowledge gained from experience—if prodded by the proper volumes of advisory literature. And at the center of these books was a troubled romance with the structure that came to typify the spirit and new architecture of communal living—the geodesic dome. Drawn from Buckminster Fuller's original design, geodesic domes were replicated across a range of communal settings, improvised from natural or discarded materials and adapted to various uses in commune settings as collective lodgings and ultimately in private settings as middle-class vacation homes.

Fuller originally devised his plan for the geodesic dome in a spirit that was anything but celebratory of untrained handicraft: part of the marvel of geodesic domes was their composition of dozens of identical parts—rods and buttresses of identical length and design, easily mass-produced in enormous volume. The domes were a marvel of mathematical measurement and computation, the product of the kind of reasoning mind, detached from execution, that Fuller envisioned as the planning genius that would "make Spaceship Earth work" and bring us back from the brink of ecological apocalypse. Indeed, geodesic domes were the paradigm of that technocratic fetish so many counterculturals rejected: efficiency. Employing a pattern of self-bracing triangles lending immense structural support with a minimum of supportive structure, the domes promised to enclose larger swaths of space at less material cost than any structure previously devised. As spheres, the domes allowed for the least amount of outside surface for the space enclosed, reducing exposure to cold and winds. Like tetrahedrons, Fuller argued, geodesic domes were closest to the fundamental structures of the universe—structure in its purest form. If the earth is round, our heads are round, and teardrops are round, one hippie suggested, certainly our homes should be round too.

These structures possessed an immense metaphorical power that outstripped Fuller's initial vision of mass-produced housing. They distributed their weight equally across all their elements, requiring no central support—a quality that seemed to take on certain democratic connotations, even if the distribution involved here was only that of structural weight between struts and braces, not social power between people and citizens. Nonetheless, domes constituted their own "whole systems," replicas of the spherical organization of the planet. Lacking corners and interior walls, right angles and vertical planes (all the fixtures of "square" housing), domes, it seemed, would usher in new possibilities of unconstrained thought and experience. "Corners constrict the mind," wrote Steve Baer, an early proponent of domes as a housing solution. "Domes break into new dimensions."[29]

Indeed, Baer early on experimented with Fuller's geodesic concepts in a series of structures he built at a Colorado commune called Drop City—skeletal geodesic forms filled in with car roofs he cut with an ax from a nearby junkyard. A year later he published his plans and reflections on domes (or on the structure whose names he coined with the neologism "zomes") in *The Dome Cookbook*, a forty-page collection published by Lama Foundation, a New Mexico commune largely composed of Baer's designs. For Baer, the dome represented an emancipated alternative to the constraints of traditional geometric housing: "These are instructions on how to almost break out of prison. The prison is the paucity of shapes to which we have in the past confined ourselves because of our technology-industry-education-economy."[30] In 1969 Baer founded Zomeworks and began manufacturing geodesic playground equipment and other applications of dome technology.

But the forbearer of the dome craze was undoubtedly Lloyd Kahn, a California architect who started building domes in Big Sur in 1966. In 1969 he was invited to supervise the construction of seventeen domes at Pacific High School, an alternative school outside Santa Cruz. Working with fifty students and a dozen teachers, Kahn experimented with a variety of materials and structures, ultimately drawing national attention and accumulating volumes of sketches and plans, together with extensive experience on what worked and what didn't. In 1970 Kahn borrowed the production facilities that the *Whole Earth Catalog* crew had used to produce their publication and put together a collection of materials under the title *Domebook I*. Like *Whole Earth*, the pages of *Domebook* were a buzzing arcade of illustrations, architectural diagrams, letters from various correspondents and participants, and photographs of domes. In 1971, the same group went on to compile *Domebook II*, which sold 175,000 copies. In a *New York Times* review comparing *Domebook II* with the *Whole Earth Catalog*, a reviewer singled out the metaphoric attraction adhering to both publications: "These books are metaphors too: metaphors disguised as how-to-do-it and where-to-find-it manuals. The deepest need they satisfy is the need for such metaphors: a need that's propelling across bookstore counters, by the hundred thousands, what only two years ago was the information exchange of a nearly invisible subgroup."[31]

Yet as appealing as they were as metaphors, domes, it turned out, were barely serviceable as architectural solutions, a realization which, as Kahn tells it, became increasingly unavoidable even as *Domebook II* was in the production stages. Many of the domes they had build had proven uncomfortable and un-

17. Page spread, *Pacific Domes: Domebook II*, pages 60–61

satisfying places to actually live: excessively hot in the summer and difficult to heat in the winter, domes, crisscrossed with hundreds of seams, were vastly more prone to leaks than were traditional structures. A year after *Domebook II*, Kahn published a pamphlet, "Smart but Not Wise: Further Thoughts on *Domebook II*, Plastics and Whiteman Technology," in which he summarized the impracticality of domes, blaming what he considered to be the industrialist spirit behind Fuller's initial conception. But Kahn's enthusiasm for creative improvisation in the design of domestic space led him to a new project: *Shelter*, another access catalogue overflowing with diagrams, letters, and photographs of a variety of preindustrial housing solutions from adobe huts to canvas yurts, included a supplemental section titled "Domebook III," a collection of testimonies and photographs of dome projects gone wrong, including photographs of Drop City after its abandonment (a ghost town of dilapidated domes, scrawled with psychedelic graffiti), and the domes of Pacific High School.

Included in *Domebook II* is a piece on one commune, Red Rockers, a group of eleven who built a sixty-foot dome for $2,500, sharing the structure over the winter months and departing to tepees or temporary housing when the weather was warmer. Reflecting on their experiences with the dome, a member describes the importance of architectural solutions in the self-transformation and renewal embodied by collective living: "We wanted to create a structure that didn't remind us of anything—a new kind of space in which to create new selves. We also needed a space that was large enough to house a lot of people and their trips—a space that was voluminous enough to assume different shapes as we changed and our needs changed." Yet, as the years in the dome unfolded, the collective life proved too compromising, leading them to plan smaller structures apart from the dome: "After three years of living in a heap," the author recalls, "most of us have decided that in order to keep becoming new people, to keep growing and changing, we need more privacy." [32] Adventures in the reconfiguration of social distance and the cultivation of new forms of trust would prove no match for the grind of everyday life, at least in the realm of domestic space. In the world of business where the basis of trust was, as any reader of Adam Smith can tell you, reinforced by well-established and mutually shared interests in profit, such adventures would yield far more lasting results.

BUSINESS

In 1979, Raymond Mungo set out to document the many counterculturally inspired small business experiments that had sprung up across the country in a rambling, Kerouacesque sojourn into the new hip market culture. Published as *Cosmic Profit*, a blurb on the book's jacket describes a "madcap migration from Seattle to Kennebunk, Maine, from New Orleans to Minneapolis: a rambunctious, informative, ultimately sanguine account of the dozens of ways— fifty-four to be exact—he found of 'making money without doing time.'" On an advance from his publisher Mungo spent seven weeks dropping in on countercultural businesses across the United States, including a cooperative cannery in California, Celestial Seasonings Teas in Colorado, a cooperative taxi service in Berkeley, a New Age publisher in New York, and a natural foods restaurant in Massachusetts, all of whose rewards were measured in what Mungo called "cosmic profit." For Mungo, cosmic profit represented a revitalized practice of entrepreneurial and economic livelihood, but also a mindful approach to consumption and materialism: "The rarest kind of profit, the gift of life, energy runaround . . . the sense of being restored and excited and energized, rather than drained, by a day's work." [33] Lavishing the largess of the graying hippie cornucopia, Mungo marvels at the range of new products, goods, and services available to mainstream and countercultural consumers in a varied market of grassroots collectives, small firms, storefront retailers, restaurants, and mail order businesses. Mungo writes: "The marketplace [today] is rife with products that we consumers never could have imagined a few years ago. There's big money in natural foods, natural soaps, weird footwear, metaphysical notions, new games, vaguely psychological self-help methods, quasi-Eastern religions, paramedical aids, 'communal' and 'collective' corporations, new magazines and newspapers catering to special interests that scarcely existed before, recreational equipment, arts and crafts cottage industries and many more" (xiv–xv).

From the mid-1960s on, the countermarket defined its own self-contained network of voluntary communities, stores, drop-in centers, crafts workshops, and community centers, increasingly centered around financial transactions.[34] Often mentioned as a progenitor of countercultural commerce is Magnolia Thunderpussy's flamboyant restaurant on San Francisco's Haight Street, which, in the early 1960s, began transforming meals into extravagant rituals for beatniks and other members of their Bay Area clientele. It is Paul Hawken, however, who is credited with pioneering the fusion of business and counterculture with Erewhon Trading Company, a macrobiotic food store he started in Cambridge, Massachusetts, in the mid-1960s. Always in search of rare merchandise (brown rice, miso, etc.), Hawken established local networks of correspondence with suppliers of organic produce and goods from local cooperative farms in the New England area and gradually began packaging and retailing in his own way, using hand-lettered labels in place of manufactured ones, with prices fixed to rounded figures ($5 instead of $4.99) in the interests of greater honesty with customers and suppliers. Into the 1970s Erewhon remained the frontrunner of countercultural business movement, pioneering management practices and customer-relations styles that affected business approaches worldwide. But the first measurable surge of interest in countercultural commerce came in the later part of the 1960s from other sources: small-scale stores, craftsmen, and businesses; successful communes able to produce a surplus of goods either for sale on the open market or for barter with other communes; hippies hawking handmade jewelry, clothing, and ornaments on the street or at countercultural festivals, and from networks of drug dealers and buyers.[35]

A handful of large-scale businesses would develop from this network, notably a tea company called Celestial Seasonings, launched in 1969 by an idealistic hippie named Mo Siegel. Siegel began gathering wild herbs from the foothills around Boulder, Colorado, with the aim ultimately of replacing Coca-Cola as the favored national beverage with a natural, herbal alternative. Starting small, he struggled for survival in the Boulder area, but with the addition of Red Zinger to its product line in 1972, Celestial Seasonings' prospects brightened and the company incorporated later that year. By 1974 sales topped $1 million. The company was also well known for innovations in management style and employee relations, staging daily, collective staff meals, lunchtime volleyball games, and meditation sessions. Similarly, such small ventures as Ben and Jerry's Ice Cream, started by two childhood friends in a renovated gas station in Burlington, Vermont, and Tom's of Maine soaps, founded in 1968 in rural Kennebunk, Maine, introduced a new business and management ideology in their rise from small hippie businesses to solid corporations, while launching successful products with direct countercultural identities.

Many of these businesses fostered close relationships between staff, management, and their clientele. The consensus management approach that had galvanized protest groups against the Vietnam War was used to create open, personal, and democratic businesses that avoided the rigid hierarchies of traditional business organizations and humanized the contact between retailer and consumer. Moreover, in place of the manipulative techniques of mainstream retailers, the countermarketers promoted a cooperative approach to commerce, stressing a deeper understanding of the real needs and interests of customers: customers were not merely sources of profit to be manipulated and persuaded, they were collaborators in a larger lifestyle project, to be advised by the retailer on the merits of assorted lifestyle practices and to be consulted as the ultimate users of products and techniques. For these purposes, new relations of trust were developed in a sprawling economic network of sensitized entrepreneurs. In many cities these networks were indexed in local countercultural listings, often called *People's Yellow Pages*. A regional *People's Yellow Pages* was a countercultural resource publication referencing a wide range of urban-based businesses, collectives, cooperatives, and other services and centers internal to the countercultural community, as well as institutions and resources to which others might turn for their needs. The first *People's Yellow Pages* was a Boston publication put out by Vocations for Social Change, a program of the New England regional office of the American Friends Service Committee.

Vocations for Social Change (vsc) was typical of the "information centers" that acted as gathering points for many countercultural communities, linked by a shared sense of the "service consciousness" described in chapter 2, maintaining a small storefront and an extensive library of literature and reference material on topics ranging from child care, housing, ecology, tenant organizing, and food co-ops to work and lifestyle alternatives. The storefront hosted weekly discussion groups on community and national issues: "We talk to people about work alternatives, lifestyle alternatives, educational alternatives etc.," they explained.[36] The 1973 edition of the *Boston People's Yellow Pages* lists these publications as affiliated, directly or not, with the larger VSC effort: *San Francisco People's Yellow Pages*, *Contact* (New Haven, Connecticut), *Women's Yellow Pages* (Boston), *Sunshine Brew* (Springfield, Massachusetts), *Changes* (Minnesota) *People's Yellow Pages*, *Missouri Living: A Guide to the Other St. Louis*, *People's Yellow Pages New York*, *Chinook Centrex* (Portland, Oregon), *Cascade* (Pacific Northwest), *Milwaukee Alternatives*, *Aquarian Unity Directory* and a list of other publications.

The *Boston People's Yellow Pages* was published by a team of staff and volunteers from the VSC storefront. Eight salaried members and dozens of volunteers spent months writing and telephoning individuals, organizations, and services in the Boston area for information and permission to list them in the *Pages*. The first edition was published in the spring of 1971, in a run of 5,000 copies, followed in November and again a year later in November of 1972 by larger editions of 20,000, of which 6,000 were donated to various groups and individuals. While the first issue grossed only $823.46, by the third edition the publication was grossing $6,050.00, which, together with grants and subsidies from foundations and agencies, allowed VSC to maintain its storefront drop-in center and modest library. In the course of two years, the price of the *Yellow Pages* went from 50 cents to a dollar, largely due to the increase in listings and the expansion to a larger format. In an introductory statement, the value of "information" is embellished with prose expressing the vitality and purpose of countercultural networks:

> The People's Yellow Pages is a way to provide information on the many social change efforts in the Boston area—information which is not easily available elsewhere. This information gives us a sense of the growth and strength these groups represent. But the Yellow Pages is more than just information. It is also an attempt to do other things: to organize and empower people by connecting them to those listed and to each other; to provide models for people who want to start alternative institutions; to facilitate more communication among the groups listed; and perhaps most importantly, to begin building here in Boston what we see as a cornerstone of a changed or new society—a real community. (2)

In addition to giving a "sense of the growth and strength" of the various members of the network, the mere fact of their connectedness serves as an end

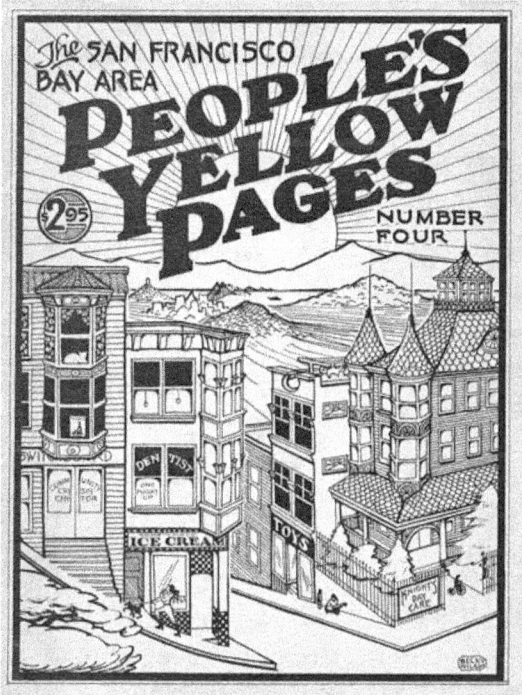

18. Cover, *San Francisco Bay Area People's Yellow Pages*, no. 4

in itself, promising personal organization and empowerment, together with the innovation of personal life and livelihood through "alternative institutions," all toward the ultimate goal of a new society. Information, it seems, was both the means and the end of a countercultural network: connectedness with other groups, who themselves provided information on groups, offered both the instruments or the "tools" through which "community" could be achieved, and the ultimate purpose of community itself.

In this sense, information about connectedness, more than a mere means of accessing commodities, is a value in itself: further into the *Boston People's Yellow Pages* we see this principle relished in listings for businesses, services, centers and other connections, all of which disavow, in their own ways, the impersonal profit motives of the mass market, assuming some alternate basis for the conducting of business interweaving trust with lifestyle counsel and advice:

> Revolutionary Rainbow Factory: A non-profit movement advertising design studio. Works solely with movement groups and attempts to get their words, ideas and/or actions to the people through visual and conceptual means. Fee is cost of materials or what you can afford. (68)

Throughout the *Yellow Pages*, we find listings of publicly funded institutions and resources—service providers in the sense already discussed—presumably not engaged in a market of any sort: the Church Society for College Work (a group devoted to exploring "experimental higher education"), the New England Committee for Non Violent Action, the Race Education Center, The East Boston Community News, Reach (a sensitivity training workshop), Community Sex Information Inc., The Community Based Welfare System: A Voluntary Alternative to Public Welfare, and a wide range of other publicly funded organizations providing community services. But where the spirit of business prevails, offerings of information, education, advice, and counsel appear alongside overt appeals of price or quality:

> The redbook: a collectively run, anti-profit bookstore . . . maintains a free book exchange program and a free "books to prisoners" program. A very nice place to spend some time! (78)

Importantly, there are, throughout the *People's Yellow Pages*, individuals offering services or goods for free, for barter or according to other forms of exchange premised less on personal profit than on reciprocity and collective betterment.

> Esther Rome: I give non-sexist body massage. Help free tensions in your muscles so more of your body energy is available to use. Price negotiable. (155)

> Joe Durland: Portraits (likes to spend enough time with the person whose portrait he is doing to capture something of the feeling that person gives him). (95)

Against the distance and duplicity of the mass market, the countermarket infused a sense of trust, concern, and involvement in the more intimate dimensions of the use of products and services.

BRIARPATCH NETWORK

Perhaps the liveliest business hub identified with the counterculture developed in the Bay Area during the 1970s, calling itself the Briarpatch Network. The *Briarpatch* business ideology began with the first issue of a subdued, glossy tabloid format magazine titled the *Briarpatch Review*, put together by Norman Gurney, a novelist whose rambling free-associative narrative, *Divine Right's*

Trip, had appeared as a running sidebar in the *Last Whole Earth Catalog*. At the same time that *Briarpatch Review* (which carried the subtitle "A Journal of Right Livelihood and Sharing Based Economics," later changed to "A Journal of Right Livelihood and Simple Living") began circulating through Bay Area networks, Michael Phillips, an influential businessman with countercultural interests, was preparing his own manuscript for what would become the countercultural business bible: *The Seven Laws of Money*.

Phillips (president of the board at the Portola institute's successor, the Point Foundation, and publisher of the *Whole Earth Catalog*) came across Norman's *Briarpatch Review* and added a promotional note at the end of his book plugging the publication. This note later generated sufficient interest among his readers to revive Gurney's effort, and the *Briarpatch Review* began publication in 1975. The second *Review* effort grew out of networks of small-business owners from the Bay Area drawn to a series of discussions and small seminars held by Point Foundation and Portola Institute staff on the ethics and opportunity of the expanding number of small businesses operating with countercultural principles in mind. In July 1974, Dick Raymond, the original Portola Institute director, and Louie Durham, organizer at San Francisco's Glide Memorial Church, put together a weekend retreat for twenty-five small-business owners to discuss their enterprises in terms of larger ethical and social issues, and the benefits of sharing resources, information, and advice in a mutually reinforcing network.[37]

Raymond dubbed the group Briarpatch, for the dwelling place of the fictional character Brer Rabbit from the popular postbellum folk stories of Uncle Remus. Just as Brer Rabbit was kept safe from predators in his thorny habitat, so Briarpatch businesses were guaranteed stable business fortunes through simple, honest, and straightforward business practices, as industrial civilization crumbled around them. Members of the Briarpatch agreed to continue meeting regularly, and to hire a coordinator, Andy Alpine (whose background was not small business but law and international business), who set about visiting and coordinating members into a cohesive business network. In the weeks following the first meeting, the Briarpatch expanded, drawing entrepreneurs and small business owners from the Bay Area to Wednesday night meetings at the Pier 40 offices of the Portola Institute for discussions with Mike Phillips, whose *Seven Laws of Money*, published by the Point Foundation's Word Wheel Press, was fast becoming the classic text on countercultural business practice and ethics.

In 1984, Phillips put together ten years of reflection and commentary on Briarpatch and other business strategies in *Transaction Based Economics*, a consideration of business that regards the pricing of goods within economic exchanges "as only one of several important components; others are service, information, quality, repair, and recourse."[38] His commentary describes the precise dimensions of the San Francisco Briarpatch membership in the late 1970s: 300 active members, another 150 associate members, and 200 former members.[39] The network included a wide range of businesses: Phillips mentions a high-fashion clothing designer, a manufacturer of massage tables, a sheep rancher, an expensive restaurant, and a circus, as well as a library, several holistic medical holistic therapists, including a Japanese acupuncturist, an Irish bar, a Mexican weaving company, an Asian theater troupe, a tea ceremony school, and an immigration lawyer.

In contrast to traditional business associations, the Briarpatch minimized formal meetings but provided workshops, parties, and an active switchboard to address the legal, informational, and technical needs of its various members. Briarpatch members with questions about their businesses were referred to each other for information and support: no permanent facilities or services are maintained beyond this simple information switchboard. Most importantly, the Briarpatch business network committed its members to maintaining open books: honesty with clients, customers, and other businesses reduced competition, built trust and, in the long term, guaranteed a deeper sense of loyalty from and a greater personal reward for everyone, even as it cut against the grain of established competitive practices for small businesses. The open-books policy encouraged businesses to maintain complete financial records in easy reach of all customers—in one case in a bound volume dangling by a rope in the bathroom. In the introduction to the *Briarpatch Book*, a compilation of the first eight issues published in 1978, Phillips lauds the openness and commitment to mutual support as a spontaneous and personal achievement of each and every member: "Our concern as Briars is the celebration of life and business. We find joy in business, and our businesses are gems radiating the excitement of our lives.... We share naturally because we love what we are doing, and we are open because our practices are honest."[40]

However, this policy also provided one of the most contentious points of disagreement in the business network, a point at which the utopian, humanist faith in cooperation ran headlong into the fundamental profit interests of the marketplace. An article titled "Open Books: Keystone of the Briarpatch Network" relates the significance of this policy to the cohesion of the network:

> One business, a natural cosmetics store, had joined the Briarpatch and was enjoying the benefits of belonging to it. Then another cosmetics store joined the network and needed information about rents and so forth. Briarpatch coordinator Andy Alpine asked the first store to share its financial records. To his shock, the proprietors refused. (Closed books is an insult within the Briarpatch.) Eventually, the first store dropped out of the network because the proprietors couldn't embrace the Briar values . . . Keeping our financial records open helps other people to start low-cost businesses where we and our friends can buy, and openness lets other people help with advice and suggestions. Sharing of information often leads also to sharing of material things such as trucks, houses and tools.[41]

Again, the word "information" is given a special meaning here: the sharing of information is a two-way process, allowing customers and competitors alike to offer suggestions and advice. Integrity, openness, and honesty are here given values that far surpass simple business ethics: in a discussion of the pricing policy for the *Briarpatch Book* (which cost $8 even), Phillips reiterates policies practiced consistently throughout the network:

> Traditionally, publishers and booksellers would recommend prices of $7.95 and $14.95 so that the books would appear to be in the cheaper $7 and $14 price ranges. Based on this kind of thinking, products sold in our culture are priced at $3.99, $6.98, etc.; so why aren't we doing it?
>
> It is important to Briars that the integrity of our lives carry over into our businesses. Following the example of Stewart Brand's *Whole Earth Catalog*, we are open and accessible in every way. The openness in business that so clearly joins us together extends to our pricing. . . . In our culture, we don't use deceptive pricing in "professional" relationships between client and supplier.[42]

For Phillips, business is revitalized as it is connected with real forms of life: it is essential for Briarpatch businesses that "the integrity of our lives carry over into our businesses." In other words, style of life is where knowledge and ethics begin, and business is only a part of that process, but a part shared with custom-

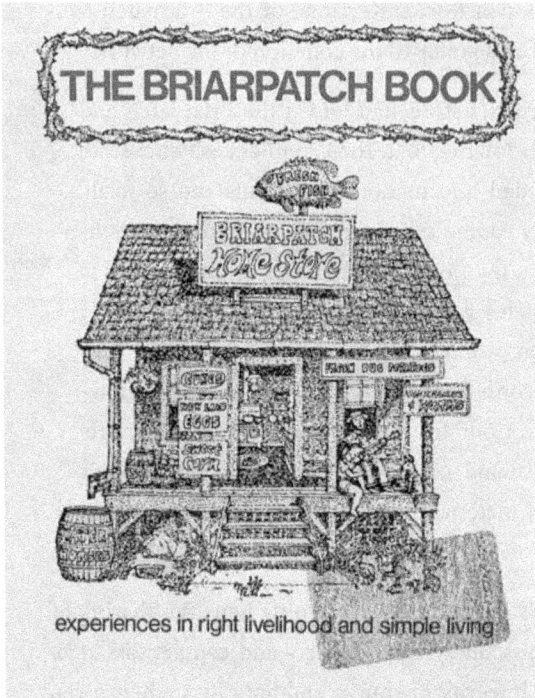

19. Cover, *Briarpatch Review*

ers who are themselves shopping for their lifestyle needs. The idea that both retailer and customer share daily life as an ethical concern redefines the commercial relationship as one built on trust between two lifestyle practitioners who share the same concerns—how to live well. And at the center of that relation of trust is a belief in the ability of the countercultural retailer to understand and speak to the deeper needs of the customer, not merely as a consumer, but as a real human being, a practitioner of a new kind of ethical livelihood. In an article titled "Demystifying Business," in the Fall 1975 issue, one author related the responsibilities held by Briar businesses toward their customers: in addition to sharing information with other businesses and with the community in general, a Briar business should feel a "concern with the people we do business with":

> A reciprocal exchange agreed upon between two people—that is, a buyer and a seller agreeing that a price is fair—is certainly a major goal. [But] in my own activities I like to go beyond this to look at the needs underlying the exchange. Why is that person really in my store? Consumption is habitual and impulsive; what people are feeling is not always directly related

to what they are buying. I like to try to find out whether the person needs the product or service I'm selling or something else entirely.[43]

The desire to understand "Why is that person really in my store?" suggests a deeper engagement with the problem of trust, and a more profound commitment to the responsibilities of a lifestyle entrepreneur as disseminator of special knowledge, than can be summarized under the production of specialist discourses. What was at stake here was a need for new forms of trust between individuals and in cultures of consumption, but also (as was the case with the marketing innovations described in chapter 2) a deeper penetration of marketing messages into the mundane significance of consumer choices in the shaping of personal identities. For several years after the demise of the counterculture, themes of honesty, understanding, and social responsibility would permeate mainstream business and management literature through sources directly traceable to the Bay Area networks, and ultimately install themselves, as we saw in our discussion of the Values and Lifestyle marketing theory, and in the mainstream of advertising and retailing vernacular.

Indeed, the evolution of a countercultural ethic of trust as a business creed is evident in the waning years of the Briarpatch network: in 1980, Stuart Brand teamed up with Paul Hawken and Michael Phillips to organize "learning expeditions," or tours of successful businesses that had, in their own ways, incorporated the principles of trust and transparency espoused by the Briarpatch. At that time the Briarpatch's roster of successful businesses was extensive: Berkeley's Buttercup Bakery (originators of "California Cuisine"); the Skin Zone (forerunner of Body Shop–style cosmetic stores), Tassajara Bakery, Ananda Village Products, and many others.[44] Out of these tours grew the Noren Institute, a Bay Area network of entrepreneurs and businesspeople, offering courses on "hands-on business learning" in various forms, which included seminars such as "Honest Consulting," "Honest Management," and "Marketing without Advertising"—a course that later developed into a highly influential marketing manifesto. Another important course-turned-book was *Running a One-Person Business*, a manual that sold nearly 70,000 copies before going out of print in 2000.[45] Graduates of the Noren Institute went on to do business consulting and to found workshops and business programs throughout the country, variously emphasizing the ethical and humanistic dimensions of business practice.

Throughout, trust was presented both as an object of organizational effort, and as a vital quality that organizations could never fully incorporate. *Market-*

ing without Advertising expressed such a faith in intimacy and interpersonal trust as a specifically extracommercial, extrainstitutional phenomenon (a point we have described first in the evolving service sector, and later in a countercultural business philosophy), yet something that could be molded into a durable business concept: social networks and word-of-mouth reputation building, it is argued, are ultimately more effective in consolidating trust in customers than advertising in an anonymous mass media.[46] Similar advice was offered on the managerial side in a book derived from the Noren workshops called *Honest Business*, authored by Phillips and Salli Rasberry and published by Shambhala Pocket Editions.[47] Here the authors describe the advantages of opening what they consider additional channels of communication in the managerial process, encouraging feedback from suppliers, customers, and a wide range of employees who are normally excluded from the management process: "When contemporary management as it is practiced in our culture is combined with the structural commitment to openness, the result is innovative business forms, extra channels of valuable information, and more effective management" (110). And one of the rewards of this structural openness, Phillips and Rasberry contend, is a transformed professional culture: an environment in which higher levels of solidarity and cooperation are assured in an environment of acceptance, empathy, and play. In a passage reminiscent of the dot-com management styles of the 1990s, the authors point out the importance of fun in the professional context. They describe a manager at Bank of America who conducted what he called Mickey Mouse Days—company parties held irregularly, signaled by the appearance of a Mickey Mouse doll on the manager's desk: "Fun is a spontaneous part of any business when the owners and managers love what they are doing and the books are open. Fun is natural where friends and relatives participate, and where the business understands its role in the community it serves" (125).

Perhaps the most recognizable trace of this legacy is apparent in the methods of such leading lifestyle brands as the Body Shop. What is now a major innovator in the cosmetics field was founded in Brighton, England, in the spring of 1976 by Anita Roddick, then an aspiring hippie entrepreneur peddling her own herbal and all-natural soaps and cosmetics in small, recyclable bottles to an increasingly receptive market. From the outset, Roddick preferred a more direct and unmediated contact with her customers. When she had only one store, she drew customers to her door not through traditional advertising but by trailing perfume down the sidewalk to lure in curious pedestrians.[48] Strictly renouncing exaggerated claims for beautification and glamour, her products asserted only the value of a distinct form of natural care directed toward the body and the self: in the form of a lettuce-and-avocado face mask, a coconut-milk moisturizer or a peppermint foot lotion, Body Shop products have always asserted a uniquely natural style of personal hygiene stemming from their use of nonindustrial products gathered from remote parts of the world from indigenous producers, under labor conditions that are humane and comparable with Western standards.

Roddick's rise to success is legendary: a year after her first store opened, more Body Shops were opened in England, followed a year later by yet more in Sweden and Greece, and by 1984 the Body Shop was a publicly traded company with a massive global presence. Throughout, Roddick's business style remained resoundingly countercultural: interviews for positions and franchise rights would consist of questions such as "What is your favorite flower?" or "How would you like to die?"[49] Body Shops would double as centers for advocacy and protest, with posters and displays supporting Greenpeace, AIDS research, and environmental activism. Its unique blend of social causes, a deft business sense, and a range of products that seemed to resonate with authenticity and naturalism encoded a new version of corporate responsibility that expressed a distinctly countercultural spirit for transparency, trust, and honesty in retail strategy.[50] Indeed, what truly distinguished the Body Shop was the retail experience itself, which was, in a word, intimate. Practicing a distinctly toned-down sales style, the Body Shop abjured the hustle and bustle of the department store, allowing customers to test lotions, soaps, shampoos, and perfumes themselves, and to read carefully placed cards explaining ingredients, origins, and precise function of all products. "People come in just to play," Michael Waldock, a company president, said in 1989.[51]

While such management and marketing gimmicks as Mickey Mouse Days and lettuce-and-avocado face masks might seem a far cry from the lofty rhetoric of "love" that floated across the airwaves that day in 1967, there is nonetheless a genealogy to be traced from the business and marketing practices of the present to the countercultural circles of three decades earlier. Indeed, the rhetoric of love itself would suffer a harsh rejection even at the hands of the counterculture's most prestigious figures. In an interview with the *Christian Science Monitor*, Stewart Brand would heap criticism on a legacy he was undoubtedly partially responsible for promoting: "I never did buy this shallow, phony love propaganda of the 1960s—you know, the hippie hug and soulful eye-to-eye contact. It became just as suspect as what it replaced. The honesty that replaced courtesy was not honesty but self-preoccupation. People would self-broadcast their mood, whether you cared to listen or not."[52]

But the spirit of love and the caring ethic it inspired, in however modified a form, would have a secret life in the many high-flying lifestyle brands and outlets that emerged in the 1990s, notably Nike, the Body Shop, Benetton, Starbucks, and several other companies where employees would be redubbed "associates," forced to wear pins that read "Hello, my name is . . . ," and taken on company retreats where they would be induced into various team building exercises, or where customers would be subjected to verbose assertions of the heartfelt concern and care of retail staff, typified by the mechanical consolation: "Your call is very important to us." These developments, it can be argued, are directly or indirectly influenced by the new management and marketing philosophies espoused by Phillips, Brand, Hawken, and others, and ultimately by a vast cultural experiment with intimacy and openness, where a looser attitude toward the other was thought to supply greater resources of personal trust between managers, employees, clients, salespeople, and customers. Moreover, it was with regard to one seminal feature of lifestyle, that of the cultivation of the body, that the injunction to loosen oneself was most readily translated into injunctions to spend money on highly varied and uniquely nuanced goods and services.

6

Letting It All Hang Out
From Mind to Muscle in the Relaxed Body

If economies of production ask us to discipline ourselves for the work regimes of a Fordist society, economies of consumption ask us to express ourselves in the phantasmagorical consumer markets that define the post-Fordist cultural order. This transition, deeply felt by the American middle classes in the early 1970s, enabled a new lifestyle culture in which the individual's relationship to both natural and human environments was developed as an object of creative manipulation and supervised care. One became looser, or more expressive, as one learned to release oneself into the domain of nature where foods were purer and one felt oneself to be part of a larger terrestrial and cosmic totality, or in social life where one dropped egoistic pretensions and shared feelings honestly and authentically. But there were other realms of self-loosening and other objects of care that defined the expressiveness of the new lifestyles: alongside the natural and social worlds, the body stood out as a thing one had to learn to relax oneself into. Indeed, the manner in which the body was experienced was quite distinct: where the Fordist compact described in chapter 1 demanded the production of "docile" bodies, smiling organization men happy in their modest functions as appendages of large, remotely administered bureaucratic machines, the culture of post-Fordism demanded the insurrectionary body of the swinger, living in the immediacy of his consumer choices, an endlessly original, personal, and expressive body of insatiable needs and manifold sensualities. The "squaring" of the body as both a functional instrument of the military-industrial complex and an other-directed symbol of a conformist, status-driven affluence was countered by the forcible and very mediated "grooving" of the body as an organ erupting with feeling, endlessly seeking opportunities to experience itself and the world afresh by overflowing the strictures imposed by the old order. The grooved body burst through the protocols of professional demeanor and shattered the abstract time of work with sensual and corporeal rhythms—opening its collar and oversleeping its alarms, growing its hair, smoking marijuana on its breaks and giggling through the day, then impulsively fleeing the city for vigorous weekends of climbing and camping. But the insurrectionary body was also a loose body: one whose sensations and capacities could be realized only by the withdrawal of the censoring functions imposed by the intellect on the body's own free flow of impulse and feeling. Against the world of work, the loosening of the body involved the deinstrumentalizing of all of its functions: in a variety of fields from sports to therapy, goals and purposes were replaced by feelings and experiences.

The grooving of the body was, in this way, a care of the body. It told the story of one's own loosening in an ethical discourse with others in which the body was treated as the source of a fundamental and irreducibly authentic self—a deep body, set against the calculative instrumentality of work, but also the shallow cosmetic body composed only of affected appearances and phony put-ons. The deep body was one whose radiance was distorted and obscured under the domination of the calculating intellect and middle class concerns with artifice and the maintenance of appearances. Such a body was an object into which one could learn to loosen oneself by relaxing the mind's tyrannical hold and accepting oneself as one truly was. By touching, massaging, exercising and working on the body, regimes of mental calculation and artifice could be relaxed and the body's authenticity could be allowed to spill out into everyday life. To be deep, in this sense, was to reclaim a wholeness of identity. It was to let oneself go into a more real and integrated mode of embodiment, to be whole, to loosen the mind into the body, to let oneself be and feel oneself in a more truthful, embodied state. For this purpose, bodywork specialists drew from a range of Eastern mystical and Western scientific sources as they advised on the reinvention of such mundane functions as breathing, standing, walking and other practices of bodily composure. By the late 1970s, a lucrative publishing bonanza had taken shape around this project, replete with titles from a variety of inventive, often uncredentialed lifestyle entrepreneurs. Books with a specifically countercultural origin include Mike Samuels and Hal Bennett's *Well Body Book*; *Our Bodies, Ourselves*; *Getting Clear*; *The Gathering Book*, a collection of articles and materials taken from annual gatherings of the Antakharana Circle in northeastern Washington; and *Spiritual Midwifery*, from the Farm's Book Publishing Company. Moreover, by the early 1980s, these themes had been reincorporated in the mainstream cultures of consumption in commercially viable discourses of somatic well-being evidenced in a new culture of athletic recreation and sporting goods, and later yoga, toiletry products, attire, food, and tourism. Getting in touch with one's body would become a characteristic aim of lifestyle consumption promulgated by some of the most influential lifestyle brands. An account of the ways in which the deep, whole body became an object of self-loosening begins with the counterculture and its emphasis on the insurrectionary body, conceived as a uniquely extrainstitutional realm of identity.

Retention and Release in the Whole Body

On the morning of January 29, 1968, Dr. Luther H. Howard, principal of the Brien McMahon High School in an upper-middle-class district of Norwalk, Connecticut, conducted a surprise classroom-to-classroom inspection of his school. He was looking at hair—specifically, at the hair of the teenage males, which had been growing longer by the season, occasionally becoming "bushy around the side," and posing a hazard, it was believed, to the boys' education and to that of others. By the morning's end, Howard had sent fifty-three boys home with letters to their parents detailing their offenses, conveying the administration's hope that parents would "impress upon your son the importance of living in a society of rules and regulations."[1]

The principal was acting on a dress code adopted by the board of education in 1964 banning blue jeans, sweatshirts and heavy boots, as well as "hair fashions and styles which are excessive and detract from a healthy atmosphere conducive to good educational practices." For the most part, the students were compliant: of the original group, most of the boys simply got haircuts and resumed classes. But others dug in, and the next day a dozen angry parents complained at a local board of education meeting that the purge was arbitrary and irrelevant to the overall objectives of education. Protesting students manned a picket line in front of the school bearing signs reading BEETHOVEN IN A CREW CUT? and IT'S NOT THE HAIR ON TOP BUT THE MIND UNDERNEATH.

One parent complained: "Jesus Christ had long hair," while a group of parents met with the local chapter of the American Civil Liberties Union, who brought the students' case to the Court of Common Pleas in Bridgeport, Connecticut.[2]

Though the judge would ultimately refuse to grant an injunction against the school, the Brien McMahon incident is illustrative of a general trend that raged across the country, and of the mix of anxiety and high moral seriousness that greeted new fashions and styles for young people. Hair stood as one of the most incendiary symbols of the new personalist challenge to the gray facade of institutional protocol—a symbol that related a narrative of personal loosening and an acceptance of one's identity as an expression of not just intellectual but physical and bodily processes. The treatment of hair stood as an allegorical figure of a more general treatment of oneself: hair, it was argued, should be let down, allowed to flow, granted its freedom and space to be itself. Letting one's hair grow related a story of letting oneself grow, of becoming more real and allowing oneself to realize one's organic, natural, and authentic tendency toward unfettered growth, to "blow in the breeze and get caught in the trees," as celebrated in the signature tune from the Broadway musical *Hair*, infusing the injunction to relax into everyday encounters and mundane spaces. Wearing long hair was to let one's "freak flag fly," as David Crosby sang in his inimitable ode to hippie hairstyles, "Almost Cut My Hair," but it was also to affirm one's confluence with natural, deeply physical processes that enveloped and permeated social and institutional life—processes embedded in the body itself.

Hair was not the only metaphor for the body's new insurrectionary presence in daily life: under the aegis of a new culture of openness, fashions grew ever sexier, more colorful, and flamboyant, making protocol for professional attire increasingly difficult to regulate. In 1975, an article on changing dress codes in the workplace described attire that would have seemed unthinkable a decade earlier: bank presidents wearing turtlenecks, medallions, double-breasted sports jackets, and flared pants; office workers in leisure suits with safari jackets, long hair, and beards. "In recent years, Americans have experienced what the more exuberant clothing writers call 'an awakening of fashion consciousness.' Which meant that people are dressing more stylishly if not outlandishly these days. 'It was inevitable,' " said a fashion editor quoted in the article. " 'People are into expressing themselves as individuals with what they wear and how they look. And for many work is the time of day when they are most concerned with their personal image.' "[3]

As any glance at a high school yearbook or company staff portrait from the period attests, looser modes of self-presentation affected a range of organizations from schools to corporate offices to police precincts. But at first, many office settings stood firm against these small but potent challenges to the hegemony of abstract labor in daily appearance. A survey of attitudes toward professional fashion in 1968 revealed that while 52 percent said miniskirts were permissible (if they were no more than two or three inches above the knee), only 25 percent approved of boots for women. Seventy-three percent disapproved of excessive makeup, and 34 percent disapproved of colorful, excessive, or exotic hosiery. A full 95 percent were against long hair for men, or other "Beatles"-like affects (with the fields of electronics, science, and education registering more lenient beliefs), and 77 percent were opposed to turtleneck shirts, in contrast to the conventional shirt and tie. Seventy-four percent were against beards.[4] These incursions provoked a series of legal spats in which dress codes, largely implicit and rarely invoked in any literal sense, were dredged up from obscure passages of professional handbooks and manuals, or in some cases hastily fabricated from scratch. But as these fetters were burst and transgressions that had seemed insurrectionary in the 1960s were absorbed into the looser dress codes of the 1970s, tensions subsided and a wider margin of expressivity was deemed acceptable. A separate study completed seven years after the Brien McMahon case noted changes in office culture: "Personnel directors say the liberal policies have robbed the rebels, who were very active in the late 1960s and early 1970s, of most of their causes. Pant suits, beards and long hair, which were the big bones of contention, were almost universally accepted today," so long as they were trim and neat.[5]

Yet if the body was treated as an object of self-loosening, the cultivation of its vitality and subversive force was part of a broader discourse on everyday life, rife with implications of subjective depth and the renewal of a core identity against the debasing encroachments of a rationalized culture of work, and a cosmeticized culture of consumption. Within the lifestyle print culture, the body was addressed by a range of authors and in a variety of domains, from New Age therapies to exercise and fitness to health, diet, and recreation—everyday realms sharing a general injunction and a broad ethical imperative: that the body was the foundation of psychic well-being, a vessel of personal meaning heretofore suppressed and unjustly restrained. The mind and the body remained tragically divorced under the regimes of modern work, consumption, and everyday life, and the overcoming of such a rending of the whole self into (sensual) body and (abstract) mind promised delivery from deep personal, spiritual, and social pathologies. The recovery of the body was related through a holistic appeal to a dissolution of this tragic rending. Countercultural body therapy was directed at emotional and spiritual bottlenecks and tangles lodged in the substance of the body itself—muscles, skin, tendons, bones, hair—often read as the locus of emotional stress, neurosis, anxiety, and hang-ups. The deepening of the body involved acknowledging the emotional content of muscle fiber, bone structure, and physical composure, treatable through exercises and programs addressed to a deeper, more profound therapeutic object—a cluster of specifically body-oriented instructional writings that can be grouped together under the broader headings of well-being, wellness, alternative medicine, or bodywork. Moreover, appeals to the deep body assumed a critique of the cold distance taken by traditional medical experts manifested in a grassroots print culture expounding the authority of experience over formal training. This tendency was pioneered in the late 1960s by a group of women in Boston who together compiled the groundbreaking collection *Our Bodies, Ourselves*.

In the spring of 1969, a group of women attending the "Women and Their Bodies" seminar at Boston's Emmanuel College recounted their largely negative encounters with doctors they found "condescending, judgmental, paternalistic and non-informative."[6] Calling their circle "The Doctor's Group," they decided to undertake a summer project: to gather as wide a range of information as possible on fundamental medical and physiological issues relevant to women, to write papers on this topic, and to reconvene for a collective course on women and the care of women's bodies the following year. The goal was to circumvent the authority of traditional medical discourse by combining first-hand testimonials and interviews with resources and medical information on a range of women's health issues.

The group met several times that summer to compile facts on a variety of issues that would form the basis of a short educational workshop and later a compendium of commentary and resources on women's health issues recounted from a deeply personal angle. Throughout, the methodology of their data collection defied the staid objectivism of traditional science, digging deeper into the personal substrate that defined their unique physical and sexual experiences: "The process of talking was as crucial as the facts themselves," the authors recall. "Over time the facts and feelings melted together in ways that

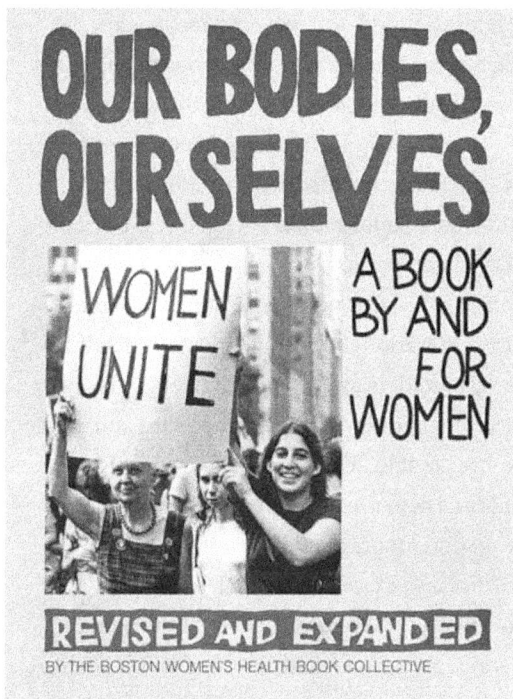

20. Cover, *Our Bodies, Ourselves*, edited by the Boston Women's Health Book Collective

touched us very deeply, and that is reflected in the changing titles of the course and then the book—from *Women and Their Bodies* to *Women and Our Bodies* to, finally, *Our Bodies, Ourselves*."[7]

Papers from these sessions were mimeographed and bound, then ultimately printed and published by the New England Free Press as *Women and Their Bodies*, a 138-page pamphlet that sold for thirty cents. The pamphlet quickly sold 250,000 copies, prompting the group to form the nonprofit Boston Women's Health Book Collective and to expand their research into what would become *Our Bodies, Ourselves*, a 276-page collection of medical advice and commentary that expanded from the earlier pamphlet's focus on sexuality and reproductive issues to include articles on aging, childbirth, nutrition, and relationships. *Our Bodies, Ourselves* became one of the best-selling books on women's health and one of the most notable publishing successes with roots in the counterculture. Published by Simon and Schuster, *Our Bodies, Ourselves* sold over 1 million copies by 1977 and inspired a genre of women's health books that included *Women's Bodies: An Owner's Manual* and *From Woman to Woman*.

Our Bodies, Ourselves is important for a variety of reasons having to do with the significance of second-wave feminism and the women's movement, but what is relevant here is the manner in which this volume set out to shape a discourse on the body that was specifically opposed to that of the traditional medical establishment. The body was primarily the realm of experiences unknowable to the distanced gaze of the traditional medical practitioner, though these same experiences held out the potential for radical personal renewal and self-knowledge. In the introductory statement to the 1973 edition, the group identifies the potential bound up in a renewed sense of embodiment as one of unconstraint and experiential release, but also of a consolidation of oneself in firmer, more "whole" sense. "Learning to understand, accept, and be responsible for our physical selves, we are freed of some of these preoccupations and can start to use our untapped energies," we are told. "Our image of ourselves is on a firmer base, we can be better friends and better lovers, better people, more self-confident, more autonomous, stronger, and more whole."[8]

In a number of fields, from athletics and exercise to sexuality, massage, and yoga, an experiential discourse on the body as an object of cultivation and care would supplant older, stodgier discourses on health and fitness. While the movement toward a democratization of health care and specifically a feminist discourse on health addressed well-being in terms of areas such as sexual reproduction, another, more inclusive discourse undertook a holistic approach to the maintenance of health in daily life.

BODYWORK

In 1977, Cris Popenoe set out to survey a range of publications relevant to the health and wellness field in an inclusive and critical guidebook. During her tenure as manager of the Yes! Bookshop in Washington, D.C. (at the time the largest source for books on holistic healing in the United States, selling more than 12,000 titles in alternative health and well-being), Popenoe published two compendiums of book reviews meant to map out the sprawling publishing category that defined the new discourse on health, variously termed New Age healing, wellness, human potential, and the growth movement. In 1976 she published *Books for Inner Development*, and the next year *Wellness: The Yes! Bookshop Guide*, under the seal of her own Yes! Books, though both titles were picked up and distributed by Random House at a price of $4.95. "I wanted to provide enough information so people could decide for themselves whether to buy a specific book," Popenoe said of her reasons for compiling the 1,500

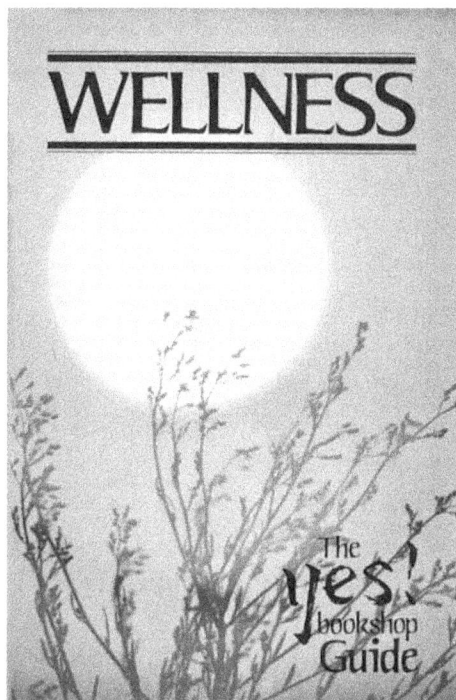

21. Cover, *Wellness: The Yes! Bookshop Guide*, by Cris Popenoe

reviews. "Wellness . . . is the result of a growing mistrust of the medical estab-lishment. As the revolt grows, people begin to look for alternatives and begin to realize that they can do more and more for themselves."[9] *Wellness* is far-reaching and inclusive, with sections covering such categories as color and aura, death, nutrition (with separate listings for raw foods, vegetarianism, and natural beauty), organic gardening, life energies (with sections on Wilhelm Reich and Nicola Tesla), and healing (including fasting, cancer, and arthritis). Popenoe begins a lengthy section of the *Wellness* guide devoted to bodywork with an excerpt from the *East-West Exercise Book* by David Smith, which establishes some of the fundamental axioms of advice literature in this publishing cate-gory. " 'A healthy body moves free and easy' begins Smith, 'It is unencumbered by aches and pains, the dead weight of sluggish organs and tensed muscles. It is light and ready to move, from the moment it opens early to the day, until its comfortable folding down for the night. Perfect health is the birthright of every body. The unity of the healthy body and its parts and functions all cooperate for the achievement of the maintenance and perfections of life.' "[10]

"Sluggish organs and tensed muscles," in this account, suppress an experience of lightness and ease, a readiness to "move" that is the result of a properly harmonized and integrated body. The body becomes the nexus of the constraining imperatives of civilization and the impulsive innocence of precivilizational vitality. As in so much countercultural discourse, natural origins are the wellspring of all life, and the bodies of babies play significantly in Smith's view of bodywork: "The type of exhilaration that emanates from a baby should be the native state of a healthy body, regardless of age. Adult good health is a sophisticated version of an infant's agility, charm, and even muscular strength." Yet grafted onto our original bodily dispositions is the anxiety and tension of modern social life, whose emotional toll is made familiar to us through that handy psycho-therapeutic moniker, "stress."

Popenoe writes, "The unhealthy body frequently reacts improperly to stress, a stimulus to the emotions that provokes the body to react. Failure to release the body responses generated by stress can cause inhibition—centers of tension resulting in colitis, high blood pressure, nervousness, headaches, ulcers, heart disease, emotional insecurity, and many other ills. When stress is internalized and not transformed into a form of action or productivity/creativity, the energy flow shuts down. Stress, having no outlet, begins to prey on the body" (18). The body, in short, as one with the same unifying framework that constructs mental and psychological dynamics, is read as the locus of these mental states. Anxieties and fears are woven into the fabrics of muscles and ligaments and can be treated through the manipulation of these muscles and through the shaping of physical composure in daily life, which work toward the restoration of a deeper logic of mental and bodily unity. The section on bodywork goes on to describe several themes that variously illustrate these general principles. Aikido is introduced as "literally the road (do) to a union (ai) with the real substance of the universe (ki). The practice of aikido aims at the refinement of our ki and its harmonious union with the ki of the universe" (20). Titles such as *Aikido in Daily Life* are lauded for their advice on "how to breathe properly, and how to concentrate one's spirit" (21). Books on the Alexander Technique are premised on the belief that "incorrect alignment of the head, neck and shoulders (which is unconscious and almost universal in modern man by the age of eleven) sets off imbalances which throw the whole muscular system askew" (23). Books on dance and movement include Howard Blanche's *Dance of the Self*, which "opens by reawakening the sense to the concept of man as a primal being composed of earth, fire, water and air, and it reorients the body in space as a completely interrelated network of energy lines and centers of force" (30), and Moshe Felden-krais's *Awareness through Movement*, which "teaches practical exercises for posture, eyes, and imagination which enable individuals to build better body habits and invoke new dimensions of awareness and self-consciousness" (33).

A section on bioenergetics is introduced by its belief in "the functional identity of the mind and body," which is disturbed when psychological strains become structured into the muscular system itself. "When this happens, they cannot be resolved until the tensions are released. To release these muscular tensions one must feel them as limitation of self-expression. It is not enough to be aware of their pain. And most people are not even aware of that. When a muscular tension becomes chronic, it is removed from consciousness, and one loses an awareness of the tension" (24). Indeed, bioenergetics, drawing freely from Freudian psychology and Eastern mysticism, insists on the possibility of affecting the alleviation of psychic stress through the restoration of a mind-body structuring logic. Books like Stanley Keleman's *Your Body Speaks Its Mind* argues that "we do not have our bodies, we are our bodies" (25), while founder of bioenergetics Alexander Lowen's book *Pleasure* argues that "the struggle for power competes with the striving for pleasure, undermines creativity and causes muscular tensions" (27). Indeed, bioenergetics provides an analysis of the body as a condensed set of metaphors for repression and release: in the introduction to Lowen's classic work *Bioenergetics*, the author describes his close work with Wilhelm Reich, and the attention Reich paid to repression manifested in the body, and in particular, in the jaw: "In most people the jaw muscles are extremely tense—the jaw held tightly in an attitude of determination often verging on grimness or thrust forward defiantly or abnormally retracted. Under pressure jaw muscles become tired and 'let go.' As a result, the breathing becomes freer and deeper, and often involuntary tremors occur in the body and the legs."[11] This "letting go" of the jaw is typical of the broader approach to the treatment of the body as a site of suppression and relaxation. Other entries in the wellness section on bodywork include titles on yoga, tai chi chuan, dance, karate, and massage, which, in their own way, reflect the same technical logic of learned release.

In the early 1970s Anne Kent Rush was an influential figure in the Bay Area publishing scene: writer, body therapist, and socialite in the Bay Area Growth Movement, she conducted workshops at the Esalen Institute in Big Sur and at the Gestalt Institute in San Francisco. She would go on to write one of the most

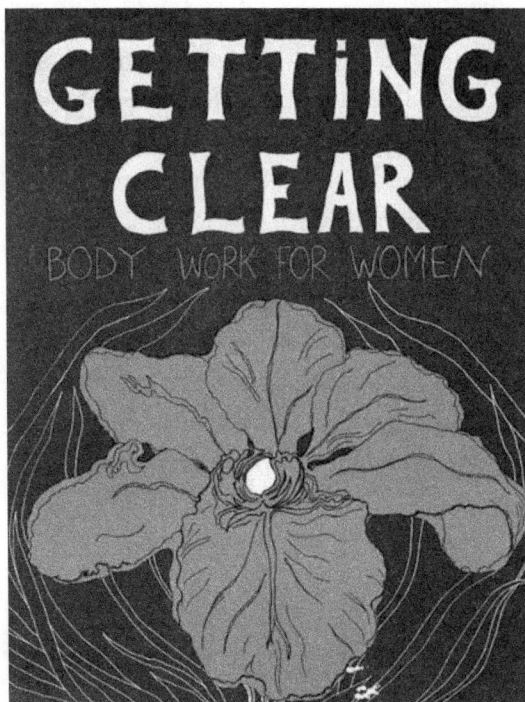

22. Cover, *Getting Clear: Body Work for Women,* by Anne Kent Rush. Copyright 1973, Random House, Inc. Reprinted by permission of Random House, Inc.

influential bodywork manuals of the counterculture, *Getting Clear: Body Work for Women.* She traces her interests in bodywork to her experiences as a twenty-one-year-old college student in Boston, "sitting in a chair feeling out of shape and tired." Rush recalls, "I began to let myself go into the way my body felt: flabby, numb, hungry, tired," though this changed with her discovery of yoga, after which she developed a greater sense of the integrity of her body as a total form, declaring: "I felt whole!"[12] Quitting her job in the East Coast publishing world, she arrived in the Bay Area in 1969, where she continued her interest in bodywork at the Free University in Berkeley. She began training in massage with an Esalen instructor in San Francisco and later taught the Esalen massage technique, emerging as one of the key practitioners of "polarity therapy" in the Bay Area scene, a technique fashioned on Chinese acupuncture aimed at releasing emotional and physical tension in the body, which she combined with her training as a Reichian therapist.

In 1972 Rush illustrated *The Massage Book* by Esalen instructor George Downing, published in 1972 by Bookworks—a title that was to reach over 2 million sales in the next decade. On the success of this project, in May of that year she began work on a collection of bodywork therapies and techniques with a feminist slant: *Getting Clear* was also completed for Bookworks in January 1973. Gathered from dozens of interviews with female bodywork practitioners and therapists of different stripes, *Getting Clear* comprised 290 pages of material on every aspect of bodywork practice. The collection inventories techniques and methods meant to cultivate a sense of wholeness within the body, to mend a gap instituted within Western cultural traditions between mind and body, and to release sensations, experiences, and potentials that were necessarily suppressed in this unfortunate divorce of mind and flesh. "What I feel and the work I do are based on the premise that mind and body are one," Rush writes. "When I use the word 'body' in this book, I am always referring to the whole person, including mental functions" (11). The collection begins with an autobiographical section, "Starting with Yourself," a collection of "physical and mental self–awareness experiments" that span topics from "Reclaiming your Genitals" to "Pain," "Food Awareness," and "Centering, Breathing and Bellypower." Other sections include "Women with Women," with items on "Closeness and Competition," and "Touching and Talking," "Women with Men," "Men and This Book," and "Back to Yourself." Throughout *Getting Clear*, exercises are provided to illustrate more general ideas and to provide direct ways of implementing ideas in practical techniques. One exercise called "Squeeze and Relax" instructs the reader to undertake a series of exercises on specific muscle groups:

> Squeeze and hold the area, then relax it . . . tense, then relax the muscles of your scalp and forehead . . . Tense, and relax the muscles around your eyes. Tense and relax your neck . . . Tighten the muscles of your thighs— and relax . . . When you reach your toes and have relaxed the muscles of your feet, tense all the muscles in your body and constrict yourself with all your effort. Intensify whatever position your body pulls into, and be aware if it seems to express some emotion. Now release the tension and relax your whole body.
>
> Let every muscle relax. Imagine your breathing can relax your muscles more and more with each exhalation, as though the tension could flow out of your body with your breath. Let your whole body sink more and more into the carpet. Let the floor support your weight. Think of the floorboards under you which are holding your weight. And think of the structure which holds up that floor, which is finally connected with the earth below. After you have gone through these steps you will be very relaxed. (20–21)

The relaxation of nerves and muscle tissue here acquires a powerful meta-phoric quality: more than a physical state, it is a reflection of a transformed mental condition in which the censoring functions of the mind are themselves made the object of relaxation. A recovered unity of the whole body allows such broad programs of treatment whereby the body itself is read as a symbol and expression of a deeper moment of the self. A careful investigation of two tech-niques of bodywork that developed from the hub of countercultural experi-mentation with body therapies—Rolfing and massage, both developed at the Esalen Institute in Big Sur, California—reveal both this principle in action as it is applied to the body itself, and the shaping of a discourse on bodywork that circulated through a countercultural lifestyle print culture.

Techniques of Uncontrol: Massage

A vibrant center for the consciousness movement of the 1970s was the Esalen Institute in Big Sur, California, an experimental think tank for the cutting edge of the lifestyle vanguard.[13] Founded in 1962 to investigate what Aldous Huxley termed "human potential," the Esalen Institute became the epicenter for experi-ments in Gestalt psychology, massage, sensory awareness, meditation, bioener-getics, Rolfing, the Alexander Technique and other body therapies loosely com-bining Eastern mysticism with Western psychology and medicine. The Esalen Institute rode a wave of interest in human potential and personal growth, whose most media-savvy product was the encounter group, a supervised session undertaken with a group of strangers whose numbers might range from half a dozen to hundreds. Encounter sessions (whose manifestations ranged from T groups, or small group sessions, to sensitivity training, sensory awareness, psychodrama, Gestalt therapy, and dozens of other variations) were broadly aimed at the removal of hang-ups and inhibitions, blockages to the sponta-neous flow of interaction with others that cramped individuals in the routine patterns of everyday social life, for which bodily contact provided an important tool. "I wanted to learn new ways of meeting people," said one thirty-year-old teacher after his visit to an encounter group. "I want to break out of the rut I'm in—relating to people on only a certain level, seeking out the safe ones and as-suming the others are dangerous."[14] Hang-ups, in this case, were described in terms of the closing of distances between others and of developing new levels of intimacy and trust—an achievement that was bound to render new depths of self-understanding: "I want to get more in touch with myself, to free myself of certain hang-ups. At least I want to learn to control them."[15]

Esalen's influence both as a publishing engine and as a hub for experimental techniques and pedagogies was immense, not only in the United States but on a global scale. When in 1970 an entourage from Esalen traveled to England to conduct two large Saturday afternoon encounter sessions, cofounder and director Michael Murphy had reservations: "We were worried that we'd meet a stiff-upper-lip, uptight reception here," Murphy recalled. But as he stood in the lavish purple carpeted ballroom of London's Inn-on-the-Park directing crowds of barefoot hippies, housewives, secretaries, and American expatriates in the various exercises of touching and embracing, sitting in small groups to share first impressions, and the asking of "What are you feeling?," Murphy was delighted by the warmth and enthusiasm of the group. "People are so out of touch with their feelings . . . this longing for a great closeness, an openness, an honesty with other people, is universal, I guess, and not just limited to the United States."[16]

Esalen was a magnet for teachers and students in these and other fields, producing several books on human potential philosophies and practices under various publishing and distribution arrangements, among them George Brown's *Human Teaching for Human Learning*, Michael Murphy's *Golf in the Kingdom*, Abraham Maslow's *Farther Reaches of Human Nature*, published in 1971, and Robert Ornstein's *Psychology of Consciousness*, published in 1973. Two books with roots in the Esalen circle offer a view of the specific techniques applied to the body as a site of loosening.

Rolfing

Ida Rolf was an unlikely candidate for countercultural celebrity: graduating with a PhD in biological chemistry from Columbia University in 1920, she was resolute in her scientific and medical orthodoxy and only marginally engaged with spirituality, psychoanalysis, or any of the varieties of mysticism that attracted many young people in the 1960s and 1970s. But her determination to treat what she considered common bodily ailments and her willingness to seek inspiration from unlikely sources led her to experiment with the then quite marginal techniques of yoga, osteopathy, and chiropractic treatment. Throughout the 1930s and 1940s, through her private Manhattan practice, Rolf evolved therapies for chronically disabled patients that developed from her early studies of osteopathy, shifting the field's traditional emphasis from the manipulation of bone structure in the correction of posture, spine curvature, and other structural problems, to that of the intense manipulation of muscle tissue. The technique she termed "structural integration," hard-tissue manipulation designed

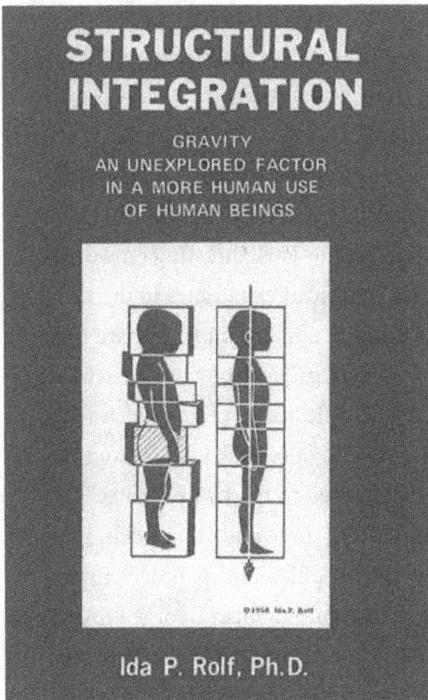

STRUCTURAL
INTEGRATION

GRAVITY
AN UNEXPLORED FACTOR
IN A MORE HUMAN USE
OF HUMAN BEINGS

Ida P. Rolf, Ph.D.

23. Diagram, *Structural Integration*, by Ida P. Rolf, 24

to restore balance, equilibrium, and a natural structural integrity to the body, would earn her international repute.

When in 1965 Rolf was invited to Esalen for a series of didactic workshops, the term "Rolfing" was coined for her approach. Rolfing focuses on fascia, the sheet-like wrapping material that envelops all human organs and muscles. Through deep and intensive massage, Rolfing loosens, stretches, and restores the fascia to its proper flexibility, allowing muscles to relax and to discharge the tensions and contortions they naturally accumulate in the course of daily stress, emotional suppression, and anxiety. Rolf's studies revealed that under the conditions of modern life, fascia hardens into tough, inflexible bands that contort the shape of muscles and tendons, ultimately deforming the skeletal structure itself. The talent of a Rolfer is in stretching and relaxing the fascia, allowing the lengthening of the muscle tissue and the restoration of the body to its original center of gravity—a natural, integrated posture and structure in which all the parts of the body find proper alignment in their correct orientation.

Rolf used the term *balance* in a way that blends the physical and emotional associations of the term: to properly align one's body was to reconcile an overall, encompassing pattern of order and symmetry into a balanced physical disposition, yielding a personally balanced outlook and sense of self. Alignment in this sense goes beyond the spinal emphasis of traditional chiropractics to include the ankles, arms, thorax, head, and pelvis—a holistic approach to the entire body. Most importantly, a well-integrated structure would enable the body to withstand the pull of gravity, a pronounced theme in her work. Gravity pulls the human form out of alignment, producing a range of maladies from physical pain and lack of feeling to a broader emotional and psychological weakening: "Since it is not possible to express a free flow through the physical flesh, the subjective emotional tone becomes progressively more limited and tends to remain in a restricted and closely defined area. Now, what the individual feels is no longer an emotion, a single response to an immediate situation; henceforth he lives, moves and has his being in an attitude."[17]

For the integrated, adjusted individual, whose composure sets him at a perfect right angle to the pull of gravity, physical freedoms are translated into states of mental well-being: "An integrated man might be defined as a person capable of free flow, free exchange, free movement . . . both in physical body and in emotional expression."[18] Rolf's classes at Esalen soon became a cult phenomenon, drawing increasing numbers of students and young people who camped out on the institute's grounds waiting their turn for the next workshop. As her popularity grew, Rolf founded the Guild for Structural Integration in Boulder, Colorado, in 1967, later named the Rolf Institute in 1973, and in 1977 published her major treatise, *Rolfing: The Integration of Human Structures*. Throughout the 1970s, and until her death at age eighty-three in 1979, she remained a favorite of the mainstream press, featured in large spreads in *Time* and the *New York Times Magazine*, while maintaining a rigorous touring and lecturing schedule.

The practice of Rolfing itself consists of a ten-stage process, broken down into one-hour sessions, conducted over a period of six to eight weeks. With each session, the Rolfer penetrates deeper into the most sensitive and contorted fascia of the body, organizing and releasing the tensions that twist the body out of its natural alignment. The first three sessions undertake a general manipulation of the whole body, allowing a freeing of superficial layers of muscle, enabling easier breathing, more flexibility, and better balance. Next, sessions 4, 5, and 6 bring about deeper changes in the pelvis to restore flexibility and balance. Session 7 goes more deeply into the neck, head, and spine, and the final sessions bring about what is termed "a higher level of integration," which engages the personal, emotional, and sensory experience of the Rolfing process itself.

Rolfing gained much of its reputation for the intensity and pain it involved:

using powerful wrenching movements, muscle tissue was twisted to enable relaxation and elongation, often sending clients into ecstatic states in which the pain of treatment was reported to give way to the sudden sensation of emotional release. Rolf describes the reactions of her clients: "The instantaneous after effect of Rolfing is a feeling of warmth and expansion—one feels open, free, more spacious, has more air." In an interview in 1978, Rolf described the process in terms that specifically reflect the holistic program of the human potential movement: "I'm dealing with problems in the body [for which] there is never just one cause. [I focus] on the circular processes that do not act in the body but that are the body. The body process is not linear, it is circular; always, it is circular. One thing goes awry, and its effects go on and on and on and on and on. A body is a web, connecting everything with everything."[19]

In contrast to the dualistic modes of traditional Western medicine, which localize problems and treat only specific symptoms, Rolfing cultivates the interconnected character of the body through a narrative of release from the constraints of anxiety, excessive repression, and self-control:

> If the forces acting around a bone are symmetrical, if it's free to swing, the bone will horizontalize itself at the joint. It's "happier" there. You are removing the restrictions, the imbalance that comes as a result of a weight above it which tends, through torque, to twist the bone. There are also forces that pull from below, and forces that hold from behind. So we try to get the pull from below to ease off a little. We try to get the holding from behind to ease a little. And then we get the contraction from within to ease a little. It's always a question of allowing. If we remove the restrictions, the bone will want to horizontalize itself. It will go to the position that is "normal"—right for that structure.[20]

Made "free to swing," the body is naturally drawn to a happier state, but only if a cultivated talent for "allowing" is brought to bear on the practice of the body in daily life. While Rolfing remained an extreme, relatively marginal therapeutic practice, its influence on the Esalen circle and on more popular approaches to massage were apparent.[21]

MASSAGE

In *Wellness: The Yes! Bookshop Guide*, Cris Popenoe lists five books in the chapter devoted to massage: two books by the author credited with introducing massage to the alternative health scene, George Downing, *The Massage Book*, a step-by-step instruction manual interwoven with philosophical reflection and sensitive line drawings, and *Massage and Meditation*; Jack Hofer's *Total Massage*, a less philosophical step-by-step study of massage techniques (which lacks, according to Popenoe, the "high feeling" expressed in Downing's book); Gordon Inkeles and Murray Foothorap's *The Art of Sensual Massage*, a popular manual for couples, illustrated with artistic photographs; and Roberta Miller's *Psychic Massage*.[22] She begins this section with an excerpt from the most influential and successful title in this category, Downing's *The Massage Book*, published in 1972 by Bookworks and later picked up for distribution by Random House: "In its essence, massage is something simple. It makes us more whole, more fully ourselves. Your hands have the power to give this to others. Learn to trust that power and you will quickly find out better than anyone can tell you what massage is all about."[23] Indeed, the effect of the massage technique is here conjoined with a mode of expertise demanded for its successful application: rather than mastering in any traditional sense the expertise demanded for correct execution, the skill demanded of the accomplished masseuse is learning to trust his or her own intuitive powers. Relaxing one's drive to instrumental mastery is coextensive with the relaxation induced in the body of the subject.

That *The Massage Book* was created in the spirit of countercultural publishing is apparent in everything from the book's cover to typography and even the color of the pages. A large-format volume, the book's cover features more of the dreamy childlike renderings that defined *Living on the Earth*'s serendipitous innocence. Against a creamy brown cover, a delicate line drawing of a sun face is partially eclipsed by a pair of hands that reach, crab like, across the cover, encompassing the book's title written in the wood-block type common to so many hippie posters and books. On the book's back cover, a corresponding pair of hands encompasses a moon face, with the words "A Book about Energy" handily noted in the corner.

At the time that he wrote *The Massage Book*, Downing was living in the Bay Area while teaching at the Esalen Institute and leading workshops at a variety of growth centers and New Age retreats. In collaboration with Anne Kent Rush, Downing took his collection of instructions and diagrams to Bookworks, for whom Rush had already done some design work. Together the two decided on a look and a feel for the book, with a rich brown paper stock and a rustic brown ink ("They felt warm to us" [183]). The volume is notable for its sparse use of

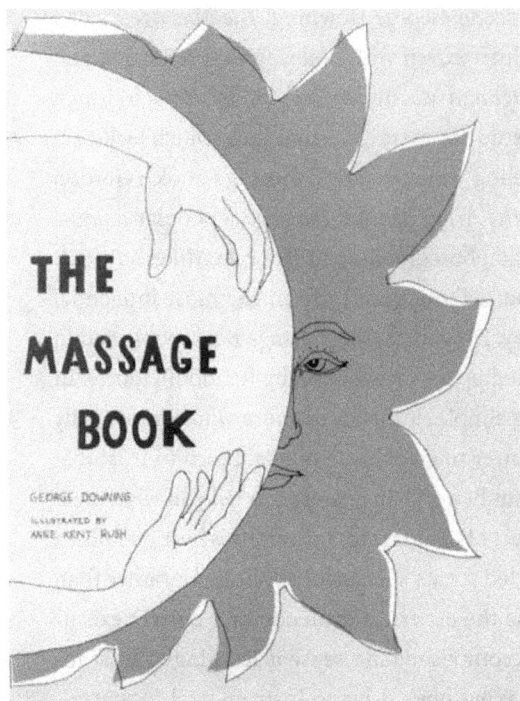

24. Cover, *The Massage Book*, by George Downing. Copyright 1972, George Downing and Anne Kent Rush. Reprinted by permission of Random House, Inc.

space and its dozens of flowing line drawings illustrating in detail the various strokes, positions, and techniques described.

The Massage Book is broken down into three sections. The first goes through the various instruments required from massage table to oils and powders. The fundamentals of massage practice are outlined, which include instruction on how to advise your friend to relax and receive the treatment: "Your job is simply to let yourself be completely taken care of. Don't try to 'help' with the massage in any way. When it is time for your arm to be lifted, let it be lifted for you. When your head has to be turned to one side, let the turning be done by your friend" (23). And this state of relaxation carries over to the hands of the practitioner himself: "Keep them as loose and flexible as possible while you are moving them. This is difficult—probably more difficult than it sounds to you—for two reasons. One is that to relax a limb while you are in the act of using it is a lot harder than to relax is while it is lying still. The other is that almost all of us, without being aware of it, carry a great deal of chronic tension in our hands" (27).

In the second section, several chapters cover a multitude of strokes and body parts: head and neck, chest and stomach, buttocks, back, full-length strokes, and so on. In a final section, a varied inventory of other possibilities are offered, including ten-minute massages, two-on-one massages, self-massage, massages for animals, and massages for lovers. The procedures espoused in *The Massage Book* are based on the Swedish massage, a technique meant to relax muscles by stimulating blood circulation through the application of pressure, using strokes of the hand, kneading, friction, shaking motions, and other methods. Downing calls his approach the Esalen massage, without theorizing its specific differences from other contrasting approaches, which he lists in the back of his book as Reichian, Rolfing, Proskauer, Shiatsu, Acupuncture, and Polarity Therapy. However, the uniqueness of his approach is implied in the broader emphasis he conveys of massage as a specifically interpersonal technique, reflective of the unique relationship between a masseur and his "friend." In an opening statement titled "Why Massage," Downing describes the ethical import of his techniques.

> To do massage is physically to help someone, to take care of them. It is for anyone with whom you feel prepared to share an act of physical caring. However, he who is giving the massage need not stop there. The more he can tune into his friend's heightened awareness, the more he can convey something of his own inner self and experience as well. The least touch becomes a statement, like drawing with a fine pen on sensitive paper. Trust, empathy and respect, to say nothing of a sheer sense of mutual physical existence, for this moment can be expressed with a fullness never matched by words. (1)

Throughout the pages of this book, a sense of intimacy is affirmed in the warm invitations to show compassion, feeling, and care in one's treatment during a massage. Illustrations consistently depict nude figures, bearded men and nubile women, unselfconsciously carrying out the activities of the massage. In the section "Nervousness, Discomfort and the Tickles," Downing advises the masseur to cover, for the sake of his friend, embarrassing parts of the body, or in the case of a complete reluctance to be touched, to ask him to concentrate on his breathing, to deepen his breath and feel his weight on the table, and, through a relaxation of his personal inhibitions, a greater receptivity to touching might be achieved. But Downing warns of other effects: "Sadness, for example; your friend may at some point find himself inadvertently [*sic*] crying, or

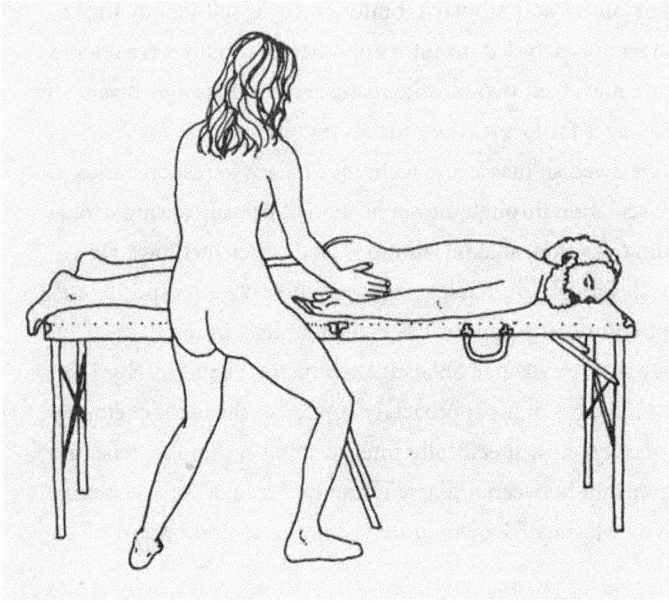

25. Massage, *The Massage Book*, by George Downing. Copyright 1972, George Downing and Anne Kent Rush. Reprinted by permission of Random House, Inc.

wanting to cry. When you are aware of this happening be sure to interrupt the massage temporarily and encourage your friend to cry for as long as he feels like it" (111). However, in the broader picture, such emotional extremes were common only in a fairly radical version of the lifestyle doctrine on the body. A more innocuous discourse on the body as a site of loosening developed around more popular recreations and sports, which in the early 1970s were being redefined according to the new culture of expressive depth and informality. Specifically, in many areas, sports were being reclassified from collective and competitive to highly individual and personally expressive activities—a shift that enhanced their significance as therapeutic practices while shaping them for the individualistic, consumption-oriented lifestyles of the 1980s and beyond.

Getting in Touch with Yourself:
From Athletics to Ascetics

By the early 1970s, the leisure market was exploding. In areas as diverse as skiing, golf, cycling, snorkeling, camping, and chess, Americans were spending huge amounts of money, about $100 billion more annually than the budget for national defense. In 1972, there was a 25 percent increase in the number of pleasure boats sold over the previous year; the number of tennis players increased

20 percent, cyclists 15 percent, and skiers 10 percent, with newer sports from hang gliding to snowmobiling broadening the range of the market.[24] Among the many novel forms taken by leisure enthusiasts was a new interest in physical fitness and athletics, though not always in traditionally defined ways and for conventional reasons. Cycling, for example, was shedding its image as a kid's diversion and emerging as a vanguard recreation for the middle class: in 1971 8.5 million bicycles were sold in the United States, compared to 5.6 million in 1965 and 3.7 million in 1960.[25] But more than the increased volume of sales, it was the swing in the demographic composition of bicycle buyers that gave cycling its changed image. A full one-third of the current sales had gone to adults, while only 15 percent of bicycle purchasers in the previous year had been grown-ups, signaling the new status of cycling as a fully adult pastime. Cycling became associated with such broad concerns as ecology and new urban planning, but also with a growing interest in fitness and the body as an object of daily care and exercise. The cycling craze suggested the legitimation of a new realm of recreation and sport, one that developed its own unique area of specialization and expertise: "Adults discovered that bikes are not toys," boasts an introduction to a Rand McNally handbook on bicycling, although, like so many other of the lifestyle developments of that time, its import was singularly unique to the individual practitioner. "No one can write about all there is to bicycling," the introduction continues; "much of the joy in riding a bike is a truly personal experience."[26]

Indeed, the wider reclassification of familiar activities from older to newer statuses (from children's pastimes to adult therapeutic activities, in the case of cycling) often implied the reclassification of an athletic pursuit from a competitive game to a solitary, ascetic exercise undertaken for irreducibly personal reasons. As a solitary practice, the goal of "winning" was divorced as a strategic aim of play from leisure practices as experiences of self-authenticity on their own terms. They became inwardly oriented techniques of self-fulfillment and authentic self-realization in which competition was read as a constraining, institutional structure imposed on the sensuality of the immediately experienced body. In this regard, amid a surge of enthusiasm for fitness and athletics in the early 1970s, a penchant for inwardness and authentic self-experience developed in the counterculture was transposed, in novel ways, onto traditional competitive athletic contests, reconceived as solitary pastimes or as noncompetitive games. Traditional, competitive sport, it was often argued, reinforced the rationalist split between mind and body endemic to Western civilization.

Mending this rupture was the aim of many new approaches to physical recreation that viewed the recovery of the body as a therapeutic task. Distinguished from the competitive recreational games of the old middle class (football, track and field, soccer), which instrumentalized the body as a tool of competition or hedonized it as a mechanism of simple fun, such recreational forms imbued the body with powerful personal sensations and transcendental moments of insight and experience. The technique of loosening, as applied to the body in vanguard leisure practices, would be accomplished chiefly through the redefinition of the body as a psychic entity, the seat of emotional and psychological feelings treatable with techniques that paralleled those of the psychotherapist. The body, as an object of immersion into which one could lose oneself, became a thing of great value and meaning whose recovered totality defined the telos of a therapeutic regime defined by a reinvented, reclassified athleticism. Toward this end, physical activity would be redefined from hedonistic relaxation or competitive play to an immersive asceticism—rather than using the body, one lost oneself into it, although this losing would require considerable focus and effort. And at the center of this pattern of reclassification was an explosive discourse on the "new sports," or "new games," much of which spun off from a variety of experiments at the Esalen Institute, often with roots in the Bay Area hippie scene.

THE ULTIMATE ATHLETE

In 1973, Esalen established a sports center on its beachside property in Big Sur. With the aim of fostering a broader understanding of the spiritual potential of organized sport, the center developed innovative programming and experimental weekend workshops to explore the relationship between noncompetitive organized play and deeper experiences of self-exploration, spiritual community, and transcendence. For the occasion, Esalen founder Michael Murphy (author of *Golf in the Kingdom*, a book on psychic phenomena in professional sports) brought together former professional football player David Meggyesy, sports coach Bob Kriegel, and running coach Mike Spino to design facilities and a program of weekend games—later expanded into a two-week summer program. The program included a session of yoga-tennis, a demonstration of Murphy's own version of Frisbee, tai chi and aikido workshops, a talk on the exploration of movement using hula hoops, and several rounds of games developed by Stuart Brand: slaughter and boffing. "What I liked," one of the organizers commented, "was the approval and understanding we got from such a broad cross section of the people there. To me there was a universal understanding of what we are trying to say—that the body and the mind are so closely related. We have to use them both together. Esalen has been saying that for years, but sports may be the best approach." The well-publicized opening of the sports center prompted one reporter to extol the historical significance of the event: "Such is the clout generated by Esalen that the occasion may be to a change in sports what the storming of the Bastille was to the French Revolution."[27]

This was not the first effort to rethink sports recreation outside the framework of competitive gaming. The Esalen revolution paralleled efforts in the Bay Area to come up with recreational forms that were aimed at the recovery of intimacy through games focused on ritual violations of social distance that called on trust, play, and bodily touching, often with players not familiar with each other. These games infused the countercultural sense of play with a therapeutic project of self-development and learning. Predating his work on the *Whole Earth Catalog*, Stewart Brand's interest in noncompetitive games began with a tournament he organized in 1966 at San Francisco State College at the invitation of the War Resister's League. Sensing that "all the peaceniks I was dealing with seemed very much out of touch with their bodies in an unhealthy way [and] consequently were starting to project a heaviness on a personal level that was just as bad as the heaviness we were projecting in Vietnam," Brand sought to create an event that would buck the pacifist trend, involving "fairly intense physical interaction between players," with experiences that were ultimately therapeutic in their aim: the intensity of conflict "instead of further entrenching people in their views and positions, would let them understand war by appreciating and experiencing the source of it within themselves." The tournament was called World War IV, though its most memorable contest was "Earthball": a competitive game involving a six-foot diameter canvas and rubber pushball, like the ones used in military training camps, painted with cloud swirls and the continents of the globe. After being inflated with breath from all participating players, Brand announced over a megaphone: "There are two kinds of people in the world: those who want to push the Earth over the row of flags at that end of the field, and those who want to push it over the fence at the other end. Go to it." And the game lurched into action. The event is recalled:

> People charged the ball from both sides, pushing and cheering. Slowly it
> began to move, first toward one end, then back to the other. The game got
> hotter. There was plenty of competition, but something more interesting

was happening. Whenever the ball approached a goal, players from the winning side would defect to lend a hand to the losers. Maybe it was, as Stewart commented, that "Berkleyites can't stand to be on the overdog team," or perhaps that's just what happens when people find themselves playing together freely. Whatever the reason, the first Earthball game went on for an hour without a score. The players had been competing, but not to win. Their unspoken and accepted agreement had been to play, as long and hard as possible.[28]

Brand's approach to what later came to be called "new games" was unique in its contention that aggression, combat, and all the competitive features traditionally manifested in athletic contest did, in fact, have some part to play in the development of personal and collective potentials: properly harnessed and contained, competition provided much of the groundwork for building a larger spirit of community and cooperation, and for extending one's own potentials to new ends. Yet it was those ends that were all important: competition would be subordinated to a program of self-development, learning, and personal growth: "I am not one who thinks competition is bad, though I agree over-obsession with losing or winning can be. It is being well-matched that makes a game take off. In a game that pits our everything against a marvelous opponent you can surpass yourself so far that you never quite return."[29]

Brand's reflections on noncompetitive sport inspired a set of experiments at Esalen whose philosophy was captured in a book by George Leonard called *The Ultimate Athlete*. A rich manifesto reflecting Leonard's effort to undo what he perceived as the cataclysmic mind-body dualism at the heart of Western conceptions of the cult of athleticism and to rethink competitive sport and physical fitness along more holistic lines, *The Ultimate Athlete* pointed the way to profound changes in professional sports, physical education, and individual recreational habits. Written in a warm first-person prose, Leonard relates observations and autobiographical accounts of physical education classes, training programs, and fitness courses to illustrate the brutality exercised on the body by rigid and militaristic command structures, manifested in high school coaches and gym instructors: "I've seen how the constricted musculature that goes with a rigid, guarded attitude toward life actually impedes the flow of life energy, how it blocks joy and empathy, how it helps create efficient monsters who can dominate nature and other people, and who may yet destroy humankind on this planet."[30]

Athleticism, reconfigured along more personal and experiential lines, could provide a vehicle for the mending of this mind-body split. Against the "cold scientific methods" that had petrified the organic spirit of true athleticism, converting the body from a vessel of experience and pleasure into an instrument of competition, the model of athleticism he proposed would release the expressiveness implicit within the body and its movements. "Athletes," Leonard argues, "can be given back their feelings and humanity at no long-term cost to performance.... Competition can be placed in the proper perspective, as an aid to achievement and as a matter of good sportsmanship."[31] The *Ultimate Athlete* offers a thumbnail sketch for a broad societal transformation of physical education and athleticism along these lines, argued within a broader philosophy of life understood as a playful pastime, or what he terms the "Game of Games." Calling on anthropologist-philosopher Johan Huizinga's writings on play in his study *Homo Ludens*, Leonard speculates on life as an irreducibly playful enterprise at once rich with philosophical import. Rifts between mind and body are mended in such new forms of adult play as jogging, gliding, skydiving, and snorkeling. Leonard devotes several pages to a discussion of Brand's experiments with noncompetitive sport in the 1960s, and to the New Games Tournaments, a series of festivals hosted by Stuart Brand in the Bay Area.

NEW GAMES

Drawing on his earlier tournaments and on the success of the Esalen sports center, in 1973 Brand began planning a large public event to be held in the Gerbode Preserve outside San Francisco on two consecutive weekends in October of that year. With funds from the Point Foundation, the nonprofit organization founded by Brand to disseminate profits from the *Whole Earth Catalog* to a variety of groups and projects, plans were drawn up for a New Games Tournament, a project that would involve dozens of organizers and volunteers, and attract 6,000 participants paying a $2.50 admission fee to an event in which anyone could get involved in any game they pleased, and all participants were invited to propose a game of their own. The event was attended by teachers, children, staff from local parks departments, and the Trust for Public Land, as well as the members of the traveling commune the Hog Farm, who catered the event, and the U.S. Army, who provided kitchens and water tanks. Among the dozens of experimental games played were Earthball, people pass, the lap game, blob, new volleyball, islands, planet pass, eco-ball, people pyramids,

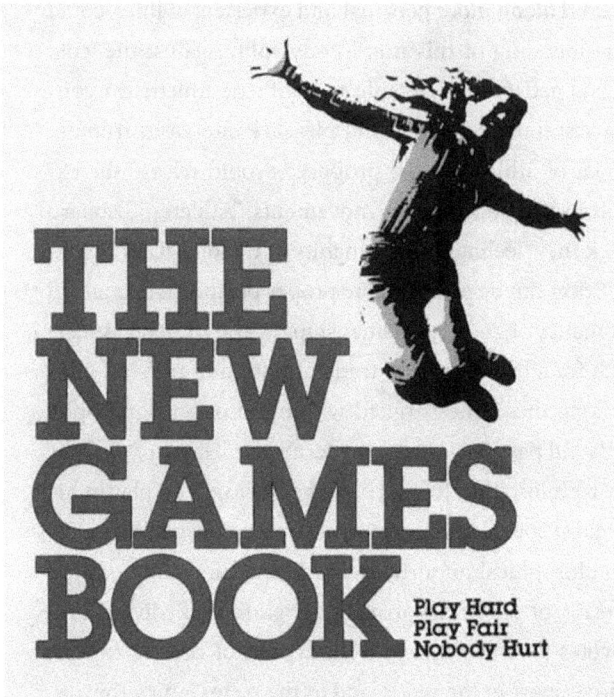

26. Cover, *The New Games Book*, by Andrew Fluegelman. Copyright 1976, The Headlands Press, Inc. Reprinted by permission of Doubleday, a division of Random House, Inc.

aura, Frisbee golf, and boffing. What is significant about the New Games, as described by participants, organizers, and game designers themselves, is the manner in which the fun of play is deepened, expanded into a grander experience of self-expression and affirmation of the bond between oneself and one's fellow players. What others might call simple fun or amusement is elevated into a more profound experience of joy in the realization of deeply personal bonds, experienced through games in which closeness is experienced through rituals of touching and bodily closeness.

Under the direction of Pat Farrington, Brand's vision of therapeutic competition was supplemented with a sense of the value of trust and cooperation in the game experience. Farrington was emphatic about the affirmative, euphoric rewards of open, unconstrained interaction and bodily contact between trusting participants, the rewards of which were the occasion for a giddy surprise in the discovery of a commonality concealed by formal roles, a joy of universal promise to anyone with the courage to let go and share experiences with others: "Games are not so much a way to compare our abilities as a way to celebrate them. I felt that by reexamining the basic idea of play, we could involve families, groups and individuals in a joyous recreation experience that creates a sense of community and personal expression. People could center on the joy of playing, cooperating, and trusting, rather than striving to win."[32]

Worlds beyond mere fun, this exultation in human community was not limited to the recognition of social trust: the New Games Tournament enabled an experience of blissful communion with nature as well as society: "The concept of a joyous and harmonious interaction between people and land resources is one of the foundations of New Games. One of our major goals is to make people aware of public lands and to promote interest in maintaining them and using them in an ecologically sound manner. New Games is attempting to bring people into harmony with their environments once again" (13). The use of "joy" in this passage asserts not only a reclassification of experience, a morally and philosophically more profound terrain than the more familiar forms of fun, it also suggests a release of pent-up vital energies in the player—a blossoming of vitality through a loosening of social prohibitions on bodily distance and personal space. With the success of the first festival, Farrington and a core group of others became the focus of an increasing trend among physical education specialists, public events organizers, parks and recreation officials on the state and federal levels, and others interested in implementing the principles of New Games in a range of settings. For a second tournament held in the same location, the organizers sought to remedy what they considered a failure to reach communities beyond the white, largely middle-class counterculturals typically in attendance at these events: "Although the participants at the First Tournament had included people of all ages, both sexes, and varied backgrounds, the majority had been middle-class, white, long-haired males in their twenties and thirties. They had probably been playing new games for years" (16). Eager to resolve this problem, the next tournament deployed an armada of tour buses to bring out groups from as many as thirty communities from across the Bay Area. With national coverage on the CBS Evening News, New Games became an international vogue, drawing lucrative speaking invitations from the governments of Australia, England, and dozens of cities across the United States.[33]

To meet the demands of this success, members of the New Games Foundation published a resource book for prospective New Games players: supported with dozens of photographs of hippies and children playing New Games at past tournaments, the book presented careful descriptions of different new games, with suggestions for how variations might be made and adapted to specific

Bug Tug

Don't have a rope? Try this version of tug of war. You can play it with two—or two hundred. *121*

It's probably easier to try it first with two. Mark a line on the ground or floor. Then you and your partner stand back-to-back on either side of it. Both of you bend forward, reach between your legs, and grasp each other's wrists. Now start tugging and see who gets pulled over the line first.

This particular version of Bug Tug looks great but doesn't last very long. If your partner outweighs you by thirty pounds, you don't stand much of a chance. The best way to get rid of these bugs is to add on a whole bunch more of them.

Stand in two lines, everyone back-to-back. Now one line stands still while the other takes a step to one side. Each of you should now be standing with a person behind you on either side. Everyone bend down and cross your arms (this is important) between your legs. Hopefully you'll come across one hand of the person on your right and one hand of the person on your left. Everyone in the line should have a grip on two different people—except the people on the ends. They had best get a grip on themselves.

Once everyone starts pulling, you may get nowhere in particular, but undulating back and forth can be mighty nice. If you get tired of just undulating and feel the urge to get somewhere, how about assembling two 50-person bugs for a centipede race? ∎

27. Bug tug, *The New Games Book,* by Andrew Fluegelman. Copyright 1976, The Headlands Press, Inc. Reprinted by permission of Doubleday, a division of Random House, Inc.

communities, or simply experimented with for the sake of fun. *The New Games Book* was initially published by Headlands Press, a San Francisco–based publisher, though distribution was handled by Doubleday. The games that filled its pages differently prescribed play situations in which competition gave way to a playful breakdown of social distance through bodily touching. One such game is Aura, in which two partners stand facing each other at arm's length with palms touching, allowing themselves to "feel the energy" they are creating. With eyes closed, they drop their hands and turn around three times, and, raising up their hands again, try to touch palms by sensing the traces of each other's energy. "This game always makes it as a spectator sport and is wildly contagious besides. Try playing it with your neighbor at the bus stop."[34] Another is Hug Tag:

> This variation on classical tag is a perfect example of how you can turn an old game into a new one. Play by whatever rules you're used to, but with one major exception—the only time a player is safe is when he's hugging another player. After playing for a while, make the frame a little more communal—rule that only three people hugging are safe. Then try four,

five . . . everyone. When you're all hugged together, why not get whoever is IT to join you and all have a go at an Amoeba Race?[35]

In the spirit of the encounter session, these games were designed to break down routinized social distances through bodily contact and were often celebrated for their effectiveness in bringing strangers into a playful, intimate experience with each other's bodies.[36] Recovering the body and mending the mind-body split through therapeutically reclassified sports enabled a utopian renewal of social bonds through a displacement of the competitive structure of traditional sports. This was not achieved through rational agreement, but by the sensual encounter of bodies. In other areas, however, the recovery of the body was defined as a more solitary task, whose aim was less social utopian than metaphysical. Jogging provides a potent example of such reclassification and therapeutic deepening of a traditional competitive sport.

FUN RUNNING

In 1966, *Distance Running News* began publication. A magazine targeting athletes and fitness specialists, the first two issues were modest twenty-eight-page newsletters filled with expert trivia, from reports on specific college and professional marathon championships across the country to long complex charts of running times and newly set records and reports from celebrity runners. Revenues were drawn from the occasional advertisement by emerging running-shoe manufacturers like Nike and Reebok. But in spite of their small size, interest was high, and by 1967, *Distance Running News* had expanded from 1,000 copies to 3,000, and as advertising revenue from merchants selling shoes, stop watches, athletic clothing, and other paraphernalia provided the necessary capital for further expansion, by 1969 the magazine had increased from a twice annual to a bimonthly publication. In January 1970 the publication changed its name to *Runner's World* and moved its offices to Northern California, where founding editor Bob Anderson began treating the magazine "much more like a business," hiring a new staff and purchasing a $5,000 IBM Composer, which enabled the magazine to launch a book series with such titles as *Thoughts on the Run, The Long Run Solution*, and the *Annual Marathon Handbook*, as well as a series of four-color Olympic posters. In addition to these advances, the magazine became active in organizing public marathons in and around San Francisco and other Northern California cities.

By 1975, with the page count up to ninety-six and subscriptions up to 30,000,

Runner's World was one of many publications that were buoyed by a rising public interest in fitness, contributing commentary, offering advice, and developing a broader discourse on the personal and practical dimensions of health and lifestyle. The deepening of running as the experience of a more meaningful form of embodiment is evidenced in the evolution from *Distance Running News* to *Runner's World*—a transformation that involved the gradual infusion of a rhetoric of personal growth loosely derived from the counterculture. A section appearing in November 1972 brings these differences to the fore: several short pieces comprising a focus on the "Science of Running" reveal the incursion of a therapeutic lifestyle agenda against the traditional authority of the physiologists and fitness experts normally consulted by marathon runners. In the first piece, titled "The Promise," one author rails against the informal information networks through which tips and experiential knowledge circulate among professional and college runners. The piece calls upon trainers and runners to pay greater attention to the increasingly expansive database on cardiovascular development, nutrition, skeletal and muscular development, and the effect of age on running: "My argument is for coaches and runners to forsake the hand-me-down cliches on training and the counsel of scientifically unsophisticated individuals, and begin understanding the lessons of the exercise physiologists. Runners should take the initiative to generate on-campus dialogues with talent in their midst. Generally, runners are too ready to believe anyone with advice on training and diet. Don't be gullible! Be skeptical! Study running from the physiologist's perspective, marshal your arguments and challenge the status quo."[37] This author's statements are aimed at a simple functional imperative defined by an expert discourse on distance running: the improvement of athletic performance. But the following article, "The Limits," discards this performance imperative and asserts instead what the author terms an ethical dimension to the discourse on running: "Methods of improving speed can only be considered ethical if they take into account what is involved in a race. A race is not merely a contest in which men discover how fast they can speed. It can and should be much more. A race is an occasion for discovering who you are—not only personally, but in relation to others and with respect to some pre-assigned task or goal."[38]

The tension between these conflicting currents was not simple: it extended to the question of the popularization of running among nonprofessionals and the degree to which casual runners deserved to be called "runners" at all. With the January issue of 1973, the scope of the magazine shifted from a restricted focus on marathon running to "the entire spectrum of running," which presumably meant a richer range of individual running habits and lifestyles undertaken by nonprofessionals. The magazine sought to address an increase in the number of nonprofessional, and most importantly noncompetitive runners, who were adapting the sport to health and lifestyle objectives that were in many ways in direct opposition to the competitive spirit fostered by the professional discourse of marathon running.

Three months after the science piece, another collection of short articles titled "The New Frontier" undertook a similar discussion of athletics as a form of personal recreation. Subtitled "Going Beyond Fitness, Beyond Competition, to a Fresh Definition of Running—'Fun Running,'" the section begins with a full-page photograph of a man, bald and slightly chubby, running with a young boy.[39] Amid pictures of figures jogging along open expanses of beach, the first article celebrates what the author calls the "Jonathan Livingston Seagulls of the running world," announcing the arrival of "fun runners," new lifestyle runners who bring a new outlook on the sport: "The running world has its Jonathan Livingston Seagulls—more of them all the time. And they're expanding consciousness of what the activity is and can be. They're pushing back the psychic limits of traditional running. . . . The Fun-Runner of the 1970s is expanding the definition of running beyond fastness and fitness by going beyond competing and conditioning into an arena of his own. Here he is an experiment of one, free to explore at will."[40] Revealing in this excerpt is the use, not only of a rhetoric of "consciousness," but of the phrase "expansion": as if a newer approach to jogging emerged not as an alternative, or in opposition to the older one, but as a transcendence of the other's limits, presenting a larger, wider, more abstracted view. Another author, discussing the differences between the "competitive athlete" and the "humanistic athlete" carries this "expansive" metaphor in a description that draws directly on Reich's typology of human consciousness discussed earlier:

> What distinguishes the competitive athlete from others is that the goal of athletic success within a competitive system and its rewards is dominant in his thinking. He is most at home in the values of Reich's Consciousness II: status, power, success, and—perhaps most important of all—the drive for excellence.
>
> What distinguishes the humanistic athlete is that he feels the major purpose of athletics is to fulfill the human potential and produce the play-

ful enjoyment and sense of achievement that comes from self-actualizing activity.... The humanistic athlete is most at home in many of the values of Consciousness III: wonder, honesty, growth, non-competitiveness, brotherhood, play. The point of competition—if indeed he does compete—is not to vanquish another but, by facing worthy opponents, to force oneself to new levels of performance.[41]

These themes were elaborated in one of World Publishing's most noted titles, *The Long Run Solution*, by *Runner's World* editor Joe Henderson, popularizer of what he termed LSD—long slow distance running, later renamed gentle running, and ultimately fun running—a philosophy that was broadly influential in new athletic and recreational discussions. By the time of *Long Run Solution*'s completion, Henderson had already proven himself a prolific writer, authoring such titles as *Long Slow Distance: The Humane Way to Train, Thoughts on the Run, Running with Style*, and other books, all philosophically inspired tracts on running, and all written for World Publications. *The Long Run Solution* offers a rich, personal reflection on running as an individual philosophy of life and a therapeutic technique, proven in cases that varied from reformed alcoholics and heroin users to neurotic housewives and depressives. This exercise is, more than anything else, a technique of managed relaxation:

> I'm never so relaxed as after I've pushed myself. If I sat here and commanded myself, "Relax!" I couldn't do it. By telling my muscles to go slack, just the opposite would happen. But if I double up my fist, make the tightest ball possible and squeeze it until my arm shakes, hold it for many seconds then let go, I'm perfectly relaxed without trying. The same thing happens in running. Running is several thousand "body clenches," done one after another, rhythmically. Tighten and relax, tighten and relax, tighten and relax. After the first 10 or 20 minutes, you feel as if a plug has been pulled and the tension is draining out through your toes.[42]

The noncompetitive sport of jogging represents perhaps the most apparent case of a competitive sport transformed into a solitary, reflexive practice. Stripped of its competitive form, running becomes therapeutic: it dissolves the calculative mind into the deep, loose body. In contrast to most games, jogging lacked any object beyond the practicing body itself, whose transformation through the exercise of jogging was thought to achieve the ends of personal relaxation and the realization of deeper, more profound dimensions of selfhood and subjectivity.

The transformation of running into jogging demonstrates the process by which a narrative of self-loosening was rehabilitated from a technique of the insurrectionary body to one intended to maximize self-potential in all realms of daily life, ultimately harnessing practices of reflexivity and lifestyle to the upward mobility of the young professionals of the 1980s. In the marketing of athletic culture, a practice of leisure defined as a realm of open-ended reflexive self-cultivation was transposed onto a disciplinary practice of competitive cultivation of physical and interpersonal skills for the labor market. One no longer ran to discover "who one was," but to unwind after work, to focus and cultivate interpersonal skills for the workplace and for heightened leisure experiences. The cultivation of the deep body was stripped of its insurrectionary form and removed from the discourse of loosening: deep bodies, in the athletic culture of the 1980s and after, would be tight, controlled bodies, and the marketing of athletic gear (most importantly shoes) would signal the paradigm by which the creativity of a loose lifestyle would be absorbed into the creative choice of a lifestyle consumer. Indeed, the Nike company undoubtedly stands at the center of this reclassification of athletics from competitive to ascetic, or from cognitive and intellectual to immersive and deep, and ultimately to prepackaged and commodified.

Like many other companies with vaguely countercultural roots, Nike started out a small firm with a generally rebellious outlook and wound up an immensely influential icon of a new style of consumption. Nike is notorious for having introduced branding and an entirely new concept of marketing to an industry that had been a relative backwater of the American consumer market. Following a surge of interest in athletic footwear after the Mexico Olympics of 1968, Phil Knight and company founded Nike in Portland, Oregon, in 1971 (Knight and his staff are remembered by fellow Oregonites as a group of "long haired, bearded flower children"). Nike quickly codified and exported the practice of athletics as one directed toward the cultivation of authenticity in the deep body, even as it repulsed the outward forms of loosening prescribed in a broader discourse of countercultural consumption.[43] Through a campaign of groundbreaking advertising in the 1980s, Nike developed a new format for addressing consumers not only as the creative agents behind their own distinctive lifestyles, but as the creative interpreters of advertising messages themselves, often coded for the savvy, media-saturated viewer. Just Do It, the motto that calls out to the reflexive lifestylist who is, above all, solely responsible for her own choices and for the resulting self that these choices produce, seemed to abjure the empty promises doled out by mainstream advertisers. Nike, in short, coded and incorporated a discourse on selfhood realized through the skilled loosening of a deep body, initially directed against a duplicitous culture of consumption dominated by imperatives of rationality and affect, into the vernacular of mainstream marketing and advertising, and ultimately into the daily practices of consumption itself.

Morning in America
Pulling in the Slack

D ecades present clumsy units of cultural measure, deceptively packaging lengthy and complex developments into neat historical parcels. Nonetheless, the ideological reversal associated with the year 1980 brought the cultural and political trends of the 1970s to such an abrupt halt as to create the impression of a decisive rupture precisely along the fault line of the decade, seemingly fulfilling a calendrical prophesy: the 1960s was a time of radical change, the 1970s one of retreat and retrenchment, and the 1980s one of reaction and backlash.[1] At the outset of the new decade, Ronald Reagan's landslide victory over Jimmy Carter signaled a sea change in the national discourse on culture and modernity: tired of the troubling doubts and insoluble social problems that seemed to follow a broad push for social democracy in everyday life, this experiment would be uprooted in its entirety with a return to traditional values, signaled by Reagan's campaign slogan: morning in America. Tired of moral seriousness and austerity in the realm of consumption, Americans flocked to the traditional signifiers of privilege, mass consumption and consumer excess. A report in *U.S. News and World Report* in 1981 greeted the forfeiture of the moral project of the 1970s by trumpeting, "Flaunting Wealth Is Back in Style": "Suddenly it's O.K. to be rich and show it." A lengthy "in" and "out" list cataloged the decline of 1960s values in the face of the new conservatism: in were wine bars, owning property, traditional weddings, Nancy Reagan red, college business courses, escapist movies, women with master's degrees in business, money-market funds, rich people. On the out list: idealism, primal scream therapy, self-realization seminars, books on politics, living together, long hair, Democrats, poor people.[2] Disenchantment with the moral legacy of the 1960s was widely felt, even among the movement's most outspoken proponents like Jerry Rubin, who in 1984 renounced his iconoclastic image and went to work as a trader with a Wall Street firm. Barely a decade after the Beatles played their rooftop concert, Elvis Costello sang "What's so funny 'bout peace, love, and understanding?" as if the answer wasn't already obvious. The moral project of the 1960s had become an object of historical curiosity—or worse, public ridicule—not only among conservatives but also among youth and cultural radicals themselves.

In the intervening years, the legacy of the counterculture—specifically the moribund version that predominated in the 1970s—has been roundly dismissed as the least memorable of cultural experiments of the twentieth century, even as its key contributions have been structured into so many aspects of daily life and personal identity. Its detractors sloganized the downward spiral of atavistic "permissiveness" that allegedly eroded the stalwartness of a once muscular American civilization. Indeed, the phrase "permissiveness," in the mouths of conservatives, would embrace a range of policies, behaviors, and attitudes, from the licentiousness of countercultural hedonism to sexual explicitness in the media, leniency in the treatment of criminals, generosity in state programs for the poor, nonaggression in foreign policy, and tolerance of cultural differences at home. "Permissiveness," writes Barbara Ehrenreich, "came to occupy the place that affluence once held in liberal critiques of America almost twenty years earlier."[3] Thus the student militants occupying the president's office at Columbia University were the spoiled offspring of misguided parents of the postwar era, elided through their permissiveness with lenient judges, cowardly and compromising teachers, prostitutes, homosexuals, pornographers, and drug users. What began as a replenishing experience of immediacy in a directly experienced modern present became the pathological mark of that modernity itself—an indolence and inability to defer sensual gratification, the sure mark of the degenerate's slouch. Indeed, since the 1980s, this reproach of the lifestyle experiments of the 1960s and 1970s has permeated every level of public discourse, lending fodder to the political offensives of the new right: describing his opponent in the 1988 bid for the presidency, George H. W. Bush quipped of

Michael Dukakis: "He probably thinks a naval exercise is something you find in Jane Fonda's workout book."[4]

In the political rhetoric of the New Right and the cultural discourse of the middle class more generally, the loose morals and permissiveness of the 1960s generation would be vanquished as America returned to the modest values of the square world, conjured up in a series of images portraying moral fortitude, obligation, and respect for public norms. What was loose would be drawn tight in a culture given to often arbitrary and sometimes hysterical calls for discipline and the reinstatement of authority in such diverse realms as family governance, corrections, education, urban policing, and foreign policy—all those public domains that, through the eyes of neoliberal visionaries, constituted the suspect domain of dependence and community. Indeed, public pining for the reassuring discipline of a strict parent commanded broad popular sentiment in the 1980s and 1990s, exemplified by Tom Brokaw's 1998 best seller *The Greatest Generation*, in which the television anchorman relates his experiences covering the fortieth anniversary of D-day for an NBC documentary. Over conversations with U.S. troops gathered on the Normandy beaches, Brokaw discovered a profound respect for the men and women of this historical generation, whom he praised for their resolve, their quiet, unflagging sense of responsibility, and their willingness to shoulder the burdens of patriotic duty without so much as a whimper of complaint. Their sturdy character and unflinching devotion to country and flag, Brokaw argued, served the country at a time of war: "The nation turned to its young to carry the heaviest burden, to fight in enemy territory and to keep the home front secure and productive. These young men and women were eager for the assignment. They understood what was required of them, and they willingly volunteered for their duty."[5] Yet, more than their iron-clad resolve, what impressed Brokaw about this generation was their stoicism and depthlessness in the face of trauma and suffering. In contrast to the boastful self-importance with which the next generation would indulge its experiences, inventing ever new languages for the airing of ever more personal wounds and anxieties while petitioning against ever more nuanced forms of discipline, the greatest generation was sparse with its words and modest in its feelings: "Although they were transformed by their experiences and quietly proud of what they had done, their stories did not come easily. They didn't volunteer them."[6] Indeed, nostalgia for such measures of self-constraint would triumph in the aftermath of the September 11 attacks, declared the "Pearl Harbor of the twenty-first century" in the president's own diary, as a new generation of Americans, conservatives told us, would rediscover the moral values so desecrated by the baby boomers. "Go forth from here and become the next greatest generation," Brokaw told the graduating class at Northwestern University in 2004—an invitation to devotion, duty, and self-sacrifice.

But like all nostalgias, this one is selective and inaccurate, reflecting more the contradictions of the present than any real relation with the past. The resolve of the Greatest Generation was grounded on a view of collective identity and the reliance of the individual on the provisioning of the state that is anathema to the high-flying individualism of the present age of neoliberalism. The soldiers who so valiantly stormed the beaches in France could look forward to long lives in unionized workforces and in firms regulated by an active government, extending more or less permanent offers of lifetime employment. They were simple in their commitments and Spartan in their needs, preferring familiarity and routine in their consumption habits. They went home to generous assistance programs provided by a powerful welfare state, many of them to communities organized around a plethora of strong civic organizations with deep roots in the New Deal's labyrinthine network of agencies and commissions. Even as conservatives since Reagan have aligned themselves with the modesty and sullen sense of duty embodied by these men who define the mythical mid-century origins of "family values," the sensibilities and styles of life through which they were practiced would hardly jibe with the fluidity and breakneck pace of contemporary market societies, with the malleability of social ties they institute and the accelerated cultures of consumption they impose, where downsizing, union busting, and frequent layoffs define loyalty as an anachronistic liability. Moreover, the brand of self-reliance trumpeted during the Reagan years as a pretext for the curtailing of welfare and assistance programs shared more lineage with the same hippies that the president himself had, as governor of California, taunted and dismissed in an ongoing public joust, going so far at one point as to attribute the shooting of Robert Kennedy to "lawlessness and permissiveness" that was gripping the country.[7]

As Daniel Bell noted, capitalism imposes contradictions on the everyday lives of people, enforcing a disjuncture between the productive and the cultural spheres. The prosperity of neoliberal economies is achieved through the exacting of political and economic concessions that cut against the self-regimentation so longingly projected onto the greatest generation. Since the

1970s, the privatization of large parts of the economy, together with the downsizing of the public sector, the cutting back of safety nets and other programs of the welfare state, the decline in civic engagement, and the replacement of traditional identities associated with civic membership and long-term commitment to a single employer with more ephemeral and reflexive identities derived from one's choices as a consumer, has left scant space for quiet devotion and a modest sense of obligation. The sternness of character Brokaw and Reagan so idolized would hardly serve to stabilize relationships that have become increasingly dependent on the securing of trust through the opening of the self to the other. The Greatest Generation would fare badly in today's tumultuous labor markets, where the fostering of impressions and the sharing of feelings rank among the most necessary assets of the modern worker. The saturation of culture and everyday life with changing images of identity and selfhood does little to encourage self-restraint and resolve. The expansion of cultural industries and the informalization of flexible employment patterns, which demand not only developed interpretive sensibilities but also skills at communication and empathy, leave little space for a workforce whose stories are difficult to coax, or for those lacking an ear for the needs and anxieties of a potential new consumer. Far from having expurgated the quality of looseness, contemporary society has incorporated it, naturalizing it as a staple of our everyday styles of life in which the self represents a sustaining object of manipulation in all of its aspects. In doing so, however, it has drained the urgency and adventure with which this project was undertaken, removing its meaning as a moment of modern possibility, the spirit of collective improvisation and caring discourse — the "new coloration" Foucault uncovered in the ethical practices of ancient Greece. The loosening project, as I have interpreted it, was colored by an experience of modernity whose meaning is not transmitted in the many forms it helped to innovate.

It has been argued throughout this study that, under current conditions, personal identity has become a project of self-production and self-reproduction—a reflexive endeavor exercised in the relatively free space of everyday choices. In recent debates, as in this volume, this assertion is made against the backdrop of an encompassing theory of social change on a dramatic scale: where once, we are told, the self was provided or imposed under the constraints of kinship and community, situated within the fixed cosmology of a closed theological worldview or derived from interactions in a normatively structured public sphere, today, under conditions of risk, commodification, cultural saturation, and flexible social arrangements, the self "bowls alone," as it were.[8] Identity today is a project of self-choosing to which all are condemned, in a Sartrean sense—one in which the management of personal autonomy composes a task demanding considerable technical prowess. The techniques of the loosening self, as described here, represented, for the groups that practiced them, ways of confronting and domesticating, or practicing and sustaining oneself within such conditions of autonomy and freedom. "In the society we live in," Bauman writes, "individual freedom moves steadily into the position of the cognitive and moral focus of life—with far-reaching consequences for each individual and for the social system as a whole."[9]

But such freedoms as we practice today are not rewards exacted from an intractable capitalism, as they were imagined in the early doctrines of the loosening self; they are conditions of life demanded of and imposed by contemporary forms of capitalism itself. The romance with the project of loosening, however it imagined itself and to whatever purposes it saw itself directed, was a forerunner to these contemporary freedoms. Indeed, the dispositions demanded for the management of today's freedoms, for converting their ephemerality into durable forms of identity, were shaped, it has been argued, in the lifestyle discourses of the 1970s. The Greatest Generation's resolve would never do for this purpose, but ultimately, neither would the loosened lifestyles of hippies. Identity today requires reflexivity and the willingness to make substance out of one's choice of oneself, but also a tolerance for the ultimately ephemeral quality of this substance, whose fragmented story one rewrites with every mundane lifestyle choice.

In both the realms of production and consumption, under the conditions of uncertainty and flux foisted on individuals in a society in which the market paradigm has eroded and displaced all other sources of collective, public authority, the maintenance of identity demands that one look upon oneself as an object of artistry and affect, but also as one of investment, endless optimization, and ongoing preparation for struggles and challenges that lie ahead. Such techniques of identity, such an appreciation for transience, was hatched in utopian enclaves in the 1960s and schematized in the 1970s into durable narratives of identity as adventures in the maelstrom of modernity, shared with contemporaneous storytellers and practitioners. They were shaped in the 1980s by yuppies and purveyors of commanding and influential lifestyle brands and extended more generally throughout the population in the decades that followed.

This study has argued that seminal features of the countercultural agenda have contributed to the shaping of techniques for coping with such measures of freedom and personal autonomy that are today taken for granted. The loose self developed cornerstone supports and skills for the lifestyle identities demanded of a society of flux and change, in which the techniques of a reflexive project of the self would become indispensable. While outward invocations to self-abandonment have been revised or neutralized, the essential structure of a self-responsible self, of a self-producing, self-choosing, and self-consuming self, have entrenched themselves in our way of life. In this world, central themes taken from the countercultural discourse on lifestyle have proven lasting: the empowerment of the individual as the sovereign maker of his or her own life and obligations have, in the years since the 1970s, penetrated deeply the fabric of American society, affecting patterns of institutional life, consumption, family, and a range of social structures. Tracing this learned flexibility to the innovators who first gave it a discursive form reveals the dependence of what often passes as an inevitable law of nature and human development to a very situated historical episode whose horizons more closely resemble our own than we are commonly led to believe. Indeed, the loosening of the self was essential to the development of much of what we take for granted in ourselves today. It is from the counterculture's adventures with self-loosening that was fashioned the flexibility and self-responsibility so deeply rooted in our contemporary self-understandings, and in the significance we attribute to the minute choices we make in daily life. Under the life-conditions of the new millennium, it is possible to assert, paraphrasing a claim once made about liberalism more generally: we're all loose now.

Notes

Introduction

1. Landy, *The Underground Dictionary*, 54, 52.
2. See Binkley, "The Seers of Menlo Park"; Diehl, "Revitalizing the National Mainstream," 36–38; and P. Holt, "Some New Directions in the Total Mix," 49–51.
3. Patricia Holt, telephone interview with the author, January 29, 2004.
4. See Bolles, *What Color Is Your Parachute?*; Bay Laurel, *Living on the Earth*; De Moll, *Rainbook*; Katzen, *The Moosewood Cookbook*; Boston Woman's Health Book Collective, *Our Bodies, Ourselves*; Downing, *The Massage Book*, Pacific Domes, *Domebook I* and *Domebook II*; Dass, *Be Here Now*; Brown, *The Tassajara Bread Book*.
5. Diehl, "Revitalizing the National Mainstream," 38.
6. See Heelas, Lash, and Morris, *Detraditionalization*; Beck, Giddens, and Lash, *Reflexive Modernization*; Bauman, *Liquid Modernity*; Giddens, *The Consequences of Modernity*; Berger, *Homeless Mind*.
7. See Bauman, *Freedom*.
8. Lovejoy, *The Great Chain of Being*.
9. See Giddens, *Modernity and Self-Identity*, 52–55.
10. See Bauman, *Liquid Life*, 80–82, and *Work, Consumerism and the New Poor*; Lash and Urry, *The End of Organized Capitalism*, 1–17; Baumeister, *Identity*.
11. See Sennett, *The Corrosion of Character*.
12. Reisman, *The Lonely Crowd*, 16.
13. See Harvey, *The Condition of Postmodernity*, 189–201; Lash and Urry, *The End of Organized Capitalism*, 285–300.
14. See Berman, *All That Is Solid Melts into Air*, 312–29.
15. Ibid.
16. Giddens, *Modernity and Self-Identity*, 36–42.
17. See Featherstone, "The Body in Consumer Culture," 171.
18. Guidelines appear in B. Henderson, *The Publish It Yourself Handbook*.
19. See Bruce-Briggs, *The New Class?*; Burris, "The Discovery of the New Middle Class"; Mills, *White Collar*; Vidich, *The New Middle Classes*; Whyte, *The Organization Man*.
20. Ehrenreich, *Fear of Falling*, 6.

21. See Kellner, "Popular Culture and the Construction of Postmodern Identities," and Bauman, "From Pilgrim to Tourist."

22. See Du Gay, "Organizing Identity."

23. See Frank, *Conquest of Cool*; Heath and Potter, Nation of Rebels.

24. See Frank, *One Market under God*.

25. See Hammond, "Yuppies."

26. See Du Gay, "Organizing Identity."

27. See Rose, "Governing the Enterprising Self" and "Identity, Genealogy, History."

28. See Bauman, "Consuming Life."

29. *Meet the Press*, NBC, February 8, 2004.

30. Sontag, *Against Interpretation*.

31. Martin, *A Sociology of Contemporary Cultural Change*.

32. Darnton and Roche, *Revolution in Print*.

1. Of Swingers and Organization Men

1. See Hurup, *The Lost Decade*; S. Miller, *The Seventies Now*; Schulman, *The Seventies*; Carroll, *It Seemed Like Nothing Happened*; Braunstein and Doyle, *Imagine Nation*; Clines, "The Celebration of Self"; Michener, "The Revolution in Middle-Class Values."

2. *New York Daily News*, October 30, 1975.

3. Lasch, *The Culture of Narcissism*; see Wolfe, "The Me Decade and the Third Great Awakening."

4. Whyte, *The Organization Man*; see Bell, *The Cultural Contradictions of Capitalism*.

5. Bell, *The Cultural Contradictions of Capitalism*, 83.

6. See S. Hall, "Cultural Studies and the Centre."

7. See S. Hall, "The Problem of Ideology."

8. See Cohen, *A Consumers' Republic*.

9. See Lamont and Fournier, *Cultivating Differences*; Hartley, "Impossibility of Dropping Out."

10. See Farber, *Student as Nigger*.

11. Scott-Heron, "Whitey on the Moon."

12. See Gitlin, *The Sixties*, 409–20.

13. See Schulman, *The Seventies*, 78–102.

14. Mungo, *Cosmic Profit*, 90.

15. Berman, *All That Is Solid Melts into Air*, 15.

16. Ibid., 90–98.

17. Bauman, *Liquid Modernity*, 2.

18. Ibid., 8.

19. Berman, "Faust in the '60's," 502.

20. See Ferguson, *The Aquarian Conspiracy*.

21. See Binkley, "Cosmic Profit."

22. See Carroll, *It Seemed Like Nothing Happened*; Miller, S.P., *The Seventies Now*; Schulman, *The Seventies*.

23. See Hall and Jacques, "Introduction to New Times."

24. Schulman, *The Seventies*, 73.

25. U.S. Department of Commerce, *American Social Attitudes*, 38–41.

26. Ibid., 7–11.

27. Ibid., 19.

28. Mermelstein, "The Threatening Economy."

29. See Lee, "Decades and Dollars" and "The '70's."

30. Sigal, "Inflation as a Deflater of the Masculine Role."

31. Corry, "The Melting Pot Didn't."

32. Carter, "The Crisis of Confidence."

33. *U.S. News and World Report*, "Is the Malaise Real?"

34. Illich, *Deschooling Society*.

35. Ibid., 78.

36. National American Student Cooperative Organization's history is discussed on their Web site, www.nasco.coop/info.html.

37. Lipnack, *Networking*, 1.

38. National American Student Cooperative Organization, *Community Market*.

39. Ibid., 8.

40. J. Todd, "The New Alchemists"; Greene, "The New Alchemists."

41. J. Todd, "Tomorrow Is Our Permanent Address," 85.

42. Students for a Democratic Society, "Port Huron Statement," 176, in Alpert and Clarvir, *The Sixties Papers*.

43. See Harvey, *The Condition of Postmodernity*, 141–72; Lash and Urry, *The End of Organized Capitalism* and *Economies of Signs and Spaces*; Murray, "Fordism and Post-Fordism."

44. Mermelstein, "The Threatening Economy," 3.

45. See Harvey, *The Condition of Postmodernity*, 125–40.

46. See Aglietta, *A Theory of Capitalist Regulation*; Amin, *Post-Fordism*.

47. Harvey, *The Condition of Postmodernity*, 135–34.

48. Ibid., 130.

49. Whyte, *The Organization Man*, xx.

50. See Slater and Tonkiss, *Market Society*, 176–81.

51. See Bauman, *Work, Consumerism and the New Poor*.

52. See Slater and Tonkiss, *Market Society*, 181–86; Lash and Urry, *Economies of Signs and Space*, 1–12.

53. See Bauman, *Liquid Life*, 80–116.

54. Bell, *The Cultural Contradictions of Capitalism*, 28.

55. See Lamont and Wuthnow, "Betwixt and Between"; DiMaggio, "Classification in Art."

56. Bourdieu, *Distinction*.

57. See DiMaggio, "Social Structure, Institutions, and Cultural Goods."

58. Radway, "The Scandal of the Middlebrow."

59. MacDonald, "A Theory of Mass Culture," 59.

60. Ibid., 64.

61. See Crane, *The Production of Culture*.

62. See D. Holt, "Poststructuralist Lifestyle Analysis" and "Does Cultural Capital Structure American Consumption?"

63. Featherstone, "Lifestyles" and *Consumer Culture and Postmodernism*; Lash, "Discourse or Figure?"

64. Bourdieu, *Distinction*, 34–41.

65. Featherstone, *Postmodernism and Consumer Culture*, 70–72; Lash and Urry, *The End of Organized Capitalism*, 285–314.

66. Bourdieu, *Distinction*, 370.

67. Featherstone, *Postmodernism and Consumer Culture*, 59.

68. Kramer, "It's Time to Start Listening."

69. Poirier, "Learning from the Beatles," 526.

70. Peyser, "The Boys from Liverpool."

71. Silverman, "Rock and Classical."

72. See hooks, "Eating the Other."

73. Von Hoffman, *We Are the People Our Parents Warned Us Against*, 101.

74. See Ehrenreich, *The Hearts of Men*; Yenckel, "And Now for the Men's Movement."

75. Mailer, "The White Negro."

76. Orwell, *1984*, cited in Wouters, "Formalization and Informalization," 4.

77. Von Hoffman, *We Are the People*, 71–72.

78. See Giddens, *Modernity and Self-Identity*; Bauman, *The Individualized Society*; Du Gay, *Consumption and Identity at Work*; Langman, "Neon Cages"; Rose, "Governing the Enterprising Self."

79. Giddens, *Modernity and Self-Identity*, 76.

80. Wolfe, "The Me Decade and the Third Great Awakening."

81. Ibid., 27.

82. U.S. Department of Commerce, *American Social Attitudes*, 52.

83. See Schulman, *The Seventies*, 78–102.

84. Gallup Poll, *Public Opinion*, 913.

85. Yankelovich, *The New Morality*, 5,251.

86. Mailer, "The White Negro," 327.

87. Reich, *The Greening of America*, 67, 72, 363–64.

88. Rubin, *Growing Up at Thirty-Seven*, 16–17.

89. Lasch, *The Culture of Narcissism*, 15.

90. Mosher, "New Pioneers in Iowa City," 16.

91. Ibid., 17.

92. Jerome, "Rumors of Change," 22.

93. Ferguson, *The Aquarian Conspiracy*, 92.

94. Frank, *Conquest of Cool*.

95. Taylor, "The Doubts Linger, But the Longhairs Are Being Trimmed."

96. R. Alexander, "Is Groovy Groovy or Ghastly over Forty?" 134.

97. Adler et al., "The Year of the Yuppie"; see Hammond, "Yuppies."

98. Ibid., 29.

99. Peer et al., "The Work Junkies."

100. See Gelman et al., "Fitness, Corporate Style."

101. "Christmas Fads"; Lewis, "Keeping Up with the Joneses' Cuisinart."

102. *Business Week*, "More Home Cooks Try Professional Equipment."

2. Experts Unbound

1. Airola, 5–12.

2. Foucault, *The Care of the Self*.

3. Ibid, 351.

4. See Foucault, "On the Genealogy of Ethics," 362.

5. Sennett, *Fall of Public Man*, 37.

6. Bauman, *Liquid Modernity*, 65.

7. Ibid., 66.

8. Bell, *The Coming of the Post Industrial Society*, 15.

9. Gartner and Riessman, *The Service Society and the Consumer Vanguard*; see also Gartner and Riessman, "The Service Society and Jobs."

10. Dass, *Be Here Now* (no pagination in original); Dowling, "Confessions of an American Guru."

11. Kent Rush, *Getting Clear*, 7.

12. Brown, *The Tassajara Bread Book*, inside cover.

13. See Binkley, "Cosmic Profit."

14. Leiss, Kline, and Jhally, *Social Communication in Advertising*, 10.

15. Hart, "Advertising Adds to Ills of Distrust."

16. P. Campbell, "Advertising in the Present Political Environment," 55.

17. Fulop, *Competition for Consumers*, 24.

18. See Strumpel, "The Future of Affluence," 75–81.

19. See Murray, "Major Federal Consumer Protection Laws"; Cross, *All Consuming Century*; Cohen, *A Consumer's Republic*.

20. See Voorhis, "The Consumer Movement and the Hope of Human Survival," 1–18.

21. See Denenberg, "Tough Consumer."

22. Everett, "70s Consumer May Spurn Status of Consumption," 36–38.

23. See Webster, "Defining the Characteristics of the Socially Conscious Consumer," 188–96.

24. Brooker, "The Self-Actualizing Socially Conscious Consumer," 107.

25. Herberger, "The Ecological Product Buying Motive."

26. See Henion, "The Effects of Ecologically Relevant Information on Detergent Sales," 10–14.

27. Fisk, "Criteria for a Responsible Consumption," 24–31.

28. Kinnear and Taylor, "The Effect of Ecological Concern on Brand Perceptions," 191–97.

29. Bunker, "Ecopornography Raises Its Ugly Head," 63.

30. See, for example, Arnold and Fisher, "Counterculture, Criticisms, and Crisis."

31. Kotler and Levy, "Broadening the Concept of Marketing."

32. Berry and Hensel, "Marketing and the Social Environment"; Steilf, "Why the Birds Cough."

33. See Bartels, "The Identity Crisis in Marketing."

34. Ibid., 75.

35. Dawson, "Marketing Science in the Age of Aquarius," 67–68.

36. Markley, Campbell, and Willis, *Changing Images of Man*.

37. Mitchell, *The Nine American Lifestyles*.

38. Elgin, *Voluntary Simplicity*, 31.

39. Elgin, *Voluntary Simplicity*, 28–29.

40. See D. Holt, "Poststructuralist Lifestyle Analysis"; and Asa Berger, *Ads, Fads, and Consumer Culture*, 81–103.

41. Mitchell, *Life Ways and Lifestyles*, 15.

42. *Advertising Age*, "VALS Undergoes Change."

43. Holman, "A Values and Lifestyle Perspective on Human Behavior," 53.

44. Townsend, "Nine Lives," 16.

45. Ibid., 25.

46. Ogilvy, "The Experience Industry," 28.

3. Book as Tool

1. See *New York Times*, "'Eastern Literary Establishment' Taken to Task at P.E.N. Meeting"; McDowell, "Small Book-Publishing Firms Flourishing."

2. *Doing It!* no. 5, back cover.

3. *Doing It!* no. 1, 22–24.

4. *Doing It!* no. 1, inside cover.

5. *Doing It!* no. 1, 18.

6. Meyrowitz, *No Sense of Place*, 76–77.

7. Ibid., 78.

8. B. Anderson, *Imagined Communities*.

9. Ong, "Orality, Literacy and Modern Media Communication," 116.

10. See Glessing, *The Underground Press in America*; Salpukas, "Underground Papers Are Thriving."

11. P. King, "Publishers Look West for New Ideas," 30.

12. P. Holt, "Some New Directions in the Total Mix," 206.

13. P. Holt, "The End of 'Me-ism' in (Western) America," 32.

14. Brand, telephone interview with the author, June 24, 2000.

15. See "Who, How, When, Where, Why They Make a Catalog," 68–70.

16. See Mitgang, "In California, Book Publishing Takes on New Forms"; Gold, "Letter from San Francisco"; Pace, "Book Publishing Is Flowering on Coast."

17. Patricia Holt, telephone interview with Binkley, January 29, 2004.

18. P. Holt, "Viewing the West as a Book Market."

19. *New York Times*, "Harper & Row Plans to Move Religious Unit."

20. Bry, "The Big Territory."

21. See Stuttaford, "Northern California's Exploding Book Market."

22. See Welles, "Steady Expansion in Southern California."

23. See P. King, "Publishers Look West for New Ideas."

24. P. Holt, "Viewing the West as a Book Market," 31.

25. Diehl, "Revitalizing the National Mainstream," 36–38.

26. P. Holt, "Viewing the West as a Book Market," 32.

27. Dietz, "Price/Stern/Sloan."

28. Collier, "For Fun and Profit in San Francisco."

29. Diehl, "Revitalizing the National Mainstream," 38.

30. Pace, "Book Publishing Is Flowering on Coast."

31. See, "California Style," 33.

32. Ibid., 32.

33. See Binkley, "The Seers of Menlo Park."

34. See Stuttaford, "Northern California's Exploding Book Market."

35. Bay Laurel, *Living on the Earth*, front matter. The author refers to Pacific Gas and Electric Company.

36. Mungo, "Living on the Earth"; see also *New York Times*, "Her Hymn to Nature Is a Guidebook for the Simplest of Lives."

37. Hodgman, "Flour Power."

38. Brown, *The Tassajara Bread Book*, front matter.

39. P. Holt, "Viewing the West as a Book Market," 29.

40. Bry, "The Big Territory," 28.

41. Hislop, "Straight Arrow Books."

42. Tetrault and Thomas, *Country Woman*, 97.

43. Mungo, "Living on the Earth," 6; S. Roberts, "Mail Order Catalogue of the Hip Becomes a National Best Seller."

44. Mungo, "Living on the Earth," 6.

4. Being One

1. Bauman, "Globalization and the New Poor," 317.

2. Bauman, 314.

3. Foucault, *The Use of Pleasure*, 14–24.

4. Foucault, "Self Writing," 210–11.

5. Lyotard, *The Post Modern Condition*.

6. Reich, *The Greening of America*, 14.

7. Ibid., 14–19.

8. Bellah, *Beyond Belief*; Bellah and Glock, *The New Religious Consciousness*; Tipton, *Getting Saved from the Sixties*.

9. Bellah, *Beyond Belief*, 142–67; Tipton, *Getting Saved from the Sixties*, 2.

10. Tipton, *Getting Saved from the Sixties*, 7.

11. "Why Another Growth Center," 25.

12. See Mowrey, and Redmond, *Not in Our Backyard*.

13. Gussow, "The Future Is Circular," 4.

14. Schumacher, *Small is Beautiful*; Fuller, *Operating Manual for Spaceship Earth*; Lovelock, *The Ages of Gaia*.

15. Fuller, *Operating Manual for Spaceship Earth*, 54.

16. Meadows et al., *Limits to Growth*.

17. Forrester, *World Dynamics*.

18. Boulding, "The Economics of Spaceship Earth," 9.

19. Belasco, *Appetite for Change*, 28.

20. Lappé, *Diet for a Small Planet*, xi.

21. Katzen, *The Moosewood Cookbook*; Robertson, *Laurel's Kitchen*.

22. Earth Shoe ad, "The Secrets of the Earth Sole." In *Runner's World*, Oct. 1975, 16.

23. Blackwell, Engel, and Spence, "Perceived Risk in Mail-Order and Retail Store Buying."

24. Gillet, "In-Home Shoppers."

25. *Business Week*, "Catalogue Sales Thrive on Inflation," 27.

26. Gillet, "In-Home Shoppers," 82.

27. Ibid., 86.

28. Reynolds, "An Analysis of Catalog Buying Behavior," 50.

29. Nelson, "Paperback."

30. Tom Bender, telephone interview with the author, October 10, 2000; Lane De Moll, telephone interview with the author, September 22, 2000.

31. De Moll, *Rainbook*.

32. Ibid., 2.

33. Sale, "Consider the Windmill."

34. Baldwin, "Rainbook," 60.

35. De Moll, *Rainbook*, 71.

36. Stuart Brand, telephone interview with S. Binkley, June 24, 2000; Binkley, "The Seers of Menlo Park."

37. Roszak, *From Satori to Silicon Valley*, 37; see also Kirk, "Appropriating Technology"; F. Turner, *From Counterculture to Cyberculture*.

38. Halstead, "Publicity-Shy Whole Earth Grows Successful Organically."

39. *Whole Earth Catalog Records*, box 25, folder 12.

40. Dick Raymond, telephone interview with Sam Binkley, May 23, 2000.

41. McClanahan and Norman, "The Whole Earth Catalog," 96.

42. *Time*, "Missal for Mammals," 75.

43. McClanahan and Norman, "The Whole Earth Catalog," 95.

44. *Harper's*, "About This Issue," 12.

45. *Whole Earth Catalog Records*, box 21, folder 2.

46. *Whole Earth Catalog Records*, box 2, folder 4.

47. *Whole Earth Catalog Records*, box 2, folder 12.

48. *Whole Earth Catalog Records*, box 1, folder 8.

49. Unidentified newspaper clipping, *Whole Earth Catalog Records, 1969–1986,* box 13, folder 3).

50. *Whole Earth Catalog Records,* box 27, folder 7.

51. Brand, *Last Whole Earth Catalog,* 40.

52. See Brand, "Editorial Comment," 15.

53. See O'Neill, "Space."

54. Brand, *Space Colonies,* 5.

55. Lears, *Fables of Abundance.*

56. Franz, "Survivors Fight for Granola-Bar Market."

57. *New York Times,* "Novelty Confections Aim for Youth Market"; Jenkins, "Health Food and the Change in Eating Habits."

5. Loving Each Other

1. Beck, Giddens, and Lash, *Reflexive Modernization,* 89.

2. Giddens, *Modernity and Self-Identity.*

3. Giddens, *The Transformation of Intimacy.*

4. Giddens, *Modernity and Self-Identity,* 58.

5. Ibid., 96.

6. Reich, *Greening of America,* 9–10.

7. Allyn, *Make Love Not War.*

8. See Ehrenreich, *The Hearts of Men.*

9. Giddens, *Transformation of Intimacy,* 61–64.

10. Blumenthal, "Pornochic," 272.

11. See *New York Times,* "Throat Cutting."

12. See Hammel, "Will the Real Alex Comfort Please Stand Up?"

13. Hutton, *The Sex Technique in Marriage,* 34.

14. Hutton quoted in Lewis and Brissett, "Sex as Work."

15. Kennedy, "The 'No-Nonsense' School vs. the 'Please-Give-Me-Back-My-Nonsense' School," 292.

16. Comfort, *The Joy of Sex,* 145.

17. Ibid., 8.

18. Masters and Johnson, *Human Sexual Inadequacy*; see also Masters and Johnson, *Human Sexual Response.*

19. King, "Sex Counseling Is Offered by at Least 3,500 Organizations in U.S."

20. See Masters and Johnson, *Human Sexual Inadequacy,* 146–56.

21. Braun, *Catalog of Sexual Consciousness,* 3.

22. See R. Roberts, *The New Communes*; Zablocki, "Communes, Encounter Groups and the Search for Community"; Speck, *The New Families*; Corr, "Getting It Together"; *U.S. News and World Report,* "Communes: A More Businesslike Style."

23. R. Roberts, *The New Communes,* 19.

24. Freudlich, telephone interview with Sam Binkley, January 12, 2001; Freudlich, Collins, and Wenig, *Guide to Cooperative Living.*

25. Freudlich, Collins and Wenig, *Guide to Cooperative Living*, 7.

26. Sundancer, *Celery Wine*, 160.

27. See *Time*, "Karma Yes, Toilets No."

28. Pacific Domes, *Domebook I*; Pacific Domes, *Domebook II*; Kahn, *Shelter I*; Lloyd Kahn, *Shelter II*.

29. Pacific Domes, *Domebook II*, 3.

30. Pacific Domes, *Domebook I*, 7.

31. Reif, "It's Taken Twenty Years, But the Dome as a Home Is Catching On," 54.

32. Pacific Domes, *Domebook II*, 138–39.

33. Mungo, *Cosmic Profit*, xv.

34. See Bender, "How to Be Profitably Hip"; Raskin, "Beads in a Time of Inflation"; Frohling, "Counterculture Capitalists."

35. See Kleiner, *The Age of Heretics*, 265–313.

36. Vocations for Social Change, *Boston People's Yellow Pages*, 75.

37. Dick Raymond, telephone interview with Sam Binkley, December 4, 2000.

38. Phillips, *Transaction Based Economics*, front cover.

39. Ibid., 39.

40. Briarpatch Community, *The Briarpatch Book*, vii–viii.

41. Anundsen and Phillips, "Open Books," 254–56.

42. Briarpatch Community, *The Briarpatch Book*, xii.

43. Warne, "Demystifying Business," 65.

44. See www.briarpatch.net.

45. Whitmyer and Rasberry, *Running a One-Person Business*.

46. Phillips, *Marketing without Advertising*.

47. Phillips and Rasberry, *Honest Business*.

48. Elmer-Dewitt, "Anita the Agitator."

49. Graham, *Current Biography Yearbook*, 103.

50. See T. Hall, "Striving to Be Cosmetically Correct."

51. L. Wells, "Boutique Chic."

52. Brand, "Uncommon Courtesy."

6. Letting It All Hang Out

1. Borders, "Norwalk School Suspends 53 in Hairline Dispute."

2. Ibid.

3. Levy, "Office Dress."

4. *New York Times*, "Management Views Office Fashions."

5. Levy, "Office Dress."

6. Boston Woman's Health Book Collective, *Our Bodies, Ourselves*; Walters, "Paperback Talk."

7. Boston Woman's Health Book Collective, *Our Bodies, Ourselves*, 3.

8. Ibid.

9. P. Wells, "Book Helps with Books That Help."

10. Popenoe, *Wellness*, 17.

11. Lowen, *Bioenergetics*, 8.

12. Kent Rush, *Getting Clear*, 3–4.

13. On Esalen, see W. Anderson, *The Upstart Spring*; Howard, *Please Touch*; Gerzon, "Countercultural Capitalists."

14. Kinnard, "A Singles Convention for the 'Aware' Adult."

15. Ibid., 22.

16. Weinraub, "Esalen Encounter Group Finds British in Touch."

17. Rolf, *Structural Integration*, 9.

18. Ibid., 10.

19. Rolf, *Ida Rolf Talks about Rolfing and Physical Reality*, 69.

20. Ibid., 196.

21. See Cant, "Our Aching Backs!"

22. Popenoe, *Wellness*, 39–42.

23. Downing, *The Massage Book*, 1.

24. *New York Times*, "Americans Spent More Money and More Time Just Playing."

25. Bender, "How to Be Profitably Hip."

26. *All about Cycling*, 9.

27. Wallace, "New Esalen Center Spurs a Sports Revolution."

28. Fleugelman, *New Games Book*, 8–9.

29. Ibid., 139.

30. Leonard, *The Ultimate Athlete*, 30–31; see Broyard, "Books of the Times."

31. Leonard, *The Ultimate Athlete*, 21, 22.

32. Fleugelman, *New Games Book*, 10.

33. Lipsyte, "Sports."

34. Fleugelman, *New Games Book*, 37.

35. Ibid., 115.

36. See Fink, "Cosmic Celebration," 3; Brand, "Theory of Game-Change" and "Battle over the Whole Earth Jamboree."

37. Boehm, "The Promise," 21.

38. Tomczak, "The Limits," 22.

39. *Runner's World*, "The New Frontier," 8–14.

40. Beinhorn, "Wishing He Could Fly," 9.

41. Mickel, "Beyond Competition," 10–11.

42. J. Henderson, *The Long Run Solution*, 37.

43. Lafaber, *Michael Jordan and the New Global Capitalism*.

Conclusion

1. See Jameson, "Periodizing the Sixties."

2. *U.S. News and World Report*, "Flaunting Wealth Is Back in Style," 61–62; *U.S. News and World Report*, "Youth," 10.

3. Ehrenreich, *Fear of Falling*, 169.

4. *Economist*, "A Lot of Hot Air," 47.

5. Brokaw, *The Greatest Generation*, 3.

6. Ibid., xxi.

7. *New York Times*, "Reagan, Scoring Courts, Links Shooting to Permissive Attitude."

8. See Putnam, *Bowling Alone*.

9. Bauman, *Freedom*, 71.

Bibliography

"About This Issue." *Harper's*, April 1974, 12.

"A Time of Learning to Live with Less." *Time* (December 3, 1973): 29–31.

Adler, Jerry, et al. "Year of the Yuppie." *Newsweek* (December 31, 1984): 14.

Advertising Age. "VALS Undergoes Change," February 13, 1989, 24.

Aglietta, Michel. *A Theory of Capitalist Regulation.* Translated by David Fernbach. London: New Left Books, 1976.

Airola, Paavo. *Are You Confused? De-Confusion Book on Nutrition and Health.* Phoenix: Health Plus, 1971.

Albert, Stewart Edward, and Judith Clarvir. *The Sixties Papers: Documents of a Rebellious Decade.* New York: Praeger, 1984.

Alexander, Jeffrey C., and Steven Seidman. *Culture and Society: Contemporary Debates.* Cambridge: Cambridge University Press, 1990.

Alexander, Ron. "Is Groovy Groovy or Ghastly over Forty?" *New York Times*, September 21, 1975.

All about Cycling. New York: Rand McNally, 1974.

Allyn, David. *Make Love Not War: The Sexual Revolution, an Unfettered History.* New York: Little, Brown & Co., 2000.

Amin, Ash, ed. *Post-Fordism: A Reader.* Oxford: Blackwell, 1994.

Anderson, Benedict. *Imagined Communities.* London: Verso, 1983.

Anderson, Bruce, and Michael Riordan. *The New Solar Home Book.* Andover, Mass.: Brick House, 1976.

Anderson, Walter Truett. *The Upstart Spring: Esalen and the American Awakening.* Reading, Mass.: Addison Wesley, 1983.

Anundsen, Eric, and Michael Phillips. "Open Books: Keystone of the Briarpatch Network." In *The Briarpatch Book*, ed. Briarpatch Community. San Francisco, Calif.: New Glide/Reed Books, 1978.

Appadurai, Arjun. *Modernity at Large.* Minneapolis: University of Minnesota Press, 1996.

Arnold, Mark, and James Fisher. "Counterculture, Criticisms, and Crisis: Assessing the Effect of the Sixties on Marketing Thought." *Journal of Macromarketing* (Spring 1996): 118–33.

Asa Berger, Arthur. *Ads, Fads, and Consumer Culture.* New York: Rowman & Littlefield, 2000.

"Authors Advocate Do-It-Yourself Typesetting for More Books." *Publishers Weekly* (October 7, 1974): 25–28.

Baer, Steve. *The Dome Cookbook*. San Cristobal, N.M.: Lama Foundation, 1968.

Baldwin, J. "Rainbook," *CoEvolution Quarterly* (Summer 1977): 60.

———, and Stewart Brand, eds. *Soft Tech*. New York: Penguin, 1978.

Baltera, Lorraine. "'New Consumer' Wants More Attention to Individual Needs." *Advertising Age* Vol. 12 (February 1977): 12.

Bartels, Robert. "The Identity Crisis in Marketing." *Journal of Marketing* (October 1974): 73–76.

Barthes, Roland. *Mythologies*. Translated by Annette Lavers. London: Hill and Wang, 1972.

Baudrillard, Jean. *The Mirror of Production*. St. Louis, Missouri: Telos, 1975.

———. *Simulations/Jean Baudrillard*. Translated by Paul Foss, Paul Patton, and Philip Beitchman. New York: Semiotext(e), 1983.

Bauman, Zygmunt. "Consuming Life." *Journal of Consumer Culture* 1, no. 1 (2001): 9–29.

———. *Freedom*. Milton Keynes: Open University Press, 1988.

———. "From Pilgrim to Tourist — or a Short History of Identity." In Hall and Dugay, eds. *Questions of Cultural Identity*, London: Sage, 1996, 25.

———. "Globalization and the New Poor." In *The Bauman Reader*, edited by Peter Beilharz. Malden, Mass.: Blackwell, 2001.

———. *The Individualized Society*. Cambridge: Polity Press, 1994.

———. *Intimations of Postmodernity*. London and New York: Routledge, 1992.

———. *Liquid Life*. Cambridge: Polity Press, 2005.

———. *Liquid Modernity*. Cambridge: Polity, 2000.

———. *Work, Consumerism and the New Poor*. London: Open University Press, 2005.

Baumeister, Roy F. *Identity: Cultural Change and the Struggle for Self*. New York: Oxford University Press, 1986.

Bay Laurel, Alicia. *Living on the Earth*. New York: Random House, 1971.

Beale, Calvin. "Renewed Growth in Rural Communities." *The Futurist* (August 1975): 196–204.

Beck, Ulrich, Anthony Giddens, and Scott Lash. *Reflexive Modernization: Politics, Tradition and Aesthetics in the Modern Social Order*. Cambridge: Polity Press, 1994.

Beck, Ulrich, Barbara Adam, and Joost Van Loom. *The Risk Society and Beyond: Critical Issues for Social Theory*. London: Sage, 2000.

Beinhorn, George. "Wishing He Could Fly." *Runner's World Magazine* (Winter 1973): 9.

Belasco, Warren. *Appetite for Change*. Ithaca, N.Y.: Cornell University Press, 1993.

Bell, Daniel. *The Coming of the Post Industrial Society*. New York: Basic Books, 1973.

———. *The Cultural Contradictions of Capitalism*. New York: Basic Books, 1976.

Bellah, Robert. *Beyond Belief: Essays on Religion in a Post-Traditional World*. New York: Harper & Row, 1970.

———, and Charles Glock, eds. *The New Religious Consciousness*. Berkeley, Calif.: University of California Press, 1976.

——, Richard Meusen, William M. Sullivan, Ann Swidler, and Steven M. Tipton. *Habits of the Heart: Individualism and Commitment in American Life*. New York: Harper & Row, 1985.

Bender, Marylin. "How to Be Profitably Hip." *New York Times*, February 1971.

Bender, Tom. *Living Lightly: Energy Conservation in Housing*. Unpublished Monograph, 1973.

——. Telephone interview with Sam Binkley, October 10, 2000.

Benson, George C. S., and Thomas C. Engeman. *Amoral America*. Stanford: Hoover Institution Press, 1975.

Berger, John. *Ways of Seeing*. New York: Viking, 1973.

Berger, Peter L. *Homeless Mind: Modernization and Consciousness*. New York: Vintage, 1974.

Berman, Marshall. *All That Is Solid Melts into Air*. New York: Penguin, 1982.

——. "Faust in the '60s." In *The Sixties*, edited by Gerald Howard. New York: Paragon House, 1991.

Berman, Morris. *The Reenchantment of the World*. Ithaca, N.Y.: Cornell University Press, 1981.

Berry, Leonard, and James Hensel. *Marketing and the Social Environment*. New York: Mason and Lipscomb, 1972.

Berry, Wendell. *The Unsettling of America: Culture & Agriculture*. San Francisco, Calif.: Sierra Books, 1977.

Binkley, Sam. *Consuming Aquarius: Markets and the Moral Boundaries of the New Class*. Ph.D. Dissertation. New York: New School University, 2002.

——. "Cosmic Profit: Countercultural Commerce and the Problem of Trust in American Marketing." *Consumption, Markets, and Culture* 6, no. 4 (2003): 231–49.

——. "The New Middle Classes and the Discourse of Caring: Toward a New Understanding of Cultural Intermediaries." In *Historicizing Lifestyles: Popular Media, Consumption and Taste Cultures*, edited by David Bell and Joanne Hollows. Burlington, Vermont: Ashgate, 2006.

——. "The Seers of Menlo Park: The Discourse of Heroic Consumption in the *Whole Earth Catalog*." *Journal of Consumer Culture* 3, no. 3 (2003): 238–313.

——. "Everybody's Life is Like a Spiral: Narrating Post-Fordism in the Lifestyle Movement of the 1970's." *Cultural Studies—Critical Methodologies* 4: 2 (May 2004).

Blackwell, Roger D., Jones F. Engel, and Homer E. Spence. "Perceived Risk in Mail-Order and Retail Store Buying." *Journal of Marketing Research* (1970): 364–69.

Blaszczyk, Regina Lee. *Imagining Consumers: Design and Innovation from Wedgwood to Corning*. Baltimore: Johns Hopkins University Press, 2000.

Blau, Judith. *The Shape of Culture: A Study of Contemporary Cultural Patterns in the United States*. Cambridge and New York: Cambridge University Press, 1989.

Bloom, Allan. *Closing of the American Mind*. New York: Simon and Schuster, 1987.

Blumenthal, Ralph. "Pornochic." *New York Times*, January 21, 1973, 272.

Boehm, Walter. "The Promise." *Runner's World* (Summer 1972): 21–22.

Bolles, Richard Nelson. *What Color Is Your Parachute?* Berkeley, Calif.: Ten Speed, 1972.

Bonham, Barbara. "Counter Culture Commune Finds Publishing Success." *Graphic Arts Monthly* (March 1978): 60–63.

Bookchin, Murray. *The Ecology of Freedom: The Emergence and Dissolution of Hierarchy*. Palo Alto, Calif.: Cheshire Books, 1982.

Booker, Christopher. *The Neophiliacs*. Boston: Gambit, 1970.

Boorstin, Daniel. *The Americans, the Democratic Experience*. New York: Vintage Books, 1974.

Borders, William. "Norwalk School Suspends Fifty-three in Hairline Dispute." *New York Times*, January 29, 1968.

Bork, Robert H. *Slouching Toward Gomorrah: Modern Liberalism and American Decline*. New York: Regan Books, 1996.

Borsodi, Ralph. *Flight from the City: The Story of a New Way to Family Security*. New York and London: Harper & Brothers, 1933.

Boston Women's Health Book Collective. *Our Bodies, Ourselves*. New York: Simon and Schuster, 1974.

Boulding, Kenneth. "The Economics of Spaceship Earth." In *Environmental Quality in a Growing Economy*, ed. Henry Jarrett. Baltimore, Md.: Johns Hopkins Press, 1966.

Bourdieu, Pierre. *Distinction: A Social Critique of the Judgment of Taste*. Translated by Richard Nice. Cambridge, Mass.: Harvard University Press, 1984.

———. *Logic of Practice*. Translated by Richard Nice. Stanford: Stanford University Press, 1980.

———. *The Field of Cultural Production*, ed. Randall Johnson. New York: Columbia University Press, 1993.

Bourdieu, Pierre, and Loic Wacquant. *An Invitation to Reflexive Sociology*. Chicago: University of Chicago Press, 1992.

Brand, Stuart. "Battle over the Whole Earth Jamboree." *CoEvolution Quarterly* (Winter 1978–79): 90–97.

———. "CoEvolution Supplement." *Organic Gardening and Farming* Vol. 24 (August 1977): 177.

———. *Cybernetic Frontiers*. New York: Random House, 1974.

———. "Editorial Comment." *CoEvolution Quarterly* (Winter 1974): 15.

———. "Note." *Whole Earth Catalog* (Spring 1969): 34.

———. "Theory of Game-Change." *CoEvolution Quarterly* (Summer 1976): 95–99.

———. "Uncommon Courtesy." *Christian Science Monitor*, August 19, 1982.

———. "Used Magazines: 63 Strange People Tell What They Read—378 Strange Magazines is What." *CoEvolution Quarterly* (Spring 1979): 72–120.

———, ed. *Last Whole Earth Catalog*. Menlo Park, Calif.: Portola, 1972.

———, ed. *Space Colonies*. Menlo Park, Calif.: Point Foundation, 1977.

Braun, Saul. *Catalog of Sexual Consciousness*. New York: Grove, 1975.

Braunstein, Peter, and Michael William Doyle, eds. *Imagine Nation: The American Counterculture of the 1960s and 1970s*. London: Routledge, 2002.

Brewer, John, and Roy Porter, eds. *Consumption and the World of Goods*. London: Routledge, 1992.

Briarpatch Community, eds. *The Briarpatch Book*. San Francisco, Calif.: New Glide/Reed Books, 1978.

Brody, Patricia. "Riding the Grey Rabbits." *California Living* (January 1976): 31.

Brokaw, Tom. *The Greatest Generation*. New York: Random House, 1998.

Brooker, George. "The Self-Actualizing Socially Conscious Consumer." *Journal of Consumer Research*, no. 3 (1976): 107–12.

Brooks, Paul. *Speaking for Nature: How Literary Naturalists from Henry Thoreau to Rachel Carson Have Shaped America*. Boston: Houghton Mifflin Co., 1980.

Brown, Edward Espe. *The Tassajara Bread Book*. Boulder, Colo.: Shambhala, 1970.

Broyard, Anatole. "Books of the Times." *New York Times*, August 12, 1975.

Bruce-Briggs, B., ed. *The New Class?* New Brunswick, N.J.: Transaction Books, 1979.

Bry, Ellen. "The Big Territory." *Publishers Weekly* (October 18, 1973): 62.

Bucaro, Frank, and David Wallechinsky. *Chico's Organic Gardening and Natural Living*. Philadelphia: Lippincott, 1972.

Bunker, Nancy. "Ecopornography Raises Its Ugly Head." *Advertising Age* (May 1973): 63.

Burris, Val. "The Discovery of the New Middle Class." *Theory and Society* (1986): vol. 15, no. 3, 317–51.

Business Week. "Catalogue Sales Thrive on Inflation," July 20, 1974, 27.

———. "More Home Cooks Try Professional Equipment," May 9, 1977, 92.

Callenbach, Ernest. *Ecotopia*. New York: Bantam Books, 1975.

Campbell, Colin. *The Romantic Ethic and the Spirit of Modern Consumerism*. New York: Blackwell, 1987.

Campbell, Joseph. *The Hero with a Thousand Faces*. Princeton: Princeton University Press, 1968.

Campbell, Patty. "Advertising in the Present Political Environment." *Journal of Consumer Affairs* (1968): vol. 23, 45–64.

Cant, Gilbert. "Our Aching Backs!" *New York Times*, February 3, 1974.

Carroll, Peter N. *It Seemed Like Nothing Happened*. New York: Holt, Rinehart, and Winston, 1982.

Carson, Rachel. *Silent Spring*. Boston: Houghton Mifflin, 1987.

Carter, Jimmy. 1979. "The Crisis of Confidence." http://www.jimmycarterlibrary.gov/documents/speeches/index.phtml.

———. *Public Papers of the Presidents of the United States* Vol. II (1979).

Chaney, David. *Lifestyles*. New York: Routledge, 1996.

Chartier, Roger. *Forms and Meanings: Texts, Performances, and Audiences from Codex to Computer*. Philadelphia: University of Pennsylvania Press, 1995.

Clecack, Peter. *America's Quest for the Ideal Self*. New York: Oxford University Press, 1983.

Clifford, James. *The Predicament of Culture*. Cambridge, Mass.: Harvard University Press, 1988.

Clines, Francis X. "The Celebration of Self—Themes and Variations." *New York Times*, December 30, 1979.

Cohen, Lizabeth. *A Consumers' Republic: The Politics of Mass Consumption in Postwar America*. New York: Knopf, 2003.

Cole, H.S.D., et al. *Models of Doom: A Critique of the Limits to Growth*. New York: Universe Books, 1973.

Collier, Peter. "Drop-out's How-to." *New York Times*, March 7, 1971: BR8.

———. "For Fun and Profit in San Francisco." *New York Times*, February 13, 1972.

Comfort, Alex. *The Joy of Sex*. New York: Crown, 1972.

Commoner, Barry. "Beyond the Teach-in." *Saturday Review* (April 1970): 50–55.

———. *Closing Circle: Nature, Man and Technology*. New York: Knopf, 1971.

———. *The Politics of Energy*. New York: Knopf, 1979.

———. *The Poverty of Power: Energy and the Economic Crisis*. New York: Bantam Books, 1977.

"Communal Living Comes in from the Woods." *Money* (November 1976): 87–88.

Community Market Catalog. Ann Arbor: National American Student Cooperative Organization, 1971.

"Continuing Do-It-Yourself Trend Gives Firms New Markets." *Industry Week*. Vol. 16, no. 2 (August 1975): 56.

Converse, Philip E., Jean D. Dotson, Wendy J. Hoag, and William H. McGee III, eds. *American Social Attitudes: Data Sourcebook 1947–1978*. Cambridge, Mass.: Harvard University Press, 1987.

Corr, M. "Getting it Together: Energy Use in Communes and Other Alternative Life Styles." *Environment* 14 (1972): 2–9.

Corry, John. "The Melting Pot Didn't." *New York Times*, December 30, 1979.

"Counterculture's Social Change Subtle but still Alive." *New York Times*, August 12, 1979, 1–32.

Crane, Diana. *The Production of Culture: Media and the Urban Arts*. Newbury Park, Calif.: Sage, 1992.

Cross, Gary. *All Consuming Century*. New York: Columbia University Press, 2000.

Darnton, Robert, and Daniel Roche. *Revolution in Print: The Press in France, 1775–1800*. Berkeley: University of California Press in collaboration with the New York Public Library, 1989.

Dass, Baba Ram. *Be Here Now, Remember*. San Cristobal, N.M.: Lama Foundation, 1971.

Davidson, Cathy N. *Reading in America: Literature & Social History*. Baltimore, Md.: Johns Hopkins University Press, 1989.

Davidson, Sara. "The Rush for Instant Salvation. *Harper's* (July 1971): 40–54.

Dawson, Leslie. "Marketing Science in the Age of Aquarius." *Journal of Marketing* (July 1971): 66–72.

De Moll, Lane, and Gigi Coe, eds. *Stepping Stones: Appropriate Technology and Beyond*. New York: Schocken Books, 1978.

De Moll, Lane, ed. *Rainbook*. New York: Schocken Books, 1977.

Debord, Guy, and Donald Nicholson-Smith. *The Society of the Spectacle*. Cambridge, Mass.: Zone Books, 1995.

DeMott, Benjamin. "On Counter-Culture and Over-the-Counter Culture." *New York Times*, January 10, 1972: E11.

Denenberg, Herb. "Tough Consumer." *Sales and Marketing Management*, April 1977, 84–86.

Denfeld, Duane, and Michael Gordon. "Mate Swapping: The Family that Swings Together Clings Together." In *Family in Transition: Rethinking Marriage, Sexuality, Child Rearing, and Family Organization*, eds. Arlene S. Skolnick and Jerome H. Skolnick. Berkeley: University of California Press, 1971.

Denzin, Norman. *Interpretive Biography*. Newbury Park, Calif.: Sage, 1989.

Desmond, John, Pierre McDonagh, and Stephanie O'Donohoe. "Counter-Culture and Consumer Society Consumption." *Markets and Culture* 14 (2001): 241–279.

Devall, Bill. *Deep Ecology*. Salt Lake City: G.M. Smith, 1985.

Diehl, Digby. "Revitalizing the National Mainstream." *Publishers Weekly* (November 5, 1973): 36–38.

Dietz, Lawrence. "Price/Stern/Sloan." *Publishers Weekly* (October 3, 1973): 42–43.

DiMaggio, Paul. "Classification in Art." *American Sociological Review* 52 (1987): 440–55.

———. "Social Structure, Institutions, and Cultural Goods: The Case of the United States." In *Social Theory for a Changing Society*, ed. Pierre Bourdieu and James S. Coleman. New York: Russell Sage Foundation, 1991.

Douglas, Mary, and Steven Tipton. *Religion and America: Spiritual Life in a Secular Age*. Boston: Beacon Press, 1983.

Dowling, Colette. "Confessions of an American Guru." *New York Times*, December 4, 1977.

Downing, George. *The Massage Book*. San Francisco, Calif.: Bookworks/Random House, 1972.

Drucker, Peter F. "The Surprising Seventies." *Harper's* No. 243 (July 1971): 35–39.

Du Gay, Paul. *Consumption and Identity at Work*. London: Sage, 1996.

———. "Organizing Identity." In *Cultural Identity*, edited by Stuart Hall and Paul Du Gay. Thousand Oaks, Calif.: Sage, 1996.

Du Gay, Paul, and Sean Nixon. "Who Needs Cultural Intermediaries?" In *Cultural Studies* Vol. 16, No. 4 (2002).

Earth Shoe advertisement. *Runner's World* (October 1975): 16.

Economist. "Christmas Fads," December 17, 1977, 42.

———. "A Lot of Hot Air," September 10, 1988, 47.

Ehrenreich, Barbara. *Fear of Falling: The Inner Life of the Middle Class*. New York: Pantheon Books, 1989.

———. *The Hearts of Men: American Dreams and the Flight from Commitment*. New York: Anchor Books, 1983.

Elgin, Duane. *Voluntary Simplicity: Toward a Way of Life That Is Outwardly*. New York: William Morrow and Co., 1981.

———, and Arnold Mitchell. "Voluntary Simplicity (3)." *CoEvolution Quarterly* (Summer 1977): 4–19.

Elmer-Dewitt, Philip. "Anita the Agitator." *Time* (January 25, 1993): 52–55.

Everett, John. "'70's Consumer May Spurn Status of Consumption,' Everett Warns," *Advertising Age* (January 19, 1970): 36–38.

Ewen, Stuart. *All Consuming Images: The Politics of Style in Contemporary Culture*. New York: Basic Books, 1988.

———. *Captains of Consciousness: Advertising and the Social Roots of the Consumer Culture*. New York: McGraw-Hill, 1976.

Fabricant, Florence. "Health-Food Stores Broaden Appeal." *New York Times*, January 18, 1981: LI8.

Falk, Pasi. *The Consuming Body*. London: Sage, 1994.

———, and Colin Campbell, eds. *The Shopping Experience*. London: Sage, 1997.

Farber, Jerry. *Student as Nigger*. New York: Contact Books, 1969.

Farrington, Pat. "New Games Tournament." *CoEvolution Quarterly* (Summer 1974).

Featherstone, Mike. "The Body in Consumer Culture." In *The Body: Social Process and Cultural Theory*, edited by Mike Hepworth and Bryan S. Turner. Thousand Oaks, Calif.: Sage, 1991.

———. *Consumer Culture and Postmodernism*. London: Sage, 1991.

———. "Lifestyle and Consumer Culture." *Theory, Culture and Society* 4 (1987): 55–70.

Featherstone, Mike, Mike Hepworth, and Bryan S. Turner, eds. *The Body: Social Process and Cultural Theory*. London: Sage Publications, 1991.

Ferguson, Marilyn. *The Aquarian Conspiracy: Personal and Social Transformation in the 1980's*. New York: St. Martin's, 1980.

———. *The Brain Revolution: The Frontiers of Mind Research*. London: Davis-Poynter, 1974.

Fink, Rita. "Cosmic Celebration." *Pacific Sun* 1–6 (September 1978): 3–5.

Firat, A. Fuat. *Consuming People; From Political Economy to Theaters of Consumption (Consumer Research and Policy)*. New York: Routledge, 1998.

Fisk, George. "Criteria for a Responsible Consumption." *Journal of Marketing* 37 (1973): 24–31.

Fleugelman, Andrew, ed. *New Games Book*. New York: Headlands Press Books, 1976.

Fonda, Jane. *Jane Fonda's Workout Book*. New York: Simon and Schuster, 1981.

Forrester, Jay Wright. *World Dynamics*. Cambridge, Mass.: Wright-Allen, 1973.

Foucault, Michel. *The Archeology of Knowledge*. New York: Pantheon, 1972.

———. *The Care of the Self*. Vol. 3 of *The History of Sexuality*. Translated by Robert Hurley. New York: Vintage Books, 1986.

———. *Ethics, Subjectivity and Truth*. Vol. 1 of *The Essential Works of Michel Foucault*, ed. Paul Rabinow. New York: New Press, 1997.

———. "The Experience-Book." In *Remarks on Marx*, 25–42. Translated by James Goldstein and James Cascaito. New York: Semiotext(e), 1991.

———. "On the Genealogy of Ethics: An Overview of a Work in Progress." In *The Foucault Reader*, edited by Paul Rabinow. Translated by Catherine Porter. New York: Pantheon, 1984.

———. "Self Writing." In *Ethics, Subjectivity, and Truth: The Essential Works of Foucault, 1954–1984, Vol. 1*, edited by Paul Rabinow. New York: New Press, 1997.

———. *The Uses of Pleasure*. Vol. 2 of *The History of Sexuality*. New York: Vintage Books, 1985.

Frank, Thomas. *The Conquest of Cool: Business Culture, Counterculture, and the Rise of Hip Consumerism*. Chicago: University of Chicago Press, 1997.

———. *One Market under God: Extreme Capitalism, Market Populism and the End of Economic Democracy*, New York: Doubleday. 2000.

Franz, Julie. "Survivors Fight for Granola-Bar Market." *Advertising Age* (February 17, 1986): 34.

Freilicher, Lila. "ABA: The Convention Goes West." *Publishers Weekly* (July 9, 1973): 20–32.

Freudlich, Paul, Chris Collins, and Mikki Wenig, eds. *Guide to Cooperative Living*. New Haven, Conn.: Community Publications Cooperative, 1979.

Freudlich, Paul. "Communications and Networking." In *Guide to Cooperative Living*, eds. Paul Freudlich, et al. New Haven, Conn. and Lousia, Virginia: Community Publications Cooperative, 1979.

Friedan, Betty. *The Feminine Mystique*. New York: Norton, 1963.

Fritsch, Albert J. *99 Ways to a Simple Lifestyle*. Bloomington: Indiana University Press, 1977.

Frohling, T. "Counterculture Capitalists." *World Press Review* 28 (1981): 52.

Frum, David. *How we got here: The 70's: The Decade That Brought You Modern Life—For Better or Worse*. New York: Basic Books, 2000.

Fuller, Buckminster. *Operating Manual for Spaceship Earth*. New York: Simon and Schuster, 1969.

Fulop, Christine. *Competition for Consumers*. London: Institute for Economic Affairs, 1964.

The Gallup Poll: *Public Opinion 1976–1977*. Wilmington, Del.: Scholarly Resources, 1978.

Garb, Yaakow Jerome. "Perspective or Escape: Ecofeminist Musings on Contemporary Earth Imagery." In *Reweaving the World: The Emergence of Ecofeminism*, eds. Irene Diamond and Gloria Feman Orenstein. San Francisco, Calif.: Sierra Club Books, 1990.

Gartner, Alan, and Frank Riessman. "The Service Society and Jobs." *New York Times*, August 25, 1974.

———. *The Service Society and the Consumer Vanguard*. New York: Harper & Row, 1974.

Gelman, David, et al. "Fitness, Corporate Style." *Newsweek* (November 5, 1984): 96.

Gerth, Hans, and C. Wright Mills. *Character and Social Structure*. New York: Harcourt, Brace & Company, 1953.

Gerzon, Mark. "Counterculture Capitalists." *New York Times*, June 5, 1977.

Giddens, Anthony. *The Consequences of Modernity*. Stanford: Stanford University Press, 1991.

———. *Modernity and Self-Identity: Self and Society in the Late Modern Age*. Cambridge: Polity Press, 1991.

———. *The Transformation of Intimacy: Love, Sexuality and Eroticism in Modern Societies*. Cambridge: Polity Press, 1993.

Gillet, Peter. "In-Home Shoppers: An Overview." *Journal of Marketing* 34 (1976): 81–88.

Gilmore, James H., and B. Joseph Pine II. *The Experience Economy: Work Is Theatre & Every Business a Stage*. Boston: Harvard Business School Press, 1999.

Gitlin, Todd. *The Sixties: Years of Hope, Days of Rage*. New York: Bantam, 1993.

————. *The Twilight of Common Dreams: Why America Is Wracked by Culture Wars*. New York: Metropolitan Books, 1995.

Glessing, Robert J. *The Underground Press in America*. Bloomington: Indiana University Press, 1970.

Gold, Herbert. "Letter from San Francisco." *New York Times*, April 4, 1976.

Goldman, Robert, and Stephen Papson. *Nike Culture*. London: Sage, 1998.

Goody, Jack, and Ian Watt. "The Consequences of Literacy." In *Communication in History*, eds. David Crowley and Paul Heyer. White Plains, N.Y.: Longman Publishers, 1995.

Graham, Judith, ed. *Current Biography Yearbook*. New York: H.W. Wilson, 1992.

Greco, Albert. "Publishers in Migration." *Publishers Weekly* (October 12, 1992): 30–31.

Greene, Wade. "The New Alchemists." *New York Times*, August 8, 1976.

Gregg, Richard. "Voluntary Simplicity (1)." *CoEvolution Quarterly* (Summer 1977): 20–27.

Griswold, Wendy. *Bearing Witness: Readers, Writers and the Novel in Nigeria*. Princeton: Princeton University Press, 2000.

Grossberg, Lawrence. *Dancing in Spite of Myself: Essays on Popular Culture*. Durham, N.C.: Duke University Press, 1997.

Grumbach, D. "Marriage, Open and Otherwise." *Commonwealth* (January 5, 1973): 305–307.

Gussow, Alan. "The Future Is Circular." *Earth Day: The Beginning*. New York: Arno Press, 1970.

Hadot, Pierre. *Philosophy as a Way of Life*, ed. Arnold Ira Davidson. Translated by Michael Chase. Cambridge: Blackwell, 1995.

Hall, Stuart. "Cultural Studies and its Theoretical Legacies." In *Cultural Studies Reader*, eds. Cary Nelson, Paula Treichler and Laurence Grossberg. New York: Routledge, 1992.

————. "Cultural Studies and the Centre: Some Problematics and Problems." In *Culture, Media, Language: Working Papers in Cultural Studies, 1972–79*, Stuart Hall, Dorothy Hobson, Andrew Love, and Paul Willis, eds. Boston: Unwin Hyman, 1980, 15–47.

————. "Cultural Studies: Two Paradigms, Media, Culture and Society." In *Culture, History and Social Process*, eds. Tony Bennett, et al. London: Open University Press, 1981.

————. "The Problem of Ideology: Marxism without Guarantees." In *Stuart Hall: Critical Dialogues in Cultural Studies*, ed. Dave Morley. New York: Routledge, 1996.

————. *Culture, Media, Language: Working Papers in Cultural Studies 1972–1979*. London: Centre for Contemporary Cultural Studies, University of Birmingham, 1980.

Hall, Stuart, and Martin Jacques, eds. *New Times: The Changing Face of Politics in the 1990's*. London: Lawrence and Wishart, 1992.

Hall, Trish. "Striving to Be Cosmetically Correct." *New York Times*, May 27, 1993.

Halstead, R. "Publicity-Shy Whole Earth Grows Successful Organically." *San Francisco Business Journal* (May 12, 1986): 3.

Hammel, Lisa. "Will the Real Alex Comfort Please Stand Up?" *New York Times*, June 2, 1974.

Hammond, J. "Yuppies." *Public Opinion Quarterly*, no. 50 (1986): 487–502.

Hart, James. "Advertising Adds to Ills of Distrust." *Advertising Age*, no. 38 (1967): 34.

Hartley, A. "Impossibility of Dropping Out." *Horizon* 13 (1971): 104–5.

Hartman, William E., and M. A. Fithian. *Treatment of Sexual Dysfunction*. Long Beach, Calif.: Center for Marital and Sexual Studies, 1972.

Harvey, David. *The Condition of Postmodernity: An Enquiry into the Origins of Cultural Change*. Oxford: Blackwell, 1989.

Hawken, Paul. "Surviving in Small Business." *CoEvolution Quarterly* (Spring 1984): 14–17.

Hebdige, Dick. *Subculture: The Meaning of Style*. New York: Routledge, 1979.

Hedgepath, William, and Dennis Stock. *The Alternative: Communal Life in the New America*. New York: Macmillan, 1970.

Heelas, Paul, and Paul Morris, eds. *The Values of the Enterprise Culture: The Moral Debate*. London: Routledge, 1991.

Heelas, Paul, Scott Lash, and Paul Morris, eds. *Detraditionalization*. Oxford: Blackwell, 1996.

Henderson, Bill, ed. *The Publish It Yourself Handbook*. Wainscott, N.Y.: Pushcart, 1973.

Henderson, Hazel. *Creating Alternative Futures: the End of Economics*. New York: G. P. Putnam & Sons, 1978.

Henderson, Joe. *The Long Run Solution*. New York: World Publications, 1976.

———. *Long Slow Distance: The Humane Way to Train*. Mountain View, Calif.: Runner's World Magazine Press, 1969.

Henion, Karl E. "The Effects of Ecologically Relevant Information on Detergent Sales." *Journal of Marketing Research*, no. 9 (1972): 10–14.

Herberger, Roy. "The Ecological Product Buying Motive: A Challenge for Consumer Education." *Journal of Consumer Affairs*, no. 13 (1973): 187–95.

Herman, Robin. "Communal Life Adapts to Endure Decade of Change." Special to *New York Times*, August 15, 1979: A20.

Heywood, Ian, and Narry Sandywell. *Interpreting Visual Culture: Explorations in the Hermeneutics of the Visual*. New York: Routledge, 1999.

Hislop, Alan. "Straight Arrow Books." *Publishers Weekly* (October 18, 1973): 40.

Hodgman, Ann. "Flour Power." *New York Times Magazine* (March 30, 2003): 32.

Hoggart, Richard. *The Uses of Literacy*. New York: Oxford University Press, 1958.

Holbrow, Charles. "Orbiting Colonies will Bring Down-to-Earth Benefits." *Rotarian* (June 1978): 56.

Holman, Rebecca. "A Values and Lifestyle Perspective on Human Behavior." In *Personal Values and Consumer Psychology*, edited by Robert E. Pitts and Arch G. Woodside. Lexington, Mass.: Lexington Books, 1984.

Holt, Douglas. "Does Cultural Capital Structure American Consumption?" In *The Consumer Society Reader*, edited by Douglas B. Holt and Juliet Schor. New York: New Press, 2000.

———. "Poststructuralist Lifestyle Analysis: Conceptualizing the Social Patterning of Consumption in Postmodernity." *Journal of Consumer Research*, no. 4 (1997): 326–50.

Holt, Patricia. "The End of 'Me-ism' in (Western) America." *Publishers Weekly* (November 23, 1978): 32.

———. "Some New Directions in the Total Mix." *Publishers Weekly* (October 17, 1977): 49–51.

———. "Viewing the West as a Book Market." *Publishers Weekly* (September 27, 1976): 31–35.

hooks, bell. *Black Looks: Race and Representation.* Boston: South End Press, 1992.

Horowitz, Daniel. *The Morality of Spending.* Chicago: Ivan R. Dee, 1985.

Horton, Lucy. *Country Commune Cooking.* New York: Coward, McCann & Geoghegan. 1972.

Howard, Jane. *Please Touch: A Guided Tour of the Human Potential Movement.* New York: McGraw Hill, 1970.

Hurup, Elsebeth, ed. *The Lost Decade: America in the Seventies.* Aarhus, Denmark: Aarhus University Press, 1996.

Hutton, Isabel Emslie. *The Sex Technique in Marriage.* New York: Emerson Books, 1933.

Hylton, William H., ed. *Organically Grown Foods: What They Are and Why You Need Them.* Emmaus, Penn.: Rodale Press. 1973.

Illich, Ivan. *Deschooling Society.* New York: Harper & Row, 1971.

Illouz, Eva. *Consuming the Romantic Utopia: Love and the Cultural Contradictions of Capitalism.* Berkeley: University of California Press, 1997.

Jameson, Fredric. "Postmodernism, or the Cultural Logic of Late Capitalism." *New Left Review* (1984): 146.

———. *Postmodernism, or The Cultural Logic of Late Capitalism.* Durham, N.C.: Duke University Press, 1991.

———. "Periodizing the Sixties." In *The Sixties without Apology,* edited by Sohnya Sayres, Anders Stephenson, and Stanley Aronowitz. Minneapolis: University of Minnesota Press, 1984.

Jay, Martin. *Vision in Context: Historical and Contemporary Perspectives on Sight.* New York: Routledge, 1996.

Jenkins, Nancy. "Health Food and the Change in Eating Habits." *New York Times,* April 4, 1984.

Jerome, J. "Rumors of Change." *Directory of Intentional Communities,* no. 22 (1978): 16.

"Jogging for Heart and Health: It's Catching On." *U.S. News & World Report* (December 25, 1967): 49.

John, Bubba Free. *Conscious Exercise and the Transcendental Sun.* Middletown, Calif.: Dawn Horse Press, 1977.

Johnson, Lee. Email Exchanges with Sam Binkley. November 2000-January 2001.

Johnson, Pyke. "Book People: A West Coast Paperback Wholesaler." *Publishers Weekly* (June 1969): 44–47.

Johnson, Stancil E. D. *Frisbee: Practitioner's Manual and Definitive Treatise.* New York: Workman Publishing Co., 1975.

Johnson, Warren B. "Battling the Environment: Conservation Turns to Ecology." In *Evolution of Mass Culture in America: 1877 to Present,* ed. Gerald R. Baydo. St. Louis, Missouri: Forum Press, 1982.

Jones, Ita. *The Grubbag: an Underground Cookbook.* New York: Random House, 1971.

Kahn, Lloyd. *Shelter I.* Bolinas, Calif.: Shelter Publications, 1973.

———. *Shelter II.* Bolinas, Calif.: Shelter Publications, 1973.

Kanter, Rosabeth Moss. *Commitment and Community: Communes and Utopias in Sociological Perspective.* Cambridge, Mass.: Harvard University Press, 1972.

Katzen, Mollie. *The Moosewood Cookbook: Recipes from Moosewood Restaurant, Ithaca, New York*. Berkeley, Calif.: Ten Speed, 1977.

Keat, Russell, and Nicholas Abercrombie, eds. *Enterprise Culture*. London: Routledge, 1990.

Kellner, Douglas. "Popular Culture and the Construction of Postmodern Identities." In *Modernity and Identity*, edited by Scott Lash and Jonathan Friedman. Oxford: Blackwell, 1992.

———. *Media Culture: Cultural Studies, Identity, and Politics Between the Modern and the Postmodern*. London and New York: Routledge, 1995.

Kennedy, Mopsy Strange. "The 'No-Nonsense' School vs. the 'Please-Give-Me-Back-My-Nonsense' School." *New York Times*, January 14, 1973.

Killingsworth, Jimmie, and Jacqueline S. Palmer. *Ecospeak: Rhetoric and Environmental Politics in America*. Carbondale: Southern Illinois University Press, 1992.

King, P. "Publishers Look West for New Ideas." *Rockford Sunday Magazine* (June 25, 1978): B30.

King, Seth. "Sex Counseling Is Offered by at Least 3,500 Organizations in U.S." *New York Times*, May 5, 1974.

Kinnard, Judy. "A Singles Convention for the 'Aware' Adult—Not the Swingers." *New York Times*, August 20, 1973.

Kinnear, Thomas C., and James R. Taylor. "The Effect of Ecological Concern on Brand Perceptions." *Journal of Marketing Research* 10 (1973): 191–97.

Kirk, Andrew. "Appropriating Technology: The Whole Earth Catalog and Counterculture Environmental Politics." *Environmental History* 6, no. 3 (2001): 374–94.

Klein, Naomi. *No Logo*. New York: Picador, 1998.

Kleiner, Art. *The Age of Heretics*. New York: Doubleday, 1996.

Kotler, Philip, and Sidney J. Levy. "Broadening the Concept of Marketing." *Journal of Marketing*, no. 33 (1969): 55–57.

Kramer, Mark. *Mother Pig and the Pig Tragedy*. New York: Knopf, 1972.

Kramer, Rita. "It's Time to Start Listening." *New York Times*, September 17, 1967.

Kremen, Bennet. "Unrequired Reading: East Meets West." *New York Times Book Review* (February 15, 1970): 5.

Kristol, Irving. "Business and the New Class." *Wall Street Journal*, May 19, 1975, 32.

Lafaber, Walter. *Michael Jordan and the New Global Capitalism*. New York: Norton & Co., 1999.

Lamont, Michèle, and Robert Wuthnow. "Betwixt and Between: Recent Cultural Sociology in Europe and the United States." In *Frontiers of Social Theory*, edited by George Ritzer. New York: Columbia University Press, 1990.

Lamont, Michèle, and Marcel Fournier, eds. *Cultivating Differences*. Chicago: University of Chicago Press, 1992.

Landy, Eugene E. *The Underground Dictionary*. New York: Simon and Schuster, 1971.

Langman, Lauren. "Neon Cages: Shopping for Subjectivity." In *Lifestyles of Consumption*, edited by Rob Shields. London: Routledge, 1993.

Lappé, Frances Moore. *Diet for a Small Planet*. New York: Ballantine Books, 1971.

Lasch, Christopher. *The Culture of Narcissism: American Life in the Age of Diminished Expectations*. New York: Norton, 1978.

———. *The Minimal Self: Psychic Survival in Troubled Times*. New York: W.W. Norton, 1984.

Lash, Scott. "Discourse or Figure? Postmodernism as a 'Regime of Signification.'" *Theory, Culture, and Society*, no. 5 (1988): 311–36.

Lash, Scott M., and John Urry. *Economies of Signs and Space*. London: Sage, 1994.

———. *The End of Organized Capitalism*. London: Polity Press, 1987.

———. *Sociology of Postmodernism*. London and New York: Routledge, 1990.

"Latest Rage: Getting People to 'Tune Into Themselves.'" *U.S. News & World Report* (February 16, 1976): 40.

Leach, W. R. *Land of Desire: Merchants, Power and the Rise of a New American Culture*. New York: Pantheon Books, 1993.

Leadbeader, Charlie. "Power to the Person." In *New Times: the Changing Face of Politics in the 1990's*, eds. Stuart Hall and M. Jackques. London: Lawrence and Wishart, 1989.

Lears, Jackson. *Fables of Abundance: A Cultural History of Advertising in America*. New York: Basic Books, 1994.

———. "From Salvation to Self-Realization: Advertising and the Therapeutic Roots of the Consumer Culture, 1880–1930." In *The Culture of Consumption: Critical Essays in American History, 1880–1980*, eds. R. Wightman Fox and J. Lears. New York: Pantheon Books, 1983.

Leary, Timothy. *Start Your Own Religion*. Millbrook, N.Y.: Kriya Press of the Sri Ram Ashrama, 1967.

Lee, John M. "Decades and Dollars." *New York Times*, January 1, 1980.

———. "The 70's: America Learns to Expect a Little Less." *New York Times*, December 16, 1979.

Leiss, William, Stephen Kline, and Sut Jhally. *Social Communication in Advertising*. New York: Routledge, 1990.

Leonard, George. "... The Games People Should Play." *Esquire* no. 82 (October 1974): 214–217.

———. *The Ultimate Athlete*. New York: Viking, 1974.

Leopold, Aldo. *Sand County Almanac*. New York: Ballantine Books, 1966.

Levy, Lawrence C. "Office Dress: Not Quite Anything Goes." *New York Times*, December 28, 1975.

Lewis, Daniel. "Keeping Up with the Joneses' Cuisinart." *New York Times*, December 30, 1979.

Lewis, Lionel, and Dennis Brissett. "Sex as Work." *Social Problems* no. 15 (1967): 8–17.

Lieblich, Amia, Rivka Tuval-Mashiach, and Tamar Zilber. *Narrative Research: Reading, Analysis, and Interpretation*. London: Sage, 1998.

Linde, Charlotte. *Life Stories: The Creation of Coherence*. Oxford: Oxford University Press, 1993.

Lipnack, Jessica. *Networking: The First Report and Directory*. Garden City, N.J.: Doubleday, 1982.

Lippert, Barbara. "Nike's 'Revolution' Is Over and Everyone's a Winner." *Adweek* (August 22, 1988): 6.

Lipsyte, Robert. "Sports." *New York Times*, December 5, 1976.

Lovejoy, Arthur O. *The Great Chain of Being*. Cambridge, Mass.: Harvard University Press, 1936.

Lovelock, James. *The Ages of Gaia: A Biography of Our Living Earth*. New York: Norton, 1988.

Lovins, Amory. *Soft Energy Paths: Toward a Durable Peace*. San Francisco, Calif.: Friends of the Earth International, Ballinger, 1977.

Lowen, Alexander. *Bioenergetics*. New York: Penguin Books, 1976.

Luckmann, Thomas. *The Invisible Religion: the Problem of Religion in Modern Society*. New York: Macmillan, 1967.

Lunt, Peter, and Sonia M. Livingstone. *Mass Consumption and Personal Identity*. Buckingham: Open University Press, 1992.

Lynd, Robert, and Helen Lynd. *Middletown: A Study in American Culture*. New York: Harcourt Brace, 1929.

Lyotard, Jean François. *The Post Modern Condition: A Report on Knowledge*. Translated by Geoff Bennington and Brian Massumi. Minneapolis: University of Minnesota Press, 1984.

MacDonald, Dwight. "A Theory of Mass Culture." In *Mass Culture: The Popular Arts in America*, edited by Bernard Rosenberg. New York: Free Press, 1965.

Maffesoli, Michel. *The Time of the Tribes: The Decline of Individualism in Mass Society*. Translated by Don Smith. London: Sage Publications, 1996.

"Magazine Survey." *CoEvolution Quarterly* (Spring 1979): 73–131.

Mailer, Norman. "The White Negro." In *Advertisements for Myself*. New York: New American Library, 1959.

Marchand, Roland. *Advertising the American Dream: Making Way for Modernity, 1920–1940*. Berkeley: University of California Press, 1985.

Markley, O. W., Joseph Campbell, and Harmann Willis. *Changing Images of Man*. Stanford, Calif.: Pergamon, 1982.

Martin, Bernice. *A Sociology of Contemporary Cultural Change*. New York: St. Martin's Press, 1981.

Masters, William, and Virginia Johnson. *Human Sexual Inadequacy*. London: Churchill, 1970.

———. *Human Sexual Response*. Boston: Little, Brown & Company, 1966.

McClanahan, E., and G. Norman. "The Whole Earth Catalog." *Esquire* (July 1970): 95–125.

McCracken, Grant. *Culture and Consumption: New Approaches to the Symbolic Character of Consumer Goods and Activities*. Bloomington: Indiana University Press, 1988.

McDowell, Edwin. "Small Book-Publishing Firms Flourishing." *New York Times*, February 23, 1981.

McKenzie, D. F. *Bibliography and the Sociology of Texts*. Cambridge: University Press, 1999.

McRobbie, Angela. *British Fashion Design: Rag Trade or Image Industry?* New York: Routledge, 1998.

Meadows, D. H., D. L. Meadows, Jorgen Randers, and William W. Behrens. *The Limits to*

Growth: The Report for the Club of Rome's Project on the Predicament of Mankind. New York: Universe Books, 1972.

Melville, Keith. *Communes in the Counterculture: Origins, Theories, Styles of Life*. New York: William Morrow and Co., 1972.

Mercer, K. "Welcome to the Jungle: Identity and Diversity in Postmodern Politics." In *Community, Culture, Difference*, ed. J. Rutherford. London: Lawrence & Wishart, 1990.

Mermelstein, David. "The Threatening Economy." *New York Times*, December 30, 1979.

Meyrowitz, Joshua. *No Sense of Place: The Impact of Electronic Media on Social Behavior*. New York: Oxford University Press, 1985.

Michener, James A. "The Revolution in Middle-Class Values." *New York Times*, August 18, 1968.

Mickel, Howard. "Beyond Competition." *Runner's World* (Winter 1973): 10–12.

Miller, Daniel, ed. *Acknowledging Consumption*. London: Routledge, 1995.

————, ed. *Material Cultures: Why Some Things Matter*. Chicago: University of Chicago Press, 1998.

————, et al. *Shopping, Place and Identity*. New York: Routledge, 1998.

————. *A Theory of Shopping*. Ithaca, N.Y.: Cornell University Press, 1998.

Miller, Peter, and Nikolas Rose. "Mobilizing the Consumer: Assembling the Subject of Consumption." *Theory, Culture and Society* 14 (1997): 1–36.

Miller, Stephan Paul. *The Seventies Now: Culture as Surveillance*. Durham, N.C.: Duke University Press, 1999.

Miller, Stuart. *Hot Springs: the True Adventures of the First New York Jewish Literary Intellectual in the Human Potential Movement*. New York: Viking, 1971.

Mills, C. Wright. *White Collar: The American Middle Classes*. New York: Oxford University Press, 1956.

Mirzoeff, Nicholas, ed. *Visual Culture Reader*. New York: Routledge, 1998.

Mitchell, Arnold. *Life Ways and Lifestyles*. Stanford, Calif.: Business Intelligence Program, SRI, 1973.

————. *The Nine American Lifestyles: Who We Are and Where We're Going*. New York: Macmillan, 1983.

Mitgang, Herbert. "In California, Book Publishing Takes on New Forms." *New York Times*, May 27, 1979.

Mosher, C. "New Pioneers in Iowa City." *Briarpatch Review* 6 (1976): 130–34.

Mowrey, Marc, and Tim Redmond. *Not in Our Backyard*. New York: William Morrow and Co., 1993.

Mungo, Raymond. "Living on the Earth." *New York Times*, March 21, 1971.

————. *Cosmic Profit*. Boston: Little Brown & Company, 1980.

————. *Total Loss Farm: A Year in the Life*. New York: E. P. Dutton, 1970.

Murphy, J. F. "Counterculture of Leisure." *Parks and Recreation* 7 (1972): 34.

Murray, Barbara. "Major Federal Consumer Protection Laws, 1906–1970." In *Consumerism: The Eternal Triangle*, edited by Barbara Murray. Pacific Palisades, Calif.: Good Year Publishing, 1973.

Murray, R. "Fordism and Post-Fordism." In *New Times: The Changing Face of Politics in the 1990's*, edited by Stuart Hall and Michel Jacques. London: Lawrence and Wishart, 1989.

National American Student Cooperative Organization. *Community Market* (catalogue). Ann Arbor, Mich., 1971.

Nearing, Scott, and Helen Nearing. *Living the Good Life: Being a Plain Practical Account of a Twenty Year Project in a Self-Subsistent Homestead in Vermont*. Harborside, Maine: Social Science Institute, 1954.

Nelson, Alix. "Paperback." *New York Times*, December 8, 1974.

New Alchemy Institute. *Journal of New Alchemy*. New York: Penguin, 1978.

"New Collar Workers." *Industry Week* (August 15, 1988): 36.

New York Times. "Americans Spent More Money and More Time Just Playing," December 31, 1972.

———. "'Eastern Literary Establishment' Taken to Task at P.E.N. Meeting," November 23, 1977, 55.

———. "Harper & Row Plans to Move Religious Unit," September 12, 1976.

———. "Her Hymn to Nature Is a Guidebook for the Simplest of Lives," March 26, 1971.

———. "Management Views Office Fashions," July 14, 1968.

———. "Novelty Confections Aim for Youth Market," August 25, 1982.

———. "Reagan, Scoring Courts, Links Shooting to Permissive Attitude," June 6, 1968, 29.

———. "Throat Cutting," March 4, 1973.

Nixon, Sean. *Advertising Cultures: Gender, Commerce, Creativity*. London: Sage, 2003.

Nixon, Sean, and Paul Du Gay, eds. "Who Needs Cultural Intermediaries?" Special issue of *Cultural Studies*, no. 16 (2004): 495–500.

Nobile, Philip, ed. *The Con III Controversy: The Critics look at the Greening of America*. New York: Pocket Books, 1971.

Office of Federal Statistical Policy & Standards, Bureau of Census. *American Social Attitudes: Social Indicators III*. Washington, DC: Federal Statistical System, U.S. Department of Commerce, December 1980.

Ogilvy, James. "The Experience Industry." *American Demographics* (December 1986): 27–29, 54.

O'Neil, Nena, and George O'Neil. *Open Marriage: A New Life Style for Couples*. New York: Avon, 1972.

O'Neill, Gerard K. "Space: A Place in the Sun." *New York Times*, June 12, 1975, 37.

———. *High Frontier: Communities in Space*. New York: Morrow, 1977.

Ong, Walter. "Orality, Literacy, and Modern Media Communication." In *Communication in History*, edited by David Crowley and Paul Heyer. White Plains, N.Y.: Longman Publishers, 1995.

Orwell, George. *1984*. New York: Harcourt, Brace. 1949.

"Outlook for the '70's: Fair with Some Showers." New York Times Book Review (February 15, 1970): 1.

Pace, Eric. "Book Publishing Is Flowering on Coast." *New York Times*, June 19, 1973, 30.

Pacific Domes. *Domebook I*. Bolinas, Calif.: Pacific Domes, 1970.

————. *Domebook II*. Bolinas, Calif.: Pacific Domes, 1971.

Packard, Vance Oakley. *Hidden Persuaders*. New York: D. McKay Co., 1957.

————. *The Status Seekers; An Exploration of Class Behavior in America and the Hidden Barriers that Affect You, Your Community, Your Future*. New York: D. McKay Co., 1959.

Peer, Elizabeth, L. Whitman, P. Simons, and J. Huck. "The Work Junkies." *Newsweek*, October 8, 1978, 87.

Penchansky, Mimi. "Alternatives in Print." *Library Journal* (February 15, 1972): 730–731.

Peppers, Don, and Martha Rogers. *The One to One Future*. New York: Double Day Sommer and Dale, 1993.

Peyser, Joan. "The Boys from Liverpool." *New York Times*, September 29, 1968.

Phillips, Michael, and Salli Rasberry. *Honest Business*. Boulder, Colo.: Shambhala, 1984.

Phillips, Michael. *Marketing without Advertising*. Berkeley, Calif.: Nolo, 1986.

————. *Seven Laws of Money*. Menlo Park, Calif.: Word Wheel, 1974.

————. *Transaction Based Economics: Small Business Lessons for Economic Theory*. San Francisco, Calif.: Clear Glass, 1984.

Plummer, J.T. "The Concept of Life Style Segmentation." *Journal of Marketing* no. 38 (1974): 33–37.

Poirier, Richard. "Learning from the Beatles." *Partisan Review* 34 (1967): 526–46.

Popenoe, Cris. *Books for Inner Development: The Yes! Guide*. New York: Random House, 1976.

————. *Wellness: The Yes! Bookshop Guide*. New York: Random House, 1977.

Potter, David Morris. *People of Plenty; Economic Abundance and the American Character*. Chicago: University of Chicago Press, 1954.

Putnam, Robert. *Bowling Alone: the Collapse and Revival of American Community*. New York: Simon & Schuster, 2000.

Radway, Janice. "The Scandal of the Middlebrow: The Book-of-the-Month Club, Class Fracture, and Cultural Authority." *South Atlantic Quarterly* (Fall 1990): 705.

————. *A Feeling for Books: The Book-of-the-Month Club, Literary Taste, and Middle-Class Desire*. Chapel Hill: University of North Carolina Press, 1997.

Raskin, J. "Beads in a Time of Inflation: Counterculture Working Class." *Nation*, October 26, 1974, 403–4.

Raymont, Henry. "Juror Quits Book Panel Over 'Whole Earth Catalog.'" *New York Times* (April 5, 1972): 35.

————. "Notes of Concern Mark Book Award Ceremony." *New York Times* (April 14, 1972): 21.

Reich, Charles. *The Greening of America*. New York: Random House, 1970.

Reid, Gary. *The Complete Book of Rolfing: Using Physical Therapy to Restructure Your Life*. New York: Drake Publishers, 1978.

Reif, Rita. "It's Taken Twenty Years, but the Dome as a Home Is Catching On." *New York Times*, November 17, 1971.

Reisman, David, Nathan Glazer and Reuel Denney. *The Lonely Crowd: A Study of the Changing American Character*. New Haven, Conn.: Yale University Press, 1950.

Reynolds, F. D. "An Analysis of Catalog Buying Behavior." *Journal of Marketing*, no. 45 (1974): 47–51.

Rieff, Philip. *The Triumph of the Therapeutic: Uses of Faith After Freud*. Chicago: University of Chicago Press, 1966.

Riessman, Catherine Kohler. *Narrative Analysis*. London: Sage, 1993.

Rimke, Heidi Marie. "Governing Citizens Through Self-help Literature." *Cultural Studies* 14, no. 1 (2000): 61–78.

Roberts, Ron. *The New Communes*. Englewood Cliffs, N.J.: Prentice Hall, 1971.

Roberts, Steven V. "Mail Order Catalogue of the Hip Becomes a National Best Seller." *New York Times*, April 12, 1970.

Roberts, Steven V. "Youth Communes Seek New Way of Life." *The New York Times*, August 3, 1970: 28.

Robertson, Laurel. *Laurel's Kitchen: A Handbook for Vegetarian Cookery and Nutrition*. New York: Bantam, 1978.

Rockefeller, Laurance. "The Case for a Simpler Life-style." *Reader's Digest* vol. 108, no. 646 (1976): 61–65.

Rolf, Ida P. *Ida Rolf Talks about Rolfing and Physical Reality*. New York: Harper and Row, 1978.

———. *Rolfing: The Integration of Human Structures*. New York: Harper and Row, 1977.

———. *Structural Integration: Gravity and the Unexplored Factor in a More Human Use of Human Beings*. Boulder, Colo.: Rolf Institute of Structural Integration, 1962.

Ronco, William. *Food Co-ops*. Boston: Beacon Press, 1974.

Rose, Nikolas. "Governing the Enterprising Self." In *The Values of the Enterprise Culture: The Moral Debate*, edited by Paul Heelas and Paul Morris. London: Routledge, 1992.

———. "Identity, Genealogy, History." In *Questions of Cultural Identity*, edited by Stuart Hall and Paul Du Gay. London: Sage, 1996.

———. *Powers of Freedom: Reframing Political Thought*. Cambridge: Cambridge University Press, 1999.

Ross, Andrew. *The Chicago Gangster Theory of Life: Nature's Debt to Society*. New York: Verso, 1994.

———. *Universal Abandon: The Politics of Postmodernism*. Minneapolis: University of Minnesota Press, 1988.

Roszak, Theodore. *The Making of a Counterculture*. Berkeley: University of California Press, 1968.

———. *From Satori to Silicon Valley*. San Francisco, Calif.: Don't Call It Frisco, 1985.

———. *Planet/Person*. New York: Doubleday, 1978.

Rubin, Jerry. *Growing Up at Thirty-Seven*. New York: M. Evans and Co., 1976.

Runner's World. "The New Frontier."

Rush, Anne Kent. *Getting Clear: Body Work for Women*. New York: Random House, 1973.

Sale, Kirkpatrick. "Consider the Windmill," *New York Times*, July 24, 1977.

Salpukas, Agis. "Underground Papers Are Thriving on Campuses and in Cities Across Nation." *New York Times*, April 5, 1970.

Schulman, Bruce J. *The Seventies*. New York: Free Press, 2001.

Schumacher, E. F. *Small Is Beautiful: Economics as If People Mattered*. New York: Harper & Row Publishers, 1973.

Schwartz, Robert. "The Countercultural Entrepreneur." *Executive* 4, No. 1 (1976): 32–35.

Scott-Heron, Gil. "Whitey on the Moon." In *The Revolution Will Not Be Televised*. New York: Flying Dutchmen Records, 1974.

See, Lisa. "California Style." *Publishers Weekly* (October 12, 1992): 32–34.

Seeger, Arthur. *The Berkeley Barb: Social Control of an Underground Newspaper*. New York: Irvington Publishers, 1983.

Sennett, Richard. *The Corrosion of Character*. New York: Norton, 1998.

———. *The Fall of Public Man*. New York: Vintage Books, 1978.

Shapiro, Stanley. "Marketing to a Conserver Society." *Business Horizons* no. 21 (April 1978): 3–13.

Shi, David. *The Simple Life: Plain Living and High Thinking in American Culture*. New York: Oxford University Press, 1985.

Shields, Rob, ed. *Lifestyle Shopping: The Subject of Consumption*. London: Routledge, 1992.

Shuttleworth, John, ed. *The Mother Earth News Handbook of Home Business Ideas and Plans*. Henderson, N.C.: The Mother Earth News Inc., 1976.

Sigal, Richard. "Inflation as a Deflater of the Masculine Role." *New York Times*, April 19, 1981.

Silverman, Stanley. "Rock and Classical: A Hairline Apart?" *New York Times*, March 9, 1969.

Simmel, Georg. *On Individuality and Social Forms: Selected Writings*. Translated by Donald N. Levine. Chicago: University of Chicago Press, 1971.

Simple, Inwardly Rich. New York: William Murrow & Co., 1981.

Sisk, John P. "The Fear of Affluence." *Commentary* 57 (June 1974).

Slater, Don, and Fran Tonkiss. *Market Society: Markets and Modern Social Thought*. Cambridge: Polity Press, 2001.

Slater, Don. *Consumer Culture and Modernity*. Oxford: Polity Press, 1997.

Slater, Philip Elliot. *The Pursuit of Loneliness; American Culture at the Breaking Point*. Boston: Beacon Press, 1970.

Sobel, Michael E. *Lifestyle and Social Structure: Concepts, Definitions, Analyses*. New York: Academic Press, 1981.

"Sociologists See Shifts in Living and Buying Habits." *Advertising Age* (April 16 1975): 23, 76.

Sontag, Susan. *Against Interpretation*. New York: Farrar, Straus & Giroux, 1966.

"Special Issue on Western Publishing." *Publishers Weekly* (October 9, 1972): 36–84.

Speck, Ross, et al. *The New Families*. New York: Basic Books, 1972.

Spigel, Lynn. *Private Screenings: Television and the Female Consumer*. Minneapolis: University of Minnesota Press, 1992.

Spigel, Lynn. *Welcome to the Dreamhouse: Popular Media and Postwar Suburbs*. Durham, N.C.: Duke University Press, 2001.

Stanford Research Institute. *City Size and the Quality of Life: An Analysis of the Policy Implications of Continued Population Concentration*. Washington, D.C.: National Science Foundation, 1975.

Steilf, William. "Why the Birds Cough." *Progressive*, no. 34 (1970): 47–54.

Stein, Barry. "Small Business." In *Stepping Stones: Appropriate Technology and Beyond*, ed. Lane de Moll and Gigi Coe. New York: Schocken Books, 1978.

Stephens, Mitchell. *The Rise of the Image, the Fall of the Word*. New York: Oxford University Press, 1998.

Stevens, Barry. *Don't Push the River*. Lafayette, Calif.: Real People Press, 1970.

Strumpel, Burkhard. "The Future of Affluence." In *Social Indicators of Changes in Economic Welfare and Behavior: 1972–1977*. Ann Arbor: University of Michigan Press, 1975.

Stuttaford, Genevieve. "Northern California's Exploding Book Market." *Publishers Weekly* (October 9, 1972): 39–46.

Sullivan, James D. *On The Walls and in the Streets: American Poetry Broadsides from the 1960's*. Chicago: University of Illinois Press, 1997.

Sundancer, Elaine. *Celery Wine: Story of a Country Commune*. Yellow Springs, Ohio: Community Publications Cooperative, 1973.

Sussman, Warren I. *Culture as History: The Transformation of American Society in the Twentieth Century*. New York: Pantheon Books, 1984.

———. "'Personality' and the Making of Twentieth-Century Culture." In Sussman, *Culture as History*. New York: Pantheon Books. 1984, 271–85.

Swenson, Chester. *Selling to a Segmented Market: the Lifestyle Approach*. Lincolnwood, IL: NTC Business Books, 1992.

Swick-Perry, Helen. *The Human Be-In*. New York: Basic Books, 1970.

Taylor, Angela. "The Doubts Linger, but the Longhairs Are Being Trimmed." *New York Times*, January 10, 1974.

Tebbel, John. *A History of Book Publishing in the United States, Vol IV: The Great Change, 1940–1980*. New York: Bowker Company, 1981.

Tetrault, Jeanne, and Sherry Thomas. *Country Woman: A Handbook for the New Farmer*. New York: Anchor Books, 1975.

"The Aging Youth Market." *Industry Week* no. 188 (1976): 26–34.

"The Embargo: Waiting for the End." *Newsweek* (March 18, 1974): 94–96.

"The Western Scene." *Publishers Weekly* (April 29, 1974): 26–30.

"The Whole Earth Catalog." *Publishers Weekly* (May 11, 1970): 20–21.

The Wild One. Directed by Laszlo Benedek. Columbia Pictures, 1953.

Thomas, William. *International Symposium on Man's Role in Changing the Face of the Earth*. Chicago: Published by the Wenner-Gren Foundation for Anthropological Research, 1955.

Thompson, William. "East Is Still East and West Is Still West." *The New York Times*, February 24, 1978, 34.

Thornton, Sarah, ed. *The Subcultures Reader*. London and New York: Routledge, 1997.

———. *Club Cultures: Music, Media and Subcultural Capital*. Cambridge: Polity Press, 1995.

Time. "Missal for Mammals," November 21, 1969, 75–76.

———. "Karma Yes, Toilets No: Counter Culture Architecture of the San Francisco Bay Area," November 5, 1973, 75.

Tipton, Steven. *Getting Saved from the Sixties.* Berkeley: University of California Press, 1982.

Todd, John. "The New Alchemists." *CoEvolution Quarterly* (Spring 1976): 55.

———. "Tomorrow Is Our Permanent Address." *Journal of the New Alchemists* no. 4 (1977): 84–88.

Todd, Nancy Jack, ed. *Book of the New Alchemists.* New York: Dutton, 1977.

Toffler, Alvin. *Future Shock.* New York: Bantam, 1970.

Tomczak, Garret. "The Limits." *Runner's World* (May 1972): 22–23.

Townsend, Bickley. "Nine Lives." *American Demographics* (December 1982): 16–18.

Turner, Bryan. *The Body and Society.* London: Basil Blackwell, 1984.

Turner, Fred. *From Counterculture to Cyberculture: Stewart Brand, the Whole Earth Network, and the Rise of Digital Utopianism.* Chicago: University of Chicago Press, 2006.

Turow, James. *Breaking Up America.* Chicago: University of Chicago Press, 1997.

U.S. News and World Report. "Communes: A More Businesslike Style" (March 3, 1980): 67.

———. "Is the Malaise Real?" (November 1974): 25.

———. "Flaunting Wealth Is Back in Style," (September 21, 1981): 61–62.

———. "Youth: Greed Gains Ground" (January 25, 1988).

Veblen, Thorstein. *The Theory of the Leisure Class.* New York: A. M. Kelley Bookseller, 1899.

Vidich, Arthur J. *The New Middle Classes.* New York: New York University Press, 1994.

Von Hoffman, Nicholas. *We Are the People Our Parents Warned Us Against.* Chicago: Quadrangle, 1968.

Voorhis, Jerry. "The Consumer Movement and the Hope of Human Survival." *Journal of Consumer Affairs* 11, no. 1 (1977): 1–18.

Wallace, William N. "New Esalen Center Spurs a Sports Revolution." *New York Times*, April 15, 1973.

Walters, Ray. "Paperback Talk." *New York Times*, April 24, 1977.

Warne, Gary. "Demystifying Business." In *The Briarpatch Book*, ed. Briarpatch Community. San Francisco, Calif.: New Glide/Reed Books, 1978.

Warner, W. L., M. Meeker and K. Eells. *Social Class in America: The Evaluation of Status.* New York: Harper Torchbooks, 1949.

Way, Bluejay. "Future Shock, Reality Shock, and Unresolved Contradiction." *Utopian Eyes* Vol. I, No. 3 (1977): 22–25.

Weber, Max. "Basic Sociological Terms." In *Economy and Society Vol I*. Translated by Ephraim Fischoff. Berkeley: University of California Press, 1978.

Weber, Max. "Science as a Vocation." In *From Max Weber.* Translated by H. H. Gerth and C. Wright Mills. New York: Oxford University Press, 1946.

———. *The Protestant Ethic and the Spirit of Capitalism.* London: Routledge, 1992.

Webster, Frederick E., Jr. "Defining the Characteristics of the Socially Conscious Consumer." *Journal of Consumer Research*, no. 2 (1975): 188–96.

Weinraub, Bernard. "Esalen Encounter Group Finds British in Touch." *New York Times*, June 15, 1970.

Weiss, Michael. *The Clustered World: How We Live, What We Buy, and What It all Means About Who We Are.* Boston: Little & Brown, 2000.

Welles, Annette. "Steady Expansion in Southern California." *Publishers Weekly*, October 9, 1972, 47–54.

Wells, Linda. "Boutique Chic." *New York Times*, February 19, 1989.

Wells, Patricia. "Book Helps with Books That Help." *New York Times*, November 29, 1977.

Welsh, Pat. "This is Earth Calling Berkeley." *Publishers Weekly* (July 5, 1971): 38–40.

Whitmyer, Claude, and Salli Rasberry. *Running a One-Person Business*. San Francisco, Calif.: Ten Speed, 1992.

"Who, How, When, Where, Why They Make a Catalog." *Doing It!* 1, no. 3 (1976): 68–70.

Whole Earth Catalog Records, 1969–1986. Department of Special Collections, Manuscripts Division, reference number M-1045, Stanford University, Stanford, California.

"Why Another Growth Center." *Utopian Eyes*, no. 5 (1977): 24–25.

Whyte, William. *The Organization Man*. New York: Simon and Schuster, 1956.

Williamson, Judith. *Decoding Advertisements: Ideology and Meaning in Advertising*. London: Boyars, 1978.

Wolfe, T. "The Me Decade and the Third Great Awakening." *New York Magazine*, August 1976, 27–48.

Wouters, C. "Formalization and Informalization: Changing Tension Balances in Civilizing Processes." *Theory, Culture and Society* 3, no. 2 (1986): 1–18.

Wuthnow, Robert. *Meaning and Moral Order: Explorations in Cultural Analysis*. Berkeley: University of California Press, 1987.

Yankelovich, Daniel. *The New Morality: A Profile of American Youth in the 70's*. New York: McGraw Hill, 1974.

Yenckel, James T. "And Now for the Men's Movement." *Washington Post*, June 18, 1981.

Yovovich, B. G. "The New Localism: Upscale Readers Scan the Scene." *Advertising Age* (April 5, 1982).

Zablocki, Benjamin. "Communes, Encounter Groups, and the Search for Community." In *Search for Community*, edited by Kurt W. Back. Boulder, Colo.: Westview, 1978.

Index

Lifestyle expertise and advice, 87–88, 106–108, 130, 143–144; in advertising, 88–89; authority of, 77–80; on body and appearance, 211–216; of caring professionals, 50, 81–84, 87–88, 93, 101; on communal living, 186–187; counselor and, 79–80; countercultural business and, 197; holistic, 154, 156, 158–159; of Jane Fonda, 80; loosening and, 77–81, 101–102, 171; relationships and sexuality and, 171–178, 182–183, 211–214; testimonial endorsements and, 88; *Whole Earth Catalog* and, 154, 156, 158–159

Limits to Growth, 139–140

"Liquid modernity," 33–34, 58, 77, 166

Living on the Earth, 118–120, 225; cover of, 120

Long Run Solution, The, 240

Loosening up, 3–13, 15, 17, 19–24, 35–36, 58–61, 101, 129; advertising and, 93; of body and appearance, 207–211; caring text and, 78–80, 130–131, 162–163; communal living and, 188; consumption and, 55, 68–69, 75, 93, 206; in contemporary society, 246–248; countercultural business and, 206; countercultural print and, 101–102, 126; cultural capital and, 55, 58–60; dress and appearance and, 69; hairstyles and, 69, 209–211; jogging and, 241; legacy of, 68; lifestyle experts and, 76–81, 101–102; massage and, 224–228; middle-class, 30, 129; middle-class youth and, 28–32, 46–47, 55–61; narratives of, 61–68, 126, 129–131; nature and, 130–133; Nike and, 241–242; in the 1980s, 68–70, 243–246; Othering and, 55, 58–61; as permissiveness, 244–246; President Bush and, 15–16; relationships and, 130, 132, 165, 168; Rolfing and, 221–224; self-identity and, 27–36, 58–75, 100–103, 126, 129–132, 246–249; sexuality and, 171, 175, 177; as "slouching,"

28, 75–76; sports and fitness and, 230, 241–242; yuppies and, 13–15, 70–75. *See also* Caring; Intimacy discourse

Love, 169; "confluent," 171; Stewart Brand on, 205–206

Lovelace, Linda, 171–172

Lowen, Alexander, 217

LSD, 94, 149; experiments with, 85. *See also* Leary, Timothy

Lyotard, Jean-Francois, 133–134

MacDonald, Dwight, 53–54

Machlowitz, Marilyn, 73

Macintosh, 73–74

Magazines. *See* Countercultural print; *and under specific titles*

Mailer, Norman, 59, 64

Malaise, 31, 36–40, 42, 47; speech, 39

Marketing. *See* Advertising

Marketing without Advertising, 204

Markley, Oliver, 94

Marx, Karl, 33

Maslow, Abraham, 91

Massage, 220–228. *See also* Body work; Rolfing

Massage Book, The, 218, 225–228; cover of, 226; illustration from, 228

Masters, William, 175–177

Me Decade, 28, 62

Meditation in Action, 120

Mellowness, 34–35

Menlo Park Group, 159

Metanarratives, 133–134

Meyrowitz, Joshua, 106

Middle class (1970s), 27–61, 129; cultural capital and, 52–55; loosening-up lifestyle, 30; malaise in, 36–40, 42, 47; modest comforts of, 46–47

Mister Charlie: defined, 2

Mitchell, Arnold, 95, 97–99

Mitchell, Fred, 123

Modernity, 27–29, 31–32, 44–45; countercultural print and, 42, 46; Faustian double-bind in, 32; liquid, 33–34, 58, 77, 166; loosening and, 35, 130; metanarratives and, 133–134; middle-class, 30, 33
Modest comfort, 46–47
Moosewood Cookbook, The, 143
Morality (1970s), 27–28, 32, 62
Muir, John, 118
Mungo, Raymond, 32–33, 193
Murphy, Michael, 221, 230
Music, 56–57

Nader, Ralph, 90
Narcissism, 28, 80
NASCO (National Association of Student Cooperative Organization), 40, 42, 45
Nature. *See* Ecology
Nelson, Alix, 145–146
Nelson, Gaylord, 137–138
Networking: The First Report and Directory, 41
New Alchemy Institute, 40, 44–45
New Games Book, The, 235–237; cover of, 234
New Games tournament, 233–236
New Glide Publications, 122
New Harbinger, 40, 42
New Life Research Cooperative, 43–44
Newsweek, 71–72
New York Times, 145–146
Nike, 206, 241–242
Nine American Lifestyles, 95
Noren Institute, 203–204
Norwalk, Conn., 209–211
Nuclear families, 27, 62–63

Ogilvy, James, 99
Ong, Walter, 107–108
Ontological insecurity, 19, 65
Organic food, 163–164
Organization man, 28, 49, 58, 207

Organization Man, The, 49
Orwell, George, 60
Othering, 58–61
Our Bodies, Ourselves, 209, 211–214; cover of, 213

Pastoral life, 41
People's Yellow Pages, 105, 195–196, 198; cover of, 197
Permissiveness, 244–246
Phillips, Michael, 199–204, 206
Phosphates, 91
Pleasure, 217
Point Foundation, 160
Poirier, Richard, 57
Popenoe, Chris, 214–216, 223
Pornography, 171–172
Port Huron Statement, 46
Portola Institute, 159, 199
Post-Fordism, 21, 47–51, 54, 207; symbolic consumer goods and, 54
"Proles," 60
Publishers Weekly, 113–116
Publishing. *See* Countercultural print; West Coast publishing

Radway, Janice, 53
Rain: A Journal of Appropriate Technology, 146–149
Rainbook, 148; cover of, 148
Ram Dass (Richard Alpert), 84–85; *Be Here Now* and, 85–86
Ramparts, 122
Random House, 117, 122
Raspberry, Salli, 204
Raymond, Dick, 199
Reagan, Ronald, 32, 70, 243, 245
Real Simple, 96
Reich, Charles, 134, 170, 239
Reich, Christopher, 64
Reich, Wilhelm, 217

Reisman, David, 97

Relationships, 181–182; communal living and, 184–185; literature on, 166; loosening and, 130, 132, 165, 168; modern versus traditional, 166–167, 182–183; "pure," 167, 170–171; trust and, 166–171, 205–206. *See also* Communes and communal living; Sexuality and sexual technique

Riessman, Frank, 82, 84

Rinzler, Alan, 124

Roche, Daniel, 20

Rock and roll, 56–57

Rockford Sunday Magazine, 109

Roddick, Anita, 204–205

Rolf, Ida, 178, 221–224

Rolfing, 23, 66, 178, 221–224. *See also* Body work

Roszak, Theodore, 150

Rubin, Jerry, 66, 71, 244

Runner's World, 237–239

Running, 66, 237–241. *See also* Sports and fitness

Running a One Person Business, 203

Rush, Anne Kent, 86–87, 217–219

Sale, Kirkpatrick, 148

Samuels, Mike, 209

Sand County Almanac, A, 137

San Francisco. *See* Bay Area; Esalen Institute; West Coast publishing

Schumacher, E. F., 95, 138

Science, 134–136; in *CoEvolution Quarterly*, 160–161

Scott-Heron, Gil, 30–31, 35

Scrimshaw Press, 122–123

Self-actualization, 91

Seneca, 131

Sennett, Richard, 79–80

September 11th, 2001, 15

Sergeant Pepper's Lonely Hearts Club Band, 56–57

Service society, 81–84, 88, 195; consumerism and, 82–83. *See also* Caring professionals; Economy

Service Society and the Consumer Vanguard, The, 82

Seven Laws of Money, 199

Sex manuals, 172–173, 175–184. See also *Joy of Sex*

Sexuality and sexual technique, 168; birth control and, 170; *Catalog of Sexual Consciousness* and, 177–184; freedom and, 170, 181–182; *Human Sexual Inadequacy* and, 175–177; *Joy of Sex* and, 172–175; loosening and, 171, 175, 177; *Our Bodies, Ourselves* and, 211–214; "plastic," 170, 177; therapy for, 175–177; trust and, 179. *See also* Relationships

Shambhala Publications, 87, 120–122, 204; *Tassajara Bread Book* and, 120–122, 121

Shelter I and II, 189–190, 192

Shoes. *See* Dress and appearance

Shopping. *See* Consumption

Sierra Books, 123

Silent Spring, 137

Simple Living, 96

Slang, 1–4

Small is Beautiful, 95, 138

Smith, David, 215

Soft-Tech, 153

Solar-powered homes, 44

Space Colonies, 153, 161–162; cover of, 162

"Spaceman economy," 141

"Spaceship Earth," 138–140

Spiritual experimentation, 63

Spiritual Midwifery, 209

Sports and fitness, 228; experiential, at Esalen, 230–233; New Games tournament, 233–236; reclassification of, in the 1970s, 228–230; transformation of running and, 237–241; yuppies and, 73

Squares, 15, 49, 52, 60, 67, 168; body and,

Sam Binkley is an assistant professor of sociology at Emerson College.

Library of Congress Cataloging-in-Publication Data
Binkley, Sam, 1963–
Getting loose : lifestyle consumption in the 1970s / Sam Binkley.
p. cm.
Includes bibliographical references and index.
ISBN 978-0-8223-3973-1 (cloth : alk. paper)
ISBN 978-0-8223-3989-2 (pbk. : alk. paper)
1. Lifestyles—United States—History—20th century. 2. Consumption
(Economics)—Social aspects—United States—History—20th century.
3. Popular culture—United States—History—20th century. 4. United
States—Social life and customs—1971- 5. United States—Social conditions—
1960–1980. 6. Nineteen seventies. I. Title.
HQ2044.U6B56 2007
306.30973'09045—dc22   2006035574

www.ingramcontent.com/pod-product-compliance
Lightning Source LLC
Chambersburg PA
CBHW050336270326
41926CB00016B/3483